AF324268

DEATH IN EAST GERMANY, 1945–1990

Monographs in German History

The complexities and peculiarities of German history present challenges on various levels, not least on that of historiography. This series offers a platform for historians who, in response to the challenges, produce important and stimulating contributions to the various debates that take place within the discipline.

For full volume listing, please see pages 233 and 234

DEATH IN EAST GERMANY, 1945–1990

Felix Robin Schulz

berghahn
NEW YORK · OXFORD
www.berghahnbooks.com

Published in 2013 by
Berghahn Books
www.berghahnbooks.com

Library of Congress Cataloging-in-Publication Data
Schulz, Felix Robin.
    Death in East Germany, 1945–1990 / Felix Robin Schulz.
        pages cm. -- (Monographs in German history)
    Includes bibliographical references and index.
    ISBN 978-1-78238-013-9 (hardback: alk. paper) -- ISBN 978-1-78238-014-6
(institutional ebook)
    1. Funeral rites and ceremonies--Germany (East) 2. Death--Social aspects--
Germany (East) 3. Sepulchral monuments--Germany (East) I. Title.
    GT3250.5.S45 2013
    393.0943'1--dc23
                                                                                2013005547

British Library Cataloguing in Publication Data
A catalogue record for this book is available from the British Library

Printed in the United States on acid-free paper

ISBN 978-1-78238-013-9 (hardback)
ISBN 978-1-78238-014-6 (institutional ebook)

For Otto and Lotti Löffler

CONTENTS

List of Figures, Tables and Graphs

FIGURES

TABLES

GRAPHS

ACKNOWLEDGEMENTS

Death in our time is regaining visibility – it might even never have truly lost it – but I still contend that much of sepulchral culture, such as the systems for disposing of the dead, remains just beyond the everyday gaze. For the historian this adds a substantial problem as this distance translates generally in dispersed archival holdings – both geographically as well as thematically speaking. This in turn makes the historical study of death, dying and disposal complex, thus explaining why much still remains to be studied for the two Germanies (and beyond). The insights that can be gained about a country through examining its sepulchral culture – about its politics, culture and society – outweigh the logistical difficulties. Moreover, the historical developments and what inelegantly might be called the structure of the sepulchral culture that operates behind the mere statistics of death reveal a lot, especially if a comparative approach is utilized to show similarities and differences. For example, the death rates in the GDR meant that from the late 1950s onwards, the state had to dispose of about 227,000 corpses a year. This was quite a challenge for the socialist state and its planned economy, and this often showed in the experience of its citizens, yet the GDR (as well as Hungary) always looked enviously at the successful sepulchral reform in Czechoslovakia. This resulting volume concentrates on the administrative side that shaped the sepulchral culture of East Germany; the personal experience of the bereaved are all too often not recorded in the state and church archives.

What can be found in these pages has been the work of more than a decade. Over that period, I learned a lot about death on an abstract as well as a personal level. Over that time I received much goodwill, and I am indebted to a great number of people. The people I tested most were the numerous archivists and librarians in East Germany, who vehemently insisted that very little could be found in their holdings on such a 'sad' topic, yet they patiently allowed me to order numerous files and books. This work would not have been possible without their work and dedication. Enthusiastic guidance and, in times of need, help was always provided by Richard Bessel and Corey Ross. Working at Lancaster and Newcastle University led to the encounter of many extraordinarily dedicated colleagues and friends. Without their generosity of spirit this volume would have been weaker. Corinna M. Peniston-Bird not only read and commented on numerous drafts of chapters but is a constant source of wisdom. Thomas Rohkrämer remains a most reliable source of encouragement, inspirational discussions and kindness. Matt Perry epitomises what is often rather vaguely described as 'research environment': he does so by being open to discussing any idea and contributing the odd joke. He further provided the most practical of all aid to the non-native writer, careful proof-reading. The final draft underwent the calm dissection of the author's language by Martin Farr who untangled the remaining vagaries and oddities; moreover afterwards out of boundless curiosity he asked many a question. All inadvertent errors and remaining oversights are no reflection on their generosity and diligence; they are simply the author's fault. Many more have helped on the way; I would therefore like to thank: Emma Vickers, Sandra Peniston-Bird, Alejandro Quiroga, Xavier Guégan, Claudia Baldoli, Ben Houston, Michelle Houston, Neelam Srivastava, Samiksha Sehrawat, Tim Kirk and Heléna Tóth. Lastly, I want to thank my parents for unwavering support in an endeavour that took longer than many non-academics can comprehend, as well as my uncle, Karly Löffler, who never ceased to be proud.

GLOSSARY

AFD
: *Arbeitskreis Friedhof und Denkmal* (Working Group Cemetery and Memorial, Kassel), the West German think-tank, advisory body and industry pressure group on sepulchral culture.

Communality
: Used in the sense of solidarity (as it is in the OED), but also specifically referring to the connotations of the German word *Gemeinsamkeit*.

Ehrenfriedhöfe
: Special cemeteries or parts of cemeteries to honour specific groups such as party members or victims of oppression; alternatively sometimes the terms *Ehrenhain* or *Ehrenfeld* are used.

Grabfeld
: Grave field, subsection of a cemetery, containing individual grave plots, normally separated by wider paths, greenery, or trees.

IfK
: *Institut für Kommunalwirtschaft*, set up in 1962 in Dresden, a think-tank for all issues concerning the municipal services, including cemetery administration and burial service providers. In those fields it mirrored the work of the AFD.

Inhumation
: This term is used to differentiate this form of disposal from the other main type of disposal: to differentiate the burial of the whole body in the ground (inhumation, as in *Erdbegräbnis*) from the burial of the cremains (urn burial).

Kissensteine
: Flat headstones.

Leitbetrieb
: Leading concern, normally the largest VEB in a region, charged with coordinating best practice and implementing policies.

Musterfriedhofsordnung
: Standard regulation for cemeteries, generally issued as guidelines prescribing the usage of cemetery space and the design of gravestones and plots. Some sections can

	be compulsory. The first regulation for Germany was issued in 1922.
Propagation	Concerted popularization and promotion of ideas through agitation, propaganda, regulations and incentives.
Reihengrabstelle	Allocated burial plot within the grid system of normal grave fields, normally for one person. Traditionally situated in the less easily accessible centre of a grave field.
Region	I use region as a translation of the East German word *Bezirk*. The regions replaced the German states in 1952 and the regional administration of state and party (BT/RdB) were the highest level of administration below the national level. In some histories of the GDR the word is translated as 'district', which I use for the German word *Kreis* (the middle level of administration), since the word denotes a smaller geographical area.
SED	*Sozialistische Einheitspartei Deutschlands*, the Socialist Unity Party of Germany.
UGA	*Urnengemeinschaftsanlage*, an anonymous communal area for the internment of urns.
VEB (st) (k) (b)	*Volkseigener Betrieb* (People's Own Concern), generally nationalized company, sometimes organized in combines. Control can be exerted from different levels of the administration, at municipal (st), district (k), or regional (b) level. Considered to be *Volkseigentum* (people's property).
Wahlgrab	A grave plot that can be freely chosen, normally for two inhumations. Traditionally on the more prestigious outer perimeter of a grave field. An *Urnenwahlgrab* is a burial plot for up to four urns. A *Familienwahlgrab* is a larger plot for up to six members of a family.

INTRODUCTION

*O*n 27 March 2002, Charlotte Ulbricht died. Her final resting place was not, as was usual, next to her husband, the first post-war leader of the GDR, Walter Ulbricht. He had been buried in the Special Cemetery for Socialists (*Gedenkstätte der Sozialisten*) alongside communist heroes Rosa Luxemburg, Karl Liebknecht and Ernst Thälmann, as well as fellow SED politicians such as Wilhelm Pieck and Otto Grotewohl, in Berlin-Friedrichsfelde. Since its reopening in January 1951 the Friedrichsfelde site had become effectively the GDR's Valhalla – not only for its politicians but also for writers and poets such as Erich Weinert, Friedrich Wolf, or Willi Bredel. However, the ashes of the 'Queen Mum of Communism', as *Der Spiegel* referred to Lotte Ulbricht, found their last resting place in an anonymous communal area for the internment of urns (*Urnengemeinschaftsanlage* or UGA) at the farthest end of the Berlin-Weißensee cemetery.[1] Her ashes were buried in a place that the workers of this ordinary Berlin cemetery refer to as 'the cauldron' or 'dell' (*Der Kessel*). Much was made in the media of the fact that she actually did not want to be buried anywhere else, and that her explicit wishes had been followed both in the ceremony as well as in the choice of her burial site.[2] Despite the humble choice, this socialist funeral was unusual in character: falling somewhere in between being a private ceremony and, in a sense, the state occasion of a defunct regime – one might possibly even call it the last state funeral of the GDR. About two hundred people had gathered to pay their respects to one of the last remaining icons of German communism, amongst them the last leader of the GDR, Egon Krenz (on day release from prison).[3] As well as former comrades and officials there were also friends, family and party members. Few fitted in the ceremony

---

Notes for this section begin on page 9.

room. The eulogy was delivered, as Lotte Ulbricht had requested, by Ursula Benjamin.[4] The whole ceremony, despite private grief and the undoubted feeling of loss, therefore had a deeply political character. Thereafter, the urn was carried to the *Urnengemeinschaft* where, to the sounds of music from a portable CD player and towards the end a single trumpeter intoning 'The Little Trumpeter', her cremains were lowered into the ground.

<table>
<tr><td>

1.

Of all our comrades
none was to us as dear and good
as our little trumpeter,
of jolly red guard stock;
as our little trumpeter,
of jolly red guard stock.

…

3.

Then came an enemy bullet
during a cheerful play;
with a contented smile
our little trumpeter, he fell;
with a contented smile
our little trumpeter, he fell.

</td><td>

4.

We took pickaxe and spade
and dug him a grave in the morning,
and those who loved him most,
they lowered him in silence;
and those who love him most,
They lowered him in silence.

…

6.

You did not fall in vain,
your work we have now completed.
We built the state,
That brought us all freedom and peace.
Therefore, let the shout be heard with honour:
Long lives the workingman's might.[5]

</td></tr>
</table>

As at other GDR funerals, this song was chosen because of its evident revolutionary zeal and the sentiment celebrating a 'fulfilled' life: that is, a life devoted to the advancement of socialism. This was precisely what Lotte Ulbricht's funeral intended to highlight, a point that Egon Krenz's final farewell accentuated. He culminated with a socialist rallying cry: 'We know that the decline of the GDR was not the death of the socialist idea. The socialist idea lives on!'[6] The whole ceremony ended, in archetypical GDR fashion, with the collective and defiant singing of the *Internationale*.

In many ways this funeral signifies more than a ritual accompanying the death of an iconic figure of German communism. It was the 'surreal' conclusion to a state and political system, in the way that Erich Honecker's death in 1994, in faraway Chile, had not been. Honecker's death could not function as a true last act, or apotheosis, of the 'collective memory' because of its timing and location. The director of Lotte Ulbricht's funeral, overwhelmed by media interest, felt forced to issue a press release; even that hints, albeit very implicitly and reverberating with that peculiarly bureaucratic German, at something definitive:

> Lotte Ulbricht was buried in a cobalt-blue decorated urn [*Schmuckurne*] with an ash capsule that, depending on the soil conditions, will have dissolved completely and without any residue, in accordance with the law, in a maximum of fifteen years.[7]

By which time the cremains will have become one with the surrounding soil; the physical remains of Charlotte Ulbricht will finally have become inseparable from the anonymous mass urn grave, and a remnant of the GDR will have gone. In the face of on-going waves of *Ostalgie,* in which views seem to have become either markedly less differentiated or highly polarized, it is timely to explore the development of the sepulchral culture of the GDR.[8]

Germany's rural conservation movement of the early twentieth century articulated wonderfully the extent to which cultural manifestations in response to death, dying and disposal have been employed as an index of the cultural development of an era:

> At all times and with all peoples, the human race has seen it as a solemn and inescapable duty to attain a decent burial for the deceased. The cult of death, although differing in its forms, is, therefore, always an interesting expression of the culture of the specific era. In a certain sense the burial sites are thus a measure of the artistic culture of an era, similar in a way to human dwellings and their interior decoration. They [burial sites] in future will continue to bear loud and clear witness to the outlook of those who brought them into being.[9]

Traditionally, such fields as archaeology, anthropology, or ethnography have scrutinized the social codes of death.[10] It took time for historians to decipher the social, economic, political and cultural responses to death. Most famously Philippe Ariès's work on death sought to chart the evolution of Western attitude to death, in order to learn more about the individual in his or her time.[11]

East Germany between 1949 and 1989 was a state that had officially adopted materialism as the underpinning of state ideology. The materialist interpretation of death is one that is as straightforward as it is technical. Death is the end of one's existence as well as the subsequent state of non-existence. Death is thus the unequivocal end. This means that, unlike in Christian theology, materialism views life not as a path – and death as redemption through a 'better' afterlife. To materialists life is a task, a challenge and ultimately an end in itself:

> For we adherents of the materialistic view of life (Weltanschauung), life is not a mere 'transit point' on the way to that 'better world' and death is not 'a redemption'. We understand the world and life as a task.[12]

Hence, the ideal of a productive life, in a political as well as a material sense, became the central point of reference and was actively promoted according to the ideals of socialist humanism. The productive individual, striving to better one's society, became the ideal to which one should aspire – what Brecht tried to reveal as the 'Good Person' (*der gute Mensch*).[13] In this secular philosophical system, a general tribute to examples of positive conduct in society had to substitute for the concept of God honouring good deeds and punishing misdemeanours. However, this intense orientation to life meant that the GDR ultimately had a problematic relationship to death as the antithesis of life.

Charlotte Ulbricht's funeral epitomizes the GDR's official attitude to death in terms of burial place, cremation as the preferred form of disposal, the music played, the tone and content of the graveside eulogy, and even the type of urn used; all have their roots in the GDR's sepulchral culture. While individual elements have a longer proletarian or socialist tradition, often stretching back to the mid or late nineteenth century, these elements only came together in the second half of the twentieth century to form the phenotype of a modern socialist secular funeral. Consequently, one is faced with a complex ideological as well as political response to death. This, in turn, formed a unique sepulchral culture. Analysis of sepulchral culture discloses much about a society and its epoch.[14]

Contemporary perceptions of death in past societies are either too romanticized, sometimes to an astonishing degree, or they follow Ariès's thesis that death has become less present.[15] These misconceptions construct a nostalgic sepulchral culture. There is a further distortion: the longing to escape the 'evils' of modern society, understood as the fragmentation or individualization of life concomitant with the realities of urban life. This expresses itself in the desire to transcend the 'relentless' advance of technology and bureaucracy into every aspect of death in all its inevitability.[16] Nevertheless, these forces have played a significant role in the development of the sepulchral culture of modernity via such phenomena as the emergence and professionalization of undertaking and later, fully fledged funeral directing. Much more research at the comparative, macro as well as the micro level is needed to provide a more coherent picture of how death has been understood and evolved in the past. Only in this way can one trace how societies responded to death: the roles played by religion, politics, ideology and economics; the balance struck between individuals and social convention; and the forces that dominated, and when.

In order fully to comprehend the 'culture of death' of a specific era, there is a clear need for a fairly broad foundation, ideally covering the spectrum from the interpretations of the meaning of death to the choice of funeral rites, on the individual level, and from the organization of the system of disposal to the prevailing design of cemetery space, on the societal. The preoccupations of these two frames of analysis are all too often diametrically opposed: personal grief and loss tends to collide with public concerns about health, order and regulation. The compulsory cremation that operates in places like Shanghai exemplifies this opposition. The case of the cemetery in the modern era further illustrates this relationship, since the cemetery itself can be defined as being both a public and a private space. Julie Rugg rightly emphasizes this as a key issue in defining the nature of cemetery space, even if her remarks primarily concern the ownership patterns of cemeteries in the Anglo-Saxon world:

> Cemetery space can be regarded as sacred, in that it acts as a focus for pilgrimage of friends and family and is protected from activities deemed 'disrespectful'. However, cemeteries are principally secular spaces: ownership is almost always by municipal authorities or private sector concerns. The sites are intended to serve the whole community, and in doing so are

closely integrated in to community history. The sites are able to carry multiple social and political meanings.[17]

The existence of church cemeteries in Germany does not fundamentally alter that relationship, because church cemeteries are, despite their ownership, essentially public spaces serving the community. A cemetery is a public space used for the disposal of a community's deceased, yet the burial site also exists as a private space for mourning and commemoration. Moreover, the addition of sites of public commemoration such as war memorials can add further public and thus political significance.[18] However, added significance does not end there; even the burial of certain individuals can complicate the balance between the private and the public function of the local cemetery. The ceremony for Lotte Ulbricht makes this point emphatically. This private farewell was held in a public space with the press in attendance. The entire ceremony had clear political overtones, and yet for some friends and family members the ceremony was primarily a means to express their shared grief. Yet it was the explicit political overtones and the quaint socialist idiosyncrasies that provoked most comment.[19] This volume will certainly draw upon the kitsch in socialist sepulchral culture, but it aims to go deeper, by eschewing antiquarianism in favour of an exploration of the sepulchral culture of East Germany in its fullness.

Since 1990, the GDR's sepulchral culture has attracted academic interest on particular details, but all too often with limited parameters and rigid assumptions, rather than on the wider cultural responses to death.[20] In 2009 Jane Redlin (who first studied funerals in East Berlin back in the mid 1980s) published her very detailed ethnographic study of the link between the public state funeral and the private funeral in the GDR. While the volume is hugely insightful and very detailed and rightly stresses the importance of state funerals as precursors and models, it suffers from the lack of a historical perspective that acknowledges change over time as well as from overemphasizing the normative nature of public funerals celebrating the death of party members in the tradition of the funerals of Rosa Luxemburg and Karl Liebknecht. That view overlooks the real diversity of ritual (see chapter six).[21] Barbara Happe stresses the totalitarian nature of the GDR and thus has primarily focused much of her work on GDR cemeteries on the two extremes of the UGA and anonymous burial, whilst only indirectly including cremation.[22] Norbert Fischer addressed cremation and the role and design of cemeteries in Germany before 1945 and contemporary issues and trends, such as virtual commemoration.[23] Gerti Maria Hoffjan published on socialist cemetery culture, though without the historian's appetite for sources.[24] Rituals and liturgy have attracted more scholarly attention. Albeit from their own largely religious perspective, Klemens Richter, Ansgar Franz and Jan Hermelink have studied the effect of GDR policy on church rituals and the extent of the proliferation of secular ceremonies.[25] With the exceptions of Monica Black's wonderful work on Berlin[26] and the work of Jane Redlin, systematic attempts to unlock the subject have been limited to shorter pieces often coming from a specific ideological angle.[27] In addition, there remain those writing on sepulchral culture in Germany, such as Fischer, Happe and Sörries, who are involved with the work of the professional association and think-tank *Arbeitskreis Friedhof und Denkmal* (AFD). It was that institution that shaped West German sepulchral culture after 1945. Hence those who formulate policy and try to steer the public tastes are close to those who write the history of sepulchral culture.[28] Furthermore, discussions of the GDR's sepulchral culture have also opened the troublesome debate on the extent to which the GDR's political *Weltanschauung* determined its sepulchral culture.[29]

In general these contributions have tended to overemphasize individual peculiarities of the GDR's sepulchral culture – such as cremation rates in east German cities and rates of secular funerals in Berlin. This tendency is not unique to the literature dealing with death, dying and disposal in the GDR – individual areas, such as cemetery design, see a disproportionate scholarly attention.[30] An approach stressing the ideological eccentricities of the GDR's sepulchral culture is an all too tempting alternative to serious comparative contextualization. Research into GDR history is further complicated by the fragmented methodology.[31] Consequently, it is no surprise that the historical literature on German sepulchral culture remains rather patchy, and the period after 1945 remains relatively neglected.[32] This leads to a curious paradox: diversity of experience has not engendered a fuller and richer literature but its opposite, a dearth.

One reason for this historiographical neglect is that increasingly during the twentieth century sepulchral culture became subject to political intervention – especially under the influence of fascism (Sabine Behrenbeck) and communism (Catherine Merridale) – ultimately making its analysis more demanding.[33] Thomas Lindenberger rightly identifies the key problem of writing a social history of the GDR as establishing the degree and scope of politicization of everyday life.[34] The historiography of the GDR has lingered over the question of the centre's domination of all aspects of life at the periphery (or the state's encroachment into the individual's private life).[35] Fundamentally this hinges on whether the party and government simply enforced their ideals through the application of political power (as in a *durchmachtete Gesellschaft*) or if there is, to any degree, an *interaction* between party and society as the concept of a consensus dictatorship (*Konsensdiktatur* – Robert Gellately) implied.[36] The latter view sees governance, even in a Leninist-Marxist state, more in terms of social practice (*Herrschaft als Soziale Praxis*) and thereby acknowledges both mechanisms of negotiation and limits of power.[37] This concept affords a less rigid base than Jürgen Kocka's initial thesis of a *durchherrschte Gesellschaft*.[38] The revised concept of a *durchherrschte Gesellschaft*, therefore, allows more room for exceptions, subtle differences, interaction, complaints and shifts, whilst it avoids the notions that this was a state that offered real freedom or actual pluralism.[39] Moreover, this view of the GDR also avoids the superficiality perception dangers of merely calling it a totalitarian state.[40]

Differentiation, despite its inherent hazard of relativization of 'structural certainties', has to underpin a more precise understanding of the history of GDR

Figure 0.1 View along the main avenue of the *Südfriedhof* Leipzig. The graves in the middle and the memorial at the far end are the remaining pieces of the SED's design.

and its sepulchral culture.[41] The evidence is not always unambiguous, but it is revealing. Hence, conscious of the dangers of relativization, this volume examines death from a broader perspective, to comprehend its peculiarities, limitations and organization, comparatively situated in relation to the sepulchral culture of other countries.[42] This has necessitated a focus on 'normal' deaths; in other words, those that can be classified as 'cases of normal or everyday mortality', specifically excluding suicide, the victims of the death penalty, those who died attempting to cross the Iron Curtain, fatalities in accidents or commemoration of the war dead.[43]

An overview of long-term regional, national and transnational processes that have resulted in the making of modern German sepulchral culture is provided in the first chapter. Such comparisons disclose the intertwined and overlapping developments of sepulchral culture in the last two hundred years and its gradualism. The subsequent chapters address individual elements of sepulchral culture: the organization of disposal, cemeteries, cremation, the UGA and ritual formation. To do justice to the diverse nature of this interplay of scales was necessary given my aspiration to write a comprehensive history of the GDR's sepulchral culture and to satisfy my explanatory ambition.

The present research into the GDR's sepulchral culture began nearly exactly a decade after 3 October 1990. In those ten years considerable change had taken place, not least with regard to the physical evidence that the GDR had left in its cemeteries.[44] The first alterations normally concerned the more overt expressions of socialism, such as memorials to 'victims of fascism' (*Opfer des Faschismus/OdF*) and other politically charged spaces – most famously the splendid main path leading towards the Leipzig crematorium.[45]

Inscriptions were modified and they were subjected to other 'metamorphoses', for example the *OdF* memorial in the city of Gotha (Thuringia) had its inscription changed from the standard phrase: 'Honour and eternal memory to our comrades, companions and friends – For Peace and Socialism' to a simple and less challenging: 'The Dead admonish'.[46] These were usually specific and politically motivated alterations. More significant in regard to this work, and less politically motivated, was the second wave of change that accompanied Western investment and management addressing the state of dilapidation of East German cemeteries. Restoration aimed at creating decent useable public spaces often necessitated serious alterations in the physical fabric of cemeteries. This, combined with legislation that allowed for the rapid re-use of burial plots, typically between fifteen and twenty-five years, meant that East German cemeteries have changed a great deal since 1990. Adding a further difficulty for the researcher in Germany, more so than in Britain (due to the abandoning of re-use of graves around 1850), German cemeteries are public landscapes in constant flux. This analysis still relies on material and impressions collected during numerous personal visits to all varieties of cemeteries in East Germany, from small Church-administered rural cemeteries in rural Mecklenburg to the largest municipal cemetery of the former GDR in Leipzig, from the cemetery of Schwerin opened in 1975, designed in strict accordance to socialist ideas about cemetery layout, to the *Stadtgottesacker* of Halle/Saale established in 1529 imitating an Italian arcade cemetery.

In order to avoid a regional distortion or a rural/urban imbalance I have consulted a wide array of state, regional, institutional and local archives, in conjunction with the archives of the churches. However, there were some lacunae in the historical record. Key papers of the Ministry of Regional Industry (*Ministerium für Bezirksgeleitete Industrie*), the body that finally received the authority to coordinate issues relating to funerals in the GDR in the 1980s, were inaccessible because of fungal growth and may be beyond recovery.[47] The files of the IfK were in private custody and those deposited in the *Stadtarchiv* Dresden had not been catalogued, and despite extensive negotiations access could not be gained – hence I had to rely on IfK papers deposited in other sections of the *Stadtarchiv* Dresden and other repositories. Church archives mostly applied a strict interpretation of the thirty-year rule. This meant that few internal church materials pertaining to the period after 1973 could be accessed, with the exception of purely administrative and synod files.

Ultimately, this evidence points to the existence of a specific East German sepulchral culture not reducible to the transnational march of modernity. It was, as the existing scholarship suggests, formed at least partly by ideological considerations. Clear ideas of how death, dying and disposal should be dealt with in a socialist environment existed and at very least informed deliberations. Nevertheless, there were other more powerful influences, such as the obstructive powers of communal and institutional traditions. The significance of these is evident in the tenacity of rural customs and in the persistence of the ideals of the late nineteenth-century cemetery reform movement that permeated institutions on both sides of the Iron Curtain. In the 1980s, ideological disenchantment began to play an important role, when more people decided to opt for silent funerals, rejecting secular, socialist, or religious alternatives. Ultimately, though, it was economics and the drive for efficiency that would prove to be decisive in shaping East German sepulchral culture. However, despite this specificity, it is also evident that many transformations of the sepulchral culture of the GDR mirrored those in other industrialized countries.[48] This underlines that German history, even that of the Germanies after 1945, should not be written 'as if it were quite unlike the history of anywhere else', since only then can we do justice to true peculiarities such as Lotte Ulbricht's funeral – with all its choices and political posturing.[49]

Notes

1. A. Smoltczyk, 'Ortstermin: Begräbnis der Witwe des ehemaligen Staatschefs Walter Ulbricht in Berlin', *Der Spiegel*, No. 17, 22 April 2002, 86; other newspapers also used variations, the left-leaning newspaper *taz* referred to her as the 'Queen Mum of the GDR' as well as the 'Queen Mum of the Majakowskirings' (the infamous secluded living quarter of the East German Politburo). The UGA is also called the 'collective for the hereafter' (*Kollektiv fürs Jenseits*).

2. B. Bollwahn de Paez Casanova, 'Kampfgruß an Queen Mum der DDR', *taz*, No. 6729, 19 April 2002, 6.

3. Lotte Ulbricht was even celebrated posthumously in print. A vivid example is a piece entitled 'Extremely Diligent', in the left wing paper *Junge Welt*, a year later, on the day that would have been her hundredth birthday: N. Podewin, 'Extrem Tüchtig', *Junge Welt*, 19 April 2003, 15. The author framed the piece in the form of a glowing recollection of her life and her achievements and finished with a polemic on the fact that a federal agency had confiscated the €3657 that were left after the funeral in an act of victor's justice to pay for the renovation of the house that had been given to her by the GDR.

4. Bollwahn de Paez Casanova, 'Queen Mum der DDR', 6; P. Ahne, 'Rote Nelken für Lotte Ulbricht', *Berliner Zeitung*, 19 April 2002, 19. Ursula Benjamin is the widow of Michael Benjamin, a prominent member of the Communist Platform and son of Hilde Benjamin the infamous former GDR secretary of justice.

5. BLHA Potsdam, Rep. 531, KL Brandenburg, No. 1295: *Kondolenzkarten*. This is the FDGB version.

6. 'Wir wissen, dass der Niedergang der DDR nicht der Tod der sozialistischen Idee war. Die sozialistische Idee lebt weiter.' This was apparently followed by an outraged shout by Krenz that those who gave their live for the GDR did not need to be ashamed: Ahne, 'Rote Nelken', 19.

7. *Der Spiegel*, 22 April 2002, 86.

8. While the term 'sepulchral culture' is infrequently used in English I find it invaluable. In the

context of this volume it offers a usefully comprehensive description of the political, social, economic and cultural response to the human condition that is death: from the transportation of the corpse via burial to the design of cemeteries and the evolution of funeral rites. On the neologism *Ostalgie* see the work of the late D. Berdahl, '"(N)Ostalgie" for the Present: Memory, Longing and East German Things', *Ethnos*, 64:2 (1999), 192–211.

9. 'Zur Friedhofsanlage' in *Blätter für lippische Heimatkunde*, No. 2 (April), 1914, 22.

10. Compare the interesting, but methodologically problematic, R. Habenstein and W. Lamers, *Funeral Customs the World Over* (Milwaukee: Bulfin, 1974).

11. P. Ariès, *Western Attitudes to Death: From the Middle Ages to the Present* (London and New York: Marion Boyars, 1976); P. Ariès, *The Hour of our Death* (Harmondsworth: Penguin, 1983).

12. G. Freidank, *Alles hat am Ende sich gelohnt – Material für weltliche Trauerfeiern* (Leipzig: Zentralhaus für Kulturarbeit der DDR, 1975), 4.

13. B. Brecht, *Der Gute Mensch von Sezuan* (Frankfurt/Main: Suhrkamp, 1982).

14. For example the innovative essay collection: J. Whaley (ed.), *Mirrors of Mortality* (London: Europa, 1981); or a revealing monograph: G. Laderman, *The Sacred Remains: American Attitudes towards Death, 1789–1883* (New Haven: Yale University Press, 1996); or on reading cemetery spaces in the modern context: B. Mann, 'Modernism and the Zionist Uncanny: Reading the Old Cemetery in Tel Aviv', *Representation* – Special Issue: Grounds for Remembering, 69 (2000), 63–95; the most outstanding example will be G. Gorer, *Death, Grief and Mourning in Contemporary Britain* (London: Cresset, 1965).

15. N. Fischer, *Wie wir unter die Erde kommen – Sterben und Tod zwischen Trauer und Tod* (Frankfurt: Fischer, 1997), 18; T. Walter, 'La Visibilité des Morts dans la Société Moderne', in *Proceedings of the Dying and Death in 18th–21st century Europe International Conference* (Cluj-Napoca: Accent, 2009), 11–18.

16. There is a sizeable literature, but an insightful place to start is R. Kegan, *In Over Our Heads: The Mental Demands of Modern Life* (Cambridge, Mass.: Havard University Press, 1994).

17. J. Rugg, 'Defining the Place of Burial: What Makes a Cemetery a Cemetery', *Mortality*, 5:3 (2000), 259.

18. C. Tacke, *Denkmal im Sozialen Raum* (Göttingen: Vandenhoeck and Ruprecht, 1995).

19. 'Whenever a piece of the GDR is set to rest, the East revives' (*Immer wenn ein Stück DDR zu Grabe getragen wird, lebt der Osten wieder auf*): Bollwahn de Paez Casanova, 'Queen Mum der DDR', 6.

20. Reiner Sörries, as chairman of the AFD *e.V.* (Working Group Cemetery and Memorial, Kassel), the German think-thank, advisory body and industry pressure group, has, as his predecessor Helmut Boehlke, continued to publish on sepulchral culture. For example: R. Sörries (ed.), *Großes Lexikon der Bestattungs- und Friedhofskultur – Wörterbuch zur Sepulkralkultur, Vol.1* (Braunschweig: Thalacker, 2002). In the context of the GDR most insightful is R. Sörries, *Ruhe sanft: Kulturgeschichte des Friedhofs* (Kevelaer: Butzon and Bercker, 2009), 188–97.

21. J. Redlin, *Säkulare Totenrituale: Totenehrung, Staatsbegräbnis und private Bestattung in der DDR* (Münster: Waxmann, 2009).

22. B. Happe, 'Anonyme Bestattung in Deutschland – Veränderungen in der zeitgenössischen Bestattungs- und Erinnerungskultur', *Friedhof und Denkmal*, 41:2 (1996), 40–52; B. Happe, 'Urnengemeinschaftsanlagen: Zur Friedhofs- und Bestattungskultur in der DDR', *Deutschlandarchiv*, 3 (2001), 436–46; B. Happe, 'Die sozialistische Reform der Friedhofs- und Bestattungskultur in der DDR – Urnengemeinschaftsanlagen', in R. Sörries (ed.), *Vom Reichsausschuß zur Arbeitsgemeinschaft Friedhof und Denkmal* (Kassel: AFD, 2002), 185–213; the clearest expression of her view is to be found in: B. Happe, 'Grabmalgestaltung in der DDR – Der erzwungene Abschied vom persönlichen Grabmal', in AFD (ed.), *Grabkultur in Deutschland: Geschichte der Grabmäler* (Berlin: Reimer, 2009), 189–214.

23. N. Fischer, *Vom Gottesacker zum Krematorium – Eine Sozialgeschichte der Friedhöfe in Deutschland* (Cologne: Böhlau, 1996); N. Fischer, 'Leitlinien einer neuen Kultur im Umgang

mit Tod und Trauer', *Friedhof und Denkmal*, 44 (1999), 3–9; N. Fischer, *Geschichte des Todes in der Neuzeit* (Erfurt: Sutton, 2002).

24. G. Hoffjan, 'Existierte eine spezifische realsozialistische Friedhofgestaltung in der DDR und was waren ihre Charakteristik?', in R. Sörries (ed.), *Vom Reichsauschuss zur AFD*, 171–84.

25. K. Richter, 'Der Umgang mit Tod und Trauer in den Bestattungsriten der Deutschen Demokratischen Republik', in H. Becker, B. Einig and P.-O. Ulrich, *Im Angesicht des Todes – Ein interdisziplinäres Kompendium I, Pietas Liturgica 3* (St. Ottilien: EOS Verlag, 1987), 229–58 (Richter is also extremely useful as a good introduction into the secondary literature on socialist rituals); J. Hermelink, 'Die weltliche Bestattung und ihre kirchliche Konkurrenz – Überlegung zur Kasualpraxis in Ostdeutschland', *Jahrbuch für Liturgik und Hymnologie*, 39 (2000), 65–86; A. Franz, '"Alles hat am Ende sich gelohnt"? – Christliche Begräbnisliturgie zwischen kirchlicher Tradition und säkularen Riten', *Liturgisches Jahrbuch*, 51:4 (2001), 190–211.

26. M. Black, *Death in Berlin: From Weimar to Divided Germany* (Cambridge: Cambridge University Press, 2010).

27. O. Groschopp, 'Weltliche Trauerkultur in der DDR – Toten- und Bestattungsrituale in der politischen Symbolik des DDR-Systems', *Sozialwissenschaftliche Informationen (SOWI)*, 29:2 (2000), 109–10 (the author is very active in the freethinker movement promoting secular ceremonies); quite outstanding is a journalisitic piece: C. Geißler, 'Unter der Erde der DDR', in K. Michel, *Todesbilder – Kursbuch 114* (Berlin: Rowohlt, 1993), 79–90.

28. See: B. Leisner, 'Zu diesem Buch', in AFD (ed.), *Grabkultur in Deutschland*, 9–10.

29. R. Schelenz and S. Meinel, '"Sozialistische" Friedhofskultur in der DDR?', *Friedhof und Denkmal*, 41:1 (1996), 12–15.

30. See for example: J. Curl, *The Victorian Celebration of Death* (Stroud: Sutton Publishing, 2000).

31. H. Gumbert, Conference Report: 'Writing East German History: What Difference Does the Cultural Turn Make?', *Bulletin of the German Historical Institute* (Washington D.C.), 44 (2009), 137–41; S. Moranda, 'Towards a More Holistic History? Historians and East German Everyday Life', *Social History*, 35:3 (2010), 330–38.

32. Fischer, *Vom Gottesacker zum Krematorium*; H. Winter, *Die Architektur der Krematorien im Deutschen Reich 1878–1918* (Dettelbach: Röll, 2001). There are exceptions such as: AFD (ed.), Raum für Tote – *Die Geschichte der Friedhöfe von den Gräberstraßen der Römerzeit bis zur anonymen Bestattung* (Braunschweig: Thalacker, 2003) but that volume gives only a limited overview, and cannot offer the depth that would be required in order to address sepulchral culture as a whole adequately.

33. For a vivid example, see: EZA Berlin, 4/563: Bundesministerum für Gesamtdeutsche Fragen, *Pseudosakrale Staatsakte in der Sowjetzone: Namesweihen, Jugendweihe, Eheweihe, Grabweihe*, pamphlet (1958).

34. T. Lindenberger, 'Alltagsgeschichte und ihr möglicher Beitrag zu einer Gesellschaftsgeschichte', in R. Bessel and M. Jessen (eds), *Die Grenzen der Diktatur – Staat und Gesellschaft in der DDR* (Göttingen: Vandenhoeck, 1996), 312–21.

35. M. Fulbrook, 'New Historikerstreit, Missed Opportunity or New Beginning?', *German History*, 12:2 (1994), 203–7.

36. K. Schroeder, *Der SED-Staat: Partei, Staat, und Gesellschaft 1949–1990* (Munich: C. Hanser, 1998); see also the debate in: P. Corner (ed.), *Popular Opinion in Totalitarian Regimes. Fascism, Nazism, Communism* (Oxford: Oxford University Press, 2009).

37. A. Lüdtke (ed.), *Herrschaft als soziale Praxis: Historische und sozial-anthropologische Studien* (Göttingen: Vandenhoeck and Ruprecht, 1991), 9–51, especially 49–51.

38. J. Kocka, 'Eine durchherrschte Gesellschaft', in H. Kaelble, J. Kocka and H. Zwahr, *Sozialgeschichte der DDR* (Stuttgart: Klett-Cotta, 1994), 552.

39. The term *durchherrschte Gesellschaft* is extremely difficult to translate, since it links certain theoretical ideas about governance (mainly those of Michel Foucault and Pierre Bourdieu) with

Max Weber's observation on the limits of power; and places them in the context of intricate interrelation between governing and governed. In doing so it rejects the idea of totalitarian dictatorship by referring to different levels of compliance and the existence of areas that were prone to non-intervention (niches). See T. Lindenberger (ed.), *Herrschaft und Eigen-Sinn in der Diktatur: Studien zur Gesellschaftsgeschichte der DDR* (Cologne: Böhlau, 1999).

40. C. Ross, *The East German Dictatorship: Problems and Perspectives in the Interpretation of the GDR* (London: Arnold, 2002), 19–68, here in particular 32–36.

41. K. Jarausch, 'Modernization, German Exceptionalism and Postmodernity', in M. Geyer and K. Jarausch (eds), *A Shattered Past: (Re-) Constructing German Histories* (Princeton: Princeton University Press, 2003); T. Lindenberger, 'Alltagsgeschichte und ihr möglicher Beitrag', in Bessel and Jessen (eds), *Die Grenzen der Diktatur*, 314; see also of the different historical perspective: D. Peukert, *Inside Nazi Germany – Conformity, Opposition and Racism in Everyday Life* (New Haven: Yale University Press, 1987), 21–25.

42. For a similar approach (following another of Ariès's research avenues) and a good discussion of the drawbacks, see the work of Peter Stearns, for example the short and informative: P. Stearns, *Childhood in World History*, Second Edition (London: Routledge, 2010).

43. Some of these topics are covered elsewhere: U. Grashoff, *"In einem Anfall von Depression": Selbsttötungen in der DDR* (Berlin: Ch. Links, 2006), while Alf Lüdtke has published: 'Blumen und Grabsteine – für alle Kriegstoten? Gedenken, Erinnern und Beschweigen in der DDR. Beispiele aus dem Berliner Umland', in I. Eschebach (ed.), *Die Sprache des Gedenkens: Zur Geschichte der Gedenkstätte Ravensbrück 1945–1995* (Berlin: Hentrich, 1999), 163–83. Moreover, the role of pastor Teichmann as a never tiring writer of letters and complaints was revealing in how the administration of the GDR could be forced into investment towards commemoration and into spending money on cemeteries altogether: see BLHA Potsdam, Rep 202, No. 498a; Rep 401, RdB Potsdam, No. 6300.

44. Not only with regard to cemeteries. Moritz Bauer and Jo Wickert published pairs of pictures taken from identical positions in 1991 and again in 2003 in an extraordinary catalogue: M. Bauer and J. Wickert, *Vorwärts immer, rückwärts nimmer – 4000 Tage BRD* (Berlin: Nicolai, 2004).

45. W. Speitkamp (ed.), *Denkmalsturz: Zur Konfliktgeschichte politischer Symbolik* (Göttingen: Vandenhoeck und Ruprecht, 1997).

46. From 'Ehre und Ewiges Gedenken unseren Genossen, Kameraden und Freunden – Für Frieden und Sozialismus' to 'Die Toten Mahnen'. See also G. Grossmann, 'Im Osten: Klassenkampf und Vergangenheitsbewältigung', *Deutsche Friedhofskultur (DFK)*, 8 (1995), 273–76.

47. Others, like a file entitled 'Undertaking and Funeral Arrangement in the Region of Karl-Marx-Stadt' (SSA Chemnitz, RdB, No. 111381) could not be found, and a number of files in the SSA Leipzig concerning health matters had suffered water damage in the 1980s.

48. See: M. Fulbrook, 'Fact, Fantasy and German History', *Bulletin of the German Historical Institute* (Washington D.C.), 26 (2000), 3–34.

49. D. Blackbourn and G. Eley (eds), *The Peculiarities of German History* (Oxford: Oxford University Press, 1984), 291.

Chapter 1

THE ORIGINS OF MODERN GERMAN SEPULCHRAL CULTURE

*H*istorically, attitudes to death have gone through manifold changes. For example, gravediggers in the cities of early-modern Germany had a status similar to that of the executioner: they were unclean persons to be avoided by the rest of society, unable ever to enter a pub without permission from all those inside.[1] Until recently, and for much of the twentieth century, the fear of the unfamiliar and the incomprehensible seemed to have been the strongest factors leading to a certain estrangement from death in modern times.[2] Despite death's inevitability and changes in aesthetics – e.g., the 'good' death in the clean white sheets of hospital beds – death was either actively and consciously or unconsciously pushed to the fringes of our thought.[3] In modern societies mortality thus increasingly became to a certain extent repressed or hidden.[4] Shifts in life expectancy (death occurs later and thus less frequently), in the location of dying, and in the complexity and organization of modern urbanized societies, has accelerated this process.[5] Repression in this context can be principally understood as a psychological defence mechanism: a mechanism to transform into mere contingencies two psychologically overwhelming and inevitable phenomena – the approach of our own death as well as the experience of the death of a loved one. The latter particularly is an experience that leaves most of us struggling or at worst utterly out of our depth.[6] This repression became more pronounced because death became externalized from the everyday environs: generally speaking people no longer die in their own beds or even under their own roof. Modern death, especially since the 1960s, happens in hospitals managed and supervised by medical staff.[7] This is a difficult process to trace, as data before the 1960s are rare. To take an example

---

Notes for this section begin on page 36.

Table 1.1: Overview of hospitals as the location of death in different regions of the GDR, correlated with population density, care home availability, and average family size, 1973–1977.

Region	Population per km^2	Care home places per 1,000 pensioners	Person per household	Percentage of deaths occurring in hospital
Neubrandenburg	58	43.5	3.0	43
Schwerin	68	39.4	2.9	46
Potsdam	89	38.8	2.7	47
Frankfurt/Oder	96	43.1	2.8	41
Cottbus	106	32.2	2.8	43
Magdeburg	113	40.8	2.7	47
Rostock	123	38.0	2.9	43
Suhl	143	29.8	2.7	34
Erfurt	170	37.1	2.8	38
Gera	185	32.3	2.7	40
Halle	216	31.8	2.7	41
Dresden	274	37.6	2.5	36
Leipzig	294	34.3	2.5	44
Karl-Marx-Stadt	332	27.0	2.5	33
Berlin	2,715	54.4	2.3	55
GDR	*156*	*36.3*	*2.6*	*42*

(Data: K. Barby-Blumenthal, *Betreuung Sterbender*, 43–44)

from the US, between 1935 and 1945 the percentage of deaths in US hospitals increased from 25 to 35 per cent. By 1970, the figure for New York City stood at around 75 per cent.[8] In the GDR in the mid 1970s this ranged from 55 per cent for the urban region of Berlin to 33–34 per cent in the less urban regions of Karl-Marx-Stadt and Suhl. This general trend was further extended by the rise of palliative medicine and the more widespread introduction of hospices has helped to sanitize death.[9]

Repression thus led to concealment and estrangement, which banished the reality of death from social life, and accentuated the professionalization of practices related to dying, death and disposal. Norbert Elias observed that this process of concealment consequently took death beyond the gaze of the individual. As a sociologist he was interested in the social repression of dying and death and criticized the increasing technical perfection of the hygienic and odourless removal of the corpse from deathbed to grave in the modern world.[10] With a few exceptions, the death of a family member, tribe, community, or village has traditionally triggered a set of events, ceremonies and rituals to cope with death, bereavement and mourning. In the modern (industrialized and urbanized) world, where death has become increasingly remote, these rituals have undergone substantial change. Some, like the washing of the corpse by the women of the neighbourhood, were often performed on the basis of mutuality;

other tasks were traditionally rewarded with a keg of beer. For instance, in rural Westphalia, it was customary until the late 1960s for an unmarried man's coffin to be carried by the village's bachelors, even if the deceased was not a friend, neighbour, or relative. Afterwards the reward was a drink at the expense of the deceased's estate.[11] The dead body is washed and prepared for the burial, a coffin or a shroud has to be made or attained, and the body has to be laid to rest. Yet the organization of this process no longer resides with the family, but with the funeral director and the specialist staff engaged to remove these burdens from the bereaved.[12]

An increased emphasis on sanitation by the administration and a shift in custom as well as a real or perceived desire to not personally deal with death further accelerated this professionalization. The growing concern for hygiene, the emphasis on public health and general tendencies of regulation, legislation and centralization led to an overall sanitation of death as a social occurrence. A key component was the emergence of professionals who dealt with the logistics of a death. The modern funeral director can be found in all industrialized countries.[13] As a dispassionate professional organizer they provide a service by taking care of everything for the bereaved. Consequently, the practical aspects of the sepulchral culture (e.g., laying out) are removed; instead they largely take place behind closed doors or in the funeral parlour. The perception and reality of death thus became divorced from everyday life, a process that Philippe Ariès describes as culminating in the 'forbidden death' – a fairly laden term.[14] In Germany, until a recent backlash, it had become unthinkable for the dead body to remain for three days of mourning in the family home; on the contrary most families asked for a swift removal of the corpse.[15] Over the twentieth century, death to a large degree became a peripheral phenomenon in most Western countries. A large number of elderly people die in hospitals and nursing homes and some, as Elias points out, lonely.[16] This is as much an expression of our modern estrangement from death as it is the sign of an underlying process of reason or progress. This process, in conjunction with increasing regulation and the desire for efficiency, has profoundly influenced modern sepulchral culture.[17] British crematoria are a prime example: with the exception of very recently built crematoria, the actual layout 'is determined neither by the requirements of religious ritual nor by a careful study of the needs of mourners, but by ease of operation and by Department of the Environment guidelines'.[18]

However, despite these trends, it would be mistaken to believe that funeral practices and rituals have simply become sterile and worldly. Even the word 'disposal', frequently employed hereafter, is merely used as a term to describe the complex organizational processes of removal, burial, or cremation. Disposal is not intended to suggest ritualistic absence in a throw-away society (*Wegwerfgesellschaft*). On the contrary, death apparently necessitates some explanation, meaning, or justification in any form of sepulchral culture, even within the GDR's Marxist-Leninist materialist paradigm. Death in every age and in every society had its own aesthetic, and that aesthetic has been influenced by many factors: from politics to practicalities. Religious beliefs often confer meaning even in countries such as Britain, France, or Germany where church attendance has declined considerably but Christian funerals have remained the norm. In 1989 in Saxony, 99.8 per cent of all Protestants chose a religious funeral, compared with 99.2 per cent in 1985, 89.3 per cent in 1976 and 84.7 per cent in 1966.[19] Death plays a central role in all religions, as it defines life by being its antithesis. It is the moment of entry into an afterlife or is simultaneously an end and a new beginning. In all religions rites of passage have been established to mark death. Whilst death neatly fits into dualistic belief systems, it does more: 'Religions give their believers an expectancy of life that defies death'.[20] The Christian view of death is difficult to summarize, but the theologian Gerardus van der Leeuw incorporated the essentials when he argued: 'Dying is not a passive experiencing of a natural phenomenon, but an art, a rite, a sacrament. One has to die and be buried in the right way, so that one gets to the other side, into the "other" world'.[21] The rise of other value systems (e.g., socialism, liberalism, atheism, new age spiritualism) has tended to challenge (or at least augment) the classic role of religion in dealing with death. These modern rivals have not, however, eroded the reliance on traditional rites of passage and conceptions of being buried in the 'proper' fashion, they have merely altered and sometimes supplemented them. In turn these alternative value systems have had the ability to reshape death as a concept; since death has become the subject matter of more than religion and philosophy. As the twentieth century vividly demonstrates, death can be reinterpreted through the optic of politics or ideology – as well as economics. Consequently, sepulchral cultures have emerged wherein aesthetics have become ever more charged with ideology and new paradigms rationalize death in ways consonant with particular political agendas.[22] This excerpt from 1934 celebrating the Nazi rise to power and the future of cremation illustrates the point:

> All departments concerned with aspects of cremation … have finally to convince themselves that burial is a sin against the German *Volksraum* [People's space], and the German *Volksboden* [German soil]. A Department for Public Health has no right to this name if it continues to allow our dead to decompose in the earth and thus poison the very soil. As a National-Socialist I have to say: If in the Third Reich so much emphasis is put upon holiness, then one has to start with the earth … In preparing the cremation law and important regulations, our Reichsgovernment has to point out how much healthy soil is contaminated by burials every day.[23]

Politicized death rituals have the ability to imbue and embed patterns of belief or ideology into moments of profound personal and social significance. Thus, Zeiss has situated the Nazi campaign for cremation as the most acceptable form of disposal within their wider ideological framework; the very act of cremation revered a sacred German soil (*Volksboden*), which was itself a leitmotif of National-Socialist propaganda.[24] Yet customs and rituals have evolved over time; propaganda may induce new rhetorics of death but new practices are not swiftly integrated into everyday life.[25]

Much longer processes are at work with the formation of customs, practices and rituals, especially with regard to death. Besides shifts in the social and cultural attitude to death, four other key developments shaped the emergence of the modern German sepulchral culture: the shift in the locality of the cemetery due to the increased desire for better sanitation, the rise of the modern funeral director, the ideas of the cemetery reformers and the changes brought about by the advent of modern cremation. The initial impetus of the emergence of much of the modern funerary culture arose when the city became the centre of growth and the motor of innovation. Ultimately, the emergence of a wider, more affluent, and better-educated middle class, and the growth of cities into metropolises, led to the breakdown of the traditional community and of the traditional sepulchral culture of the Church.[26] The expansion of the urban population highlighted novel problems in sanitation and hygiene and led directly to a fundamental change in the perception of their importance and even more importantly to the formulation of plans, polices and legislation. Traditional forms of disposal swiftly became unviable. It was initially the bourgeoisie, in the form of rich merchants and learned scholars, mainly in the aftermath of the German Reformation, that advocated the separation of church and cemetery. From the middle of the sixteenth century the churchyard as a place of burial declined in favour of cemeteries outside the city wall: for instance, in Freiburg (1511); Nürnberg (1519); and Leipzig (1534).[27] It was the city governments that continued to drive this process. The change of location as well as urban wealth made new designs possible. One of the earlier designs was the '*Camposanto*', a cemetery with walled Italian-style arcades. The *Stadtgottesacker* (1529) in Halle an der Saale is a prime example of this expression of German renaissance.[28] The later idea of park cemeteries reflected the prevalent contemporary bourgeois cultural ideal of the urban elite. The working class would later rebel against certain aspects of such a funerary culture, for example insisting on a more egalitarian cemetery and grave design.[29] In early nineteenth-century Britain, opposition emerged against overcrowded burial grounds. Between 1832 and 1847 eight commercial cemetery companies were set up in London to alleviate conditions described by Lord Lansdowne in 1830 as 'leading to consequences injurious to health and offensive to decency'.[30] This evolution saw a dramatic proliferation of cemeteries with the onset of industrialization. The population explosion and the extreme deprivation in urban areas resulting from rapid industrial growth made changes in public sanitation necessary. Besides ensuring the water supply, engineering sewage systems and organising waste collections, the cities needed to reform the system for the disposal of human remains.

When on 12 August 1827 the Prussian *Oberpräsident* and Minister of State Wilhelm Anton von Klewiz signed legislation that disallowed the use of churchyards in Magdeburg as places of burial, it was because in the new environment of a steadily growing city the old means of burial were no longer feasible. New and larger cemeteries were needed to accommodate the growing number of graves required. The new regulation stated that the new cemeteries had to be placed under state control.[31] Other cities had made similar changes much earlier. In 1715 the Elector Joseph Clemens had ordered that burials should be moved out of the city of Bonn and a new cemetery should be built nearby. In Münster in Westphalia there were similar plans in 1729, when the ruling Bishop Clemens Augustus of Bavaria complained that corpses were often buried less than a foot deep, which, he noted, caused a terrible smell and led to contagious diseases.[32] This resulted in an order that bodies should be buried no less than six feet deep, and led to the planning of two new cemeteries outside the city walls. However, in both cases these plans were not realized because of heavy resistance from local citizens against the resting places being moved away from churches. The idea of salvation and of a godly burial was, despite reforms elsewhere, still closely linked to a burial on *Gottesacker* (God's acre, meaning the churchyard). In 1775, Parisian authorities promulgated the first law to ban burial within its city walls – this set an important precedent. Further impetus came from Joseph II of Austria's partially successful burial reform in 1785, which tried to remove the control of the Catholic Church over secular matters. It prohibited internment in town centre cemeteries, and tried to establish a civic authority to oversee cemeteries.[33] However, it was not in Habsburgian lands that the reform really took roots, it was in neighbouring Bavaria. In Munich in 1789 the same set of reforms proved successful because of prior consultations and multiple compromises. The opening of the new central cemetery outside the city, *vor dem Sendlinger Tor*, on 26 June had a marked effect on German sepulchral culture. This was not a new idea, but what distinguished the Munich case was its success, and especially success in a Catholic area. In many places the Austrian reforms proved short-lived. In Munich, where the ideas of the Austrian bureaucracy were seen as a way forward, the idea of a new central cemetery was made possible by the compromise which retained the old differences between the rich and the poor. The graves were classified, with family crypts at the top of the hierarchy and simple holes in the ground marked with a wooden cross at the bottom. Prices were fixed accordingly, thereby retaining the hierarchy, exclusivity and status with regard to each grave category and location.[34] This revealed two forces important to future reforms: economic constraints and an inherent traditionalism (conservatism) regarding disposal. Local as well as national governments could not ignore economic realities of disposal, even when planning and executing ideologically driven radical change. Moreover, the elaborateness of the burial ritual, the location of the grave plot, the choice of coffin and the design of the grave have been (as well as expressions of culture and aesthetics) powerful status symbols. A family plot with an outsized granite family crypt on the main avenue or another highly visible location in the local cemetery was a clear sign of station. Therefore, the propagation or imposition of more uniformity and egalitarian ideals on the cemetery has traditionally encountered rigid opposition, the only exception being when proposed by a voluntary social movement.[35]

The success of the Munich reforms, moreover, also underlines the importance of the government in the organization of disposal. The physical separation of church and cemetery aided increased legal and administrative control over burials. In times of plague and pestilence, the government had already regulated and legislated the disposal of the deceased in order to safeguard public health. With the desire to improve public hygiene and levels of sanitation, the involvement of the government or state in the organization of disposal became pressing. With the late eighteenth-century reform in Munich general legislative control was passed to the city. The 1789 edict stated three rules for any burial: a grave had to be six feet deep, a burial space could not be reused for at least twelve years, and the body should have been dead for at least thirty-six hours, ideally forty-eight hours, before burial.[36] The state, in the form of the local council, had taken responsibility for and control of appropriate forms of disposal, and this included the organization of all its technical details by specialists. This encroachment into religious custom in the name of sanitation marked a change, unthinkable without the inventions of modern science, but born out of the initial erosion of tradition. Necessity, scientific explanation and legislation began to exert their power. The German city thus saw death increasingly become an organizational, technical and administrative challenge.

This is not to say emotional assistance drawn from the wider social surrounding became absent, but this shift meant that it became rarer, as did communal and neighbourly help of a more practical nature. What started with the regulation of burial space in the city, spread and started another altogether different incremental process – the professionalization and specialization of the organization of the processes leading to the he burial. Although professional undertakers at first complemented customary neighbourly assistance, in due course the help, expertise, services and products provided by professionals of the undertaking industry replaced the help of neighbours. One of the first steps was that the municipality employed official layers out (*Leichenfrauen*, as only women were employed). In the city of Bielefeld, for instance, regulations regarding layers out date back to at least the 1850s; in other cities like Munich, this tradition goes back to the early 1800s and, in the case of nuns fulfilling this task, as far back as the late Middle Ages. Municipalities set strict guidelines for these women and fixed their fees. Their employment was only viable in urban areas; in the countryside their tasks were still fulfilled (often until the 1960s) by the extended family, neighbourly help, or informal professionalization (like a woman who was called upon for every death). The layer out became the first line of defence in fighting against epidemics and the growing threat of rapid spreading diseases. In cities, population density and public sanitation provided an ideal environment for cholera and typhoid. The increased emphasis on hygienic standards and prevention of epidemics was exemplified by a decree of February 1871 in Munich, which made it illegal to take any coffin decorations home for fear of carrying infectious material.[37]

The new regulations repeatedly stressed hygiene and the role the new professions in policing public health. Layers out, gravediggers, or undertakers were required by law to notify the local administration of contagious illnesses or suspicious circumstances.[38] The duties of the new professionals also extended to disinfecting the room in which the deceased had died. Predominately Catholic Munich was able to reconcile religion and modernization as it also pioneered another development: the building of one of the first mortuaries in Germany.[39] Mortuaries improved hygiene and were based upon increased scientific knowledge of disease. Laying out at home had become (until very recently) an anachronism and removal to the mortuary (*Leichenhallen*) became compulsory in most cities.[40] This meant that from the second half of the nineteenth century death in urban areas not only led to burial in a municipal cemetery but also became the domain of professionals. Moreover, it also became incrementally removed from its association with the churches and religion. While most mortuaries had an annexe for the celebration of burials, they were municipal buildings. This provided essentially non-denominational space for funeral ceremonies in most urban areas. Moreover, in Germany the new cemeteries were city property. In Britain or the United States, on the other hand, they were often run by companies and were normally privately run, or at least partially municipally owned.[41] In any case this meant that the state had greater control, and in Germany this meant it could exercise direct legislative and fiscal control. From 1814 onwards, irrespective of the predominant denomination, there is a profusion of regulations. The new *Friedhofsordnungen* reflected the modernizing trends and enshrined intricate regulations that prescribed everything from pricing to the exact dimension of a grave plot. These rules were meant to cope with growing populations and increased urbanization. Municipalities also needed to regulate the ever-growing scope of professional funeral direction.[42] Moreover, further cemetery space was needed towards the end of the nineteenth century as industrialization expanded cities enormously. Civic-minded local governments could establish grand landscaped park cemeteries with even stricter regulations. These were built even further away from the city centre, on the city's outskirts. To make the new cemeteries accessible to the public, tramlines were laid in such cities as Munich, Bielefeld, Leipzig and Magdeburg. Given that the cemetery is public site that acts as a physical reminder of death, there is a spatial significance to this removal further away from the bustling market squares that epitomized the everyday life in the cities. Nevertheless, the new location meant that cemeteries assumed an altogether different and slightly unexpected role of being used and seen as recreational spaces, offering greenery and space to saunter. The park cemetery, characterized by broad, tree-lined, axial avenues, was born.

Magdeburg, despite not being at the heart of the German industrial revolution, is a good example of these trends. Magdeburg gained increasing importance as a transport hub, being well connected by canals, the Elbe, and major railroad connections. The city grew rapidly in the 1840s with the small local steel industry and river-ship building playing an important role. The resulting population growth led to the construction of a large cemetery of fourteen hectares in the 1850s, because the capacity of the old *Nordfriedhof* (built in the 1700s) was exhausted. However, even this large new cemetery proved inadequate. On 11 October 1898, the third and largest cemetery was opened. The new *Westfriedhof* was thirty hectares in area and a new tram line directly connected it to the town centre. The cemetery of the industrial age had arrived. A contemporary source hinted at the emerging modern character of the cemetery:

> The main paths were built in order to be driven on, to allow older persons to get as close as possible to the graves of their deceased … garden elements to decorate the cemetery are situated at the main entrance and in front of the chapel, moreover the middle section of the main paths are planted with decorative elements … the planting [of trees] gives the cemetery a closed forest-like appearance, mainly fir trees were used … establishing a nursery has the advantage of being a considerable source of income to the city.[43]

The *Westfriedhof* was thus modern by design in terms of its locality, form, function and aesthetics. In other words, the parish churchyard had given way to a smoothly and efficiently run municipal cemetery. The result was a large park-like cemetery with a chapel and two adjacent mortuaries (each holding up to twenty-one bodies in cooling chambers), along with a number of administrative buildings. The cemetery had become a municipal institution providing dependable services, their scope and costs enshrined by regulations and price lists set by the local councils. In time of economic crisis this service could easily be expanded into a municipal industry, once private funeral directors were no longer permitted.[44] Magdeburg also underlines the aesthetics which coincided with the emergence of large park cemeteries (see below). Form and function became important, indeed in the 1890s Magdeburg's *Nordfriedhof* was turned into the *Nordpark* in order to provide recreational green space – a practice that became increasingly common and later became a favoured practice with regard to old cemeteries in the GDR. As with urban planning, parks and public buildings, the design of cemeteries tends to express a specific aesthetic and ideological inclination, often mixed with a predisposition to social engineering. References to cemeteries, gravestones and ceremonies as mirrors of German nature became a motif:

> The cemetery, a site of the dead, is a mirror image of the culture of a people. The German character is unpretentious, true and deeply imbued with soul.[45]

The cemetery had become a domesticated cultural space (*domestizierter Kulturraum*). In turn, with ever more planning the cemetery had been turned into works of art (*Gesamtkunstwerk*).[46] Using the traditional form of a park or the garden of a stately home, the typical design for a cemetery in the first half of the nineteenth century was thus isometric – a square separated by pathways into four smaller squares.[47] Generally the more expensive family plots (*Familiengrabstätten*) were located alongside the main paths and around the encircling wall. The cheaper plots were in the centre of the squares along the paths (*Reihengrabstellen*). The second half of the nineteenth century saw more open and relaxed designs introducing the curved (or meandering) line (*Krumme Linie*) for the main paths. German cemeteries took inspiration from abroad – John Claudius Loudon and the Anglo-Saxon garden cemetery movement inspired this design.[48] This articulated bourgeois sepulchral culture and created a cultural space where the bourgeoisie could freely express its own (rather than earlier aristocratic) aesthetic ideas and identity. The American rural cemetery (1834) was also imitated; a prime example is the famous Mount Auburn cemetery in Cambridge, Massachusetts, which incorporated a series of hills and other natural features in the design. In this form, the layout of cemeteries no longer looks violently imposed on the landscape and the garden is more unified with the surrounding landscape. This was far removed from the strong geometrical forms and designs of earlier periods, such as the City of London cemetery near Epping Forest (1854) with its delineated vistas.[49] These precedents led to the design and construction of cemeteries that became the models for large urban cemeteries in many European cities and synonymous with bourgeois cemetery design.[50]

Towards the end of the nineteenth century Germany saw the design and construction of two large urban cemeteries that were to have a fundamental impact on the prevailing taste and the way that the German cemetery space was to be regulated in order to preserve an aesthetic. First, Wilhelm Cordes planned and supervised the construction of Hamburg-Ohlsdorf between 1879 and 1914. Ohlsdorf is a gigantic park cemetery incorporating natural features such as woodland and hills as well as constructions such as artificial lakes. Cordes had created an enthralling symbiosis of architecture, sculpture and landscape design. Moreover, he addressed a certain need for reform and the establishment of order – a term that was about to dominate German cemeteries for the next hundred years.[51]

> How plain and without charm … all the cemeteries appear which were built immediately after the wars of unification. What makes them so ugly is not that they were merely created to fulfil a purpose, nor that in order to make the fullest use of the space available, there was no space for greenery left between the graves, but the fact that the soulless mass-produced gravestones have a repugnant effect. The output of the machine saw replaced artistic craftsmanship; mass-produced railings replaced luxuriant greenery … Soon people began to understand that things had to change, if we did not want to expose ourselves to the devastating judgement of later, more discerning, generations. The cemetery of Hamburg-Ohlsdorf thus came into being. Its brilliant creator Cordes planted an extensive wood and set the graves in this.[52]

Georg Hannig, the author of this article published in 1925, was the director of the cemetery in Stettin and a keen supporter of reform through the positive examples set by the *Reformfriedhöfe*. The idea was to show what could be done in terms of orderly cemeteries and thus instigate reform by example. Hannig, therefore, turns to the second individual and the second cemetery that was to be formative.

Thus, in Munich, under Grässel's supervision, in Bielefeld, in Darmstadt … cemeteries were created in existing woods, which all turned into sights in their respective cities.[53]

Hans Grässel's *Münchner Waldfriedhof*, built between 1905 and 1907, still influences perceptions of modern German cemeteries and beyond. Grässel created the Wilhelmine ideal of the *Waldfriedhof* – the original German woodland cemetery.[54] The design concept encompassed a semiotic order: German trees, Germanic traditions and later the idea of the German oaks were easily fused with the oaks as symbols of heroism in the World Wars.[55] Similar cemeteries were built on a large scale and continued to be built for a long time. The *Waldfriedhof* of Münster was, for example, opened as late as 1935.[56] The examples set by Cordes and Grässel proved persistent, because of their design and their timing. Many German cemeteries were designed or extended in the last decades of the nineteenth and the first half of the twentieth century; this has meant that fundamentally, most German cities to the present day operate the cemeteries (and in many cases the buildings) built and opened between 1870 and 1930. This has been one reason that allowed the reformist design of the time to leave enduring traces in the German cemetery landscape.

The third reason has been the persistence of its regulation. The reform movement's main aspiration was an aesthetic integrity achieved through order and homogeneity. By the early 1920s the advocates of reform believed that many cemeteries suffered from either aesthetic eclecticism in combination with an overabundance of kitsch, or cold mass characterless efficiency in the form of chessboard layouts.[57] Both extremes clashed with their aspiration to integrate cemeteries into the natural landscape. The grave ornamentation industry had created large concrete angels, and contemporary photographs disclose a vast array of lavish and fantastic ornaments. This caused some directors of cemeteries to aspire to the widespread introduction of the rather strict and more austere rules that amongst others Grässel, as one of the fathers of the *Reformfriedhöfe*, had insisted upon. The new regulations increased insistence on order, imposed height regulations and introduced processes of supervision and prior approval of gravestones and their inscriptions. The ubiquitous plot within the grid system of the cemetery (*Reihengrabstelle*) would become homogeneous once more.

> The accomplishment of having conducted the fight against disfigurement and (aesthetic) impoverishment of cemeteries and graveyards by mass-produced grave-furnishings is primarily to the credit of *Stadtbaurat* Grässel, Munich. His 1907 regulation on the erection of memorials and the treatment of graves in the *Waldfriedhof* of Munich delivered the tools to fight against broken remains of columns, concrete dripstones, pigeons, angels, dogs, cement tree trunks … and more of the same developed by the grave-furnishings industry and repeated a thousand times, and which heedlessly resists every move to eliminate this gravestone anti-culture. Grässel was completely successful in this struggle, and thus secured a broad foundation for serious art, artistic community spirit, and sensitive consideration of the overall impression made.[58]

Thus, in the 1920s, a wave of stringent aesthetical reform of cemeteries ensued, which is even persistent today – most German cemeteries still dictate a maximum height of either 80 cm or 120 cm for gravestones.

In 1922 the *Reichsausschuß für Friedhof und Denkmal* (Reich Committee for Cemetery and Memorial) was founded and chose Dresden as its seat. It subsequently published its standard for a cemetery regulation (*Musterfriedhofsordnung*). This standard was followed by many cities and communities taking up the suggestions and restricting many aspects not previously considered. The Committee influenced the design of cemeteries well into the 1950s and beyond (see next chapter).[59] Some of its writings and many of its ideals proved influential on both East and West German cemetery design and aesthetics in the post-war era. The Nazi interlude made some impression on developments of cemetery design, particularly the introduction of pronounced anti-church sentiments:

> The cemetery, according to current understanding, is a public institution serving the community, and is therefore – without consideration of whose possession it finds itself in – open as a burial site to every *Volksgenossen* … At burials in cemeteries belonging to a religious community even persons who do not belong to that particular religious community can deliver speeches and addresses that are dedicated to the commemoration of the deceased. They have to abstain from any remarks relating to church policy.[60]

Although the terminology may differ, the vehemence of these remarks is comparable to equivalent statements from the GDR. But, as with Joseph II's cemetery reform, those keen to reform cemeteries often overlooked the role of the churches and religion, believing more often than not that rationality would overcome obstacles of a legal, traditional, or practical nature. Since the French Revolution, in conjunction with secularization, more regulatory powers had been established with regard to public space. However, ownership of cemeteries in Germany, with the exception of urban cemeteries, remained with the churches. This meant that changes in the sepulchral culture of Germany nearly always showed a marked difference between the urban and the rural.

This same divide can be clearly seen in the next development that proved ultimately to be of even greater significance than the rise of the urban cemetery. Modern cremation advanced during the twentieth century to the point that cremation not only represented a viable alternative to burial but actually became the ultimate expression of secularism and dovetailed with the other influential processes of sanitation and rationalization. On 4 April 1929, the ninetieth crematorium in Germany opened in Bielefeld. This might seem a rather arbitrary event, with no significance except, perhaps for local historians. However, in the longer time frame of German sepulchral culture since the late eighteenth century, this event clearly marks the point of convergence of two key developments, insofar as the new crematorium was built on the *Sennefriedhof*, the central cemetery in Bielefeld, which itself had only been established seventeen years earlier in 1912 as an example of a well-coordinated and well-proportioned *Waldfriedhof*. Bielefeld underlines the fact that in many cemeteries the crematorium had not only become part of the landscape, but also introduced a hitherto unknown form of sepulchral culture to an ever larger catchment area.

Ever since the discursive and medical imperative of hygiene had conquered the public sphere, individuals were looking for new and progressive means of corpse disposal. An anonymous painter in Munich made possibly one of the oddest suggestions of the mid nineteenth century. He based his idea on the work of Italian scientist Paolo Gorini. The Italian had numerous ideas on how to modernize the disposal of human corpses and invented the cremation oven. The German painter proposed that the coffin should be buried as usual but that it should be connected to a funnel above the ground, through which a mixture of acids could be poured, dissolving most of the body in about twenty minutes.[61] This represented a scientific solution to the problem of slow and repulsive decay. A rather less novel and radical way to dispose of the body was through burning.

The keys to the success of cremation in Germany are the particularism of the German lands as well as the fact that both the middle class and the working class became supportive of the form of disposal. On 10 December 1878 the first cremation of a body occurred in the new crematorium of Gotha, signalling the dawn of a new era. The event was entirely due to the liberal and tolerant views held by the ruler of Saxony-Coburg-Gotha, one state of the Thuringian Union (*Thüringische Staaten*).[62] This crematorium, like all in the late nineteenth century, had been proposed by a private cremation society (*Feuerbestattungsverein*) which advocated a far more pragmatic approach to the problem of disposal. This dynamic idea stemmed from an initially bourgeois, deeply secular and reformist agenda that based its reasoning on the principles of the Enlightenment and rationalism. Technology was increasingly seen as the new cure-all. No source underlines this more emphatically than a small leaflet written by Georg Müller on behalf of the *Volks-Feuerbestattungs-Verein* (the working-class cremation society) in 1927. It repeatedly advocates crematoria even in smaller communities on the grounds that they would not only save space but money. It emphatically asserts that 'cremation, apart from its other advantages, and considering the great economic benefits which it delivers when compared to inhumation, is also the most expedient form of disposal for small communities'.[63] This rational argument of a dozen pages is ultimately followed by a compassionate dimension shown in a rather powerful poem promoting the ideals of cremation:

> Beautiful may dying be: To descend as victor into Hades' night
> To incline the head to a long slumber, after the day's work is done.
> Yet ever daunting it remains, to think that into the earth they lower us.
> That this breast, so full of deeds, in a cold grave is to rest.
> You can gaze smilingly into death's bony visor,
> Yet you ask in silent horror: What will become of me down below?
> After a proud life's journey on earth to be crudely buried,
> That remains an abominable picture which I shudder to behold.
> Your most beloved you always like to lay to rest in the shroud of resurrection,

> To rescue the godlike [plural as in gods] body from the worm, who gnaws on the coffin's
> wall,
> Let giant fire wreaths flicker! It is surely better than to moulder in death's field:
> In the play of flames, to reach the final destination!
> Into dust and ash you turn! – In the crimson glow of the evening embers
> You fly forth on fiery horses, and every lamentation rests silently on the graves.
> Instead of sleeping under the damp turf, life's remains in the round shape of the vases
> [urns];
> That which is so small, enclosed in our hand, encompasses a world of love![64]

This poem hints at the vehemence and passion of the philosophical and social argument made for cremation. These sentiments shed light on the ideology behind the frequent use of such phrases as *Verwesungsgruben* (decomposition hole) as the synonym for grave, and *Madensack* (maggot sack) for corpse. 'Innovative and intellectual' members of the bourgeoisie saw traditional inhumation as anachronistic, unhygienic and even barbaric.

In the German context, however, Norbert Fischer and Sabine Ameskamp rightly stresses that the origins and motives for this movement are often overlooked.[65] Inhumation was only challenged because of a peculiar mixture of scientific interest, the Enlightenment leading to secularization and an increasing interest in classic and ancient cultures. The prevalence of neoclassical ornaments found on crematoria demonstrates the centrality of this latter dimension.[66] Another important influence was romanticism. One of the earliest recorded modern cremations in Western Europe was that of the poet Percy Bysshe Shelley in 1822. Nevertheless, only in the second half of the nineteenth century did attitudes to death change. Death became medically better understood and pragmatic and material philosophies, such as the secular thoughts of Ludwig Feuerbach, were in vogue, combining to form a potent rationality challenging religion and myth alike.[67] It was also the time of scientific experiments, and implications of the industrial revolution contributed to a contemporary fear of decay and pollution. In 1872, Gorini, Pollini and Brunetti conducted a famous and influential cremation in Padua, experimenting with a workable apparatus, and Brunetti exhibited the resultant ashes at the 1873 Vienna Exhibition. In 1879 it would be Gorini who would built the British Cremation Society's crematorium in Woking, England. Two years later, in 1874, Pieper and Lilienthal conducted experiments with a closed Siemens furnace – a gas-fired oven with air valves achieving the necessary temperatures leading to incineration rather than mere burning. This led to one of the first modern cremations in Milan in 1876.[68] The first German cremation societies were formed in the early 1870s in Gotha, Dresden, Berlin, Hamburg and Frankfurt/Main. This list indicates one pivotal factor in the dissemination of cremation throughout Europe; all these cities were Protestant (and the earlier Italian influence was explicitly scientific and secular). Religion became a determinant in the spread of cremation. These societies used their influence and their publications to promote cremation. They had little initial success. The second crematorium was only built in Heidelberg in 1891, a further one in

Hamburg in 1892. The new technology had to overcome theology and tradition. Objections included whether a corpse was needed for resurrection, and whether the ashes could be contaminated with the remains of other people. Burning was traditionally seen as the punishment for witches and many conservative commentators referred to metaphor of roasted flesh.[69] Entire religious denominations – the Greek-Orthodox Church and the Catholic Church – resisted the new technology of disposal in their fight against modernity. In reaction to the largely secular nature of the cremationist movement, the Catholic Church decided to ban cremation for Catholics in 1886 by the use of Canon Law.[70]

Despite these obstacles, two developments assisted the proliferation of cremation. The first was the introduction of the mortuary, associated with the compulsory, albeit mostly superficial, post-mortem (as in necropsy or *Leichenschau*, not as in the fully invasive autopsy or *Leichenöffnung*). This dispelled the fear that evidence of criminal events could be lost or that somebody could be cremated in a state of suspended animation. Secondly and of far greater importance was secularization. In Germany the state took over key elements of the Church's administrative control over schooling in 1873 and introduced civil marriage certificates in 1874, by which time many cemeteries in urban areas had become municipal property.[71] The Catholic Church argued that cremation as a practice was contrary to Christian funeral tradition. Priests were, therefore, not allowed to administer the last rites nor take part in the burial of the ashes. This ban was not lifted until 1963. The Catholic Church now permits cremation, provided that it does not demonstrate a denial of faith in the resurrection of the body.[72] The Protestant Churches took a more plural and more liberal view. The Protestant Church, due to its decentralized organization into *Landeskirchen*, soon discarded an initial scepticism. Amongst the most liberal churches were those of Saxony-Coburg-Gotha, Badenia, Hamburg, Hesse, Saxony-Weimar-Eisenach and Württemberg.[73] With the exception of Badenia and Württemberg, all these churches are in the Protestant north. It is no coincidence that cremation was first made possible in the state of Thuringia with its predominately Protestant population. Crematoria statistics for 1926 make this obvious. The three crematoria with the highest number of cremations in 1926 were all located in the Protestant area of central Germany, whilst Augsburg, the only city listed which is in predominantly Catholic Bavaria, has the lowest rate of cremations of all cities listed (see Table 1.2). This correlation remains. Moreover, as the detailed statistics of cremations in Eisenach also underline, because crematoria were rare in many regions, many vehement supporters of cremation asked to be cremated far away, only to encounter more problems when the ashes were returned to the family (see Table 1.3).

A pamphlet of the *Verein für Feuerbestattung* in Hagen (Cremation Society of Hagen in Westphalia) draws a vivid picture of the difficulties faced by those favouring cremation but without a local crematorium. The society encountered resistance from the local parish and, with pending legal action, had to bury the ashes in the cemetery of a nearby parish which was more sympathetic.[74] The

Table 1.2: Cremation rate of selected German cities in 1926.

City	Population	Cremations	Cremations per 100,000
Augsburg	162,000	78	48
Lübeck	120,000	122	102
Mainz (1903)	107,000	138	130
Karlsruhe	145,000	192	130
Krefeld	129,000	173	134
Plauen	110,000	320	290
Wiesbaden	104,000	318	305
Halle/Saale (1915)	192,000	624	325
Erfurt	133,000	453	340
Braunschweig	144,000	814	560

(Source: Letter from Stettiner Chamottefabrik to the City Council of Bielefeld, 27 January 1927, StA Bielefeld FW 152)

same document gives a rather interesting insight into the social composition of these societies. The president of the society was a doctor, the secretary a police inspector, the treasurer a merchant. Also included were four businessmen, a bookshop owner, the director of the local tram service, a journalist, an architect, two high-ranking local civil servants, a banker and a retired officer. Altogether this constituted a good number of local notables with above average education. These people promoted cremation as the clean, logical, technical solution to the problem of disposal. It is this frame of mind which made the cremation movement so successful in most of the Protestant regions of Germany.[75] Thus, it is not surprising that one finds this kind of strong rationalist pro-cremation movement in nearly all industrialized communities with a considerable Protestant population.

In other Protestant countries the development of cremation differed. The British Cremation Society was formed in 1874 under the influence of Sir Henry Thompson's writings. The society built a crematorium in Woking in 1879. However, it did not use the crematorium until 1885, when a court case finally ruled that a crematorium was not a nuisance if distanced from dwellings. Two further crematoria were built in the cities of Glasgow (1895) and Liverpool (1896). The first municipal crematorium was built in Hull in 1901. Despite other arguments, it was not until well after the First World War that cremation successfully took root in Britain. The war itself had very little impact on the cremation rates.[76]

In the United States, the New York Cremation Society was founded in 1881 and the first two crematoria opened in 1888, both of which included columbaria.[77] Stephen Prothero has observed that German literature on cremation was widely available in the US and that German Americans gave cremation a boost by forming such entities as the *Allgemeine Feuerbestattungsverein* of New York; he also notes the significance of the German Workingmen's Cremation Association

Table 1.3: Cremation rate in Eisenach 1902–1925.

Year	Cremations	Of these locals
1902	17	11
1903	43	23
1904	57	39
1905	59	37
1906	93	32
1907	96	46
1908	85	51
1909	100	60
1910	164	106
1911	162	98
1912	167	107
1913	156	105
1914	159	107
1915	194	133
1916	212	155
1917	233	175
1918	283	218
1919	200	157
1920	229	186
1921	198	152
1922	216	167
1923	318	295
1924	349	307
1925	410	350

(Source: Eisenacher Tagespost, 31 December 1926, StA Bielefeld, FW 152)

of Buffalo.[78] His works emphasized the importance of the precedent set by some German states.

This last cremation association points to a second social class supporting the idea of cremation – the working class. A number of Social Democrats supported the idea of cremation because it represented a new secular form of dealing with death. This political party emphasized the pragmatic rather than the dogmatic aspect of cremation. Despite being well structured, the SPD was initially slow to propagate the idea of cremation. In conjunction with the unions, the SPD and the *Freidenkerbund*, which viewed cremation as atheistic and egalitarian, the *Volks-Feuerbestattungsverein von Groß-Berlin* was founded in 1913. When August Bebel died in August 1913, his body was cremated in Zürich. He had stated that his decision was based on anti-clerical sentiments.[79] His precedent was to have strong reverberations for many decades to come. By the end of 1917 the *Volks-Feuerbestattungsverein* had 3,600 members, and by 1925 it had amassed 600,000 members. This indicates that these societies grew through a second wave in the popularization of cremation. During the first few years of the

Weimar Republic cremation had thus acquired a broad two-tiered social base. This was amplified by the strong desire to rationalize (in the sense of both connotations) disposal, especially in the major cities of the country. The percentage of workers amongst the cremated rose from roughly 12.5 per cent in 1920 to 45 per cent in 1926.[80] The 1920s also saw a growing number of regional *Vereine für Freidenker* or *Proletarische Freidenker* (Association for Freethinkers or Proletarian Freethinkers). These officially merged in 1927 and the amalgamated society proposed a crematorium in Magdeburg.

This effort was successful. In December 1925 it created the first mass urn burial site (*Urnenhain*). This site comprised of a central memorial, a bench made from red brick, and a large grey stone torch marking the place and the purpose, but where the urns were buried without individual markers. The society called it *Neue Deutsche Bestattungsklasse* (New German burial class). This new form of burial challenged the conservative and conventional ideas so inherent in the lease of a normal burial plot (*Wahlgrab-* and *Familiengrabstelle*). The anonymous burial, the ultimate egalitarian and atheistic form of burial, was created.[81] This was an idea that took a long time to find really widespread usage. Cremation was initially more successful, because it could be reconciled with the continuation of other traditions. Socialism and the proletariat had not invented their own form of disposal, nor did they promote anonymous burials, but they shared their ideals with a number of other organizations – many of bourgeois orientation. While this anonymous burial was not widespread, its local acceptance grew progressively. In Magdeburg it proved so successful that the designated field did not last the intended thirteen years; the space was filled in less than five.

Although cremations gained popularity in Germany, geography has remained a key determinant. Initially cremation was successful in places with strong left-wing majorities, such as Berlin, or in places with a strong liberal, Protestant, or enlightened traditions, such as Hamburg, Heidelberg and Lübeck. In other places the picture was different. Cremation did not spread in rural areas and especially in conservative or Catholic areas such as Bavaria or Paderborn. In the late 1920s, fifty years after the battle for the construction of the first crematorium, the decision to build a crematorium was not much easier. Like all its predecessors, the crematorium of Bielefeld was the product of intense and repeated lobbying by the local cremation society.[82] This group of local dignitaries and intellectuals had already unsuccessfully attempted to introduce this idea to the local council in 1923 and 1925. Two years later, they finally succeeded with the strong support from the SPD councillors, referring to the precedent set by August Bebel, their revered former party leader. The decision of the council recommended that the task should be dealt with as soon as possible. However, the department responsible for the implementation of this decision (*Amt für Friedhofswesen*) took a considerable time approaching all possible contractors and trying to organize the astonishingly complex technical details. Special attention was given to solving the question of the most economical process for the cremation.[83] One explanation of this might be found in the difficult economic situation of the late 1920s. Another factor was the role economic considerations played in changing sepulchral culture. A third reason was one of a more practical nature. Local officials were well aware that crematoria were often slow to establish economically sustainable levels of acceptance. In the files concerning the construction there is one newspaper clipping quoting the slow rise of cremation rates in Eisenach. The crematorium was opened in 1901 and saw a rather slow, hesitant and uneven rise in the numbers of cremations. It took twenty-two years before cremations in Eisenach reached an economically viable level of cremations per week.

However, there are also some examples of the more successful evolution of crematoria. The developments in the city of Jena were quite remarkable. Norbert Fischer stresses that Jena illustrates that with the political will to promote cremation it can be extremely successful. The local government above all kept costs for the citizens low.[84] The local *Feuerbestattungsverein*, in conjunction with a progressive local government, was able to establish a new tradition and a general acceptance of cremation. In Jena by 1910, when there were only twenty crematoria in Germany altogether and the crematorium was only twelve years old, there were more cremations than earth burials in the city. In the 1920s, cremation had become the most common way of burial in Jena by far. This figure would rise to the figure of 90.8 per cent in 1995. In this day and age, the home territories of the German Reformation are still the places with the highest cremation rates in Europe.

Not all cities were so swift in adopting the new method of disposal. For a long time uncertainty was the rule rather than the exception. It was difficult for the families of many who were cremated to find a final resting place. Some societies, like the *Volks-Feuerbestattungsverein* Groß-Berlin, decided to avoid legal arguments by buying their own private cemeteries reserved for their members. In Hagen the same decision was taken. However, the club also insisted upon asserting the general legal rights of the society's members and went to court in order to ensure the wishes of their deceased members. Nevertheless, it would take more than thirty years to establish a unified legal basis for cremation in Germany. In 1934, one year after Hitler became chancellor, after a prolonged period of discussion, which as one document suggested had been well underway as early as 1921, the *Reichsgesetz über die Feuerbestattung* became statutory law.[85] The press release of the *Lippische Landesregierung*, for example, stressed the major changes:

> The most important advance with regard to the previous legal framework is the fundamental equality of cremation and conventional burial. The form of burial, whether cremation or conventional burial, depends only on the choice of the deceased ... The cremation of a corpse is only admissible in a crematorium. The ashes [cremains] of every corpse are to be placed in an officially sealed container, and have to be laid to rest in a columbarium, an urn field, or a grave. Keeping the ashes in private rooms is not allowed.[86]

This legislation marked a turning point. The new Nazi rulers had not been shy to promote some of their own ideas regarding cremation, such as its representation as a great Nordic tradition. On the contrary, the law of 1934 simply made cremation legitimate and regulated.[87] The cremation legislation of 1934 is merely technical and devoid of ideological language. There might have been an element of anti-Church sentiment, as supporting cremation was often seen as counteracting Catholicism, but the core of the legislation went back to the ideas of the Weimar administration. The crematorium had established itself as a key component in the running of many urban cemeteries – it had become a beacon of technical modernization. This is reflected in architectural change. The early crematoria, before 1914, were distinguished by what was essentially an attempt to camouflage their purpose – the impious combination of death and technology – by means of neo-classical or even gothic design.[88] They looked like temples or chapels. Their quintessential design feature was embedded in the surrounding park landscape of the *Waldfriedhof*. A prime example is the crematorium of Heilbronn which was built in 1905. Even the brochure of Fritz Schumacher's new monumental crematorium in Dresden (1911), whilst admitting that the building dominated the wooded landscape, still emphasized the important unity of form and space (*Form und Raum*).

> In the middle of a pine wood on an area south of the *Johannisfriedhof* in Tolkewitz stands the impressive sandstone building of a new crematorium … The location of the new institution has two special and attractive features, the impact of the dense dark pine wood and the view of the friendly banks of the Elbe. A connection has been established between

Figure 1.1 View towards the crematorium of Dresden-Tolkewitz with the reflection pool.

Figure 1.2 The decaying reformed urn field of Dresden opened in 1926 and encapsulating the key idea of the cemetery reform movement: 'Order is already beauty'.

both of these and the building. The building has been set back so far on the site that a long dark tree-lined avenue, reflected in a narrow pool leads to it, whereas at the rear there is a cloister-like urn yard with archways which open up to the friendly landscape on one side.[89]

By 1911, the general opinion of how a cemetery should be designed was about to change, and so was the design of crematoria. The ideas of classic modernity beckoned – the crematorium of Dresden-Tolkewitz marked the departure from historicism and neo-classicism.

This new building was monumental, combining many different elements but retaining clear lines while avoiding references to sacral or classical temple architecture. This trend would continue with crematoria built after 1920, like the grand brick structure in Hanover which, with its bold triangular pillars, looks more like a theatre than a functional building in a cemetery. The reformed urn field of Dresden (1926), with its long grey banks, signified better than any other form of burial the loneliness of the dead. More fundamental changes in the design of crematoria or cemeteries would only come sporadically in the new era after 1945. It was then that concrete and glass finally conquered the realm of sepulchral architecture.

In the less densely populated countryside a different pattern existed. Some reforms took a very long time to filter through. The most obvious reason is that

Figure 1.3 Traditional family grave from the Baltic coast area. They have been characterised by the inclusion of a bench within the confines of the grave plot.

owing to the smaller population cemeteries did not run out of space so soon. Therefore the communities did not need to extend old cemeteries or build new ones as frequently. This might also explain the obvious contrast between urban rates of cremation and rural rates. In the countryside cremation remained far less common, and only recently do we see a change in that trend. One reason has to be that the countryside as a whole, because of its closer community and more rigid customs, remained conservative longer. Most rural undertakers will testify to the importance of the oak coffin (*Eichensarg*) for many of their customers.[90]

The steady stream of reforms, setting clearer and more restrictive regulations and guidelines, was born out of a wide array of factors, chief amongst them urbanization, industrialization and population growth, as well as sociocultural problems that arose mainly out of a larger population density. The city played the key role, because issues of hygiene and organization were predominately urban in origin, as were more complex problems such as the loneliness of the dying. Since the 1970s, some of this has changed, as general awareness has increased. The hospice movement, the natural death movement, and since 1990 debates about restrictions on cemeteries, all bear witness to an increasing engagement with issues related to death.[91] Additionally, urban areas face growing cemetery crises – as sites get older there is a general lack of space for burials. This is often paired with an explosion in costs – sooner or later these facts will have to be faced.[92] Given that the decomposition of a human body can take up to sixty years and that in most European countries burial plots are reclaimed after 25–50 years (although in Britain it is still illegal to re-use a plot) the strains on the system have become clear. This fact also underlines the continuing importance of cremation as a means of disposal. One of Europe's newest crematoria was open in Berlin in 2001 with a large spare capacity (25,000 cremations a year). The director is expecting increasing cadaver-tourism (*Leichentourismus*) from the surrounding rural countryside of Brandenburg in order to operate on a cost-effective level.[93] This fact once again underlines the importance of economics and efficiency in disposing of the dead. Similar forces shaping sepulchral culture were at play then as now.

By 1945 the fundamentals of the modern German sepulchral culture were to a large degree already established. Of the crematoria used in the GDR all but one were built before 1945. The cemeteries, with few exceptions, were built before 1930, and the modern funeral director had already emerged during the Weimar Republic. Similarly, the municipal nemesis of private companies profiteering from death had already emerged as an alternative, especially in the light of economic hardship. Germany saw similar developments to other countries, but also many differences. The major factor in the evolution of modern sepulchral culture was the human tendency to repress unpleasant tasks, creating what is termed the 'death-care profession' but what might actually be better called the 'death-care structure'.[94] The need for better public sanitation in the face of rising population density and urbanization accelerated this process, and also caused an explosion of regulations. In Germany this was then combined with the emergence of a bureaucracy ensuring adherence to regulations, making the German sepulchral culture one of the most rigidly legislated in the world. This in turn allowed for the implementation of ideological and/or aesthetic ideas held either by the state, by technocratic civil servants, or by interest groups. This meant that death, dying and disposal became increasingly engineered, and thus subjected to an increasing need for economic efficiency. Disposal of the dead in particular had become a huge, inescapable organizational necessity. The crematorium, the modern municipal park cemetery, the mortuary, the professional undertaking service or the municipal burial service, even secular funeral rituals and mass urn graves have all evolved as a result of these developments and the underlying need to dispose of the human corpse in an 'appropriate' way.[95] Therefore, even before the great cataclysm of the Second World War, the components of a modern sepulchral culture had appeared. There was still a large gulf between the city and the countryside, and certainly differences between individual countries, but ultimately Western countries shared a sepulchral culture dominated by individualization, professionalization, secularization, sanitation, regulation and rationalization. When Germany emerged from the ruins of that War, the post-war sepulchral culture of the West as well as the East would have to be built upon these foundations, and both would find it difficult to break quickly with a number of these established traditions and trends.

Notes

1. O. Beneke, *Von unehrlichen Leuten: Kulturhistorische Studien und Geschichten aus vergangenen Tagen deutscher Gewerbe und Dienste,* Second Edition (Berlin: Hertz, 1889), 231–40. It was part of the executioner's duties to bury those who committed suicide or others who did not warrant a proper (*standesgemäß*) burial.

2. T. Macho and K. Marek (eds), *Die neue Sichtbarkeit des Todes* (Paderborn: Wilhelm Fink, 2007); in the context of the suicide of Robert Enke see the thoughtful piece by T. Assheuer, 'Die neue Sichtbarkeit des Todes', *Die Zeit,* 19 November 2009.

3. For a theological introduction see: D. Davies, *A Brief History of Death* (Oxford: Blackwell, 2004) and as a philosophical introduction, K. Lacina, *Tod* (Vienna: Facultas WUV, 2009).

4. T. Walter, 'Death: Taboo or Not Taboo', *Sociology,* 25:2 (1991), 293–310.

5. U. Gebhard, 'Todesverdrängung und Umweltzerstörung', in U. Becker et al. (eds), *Sterben und Tod in Europa* (Neukirchen-Vluyn: Neukirchener, 1998), 146–51.

6. N. Elias, *The Loneliness of the Dying* (Oxford: Blackwell, 1985), 8–10.

7. F. Hartmann, 'Grenzen ärztlichen Vermögens am Lebensende', and K.-H. Wehkamp, 'Lebensende: Zwischen Medizinisierung und Sterbekultur', both in Becker et al. (eds), *Sterben und Tod in Europa.*

8. K. Blumenthal-Barby, *Betreuung Sterbender: Tendenzen, Fakten, Probleme* (Berlin: VEB Volk und Gesundheit, 1982), 40.

9. For a very brief overview see: D. Bennahum, 'The Historical Development of Hospice and Palliative Care', in W. Forman et al. (eds), *Hospice and Palliative Care: Concepts and Practice* (Sudbury, MA: Jones and Bartlett, 2003), 2–11.

10. Elias, *The Loneliness of the Dying,* 23.

11. A good explanation for this communal washing ceremony of the corpse might be found in the fact that a shared task did not leave one woman of the neighbourhood untouched by the task. See also: B. Wrede, 'Das Familiengrab ist voll', *Süddeutsche Zeitung,* 20/21 November 2004.

12. There have been notable exceptions: some Swiss cities (Bern, Geneva, etc.) have a standard coffin (*Standardsarg*) to which every citizen of the city is entitled. Despite their rather dire name, these coffins are not as depressingly plain as their name might suggest, and are a far cry from the cheap and crude pine coffins, reminiscent of a 'tea chests', sometimes used for cremations in the GDR.

13. N. Fischer, 'Zur Geschichte der Trauerkultur in der Neuzeit – Kulturhistorische Skizzen zur Individualisierung, Säkularisierung und Technisierung des Totengedenkens', in M. Herzog (ed.), *Totengedenken und Trauerkultur – Geschichte und Zukunft des Umgangs mit Verstorbenen* (Stuttgart: Kohlhammer, 2001), 49–50.

14. Ariès, *Western Attitudes to Death,* 85–108.

15. G. Schiller, *Die Tätigkeit eines Bestatters: Versuch einer Beschreibung,* available at <http://memopolis.uni-regensburg.de/lekt…texte/tod_und_gesellschaft/shiller.html> (accessed 10 March 2003); one should, however, note that there is also an increasingly active movement that advocates a return to older practices alongside a more 'natural' attitude to death and dying in order to aid the mourning.

16. Elias, *The Loneliness of the Dying,* 86–88. For a useful and comprehensive sociological overview see: K. Feldmann, *Tod und Gesellschaft: Sozialwissenschaftliche Thanatologie im Überblick* (Wiesbaden: Verlag für Sozialwissenschaften, 2004).

17. Many factors are entangled in the process of modernization. For a critical view see: J. Scott, *Seeing Like a State – How Certain Schemes to Improve the Human Condition Have Failed* (New Haven and London: Yale University Press, 1998), especially 87–102.

18. T. Walter, *The Revival of Death* (London and New York: Routledge, 1994), 11.

19. Figures for entire populations are sadly rare. See: E. Winkler, *Tore zum Leben: Taufe, Konfirmation, Trauung, Bestattung* (Neukirchen-Vluyn: Neukirchener, 1995), 172; and to a lesser extent: C. Brown, *Death of Christian Britain* (London: Routledge, 2000).

20. C. Ratschow, 'Erwarten wir noch etwas jenseits des Todes?', *Neue Zeitschrift für systematische Theologie und Religionsphilosophie*, 14:1 (1972), 116.

21. G. van der Leeuw, 'Unsterblichkeit oder Auferstehung', *Theologische Existenz*, 52 (1956), 8, as quoted in F. Johannsen, 'Auf der Suche nach dem Sinn von Sterben und Tod – Der Wandel von Deutungsmustern aus theologischer Perspektive', in Becker et al. (eds), *Sterben und Tod in Europe*, 12.

22. J. Baird, 'Goebbels, Horst Wessel and the Myth of Resurrection and Return', *Journal of Contemporary History*, 17:4 (1982), 633–50.

23. THSA Weimar, Thüringischen Ministeriums des Inneren, Akten E 1551: H. Zeiss, *Feuerbestattung und Nationalsozialismus* (Berlin: Selbstverlag des Großdeutschen Verbandes der Feuerbestattungsvereine, 1934).

24. See also: S. Friedländer, *Kitsch und Tod – Der Widerschein des Nazismus* (Frankfurt: Fischer, 1999), 31–59.

25. Another splendid example was the short-lived attempt to rid the language of undertaking of words without a German origin in 1933. M. Opitz, 'Können wir in der Bestattungswirtschaft mit der deutschen Sprachen auskommen oder müssen wir uns der Fremdwörter bedienen', in *Zeitschrift der Deutsche Bestattungswirtschaft*, 1933, 119–21, to be found in StA Dresden, Rep. 9.1.14, No. 825.

26. I. Wilhelm-Schaffer, *Gottes Beamter und Spielmann des Teufels – Der Tod im Spätmittelalter und früher Neuzeit* (Cologne: Böhlau, 1999).

27. N. Fischer, 'Zur Geschichte der Trauerkultur in der Neuzeit', in M. Herzog (ed.), *Totengedenken und Trauerkultur*, 42; AFD, *Die Geschichte der Friedhöfe*, 63–79.

28. StA Halle: *Gebäudeakte Stadtgottesacker*, offering a comprehensive collection of material and press cuttings on the cemetery, especially the threat of being demolished and turned into a socialist park.

29. The best example here is the rise of cremation in interwar 'Red Vienna', see: I. Langer, *Das Ringen um die Einführung der fakultativen Feuerbestattung im Wiener Gemeinderat*, Diplomarbeit, Universität Wien, 2008.

30. Curl, *The Victorian Celebration of Death*, 212.

31. H.-J. Krenzke, *Magdeburger Friedhöfe und Begräbnisstätten* (Stadtplanungsamt: Magdeburg, 1998), 67 This legislation was born out of earlier changes, especially which lead to the construction of Magdeburg's first of three main cemeteries (*Nordfriedhof*) in 1823.

32. S. Dethlefs, *Zur Geschichte der Friedhöfe und des Bestattungswesens in Münster* (Münster: Regensberg, 1991), 45.

33. H. Boehlke (ed.), *Wie die Alten den Tod gebildet – Wandlungen der Sepulkralkultur 1750–1850, Kasseler Studien zur Sepulkralkultur Vol. 1* (Mainz: Böhlau, 1979), 232–33.

34. C. Rädlinger, *Der verwaltete Tod – Eine Entwicklungsgeschichte des Münchner Bestattungswesen* (Munich: Buchendorfer, 1996), 63–86.

35. For example the collective uniform urn graves of Freethinker Clubs advocating a very restrained but dignified communal form of burial in reaction to pomp. From the late eighteenth century there was an increasing discourse of the pomp and exuberance of upper-class funerals, while the majority of the population could not afford a decent burial. See Fischer, *Vom Gottesacker zum Krematorium*.

36. Rädlinger, *Der verwaltete Tod*, 69.

37. Ibid., 140.

38. For example: 'Begräbnis-Ordnung der Stadt Jena vom 28. Februar 1889', published in *Statuen betreffend das Begräbniswesen der Stadt Jena* (Jena: Universitäts-Buchdruckerei Neuenhahn, 1908), 3–6.

39. Fischer, *Wie wir unter die Erde kommen*, 80–93.

40. In Munich, by 1862, in the smaller cities and in rural areas mortuaries were less common. The provincial city of Detmold built one in 1912 and in rural Westphalia laying out at home was common until after 1945. In the countryside large blocks of ice were provided by the local

undertaker to be placed beneath the coffin in order to prevent rapid decomposition. NWSA Detmold, D 106 Detmold No. 2128.

41. See for example: C. Arnold, *Necropolis: London and its Dead* (London: Simon and Schuster, 2007), 123–51.

42. It would go well beyond the scope of this chapter to cover all aspects this development, however, for an introduction in regard to Germany see: G. Howarth, 'Professionalising the Funeral Industry in England 1700–1960', in P. Jupp and G. Howarth (eds), *The Changing Face of Death – Historical Accounts of Death and Disposal* (Houndsmill: Macmillan, 1997), 120–34. With regard to Germany there is still a lacuna of historical knowledge.

43. Magistrat der Landeshauptstadt Magdeburg, *100 Jahre Westfriedhof Magdeburg* (Magdeburg, 1998), 4–5.

44. The 1920s (especially 1923 and 1929) saw times of great crisis which saw a number of cities declaring burials a municipal remit, and banning private companies. Characteristic were also attempts to save wherever feasible, for example a vast number of advertisements were sent out praising wood-conserving coffins made from cardboard and bitumen, *Rapitz-plaster* coffins (using plaster rather than wood), or the wonderfully named half-wooden-coffin (*Halbholzsarg* – 1923): NWSA Detmold, D 106 Detmold No. 2152.

45. NWSA Detmold, File D 106 Detmold No. 436, *Verkaufsborschüre W. Thurst: Marmor-, Syenit-, Serpentin-, Kalk-Werke Groß-Kunzendorf (Neisse)*, January 1930, 3. But this is only one example taken from an especially troubled time in German history, similar references can be found earlier and later, as further quotations will show.

46. S. Koch, 'Geschichte und Bedeutung des Friedhofes im Abendland', *Zeitschrift für Semiotik*, 11:2–3 (1989), 131.

47. Such as the Hauptfriedhof Kassel, Dresdner Nordfriedhof.

48. A prime example is the South Metropolitan Cemetery in Norwood. See also Curl, *Celebration of Death*, 244–64. Another is York Cemetery, see: H. Murray, *This Garden of Death – The History of York Cemetery* (York: Friends of York Cemetery, 1991).

49. D. Sloane, *The Last Great Necessity – Cemeteries in American History* (Baltimore: John Hopkins University Press, 1991), 48–51.

50. M. Felicori and A. Zanotti, *Cemeteries of Europe – A Historical Heritage to Appreciate and Restore* (Bologna: Commune di Bologna, 2004).

51. H. Schoenfeld, *Der Friedhof Ohlsdorf: Gräber – Geschichte – Gedenkstätten* (Hamburg: Christians, 2000); N. Krieg, *'Schon Ordnung ist Schönheit': Hans Grässels Münchner Friedhofsarchitektur (1894–1929), ein deutsches Modell?* (Munich: Herbert Utz, 1990).

52. G. Hannig, 'Alte und Neue Friedhofskunst', *Der Friedhof*, 21:4 (1925), 46.

53. Ibid.

54. Fischer, *Vom Gottesacker zum Krematorium*, 54–59; the city of Stockholm began to plan the famous *Skogskyrkogården* in 1912, and UNESCO declared it a world heritage site in 1994.

55. See A. Lehmann, *Von Menschen und Bäumen: die Deutschen und ihr Wald* (Hamburg: Rowohlt, 1999); A. Lehmann, 'Der deutsche Wald' in E. Francois and H. Schulze (eds), *Deutsche Erinnerungsorte Vol. 3* (Munich: C.H. Beck, 2003), 187–200.

56. Dethlefs, *Zur Geschichte der Friedhöfe*, 73–74.

57. Some of the reforms did work in war cemeteries, and these ideas are clearly present in the more extreme suggestions of uniformity (as opposed to homogeneity). Also we see a very clear return to arts and crafts, a move away from machine-produced gravestones. See: Fischer, *Vom Gottesacker zum Krematorium*, 172.

58. NWSA Detmold, D 106 Detmold No. 2128: W. Hellweg (Oberbaurat), 'Ohlsdorfer neue Grabmalkunst', in *Hamburger Fremdenblatt – Rundschau im Bilde*, Jg. 94, No. 198, 28 April 1922, 1.

59. Fischer, *Vom Gottesacker zum Krematorium*, 129–31.

60. NWSA Detmold, D1 Dezernat 24 No. 225: *Schreiben des Reichsminister des Inneren an die Regierungspräsidenten*, 31 October 1940.

61. Rädlinger, *Der verwaltete Tod*, 141–43; Curl, *Celebration of Death*, 304.

62. Fischer, *Wie wir unter die Erde kommen*, 98.

63. 'Die Feuerbestattung ist also abgesehen von ihren sonstigen Vorzügen, mit Rücksicht auf die großen wirtschaftlichen Vorteile, welche sie der Erdbestattung gegenüber bietet, auch für kleiner Gemeinden die zweckmäßigste Bestattungsform': G. Müller, *Empfiehlt sich für kleine Stadtgemeinden die Errichtung von Krematorien?* (Third Edition) (Berlin: Volks-Feuerbestattungs-Verein, 1927), 12.

64. '*Funerale*' von Alfred Beetschen, journalist and poet, who lived in Aarburg, Switzerland: quoted in Müller, *Die Errichtung von Krematorien*, 12.

65. S. Ameskamp wrote a PhD thesis at Georgetown University, Washington D.C. on a more detailed and revised history of the origins of cremation in Imperial and Weimar Germany. See: S. Ameskamp, 'Fanning the Flames: Cremation in late Imperial and Weimar Germany', in: A. Confino, P. Betts and D. Schumann (eds), *Between Mass Death and Individual Loss: The Place of the Dead in Twentieth-Century Germany* (New York: Berghahn, 2008), 93–112. See also: T. Pursell, '"The Burial of the Future": Modernist Architecture and the Cremationist Movement in Wilhelmine Germany', *Mortality*, 8:3 (2003), 233–50.

66. Such as Columbaria, classic stone urns and the design of many gravestones marking urn burials, all reflect classical design.

67. Fischer, *Vom Gottesacker zum Krematorium*, 94–98.

68. Modern cremation refers to cremation in a dedicated cremation furnace, not on an open pyre: Curl, *Celebration of Death*, 304–5.

69. R. Thalmann, *Urne oder Sarg? – Auseinandersetzung um die Einführung der Feuerbestattung im 19. Jhrt.* (Bern and Frankfurt: Lange, 1979), 71–74.

70. D. Davies and L. Mates (eds), *Encyclopaedia of Cremation* (Aldershot: Ashgate, 2005), 107.

71. Fischer, *Vom Gottesacker zum Krematorium*, 98; Winkler, *Tore zum Leben*, 171–72.

72. Code of Canon Law of 1983, Canon 1176 §3: 'The Church earnestly recommends that the pious custom of burying the bodies of the deceased be observed; nevertheless, the Church does not prohibit cremation unless it was chosen for reasons contrary to Christian doctrine.' The change happened in 1963 and was enshrined in the above law in 1983.

73. Fischer, *Vom Gottesacker zum Krematorium*, 98.

74. NWSA Detmold, D 106 Detmold, No. 2146: *Rundbrief des Vereins für Feuerbestattung in Hagen in Westfalen*, 5 June 1900.

75. See the concept of *Bildungsreligion*: T. Nipperdey, *Deutsche Geschichte 1866–1918, Vol. 1 – Arbeiterwelt und Bürgergeist* (Munich: C.H. Beck, 1994), 476–79 and 504–7.

76. P. Jupp, 'Why was England the First Country to Popularize Cremation', in K. Charmaz, G. Howarth and A. Kellehear, *The Unknown Country: Death in Australia, Britain and the USA* (Houndsmill: Macmillan, 1997), 141–54, see also: D. Schumann et al., 'Death in Germany', *Bulletin of the German Historical Institute* (Washington D.C.), 34 (2004), 210.

77. Curl, *Celebration of Death*, 309.

78. S. Prothero, *Purified by Fire – A History of Cremation in America* (Berkeley, Los Angeles and London: University of California Press, 2001), 138.

79. Fischer, *Vom Gottesacker zum Krematorium*, 115.

80. Ibid., 116–17.

81. Krenzke, *Magdeburger Friedhöfe und Begräbnisstätten*, 101.

82. StA Bielefeld, Akte FW 152–54: *Krematorium Sennefriedhof Vol. I–III*.

83. Ibid.

84. N. Fischer, 'Vom Krematorium zum "Flamarium"? Über die historische Entwicklung der Krematoriumsbauten, Vortrag auf der Eternity 2001' [the aptly named annual trade fair for the funeral industry] in Ulm, Bernd Bruns: available at <http://www.postmortal.de/Impressum/DrNorbert_Fischer/drnorbert_fischer.html> (accessed 7 June 2001).

85. NWSA Detmold, L 80 IC (Medizinalwesen Minden), Fach L.5, No. 9: *Schreiben des Reichsminister des Inneren an die Ausserpreussischen Landesregierungen vom 21. Dezember 1921,*

contains the minutes of a meeting of emissaries of miscellaneous Prussian ministries and of the states of Bavaria, Saxony, Württemberg, Schwerin, Oldenburg, Bremen and Lübeck.

86. NWSA Detmold, L 80 IC, Fach L.5, No. 9: *Lippische Landesregierung Abt.1 an die Lippische Presse*, 27 June 1934.

87. Fischer, *Vom Gottesacker zum Krematorium*, 113.

88. Fischer, *Wie wir unter die Erde kommen*, 104–6.

89. StA Magdeburg, Rep. 41, No. 37: *Eröffnungsbroschüre Krematorium*, 1911.

90. Turnout is equally important. In general the role of funerals in ascertaining status in the countryside remains high, while we see a trend to save money in urban funerals.

91. <www.postmortal.de> is an internet portal that stands as a vivid example of the scope of current debate, or for the more academic debate see: K. Feldmann, *Tod und Gesellschaft*, 272–96.

92. 'Sensitive Britons Try to Bury Cemetery Crisis', *The Guardian*, 2 September 2000, 7.

93. 'Die Hadesmaschine', *Die Tageszeitung*, 21 May 2001.

94. M. Foucault, 'Des Espace Autres', in *Architecture/Mouvement/Continuité*, October 1984, 46–49.

95. For example, the crematoria of the northern regions of the GDR where cremation was not that common were built: Rostock (1928), Greifswald (1913), Schwerin (1930), Potsdam (1930), Brandenburg (1926), Fürstenberg (1934), Frankfurt/Oder (1930), Forst (1930), Magdeburg (1923).

Chapter 2

AFTER DEATH
THE ORGANIZATION OF DISPOSAL

When the surrender terms were signed in Reims on 7 May 1945, Germany lay in ruins in more than one sense. The war had left its physical and psychological marks upon the country and its people. Aerial photographs of the five largest cities, Berlin, Hamburg, Munich, Cologne and Leipzig, bear witness to the extent of the devastation. The death rates for Berlin showed the extent of the human losses, while additionally there was the devastation of the physical environment. A census of the available habitable space in Berlin on 16 April 1946, nearly a year after the end of the war, showed 1,065,258 useable flats and houses, with 3,140,603 available rooms, a 39 per cent loss compared to 1943, and in Berlin-Mitte and Tiergarten the decline was as much as 61 and 59 per cent.[1] Nonetheless, the magnitude of disruption and the political changes notwithstanding, everyday routines (*der Alltag*) showed remarkable continuity and resilience. In the face of dramatic change or hardship the core workings of the individual as well as society have to continue. It might sound like a truism, but that does not alter the fact that it is precisely this continuum of time, of coping with life, that represents one of the more fascinating aspects of studying the aftermath of any conflict. Alon Confino, in asking why some Germans thought of tourism on the day of the unconditional surrender, approaches the complex issue of normality and its perception in historiography.[2] It seems odd that even before the immediate post-war reconstruction and during a period of many other pressing issues, some people lobbied the military administration for the creation of a tourist union (*Fremdenverkehrsverband*). This dissonance between historical reality and individual or collective perception of reality illuminates human nature in the face of fundamental change and our ability, indeed need, to construct 'normality'. As much as human beings are capable of constituting complex social structures, they remain compelled by a number of core necessities of life. People had to organize food and shelter in more or less damaged cities and towns in order to sustain life and survive, and had to dispose of the increasing number of corpses. In this, the situation before May 1945 did not differ from the period immediately after the surrender (both in March and June 1945 about ten thousand people needed to be buried). This, in conjunction with the continuum of everyday life, stands in stark contrast to the myth of '*die Stunde Null*' (Zero Hour, an emotionally charged concept of the initial moment of renewal often used with reverence). The phrase has evoked a mental image contrary to any continuity, namely that of a fixed starting point at which all began anew.[3] It is precisely this metaphor of an absolute beginning which unburdened the present from the past, thus allowing a certain sense of German victimhood, that accounts for the reverential qualities that often reverberate in the usage of the phrase. However, it is this notion of the *tabula rasa* which is strongly negated by the persistence of everyday life in 1945: that everyday life goes on (*Der Alltag geht weiter*).[4]

In this atmosphere of destruction, despair, disarray, malnutrition, insalubrious hygienic conditions, suicide and the legacy of Nazism, death added yet another ubiquitous problem.[5] Like housing shortages, scarcity of supplies and the threat of cholera or dysentery, death rates in many urban areas were worsening. Those who had perished in the last acts of futile resistance as well as those who had simply died of old age, weakness, malnutrition, or illness, all needed to be buried.[6] Moreover, the army had suffered the highest casualties in the last months of the war.[7] This overwhelmed undertakers and cemeteries in nearly all cities. The system of disposal, already stretched by the bombing campaign, came close to collapse in many places.[8] It had to cope with too many corpses in too short a period, while suffering itself from neglect and destruction. An official within the provincial government of Brandenburg wrote a memorandum about public health and a letter to the city of Potsdam that provides a rare insight into the situation prevalent across the country. Archival evidence of similar conditions remains scarce due to the chaotic situation of the eighteen month after the surrender.[9] The official noted that both parts of the Potsdam cemetery – which had been divided into a new (late nineteenth-century) and an old part – contained approximately fifty bomb craters, and that repair work was being carried out only at a very slow pace. On the positive side, it was noted that there was only light damage to the structure of the administrative building, the crematorium and the mortuary.

> Many of the doors, however, are damaged and nearly all the windows are shattered. This had the particularly unpleasant consequence that rain, dust and wind penetrated right up to the storage chamber for the corpses, and birds were flying around there, which could be dangerous as carriers of infection; I saw large numbers of them flying around.[10]

The threat of infectious diseases, such as typhoid, was seen as a very serious problem, and thus of immediate concern for those charged with running rudimentary services while most urban mortuaries were full. The mortuary in Potsdam in the first days of August 1945 was completely full with twenty-seven bodies: six men, seventeen women and four children – including three corpses that were deemed to be infectious. These numbers meant that between the delivery of the corpses and the funeral there was a delay of five to eight days, and sometimes much longer. The administration also had to cope with recording the location of the burials, and sometimes with exhumations; about 1,100 corpses had been buried outside the city's cemeteries. In addition, there was the problem of removing corpses and body parts unearthed at bombsites (the so-called *Trümmerleichen*), many of which were in an advanced state of decomposition.

> Over half of the bodies in the storage chambers were placed in coffins or coffin-like crates, the lesser half, however, lay close together, sprinkled with a little lye [chlorine-chalk], some dressed, some undressed, on the concrete floor, emitting a very repulsive odour. In one room exhumed bodies from outside the cemetery lay without coffins; in another [room] I saw the remains of 5 dead bodies dug out of bombing sides, partly charred, partly putrefied, also without coffins.[11]

Such a picture was certainly not exceptional. Many other cemeteries, especially those in fairly close proximity to the larger cities or industrial towns, were hit harder, and additionally had to deal with larger numbers of corpses. For instance, the yearly report of the burial service of Dresden as late as 1950 identified the disposal of *Trümmerleichen* as one of its key tasks.[12] As with the experience of 1923 and with their economic hardships, 1945 gave cause to consider what constituted a 'proper' burial. Many innovations and customs that had surfaced in the era of economic uncertainty and the depression in the 1920s, such as the rented, or the light-weight coffin (*Leichtsarg/Sparsarg*) – made from as little wood as possible – resurfaced during the later stages of the war. Coffins made from wood replacement products and rented ones might explain, to a degree, the German obsession with the 'proper' oak coffin (*Eichensarg*); the reality of the immediate aftermath of the war, however, meant that attitudes towards corpses in some cases became utterly utilitarian:

> The next-of-kin of the deceased frequently deliver such [corpses] to the cemetery even without a coffin; the companies bring them in rental coffins, if the coffins are not the property of the next-of-kin; the rental coffins are either brought to the grave, if this has already been prepared, and are then emptied; most however are emptied in the mortuary and the rental coffins are taken away again; then when the grave is ready, normally at night time, the corpse will be wrapped in clothes brought to the grave usually on a cart, is placed in the grave and covered with a some earth, until the burial ceremony, if one takes place at all.[13]

Some aspects of this behaviour are reminiscent of the fictional scenes in Camus's existentialist masterpiece *La peste*.[14] This is not an inapt comparison, as utterly utilitarian solutions represented the only answers to the problems posed. The situation in Potsdam cemetery – where owing to bombing only a single tap was working serving the entire cemetery and the mortuary – represented as serious a problem of hygiene as could be imagined. Moreover, the number of deaths had nearly tripled (the mortality of children had actually quadrupled): whereas in the month of July 1944 there had been 160 funerals (67 men, 73 women, 20 children), in July 1945 there were 417, including some exhumations (167 men, 166 women, 84 children).[15] Under such conditions it seems that these measures resulted from sheer necessity. The number of new corpses reached a level beyond the capability of the mortuary and the staff to cope. In other cities, such as Dresden, the situation was far worse and went well beyond any comparison with Camus's literary depiction.

The essential strategy for coping with the extraordinary number of corpses requiring disposal was the immediate repair of the cremation ovens, the reduction of the waiting periods and the organizational problems of burials. As after the First World War, cremation was advocated as the principal means of avoiding the breakdown of the disposal system. During the Weimar Republic, cremation had lost its initial 'exotic appeal' expressing a particular aesthetic, social or political agenda, at least in urban areas, and crematoria had been built in nearly all the larger cities.[16] The availability of crematoria eased the situation considerably, as cremation increasingly represented the pragmatic answer to the problem of disposal of many corpses during, as well as after, the war.[17]

The larger cities and some towns faced even bigger problems of disorganization and disruption. Berlin, for example, was a city devastated by aerial bombardment, fires and street fighting. However, the conflict not only left obvious marks of violence. The city's infrastructure suffered from a combination of simple neglect, a general war-time lack of repairs and maintenance and the necessities of an economy geared mainly to one purpose: to sustain war. Berlin's population had dwindled from 4.4 million before the war to 2.8 in 1945; eighty million cubic meters of rubble were obstructing the reconstruction effort; its 2,200 hectares of cemeteries, parks and greenbelts were largely devastated.[18] This meant hardship for its inhabitants and trouble for those trying to run rudimentary public services after the end of the fighting. While some rural areas also witnessed widespread devastation, in general the destruction was not so great, and reverting back to normal life seemed far swifter, as, for example, food supplies were more steady and the housing shortage less acute. The countryside lent itself more readily to the improvisations that were needed due to the disruption of normality. The picture of families carting their deceased to the local cemetery in makeshift coffins – for example in the case of an old grandfather clock – hints at the extent of disruption in urban areas.[19] It is literature and recollections, such as those of Heinrich Böll, Wolfgang Borchert, or Walter Kempowski, that can convey some of the conditions suffered by ordinary inhabitants of the cities after the war.[20] Amongst these, Bochert's emotive short story *Nachts schlafen die Ratten doch!* takes an iconic position: it describes a stranger meeting a young boy who is guarding the ruins of the house that have buried his brother. The boy is adamant about not leaving in case the rats come to desecrate the corpses, and only finds rest when the stranger lies to him about the fact that rats sleep at night.[21]

There is, as Alon Confino points out, 'nothing normative about normality' and '[t]he normal is not an appraisal of reality; rather, it is an appraisal of value'.[22] Moreover, that appraisal is conducted by individuals. Individuals are not, as such, concerned with the state of the society as a whole, human beings are concerned with the state of their immediate affairs, experiences and expectations. Their perception is thus governed by their small field of expertise. Therefore, 'normality' returns swiftly, because it is nothing more than a perceived entity made up like a mosaic: those concerned with death judged normality by the fact that the burial service operated nearly as before. Others might have defined normality through food supplies or the resumption of the tourist trade.

By October 1946, the administration of the parks and cemeteries in Greater Berlin (*Groß-Berlin*) acknowledged that for the previous six months the demand for coffins had been met completely by the private undertaking sector – normality had returned. By late 1945, the private undertaking guild (*Innung*) was already complaining about these institutions, through Rudolf Diesing, the proprietor of a company producing coffins:

> When building anew or when reconstructing Berlin, the reorganization of the burial system of Berlin should not be considered of secondary importance. This is a matter of a relatively small profession, with which the public never or very seldom concerns itself. Only in the last few months did the question of the burial of the deceased naturally warrant more discussion. What was responsible for this was the lack of coffins which had existed since the aerial bombardment of 3 February … A central burial department and 20 district burial departments were created, which were only to allocate the coffins to the next-of-kin … The relatives who were already to be pitied having had, from one minute to the next, their healthy loved ones suddenly snatched away through the Hitlerian war of extermination and nazistic [sic] insanity, were informed in the coldest and most indifferent official tones: 'There are no coffins, burials must to be carried out without coffins.' Until the end of February the burials of the victims of aerial bombardments were organized by professionals and until then everybody who died in Berlin got his/her coffin. That ended on the day the burial departments were set up.[23]

This statement hints at the curious nature of the profession: while offering an essential service to the public, undertaking is largely ignored until the necessity arises. In times of crisis the proper burial of the deceased easily gains a high degree of importance, not least because of the psychological and cultural significance of a 'decent' (*anständige*) burial. However, the statement suggests that those who formed the private undertaking industry feared the permanent existence of a local government office that would interfere with their business interests. The 'threat' of socialization or municipalization, promoted by the KPD/SPD, loomed. The party policy was that many utilities and local services should be under the control of the local councils, in effect municipalizing the local service

Table 2.1: Total number of deaths, the mortality rate and distribution between the sexes in the Soviet Sector and from 1949 onwards in the GDR.

	Total number of deaths	Death per 10,000 of population	Male	Deaths per 10,000 males	Female	Deaths per 10,000 females
1938	–	119	–	–	–	–
1939	–	126	–	–	–	–
1946 (July onwards)	178,812	198.8	89,832	226.7	88,980	166.1
1947	358,035	189.5	185,550	228.2	172,485	160.3
1948	289,747	152.0	147,829	178.2	141,918	131.8
1949	253,658	134.3	125,679	151.2	127,979	121.0
1950	219,582	119.4	108.428	132.8	111,154	108.6
1951	208,800	113.8	103,083	126.4	105,717	103.7
1952	221,676	120.9	108,609	133.2	113,067	111.2
1953	212,627	117.1	104,753	129.4	107,874	107.0
1954	219,832	121.1	107,428	133.4	112,404	112.4
1955	214,066	119.3	104,843	130.8	109,223	110.0
1956	212,698	120.1	105,122	132.7	107,576	109.8
1957	225,179	128.6	111,422	142.1	113,757	117.6
1958	221,113	127.4	107,963	138.8	113,150	118.2
1959	229,898	132.9	112,470	138.8	117,428	123.3
1960	233,759	135.6	114, 496	147.5	119,263	125.8
1961	222,739	130	108,608	141	114,131	121
1962	233,995	137	113,049	146	120,946	129
1963	222,001	129	107,411	138	111,590	122
1964	226,191	133	109,235	141	116,956	126
1965	230,254	135.2	111,129	143	119,125	129
1966	225,663	132	107,849	138	117,814	127
1967	227,068	133	108,541	139	118,327	128
1968	242,473	142	115,156	147	127,317	138
1969	243,743	143	115,538	147	128,194	139
1970	240,821	141.2	112,721	143.6	128,100	139.1
1971	234,953	137.7	108,945	138	126,008	137
1972	234,425	137.5	108,536	138	125,434	137
1973	231,960	136.6	107,991	137	123,969	136
1974	229,062	135.3	106,101	135	122,961	135
1975	240,389	142.7	110,117	140.8	130,272	144.3
1976	233,733	139.2	106,756	136.7	126,977	141.4
1977	226,233	134.9	103,738	132.8	122,495	136.8
1978	232,332	139	106,235	136	126,097	141
1979	232,742	139	106,670	136	126,072	141
1980	238,254	142.3	107,908	137.5	130,346	146.6
1981	232,244	138.8	104,167	132	128,077	144
1982	227,975	136.5	102,090	130	125,885	142
1983	222,695	133.4	99,255	126	123,440	140

Table 2.1: (continued).

	Total number of deaths	Death per 10,000 of population	Male	Deaths per 10,000 males	Female	Deaths per 10,000 females
1984	221,161	132.7	97,869	124	123,312	140
1985	225,536	135.4	99,370	126.3	125,983	143.6
1986	223,536	134	97,713	124	125,823	144
1987	213,872	129	94,083	119	119,789	137
1988	213,111	127.9	94,489	119	118,622	136
1989	205,711	123.8	91,090	114.5	114,621	132.4

(Data: Statistische Jahrbücher der DDR 1949–1990)

industry. On a long-term basis, the very existence of departments to coordinate the undertaking industry could easily be seen as the precursor of a pending complete municipalization: that is, the nucleus on which to construct a municipal burial service. The municipalization of the undertaking industry has taken many forms, but generally there are two extremes: a complete municipalization means that a city would legislate that only a city-owned undertaking service would be allowed to arrange funerals, which are either privately financed or paid for in part or in full out of city coffers. Alternatively, the other constitutes a kind of cooperative model in which a restricted number of companies would have to follow strictly the guidelines and prices set out by the local cemetery administration – ultimately representing a state-run but privately owned undertaking sector. Both options would end the free market for private undertaking companies. The concept and enactment of municipalization was familiar to the Berlin undertakers as it had taken place in other cities (predominately in Southern Germany and Switzerland) since in the 1920s. Together with the new political dominance of the left, which traditionally had had a tendency towards municipalization, this explains the emphasis put upon the expertise within the industry and the coldness that would be the 'inevitable' result of a municipal (and thus bureaucratic) undertaking service.[24]

The undertaking industry in Berlin, unlike those in a number of municipalities and cities, most prominently in Saxony, Thuringia and Baden, had not been municipalized in the 1920s. In general, this idea had its inception in the 1890s, when a political movement in the canton and the city of Zurich succeeded in establishing a legal basis for a free burial for all its citizens (not a pauper burial, but a simple bourgeois funeral).[25] In Germany, the goal was even enshrined in the Erfurt programme of the SPD in 1891. After the revolution of 1918, this idea was enacted by a number of local governments.[26] As a popular movement, its intellectual roots were diverse: some proponents were socialists, others conservative moralists, but in general the sentiment most vehemently advocated was that:

For the capitalist undertaking institutes, coffin producers, etc., however, the burial of the dead is naturally only a business matter, through which they seek to achieve the highest possible gain, and in their competitive hunt for the dead they pounce upon the bereaved in the moment of their greatest suffering with their offers and their pushiness. It was principally for these reasons that the cities for many years have been endeavouring to liberate the burial of the dead from the interests of church and capitalists by taking the burial service into their own administration.[27]

This indicates that in Germany the sentiments that were to resurface in 1945 had a tradition connected with Socialist thought – a crucial point considering that many of those who laid the foundation of the GDR were steeped in that tradition.[28] Moreover, pre-war Dresden, ruled by the Social Democrats, proved that a municipal undertaking department with a share of over half of all funerals (the rest were organized by private companies) could achieve profits and add to, rather than deplete, city funds. Other cities, such as Gera in 1923, had municipalized all the burial services and covered all the expenses for their citizens. These instances of communalization were generally perceived positively and widely accepted by their citizens. After May 1945 the remaining municipalized burial services would be represented increasingly by those with an interest in municipalization as examples that should be followed.

In Berlin the undertaking industry had not been incorporated into a municipal company in the 1920s, but instead remained a service organized by a large number of highly specialized and often local companies of variable size and long standing.[29] That legacy of tradition and service to the community was deployed pre-emptively to rebut any allegations of amoral practices and 'capitalistic profiteering'.[30] Hence Rudolf Diesing's proposal to dispel these 'misconceptions' and his lobbying for a licensing agreement in order to avoid municipalization:

For many years I have had in mind as the most ideal solution, a *licensing system for the undertaking industry*, like that of pharmacies. The city thereby has, in regard to the undertaker, every possibility to see the profession conducted as it wishes. Moreover, licensing means that not just anybody can change into this profession. No funeral director should get a licence who has a shop next to a hospital. That is tasteless. The license has to be withdrawn from any funeral director who puts advertisements on streetlamps in front of hospitals or in their immediate vicinity. The whole profession should only be granted the type of advertisement that is granted to doctors and pharmacies.[31]

The report does not represent a picture of the abnormality one would have expected in May and June 1945; in other words, discussing ethical rules of advertisement for undertakers at such a time was clearly a pre-emptive measure against the threat of municipalization, but also once again spotlights the issue of normality.[32] A system of licensing and concessions was seen as a way to avoid what many craftsmen, shopkeepers and proprietors of small companies foresaw on the horizon: a Soviet-style economy. Furthermore, it had also the lure of creating equally profitable *de facto* cartels such as had been created with regard to the regulation and curtailing of the numbers of pharmacies. The return to normal conditions in regard to the coffin question led in 1946 to the abolition of the burial departments (*Bestattungsämter*) in Berlin that had been set up a year earlier to cope with the danger of epidemics and the lack of proper coffins.[33] Indeed, in an answer to a questionnaire sent out by the city of Munich to the other big cities about the state of their undertaking industry, the Berlin Department for Parks and Green Spaces (*Magistatsabteilung für Park- und Grünanlagen*) stressed the efficiency of private industry in coping with initial post-war difficulties.[34] By 1 October 1947, the coffin shortage had eased to such an extent that even those buried on behalf of the city – the poor; the so-called social corpses (*Sozialleichen*) – were no longer buried wrapped in paper but in proper wooden coffins. This change confirms the original argument of opponents to burial departments who stressed that their abolition would not undermine the quality of the funerals of the poorest of society.[35] In all these sources the language hints at an inherent ideological dimension of the organization of the undertaking services: the way society disposes of the dead, how it buries its dead, is not only an indicator of the state of society but also of the political, moral and ethical principles and the cultural practices that govern it.[36]

The organization of disposal and the administration of cemeteries in Germany have traditionally been the remit of local councils or, especially with regard to health regulation, state (*Länder* or *Provinzial*) governments. The ability of local governments to enact radical legislation is underlined by Grässel's reforms in Munich as well as the massive success of Munich's *Waldfriedhof* in forming a general perception of an ideal cemetery. Therefore, after the war, and especially after 1947, the organization of the local undertaking industry became the subject of sometimes intense political deliberations. As disposal was classified as a municipal responsibility, a determined local council could enact legislation or simply change the guidelines for the local cemeteries and thus affect the status of the local undertaking industry. However, the scope of change was not restricted to the traditional patchwork of local legislation. As early as May 1946, the local policy unit (*Kommunalabteiluvng*) of the president of the province of Sachsen-Anhalt (until 21 July 1947) gathered information regarding a proposed nationalization or communalization of undertaking services (*Bestattungswesen*). Article 10 (5) of the Weimar constitution of 1919 allowed the government to legislate on everything to do with funerals and undertaking.[37] This article of the constitution was never really invoked – but nonetheless hints at the progressive, liberal thoughts of the authors of the constitution.[38] When elaborating the legal framework of sepulchral culture and dealing with the problem of church property, the discussion paper of the local policy unit arrived at a crucial conclusion:

> The greatest obstacle to the municipalization of the funeral services is probably the fact that for the most part the cemeteries in the region are in the possession of the parishes, and that these will not voluntarily relinquish their property. When assimilating private funeral services into the administration of the city, the first thing to do would be to check

in which cities such institutions exist, and whether in these municipalities the appropriate usage of the municipal burial service is not being made compulsory. The issuing of a statutory order by the province is not required for this. On the basis of paragraph 18 DGO [*Deutsche Gemeindeordnung*, passed 30 January 1935] and through a local statute, the municipalities can make the usage of such a burial service for any member of the community compulsory.[39]

This legal view and the problems indicated above were symptomatic of the whole attempt to reorganize the East German undertaking industry after 1945. Local councils could legislate on the organization of the disposal, but they could not dispossess the churches of their cemeteries outright. From the beginning, this meant a separation between the two areas of disposal: undertaking and cemeteries. The reorganization of undertaking services and the ownership (and to a lesser degree judicial control) of cemeteries were tackled differently and separately. Ultimately, it would take a considerable amount of time until the SED, the emerging East German state, and its legislative bodies at different levels of government were able to gain some form of direct control of both undertaking and the cemeteries.

Nevertheless, one thing was clear: ideology was going to play a central role. A shift of paradigm was underway; the local and state elections of autumn 1946 in the Soviet zone had already taken place in a partisan atmosphere.[40] The Soviet Military Administration of Germany (SMAD) took great care, for example, in using its propaganda machinery and restricting the propaganda of the other parties, to facilitate a SED victory. Measures were taken to ensure that East Germany and a prospective East German state would be built upon a different footing from that in the Western zones. On 8 May 1948, the SMAD charged the SED leadership with the task of constructing an East German state. An important step in that direction was the introduction of a Soviet-style planned economy. The German Economic Commission (*Deutsche Wirtschaftskommission* or DWK) was the main instrument for advancing this aim. Founded in February 1948, it only had jurisdiction in the Soviet zone, but it formed in effect the foundations on which the East German government was to be erected. On 24 November 1948 the DWK, after having nationalized the heavy and chemical industries, decided to tackle the economic activities that could be taken over by the local authorities in 'municipal holding companies'.[41] The decree on the regulation of the local economy (*Kommunalwirtschaftsverordnung*) was one of the first stages in the nationalization of the whole economy: as paragraph 2 makes unmistakeably clear, the newly formed municipal companies (*Kommunale Wirtschaftsunternehmen* or KWU) were 'people's property' (*Volkseigentum*). Thus, these KWUs had a very different legal status from the hitherto prevailing municipal utility companies, the so-called *Stadtwerke*, which were mostly limited companies or, in the case of big cities, publicly listed companies in which the city was the majority stakeholder. The new KWU placed many of the local economic activities under the direct political influence of the provisional local political councils elected in autumn 1946 and increasingly dominated by SED function-aries.[42] In addition the local councils could decide to incorporate into the new entities a far wider spectrum than the traditional public utilities (water, sewage, waste and sometimes electricity) and local transportation companies; the new law foresaw the incorporation of everything from parks, theatres and hospitals to hotels, restaurants, printing shops, swimming pools, cemeteries and undertak-ers.[43] Whereas the SMAD had begun to expropriate industrial companies as early as autumn 1945, and by 1948 had nationalized over ten thousand companies, most of these were medium to large ones.[44] Hence, with this legal change in ownership, a major step in the direction of changing the economic fabric of East Germany had been taken. However, it would be a mistake to assume that this was a decisive and orchestrated move from the beginning. The legal text was very unclear as to which institutions could and should be incorporated and which could not, leaving the need for considerable clarification – and thus room for legal manoeuvrability. This meant that as early as 1948, in many communities and especially in cities in the south of the GDR where the undertaking industry in part or as a whole had already passed into the hands of the cities, substantial portions of the undertaking industry came under fairly direct political influence and control: that meant, to a lesser or greater degree, being under SED control. In the cities where municipalization had not taken place, like Berlin or Leipzig, the incorporation and thus direct influence was not established in 1948. This fact alone suggests that local and regional differences and idiosyncrasies in the admin-istration of disposal in Germany before 1945 therefore still continued after such a profound political change. Consequently, these regional variations contributed to a substantial and persistent lack of conformity in the organization of burials as well as the wider practices that constituted the specific sepulchral culture.

This is not to say that some municipalities did not decide to be bold and to go forth with municipalization. A good example for this was Dresden, as Saxony had a strong tradition of municipal funeral arrangements.[45] In 1948 the city's undertakers were municipalized in very much the same way that undertaking in Gera had been communalized twenty-three years earlier: that is to say entirely. The remaining private companies were dissolved. The yearly report for the KWU for 1950 acknowledged that:

> After the breakdown of the Nazi empire, through the municipalization of the entire burial service, the sepulchral service in Dresden was finally placed in the hands of the city admin-istration. With this all the processes occurring during a burial were, with one exception, reserved for the city. Attempts to include the church cemeteries in this municipalization had not been successful; it had only been possible to reach certain agreements as to burial times in the individual cemeteries.[46]

The administration of burials, the city-owned cemeteries and the local cremato-rium (including its dedicated 'urn cemetery' at Tolkewitz) were all placed in the hands of a single department. This was the bureaucrats' favoured administrative model for the organization of the major cities' burial services. However, the report also highlights the problem of church cemeteries, which could not be municipalized. The only option to establish an effective communalized burial service was to arrange for agreements with the individual parishes or the administration of the church province (*Landeskirche*). The city of Dresden had certain regulatory mechanisms, especially via health legislation, on church cemeteries, but no right to unsolicited access. The issue of access needed to be settled, since no funerals could take place without the cooperation of the city's burial department as well as the permission of those who owned the cemeteries. The solution was to arrange set hours with the churches within which the employees of the burial service could legitimately access the cemeteries and conduct secular funerals on church property. This represents a prime example of how limited the application of state authority, albeit via the local government, could be in the Soviet-occupied sector and during the early years of the GDR. However, that was only a temporary *modus vivendi*; the real answer in Dresden was to enlarge the central cemetery (in the north of the city) thus allowing the KWU to rely as little as possible on cooperation with church institutions. Nevertheless, the KWUs did not survive for long.

On 30 September 1948 the 'spontaneous' (Soviet-instigated) East Berlin city council was formed. From that point Berlin had two governments, effectively separating the city into West and East. The SED was quick to bring East Berlin in line with the changes that had taken place in the rest of the Soviet zone. In its second session on 2 December 1948, the new city government of East Berlin decided to municipalize in order to integrate Berlin into the Two-Year Plan (East Germany's first concerted step towards a planned economy). Berlin, as a jointly administered area, was not covered in the original plan in 1948.[47] Ultimately, the proclamation of the Basic Law (*Grundgesetz*) by the West German Parliamentary Council on 23 May 1949 and the subsequent West German elections in August were followed by the formation of the German Democratic Republic by the People's Council (*Volksrat*) on 7 October in opposition to the West German state. With the foundation of the GDR in 1949, the SED swiftly and firmly took over all institutions of the state, creating a centrally governed state in which all rules and guidelines were handed down from Berlin, despite the initial warning from Moscow not to fetter the system with red tape.[48] All levels of the administrative system, as well as the Party institutions, became means of asserting direct control and influence.[49] A major step in this direction was the adaptation of the first Five-Year Plan. As a part of this reorganization the KWUs were dissolved by 31 March 1951. A new statute (*Verordnung*) was published on 28 February 1951, charging the local authorities with the task of establishing a local state-owned industry, the so-called locally administered People's company – VEB(ö).

> In order to support limited tasks in the local area, and to advance the local social initiative, the people's industry is established, and the local economy reorganized. The task of developing profitable people's businesses falls to the city and the administrative district and the

municipality, as well as that of developing economic and progressive municipal institutions and building up their organization.[50]

This meant that the management of the municipal burial services and that of the cemeteries, where they belonged to the local council, came under the direct economic control of the local council, and were run by the department charged with planning and financing these institutions. The SED was the governing party, due to Soviet support, and took over control of the entire state. In general this meant, primarily due to the degree of specialization, that the same people who had run the KWU also ran the VEB or the new cemetery departments (*Friedhofsämter*). What changed was the integration within the administrative framework: cemeteries returned, in most cases, to the control of the local council, either to its committee for reconstruction (*Aufbau*), local utilities (ÖVW), or locally administered industry (*örtliche Industrie*). With the administrative reform of 1952 (the abolition of the *Länder* and the introduction of the 14 districts [*Bezirke*] of the GDR), came the new 'principle of double subordination' (*Prinzip der doppelten Unterstellung*). The local councils, their committees and departments, were supervised by both the region (*Bezirk*) and district (*Kreis*), as well as by the specific ministry in Berlin.

All this was part of what was called the democratic reconstruction (*Demokratischer Aufbau*) of the GDR: the attempt to penetrate as much as possible of society, politics, culture and economics with Marxist/Leninist and Stalinist ideas.[51] Seeing itself as a 'party of the new type', the SED was very clear about its role in conducting a revolution from above. In a lecture given to the party faithful explaining the motives and deliberations of the 1952 reforms, Willi Barth, head of the working group for church questions at the central committee, explained bluntly:

> The territorial area of operation of the local institutions of the state authority has to be determined in such a way that these institutions can realise completely the running of economic and cultural reconstruction. The effective management and control of the lower institutions through the superior [institutions], as well as through the people themselves, have to be safeguarded.[52]

The idea of a democratic reconstruction was not merely superficial in its scope; it was taken rather seriously. With regard to those elements that touched upon sepulchral culture the issue becomes instantaneously more complex. It would be a gross exaggeration to argue that sepulchral culture *per se* became a prime focus. Nevertheless, on different levels many institutions were deliberating how to overcome the complexities in the existing organization and legislation in order to establish institutions and traditions that conformed to the new state. The decentralized and federal structure as well as traditional German particularism, which has had amongst other points an important influence on the administrative organization of the churches, meant that not a single level of government had ever had overall administrative control, jurisdiction, or even a legislative overview. Health regulations had been the domain of the states and provinces, while the specific legal framework was made by the local councils. These general shortcomings were seen when the administration of the GDR was established. The ambitious aim was not only centralization with regard to organization but also central political control and in due course the reshaping of the whole sepulchral culture: essentially to propagate a 'socialist' attitude to life and death and 'socialist rituals'.[53] In the 1880s, when the cemetery reform movement had gathered momentum and achieved a kind of uniformity regarding cemetery design (as epitomized by Hamburg-Ohlsdorf), or when the municipalization movement accelerated after the 1923 inflation, it was a small vanguard that had had both the vision and the desire for change in regard to the sepulchral culture. With strong reverberations of the cemetery reform movement, the most important means to expound and promote the 'socialist' ideas was the setting of 'virtuous' examples to be emulated. It was judged that well-trained and smartly dressed personnel (orators and officials) and well-decorated rooms were key in making secular rites more attractive.[54] However, during the early 1950s the nature of the momentum for change in the GDR was initially entirely different and far more ambitious: the momentum was the product of the intrinsic ideological and political values of the centralist Stalinist state and its governing party. The political system was thus, one might argue, destined to challenge regional variations and traditions, to organize undertaking and the legal status of cemeteries uniformly throughout the country, and ultimately to impose its own ideology on sepulchral culture.

As the 1952 organizational reform had overcome the separation of powers between regional and national government and allowed the Party direct influence on all levels of government, the obvious next reform envisaged the abolition of local differences through the imposition of a uniform framework upon the whole society and the whole country. There were two approaches to the initiative: one was primarily politically motivated, and the second driven more by the desire for uniformity based on sound economic considerations. Nevertheless, it is essential to understand that neither of these schools was dogmatically deterministic in its approach; even the latter, more economically motivated, argument acknowledged the political motives rooted in socialist thought and the ideological benefits of eventually establishing a uniform socialist cemetery culture. It simply put more emphasis on the short-term economic benefits as being more essential. What remained, more often than not, was mere ambiguity leading to ideologically motivated language in order to advocate economically motivated changes.

Two documents in the files of the Ministry of the Interior of Mecklenburg reveal the economic considerations of the regime concerning the organization of disposal. In June 1950 directors of cemeteries of one hundred and twenty cities and communes of the GDR met in Halle to discuss the reorganization of their institutions and the undertaking industry. A major topic of discussion was the introduction of work norms and performance-orientated salaries (*Arbeitsnormen* and *Leistungslohn*). These had only been introduced in the Thuringian city of Altenburg, where, according to the calculations of Kuhn (director of Altenburg cemetery and crematorium) they were a success. They reduced the number of employees by about thirty per cent resulting in raised turnover per remaining employees, thus doubling the rate individual graves were tended to from four to eight times a year. Technical changes had cut the required amount of gas per cremation by two-thirds. The reform thus had raised revenues and thereby reduced the need of subsidies by the city council.[55] The list of achievements culminated in the demand for similar measures for all cemeteries and for the strict planning of all cemeteries to maximize their efficiency and general utility. In the second document, also based on the concepts introduced in Altenburg, the author demanded the restructuring of the entire funeral organization:

a) Municipal burial services shall be set up in all cities of the GDR. If there is no municipal cemetery, then these departments shall be put under the control of the garden and park administrations.

b) The provision of coffins, urns and shrouds, even if the burial takes place in the cemetery of the parish, may only take place through the garden departments subordinated to the municipal cemetery.

c) The issuing of corpse licences and the related fees are to be abandoned …

d) The coffins – two or three types for burials, two types for cremations – shall only be made from softwood and, to save wood, be produced in the people's own coffin factories or large cooperative carpentry shops.

e) [Transportation is to be restricted to vehicles owned by, and personnel employed by the city.]

f) The ordering of musicians or decorations, in general the organization of the funeral ritual, may only be conducted by the municipal burial services …

Suggestion II enables for uniform pricing and lowers the burial costs for the population, the subsidies for the municipal burial services and garden departments are reduced, and the so-called *piety institutions (Pietäts Institute)* would be deprived of their easy and partly inappropriate earnings, for little work. The state would receive its taxes more easily.[56]

This prophetic summary reveals the reason for the creation of a uniform organization of the undertaking industry, namely that the objective was to reduce funeral costs for the individual as well as the state. This main objective nicely combined with administrative streamlining measures and a reduction in amoral behaviour, as exemplified by the 'so-called piety institutes' and 'easy and partly incorrect earning of money', and the abolition of profits (see earlier use of the term profiteering) for private companies.

Considerations of increasing efficiency might have been the main driving force in replicating the Altenburg model enacted, and thus it is significant that in February 1952 a delegation from Wismar and Schwerin was sent to inspect the Altenburg system, and to report as well on those in Leipzig and Halle.[57] The state of the cemeteries in Halle was depicted as appalling, and the idea of work norms received a hostile reception, whilst the good condition of the Altenburg cemetery and its exemplary cleanliness were praised. However, the report also noted that the latter cemetery was comparatively small, only covering 6.5 hectares, and was serviced by nineteen personnel – a high number for a cemetery of that size. Moreover, it was also critical of the work norms, indicating that a number of employees thought them too high and demanding; and it stressed that most of the administrative changes in favour of uniformity had been taken in conjunction with the opening of the town's crematorium in 1928. This fact does not minimize the significance and breadth of the proposed measures in regard to reorganization, but hints at the deep roots of the socialist tradition. The combination of strong ideological sentiments, such as giving free or cheap funerals to all citizens, with the allure of savings and efficiency gains, proved potent – efficiency was also a watchword of socialist economic renewal, not merely of late-twentieth-century capitalist economics.[58] This latter point is strengthened by the juxtaposition of the negative example of Halle, with its private undertaking business, with the two positive examples of Altenburg and Leipzig.[59] In both Halle and Leipzig all undertaking was in the hands of private companies. However, the city's cemetery department had to approve every customer invoice to prevent 'immoral' overcharging. Furthermore, the cemetery department of the City of Leipzig harboured definite plans to introduce the reorganization along the above-mentioned lines, thus demonstrating that there was a gathering impetus for change. The undertaking industry's repeated reference to its efficiency and its great professionalism countered the purely economic rationale for socialization. Against the contemporary ideological impetus, the reference to tradition, professionalism and efficiency proved far less successful.

There was also a very compelling political case, at least in the eyes of those party officials who took an interest, for the restructuring of the whole sepulchral culture, namely organization of disposal, control over cemeteries, formation of rituals, and later from the late 1960s even the form of bereavement.[60] Disposal does not equate mere discarding, but entails a prescribed process or ritual. It has entailed manifold responses like the purchase of a resting place within a cathedral or the organization of a specific ceremony.[61] However, in the twentieth century, after death has been certified, it became customary for professionals to be called to assist: the layer out dealt with the body, as the carpenter, or later the undertaker, began to build or prepare the coffin. Later, the funeral director would have the body taken away and thus begins the often elaborate process of organising the funeral. This professional involvement in the process of disposal has had implications beyond the fact that fees were to be charged for services rendered. First, the creation of such a profession in a modern state elicited regulation, thus necessitating an administrative and political process. As a corollary the door was opened for moral, aesthetic (and ultimately, especially in a Marxist-Leninist environment), ideological considerations by those setting guidelines and establishing frameworks. The scope of these ideological considerations varied, but where communist governments were concerned, any aspect of life that was traditionally in the churches' sphere of influence or had a sizeable social significance (such as education and rituals) very quickly became politicized. The term 'cultural reconstruction' (*kulturellen Aufbau*), in the above-mentioned quotation from the

Party school lecture, suggests the scale of the task and its aims. The atheist and materialist dimension of the GDR's Marxist-Leninist ideology meant that the Party ideologues had a very clear view of the place of religion in the new socialist society.

While there were no further legislative changes for the industry after 1952, throughout the whole of the 1950s and well into the 1960s an increasing number of communities, towns and cities followed the examples set by cities like Dresden and wholly municipalized their undertaking industry.[62] A second more indirect way of establishing a degree of control was by forcing local undertakers and craftsmen such as carpenters and masons to sell a share of their business to the local government, which then received a percentage of the profit at the end of the year.[63] From 1956 onwards, pressure on these medium- and small-sized private companies grew substantially, and taxation was increased to force companies to sell part of their businesses to the government.[64] In 1958 there was a further wave of nationalization, which had its origins in this desire to socialize the traditional small and medium-sized businesses which formed the core of many local economies. On 10 January 1958, the Liberal-Democratic Party (LDP) called upon artisans and small business members (*Handwerk und Mittelstand*) to unite into so-called *Produktionsgenossenschaften des Handwerks* (PGH) – production cooperatives for craftsmen. Although this call came from one of the 'block parties', it nonetheless represented the SED's policy to nationalize as much of the economy as possible. Initially the move was voluntary, yet tax reductions and improved access to raw materials were used to soften the decision. However, as with most East German policies, it can be assumed that a fair amount of pressure was exerted via local party officials. For an industry such as undertaking, this meant the indirect or partial nationalization of private sector companies. Few companies, mainly in rural areas, were willing and able permanently to resist this pressure and obstacles like delays in orders for coffins. In an increasingly centralized economic system, these pressures could be easily exercised.

The city of Greifswald demonstrates this process of communalization. In 1948 the city cemetery was included in the assets of the KWU. When that organization was dissolved in 1951, the ownership of the cemetery reverted back to the *Friedhofsamt der Stadt Greifswald*. In 1958 the private undertaking company Hofmann negotiated to be re-established as the *VEB (st.) Bestattungshaus* with the prior owner Walter Hofmann as director. In 1965 the cemetery and its administration were combined with the running of the undertaking business, and the *VEB Friedhof- Bestattungswesen Greifswald* was founded. A year later, in 1966, it was renamed *VEB (ö) Gartengestaltung und Friedhofswesen*.[65] This meant that in Greifswald, after 1959, there was only one city-owned undertaking company and two small private ones, operating mainly in the surrounding villages. This centralization, and to a certain degree monopolization, had serious implications for the local craftsmen, as the new city-owned undertaking company planned to supply its coffins from a central regional source, rather than many small ones as had been the custom hitherto. This was the first real attempt to centralize as much of the production for and organization of the undertaking industry as possible, at least within the region. This inevitably resulted in the transition from artisanal to industrial methods in the production of coffins in the region. However, this socialist process of rationalization that characterized industrial production in the GDR led to constant and characteristic shortcomings in quantity and quality with regard to many items.[66] Coffins posed one of the pressing problems. In that distinctive East German lexicon there was even a specific term for it: '*die Sargfrage*' (the coffin question). In 1960 approximately 180,000 coffins were industrially produced, while there were 233,759 deaths in the GDR; the shortfall was made up by local craftsmen or small companies, leading to numerous temporary shortages and imbalances.[67] More coffins than needed could be produced in Thuringia and Saxony, due to the ready availability of wood, whilst, especially in the north, a permanent shortage of coffins remained the norm. The perceived remedy lay within central planning and in the central allocation of production quotas, standardization of products, and in 'more efficient utilization of materials'. This last term was official shorthand for the reduced use of solid wood for coffins, often in favour of paper, cardboard and plastics. Once again, as in the 1920s, the idea of using MDF instead of solid wood and the utilization of a solid wooden coffin lid (that was removed and reused after the coffin was in the grave) was put forward, and experiments undertaken.[68]

The scope for centralization and increased efficiency also affected other areas. Especially in the larger cities, particularly Leipzig, Rostock and Berlin, undertakers were perceived as requiring reform. There had been little initial political impetus in the councils of these cities to communalize or nationalize the undertakers. In Leipzig in 1958, for example, there were twenty-nine private undertaking companies operating, which had fifty-five outlets. However, sixteen were so small scale that they did not have a hearse, this was seen as wasteful.[69] In Berlin, a plan to municipalize all undertakers was considered, but in 1958 a debate broke out between two departments of the East Berlin city government; both the Department for the Local Economy and the Department for Agriculture and Forestry thought that they should take over responsibility for the five flower shops at the entrances of Berlin's cemeteries, providing the public with flowers and grave decorations. Both argued that these were integral parts of their sphere of interest and a considerable source of revenue. However, a statement by the Department for the Local Economy suggests an even broader socialist (even international) agenda of what it thought would be the ultimate scope of its reorganized burial industry:

> In the further development of the cemetery and burial system in Berlin a people's-own corporation is to be formed, analogous to the organizational form of the cemetery and burial systems in the larger cities of the Republic and in Moscow. This corporation will conduct all services that are required in the case of a death. This includes, besides dealing with formalities, the delivery of coffins, transportation, the selling of grave plots, the planning of burial ceremonies with vocal and instrumental performers, the decoration, the closing of

the grave and planting, the production of floral wreaths and the selling of plants to decorate the grave plots. We are also of the opinion that, in addition, the manufacture of gravestones must be conducted within such a corporation.[70]

The idea was to create an institution that would conduct the whole process of disposal from picking up the corpse to organizing all aspects of the funeral ceremony. Essentially this paralleled the development of funeral directors in the capitalist West. Repeatedly portrayed as the inspiration, the Dresden model was to be established in Berlin and in this specific case, even the production of gravestones that in Dresden (and many other places) remained in the hand of PHG was to be incorporated.[71] This burial service was not a mere undertaking service; it was a socialist funeral directing service. This funeral direction service was to offer a comprehensive approach to undertaking, providing more than the sale of a coffin and other sepulchral paraphernalia, including large transportable silver candelabra and many metres of black cloth for draping purposes. The municipal burial services began to offer much more; the East German definition implies the comprehensiveness of the service:

> **Cemetery and Burial System:**
> [Part of the economy within the group of local utilities, municipal or communal service provider, part of the service industry within the national economy.]
> Tasks:
> Conducting or arranging all the necessary and desired services after the occurrence of a death up to the orderly, hygienically impeccable and culturally dignified burial.[72]

The significance of the word *Dienstleistung* (service) came through its representing an important political catchphrase in the GDR.[73] The *Dienstleistungsbetriebe* (service providers) were intended to demonstrate to citizens the efficiency and superiority of the socialist approach, as well as a way to reflect the advances of socialism.[74] Extending services to transport, laying out, the arrangement of official formalities, the coordination of the different elements of the ceremony and the funeral meant that the municipal burial services were essentially offering the same level (with the unavoidable aftertaste of 'real existing socialism') of services as provided by the funeral directors in the capitalist West.[75]

The rise of large municipal burial services, at least in the cities and larger towns, mirrored the development that undertaking went through in the capitalist West. There, similarly, undertaking had become a full-time business, rather than a way for carpenters to augment their income.[76] Together with the growing estrangement from death in modern western culture, increasing bureaucratization (further aided by the scale of deaths between 1945 and 1947) was the basis for such a development, since it made professional funeral direction economically viable. The reluctance to deal personally with death-related matters within the family, in conjunction with the widespread inability to act positively in the face of bereavement, gave further credence to the increasing scope of the role of the funeral director. In the course of the twentieth century, he not only became the paid service provider and master of ritual, but also the organizer of the bureaucratic formalities as well as the painful and the distasteful tasks associated with death, such as the washing and clothing of the deceased.[77] Queuing for death certificates and dealing with initial pension paperwork had become second nature for the funeral director both in the West and the East.[78] This resonates with H. Gordon Skilling's hypothesis of convergence between capitalist and communist countries.[79] Skilling's case revolves mainly around the role that interest groups played within the communist state. Despite the 'totalitarian' nature of the state, interest groups with conflicting goals were able to exert an influence on policy making, if not in a fully pluralistic sense, then nonetheless not truly dissimilar in pattern to what occurred in other industrial societies.[80] The organization of disposal in this context is a field that is dominated by special interests. It is an arena in which individual professionals have consulted each other and thus functioned, especially with the help of an umbrella organization, as a 'quasi-pressure group'. This results in the coordination of policies and reform efforts, but also in the collection of data, recommendation of legal changes and suggestions of certain investments; in other words, to the operation of an entity pressing for change. Skilling's theory, therefore, explains the similarities in the emergence of funeral direction in the East as well as the West, since the theory avoids totalitarian assumptions that a communist government simply asserts its knowledge of the 'real' needs of society, and allows for a professional policy-formation process mediated by interest groups, driven by individual motivations and subjected to political influences and economic pressure – a process not altogether dissimilar to that found in democratic, capitalist countries. The only major difference in the GDR was that investments required the state and party to sanction them, and that this became increasingly difficult in the face of other spending, at least if the suggested investment did not converge with the current interest of party and state organizations.

While in 1958 many elements of socialist undertaking were still embryonic and it would take a while for many of the ideas to materialize, in 1985 Jane Redlin, an East German ethnologist, summarized the trend in funeral direction in East Berlin by arguing that:

> The range of services of the municipal burial system in Berlin is so extensive that it can undertake all the necessary tasks and measures subsequent to the ascertainment of death and the issuing of the death certificate by a doctor. It carries out all the commissions itself, or arranges them with the cemeteries and affiliated institutions (florists, masons).[81]

The case of Berlin underlines the last important limitation that was imposed in the socialist environment: that many ideas only ever existed on paper. Aspiration and reality tended to diverge in the early years of the GDR (but not only then). Hence, the plan for Berlin was not carried out to the extent envisaged. Berlin retained its eight semi-private undertaking companies. They coexisted with the *VEB Bestattungsdienstleitungen* (funeral services) that was founded only in 1959 and operated fifteen outlets. Later, in 1981, the *VEB Bestattungsdienstleitungen* was incorporated in the *VEB Kombinat Stadtwirtschaft* (municipal economy).[82] This confirms that despite all the reorganization, most of the initiatives remained at best piecemeal regional or local reforms. Until 1957/8, with the exception of the creation of the VEBs in 1952, aspects of disposal and undertaking and its organization had largely remained a peripheral concern for the central ministries and party committees, left to the regional, local municipal government or parish levels. This meant that in 1957 cities such as Leipzig, Berlin, Halle and Rostock did not have a municipalized burial service, while in Schwerin and Magdeburg private companies still supplied coffins and other paraphernalia. Moreover, the private undertakers of Leipzig saw themselves at the frontline against further municipalization, and were reputedly well connected within the trade. They actually advocated an independent undertaking industry like that of West Germany where a number of municipal burial services had been re-privatized. The greatest success of their political lobbying was that a decision made by the council of the city of Halle to municipalize its burial service was reversed. An internal report highlights the central role assigned to Leipzig's undertakers in resisting reorganization:

> The undertakers of Leipzig in particular consider themselves as the advance guard of their profession, and have connections to undertakers in the whole Republic … [I]n one of their last discussions [they] have openly expressed their contentment with the conditions in West Germany … They speculate on the lack of knowledge within the departments with regard to the conditions in the burial services in general, and they point to the new course [policy] despite the fact that municipalization of the burial services is an old demand of the progressive [elements] of our people.[83]

A lack of widespread knowledge and the ability of regional councils to work out different legal frameworks in fact amplified the manifold ambiguities that prevented any strict organization of the undertaking sector. Thus, the GDR did not overcome the traditional particularism that had governed the burial services in Germany. In turn, this inability to achieve any systematic socialist reform of disposal frustrated those few officials who saw it as their duty. It was precisely this mentality that induced Dr Ulrich Krüger of the Institute for State and Administrative Law of the University of Leipzig to write a report informing the SED central committee about the legal and organizational disarray. His style conveys the level of personal frustration of someone personally invested in this specialist field:

> In the sphere of burial and cemetery systems there are no uniform conditions in the GDR. Owing to the existing regulations that is not even possible.
>
> In Saxony the burial service is more or less still governed by a law from 20 April 1850.
> …
>
> A whole host of local statutes and cemetery regulations devised by the municipalities have made for a difference in fees, tariffs and supplements that must absolutely be

reduced to a common denominator. Even the organization with regard to trade unions and economic relations shows more diversity than almost any other field of our state-run life. Since 1952 the municipally owned service industry has proved to be the best economic organizational form for the burial and cemetery system in the larger and medium cities.[84]

The thirteen pages of his report outlined in detail the problem of legal and organizational diversity, and the obstacles presented by local legislation that was in some cases hundred and twenty years old. Yet the report also acknowledges that the issue was not crucial at that time and that other areas of policy making might be prioritized.[85] This last proviso explains why so much of the reorganization lacked overall coherence. No doubt the central institutions of party and state saw the exodus to the West as more pressing and perceived more promising areas of political activity than the question of socialist undertaking, which was at best a secondary issue, sparking only sporadic deliberations and even fewer deeds. Nothing illustrates this more effectively than the fact that no single ministry possessed overall responsibility for cemeteries and burial services, and that consequently any consideration of policy necessitated inter-ministerial dialogue.[86]

The best case of alternative prioritization is the introduction of the *Jugendweihe* from 1955.[87] From 1957 onwards, pressure on individuals and families increased, and the choice to abstain from the *Jugendweihe* became increasingly a parental statement of political non-conformity.[88] Under Ulbricht's personal supervision, the *Jugendweihe* rapidly became almost universal: before 1957 a mere fifth of fourteen-year-old children went through it, a year later it was nearly half; by 1959 more than 80 per cent experienced the socialist rite of passage into socialist society. In every *Bezirk* the SED set up committees that supervised this development closely and assisted in the organization. These commissions, most of which were later also to oversee all socialist rituals, collected statistics and additional information to report back to Berlin. This showed how seriously the *Jugendweihe* was perceived as a significant index of secularization and modernization.[89] The most important distinction between the socialist burial service as well as the socialist funeral ritual and the *Jugendweihe* was that the latter was youth policy, in other words it pointed towards the future, rather than the past. Nonetheless, the *Jugendweihe* was only a point of departure. Ultimately, the state provided a whole range of '*lebensbegleitenden*', secular socialist rituals that accompanied the stages of life, such as name giving, marriage and death. The 'real existing socialism' had to be percolated into the natural life cycle. This premise became a central element in the rituals and traditions that were invented for a socialist everyday life – *Sozialistische Alltag*:

> The socialist means of production changed the entire societal [sic] life in our Republic, and also resulted in the awareness of the continuous development of our people. This is demonstrated in the process of communal labour by working people, and the realization is growing that personal [interests] must correspond to societal interests. This, amongst other things, is expressed in the fact that there is a desire to celebrate the beginning of a phase in life or its ending, the different high points and occasions in life, such as birth, marriage and

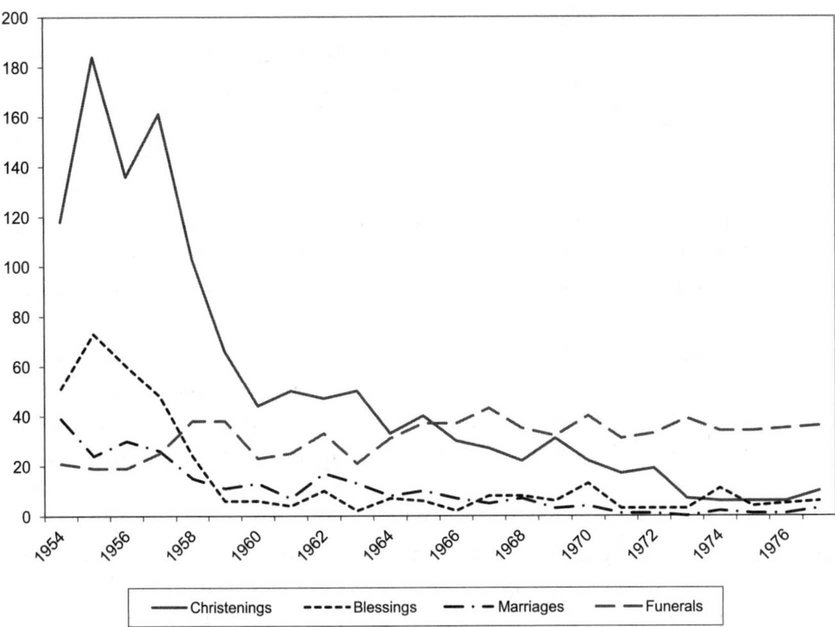

Graph 2.1 The four major Protestant rites performed by Hans Bräuer, the pastor, in Stalinstadt/Eisenhüttenstadt between 1954 and 1977.

(Data: Appendix 4, H. Bräuer, 'Die Ersten Jahrzehnte der Ev. Friedenskirchengemeinde Eisenhüttenstadt', im StA Eisenhüttenstadt, Sig. S 77)

burial. It is also necessary to create such a possibility for phase-of-life-celebrations and to fill these with our new socialist content.[90]

This meant that issues that had customarily been of limited and specialist consideration and discussion were henceforth to be subjected to broader political and ideological consideration. In this regard the end of the life cycle was not afforded the highest priority. Therefore, it will not be unexpected to find an absence of widespread enthusiasm to tackle something as peripheral as legislation on undertaking and cemeteries before the early 1960s. Proper, all-encompassing change, one might argue, could only be expected in the hermetic environment that emerged after the building of the Berlin wall in August 1961.[91]

The first decisive step to coordinate reform was taken shortly after the physical separation of East and West Germany, when the *Institut für Kommunalwirtschaft* (IfK, the Institute for Local Economy) was set up in 1962. Significantly, Dresden was chosen as the institute's location. The city had been home to the former *Reichsausschuß* and the most exemplary socialist funeral direction service of the GDR. The IfK was to be the East German equivalent to the *Arbeitsgemeinschaft Friedhof und Denkmal* (AFD) that was founded in 1951 in Bonn (and later moved to Kassel). The AFD brought together, on a voluntary basis, those professionally concerned, the academically or otherwise interested, and those involved in the practice of sepulchral culture – thus keeping in the tradition of the *Reichsausschuß*. However, the IfK was a different kind of institution: the modern term 'think tank', albeit with direct and strong connection to state and party, is possibly the best way to describe the role of this institution within the GDR. Specialists who had previously published or worked on waste disposal, street cleaning, urban lighting services, maintenance of greenbelts and recreation areas and on cemeteries and burial services were assembled under one roof to discuss issues of socialist municipal services (*Stadtwirtschaft*).[92]

Since the demise of the GDR, there has been a debate about the role of the IfK, in particular whether it was influenced merely by socialist thought, or whether the regular contact with the West German AFD, and especially its former director Hans-Kurt Boehlke, meant that both carried, at least to an extent, the same reformist ideals.[93] Schelenz and Meinel (one a municipal official and the other a church administrator for cemeteries within the GDR) have argued against a socialist agenda on the basis mainly that the GDR exhibited a continuation of pre-existing reformist tendencies. Furthermore, they also maintain that the West German AFD influenced the sepulchral culture of the GDR to a considerable degree. Central to their case is the role of Marxist ideology: they stress that the publications of the IfK were only interspersed with party-political phraseology, and the practical side of its affairs were heavily influenced by individuals (and 'reality'). By contrast Reiner Sörries stresses the integration of reformist thought into a socialist cemetery culture.[94] Both institutions had very similar views on the aesthetics of cemeteries, yet this argument oversimplifies the role of these publications as well as ignoring a good deal of the physical evidence that documents the sepulchral differences between the GDR and the FRG. Nevertheless, both interpretations represent very much an insiders' (practitioners' and technocrats') perspective: the view that institutions can influence culture and each other, and neglecting the fact that they themselves are prone to be influenced by society: and in this case, ideology and politics, a common reformist culture, an institutional-corporate ethos and most crucially by the particular economic realities. Skilling made this last point himself in order to avoid exaggerating the heuristic force of the concept of convergence.[95]

Only the integration and acceptance of all these factors into a comprehensive explanation will reveal the complex relationship between the two think tanks separated by the Iron Curtain and their respective environments. Moreover, similar aesthetic sensibilities, arising out of the shared reformist tradition, especially in regard to the design of gravestones and cemeteries, explain the 'proximity' of the institutions, and some comparable practicalities. Nonetheless, reformist thought – by definition very compatible with both West German and East German specialist ideas of cemeteries – also related to many elements of socialist aesthetics and especially the insatiable desire for efficiency. This is ultimately why Sörries arrived at following conclusion:

I, however, emphatically insist that the aims and structural methods (design) of the IfK to realize socialist cemetery culture, are unacceptable in the now unified Germany due to philosophical (religious) and political (democratic) reasons.[96]

Consequently, what this reformist tradition does not explain are the fundamental differences, like the degree of centralization or, more crucially, the painstakingly planned propagation of socialist ideals that is at least part of the initial move towards the establishment of burial services in urban centres. Nor does it explain East German idiosyncrasies: perfectly summed up by the IfK's attempted insistence on grey clothes for personnel (employees of the burial services and socialist funeral orators) in contact with the bereaved as signs of grief, and the explicit emphasis that black clothes should not be used as they are part of a religious tradition of grief. The IfK in their pamphlet even advocated there being different summer and winter dress.[97] Even if the institutional independence of the IfK remains debateable, the role of socialist municipal burial services and their aims were clearly politically delineated: to increase hygiene, cleanliness and order and to provide the atmosphere necessary for a socialist approach to life (*sozialistisches Lebensgefühl*).[98]

Any argument that suggests that these were merely empty phrases ignores the seriousness, even if it was that quintessentially ludicrous and often absurd East German seriousness, attached to some of these services – e.g., the *Texitlreinigungsleistung* (washing and cleaning service) and its earnest desire to ease the strain on working women – in advancing equality and socialism, even if the achievements ultimately remain doubtful.[99] In order to fulfil its role in this task the IfK undertook research into the practicalities and efficiency of cemeteries and undertaking, published guidelines and suggestions and a journal (from 1971) which gave those working in the field the opportunity to report on innovations and discuss alternatives.[100] With the formation of the IfK, there was finally a nucleus around which a specific East German (but not necessarily socialist) sepulchral culture could be constructed. One institution had taken charge, working as a catalyst, allowing for a certain degree of coordination of existing responsibilities and expertise.

This meant that, like the AFD, the IfK pooled those who had ideas and opinions on how to design, run and organize cemeteries and burial services and gave them an institution to lobby and one that would lobby on their behalf. All too often there are monolithic ideas about East German institutions, ideas of state machineries executing orders passed down from the Central Committee. In many cases such a view is entirely misleading; the convergence theory looks more compatible with the East German reality. Whilst the IfK mainly issued suggestions and guidelines (rarely directives), it gave shape and focus to many campaigns that had taken place locally before. A major step to create a specifically East German sepulchral culture was taken when in 1963 the IfK published a revised edition of the standard cemetery regulation (*Musterfriedhofsordnung*), thereby essentially replacing the *Musterfriedhofsordnung* of 1937. In the same year it also published an innovative guideline to socialist cemeteries and how their design should reflect socialist society.[101] A number of contributors had already lobbied for change as early as 1958: this clearly indicates that from the second half of the 1950s concerns were growing about the traditions and values that were reflected in the existing sepulchral culture. But this did not necessarily signify that this situation was caused by the 'capitalist' tradition, and that a socialist alternative was needed, even if some of the language suggests precisely that. Too many of the IfK's early publications were indeed written by individuals from a reformist viewpoint, suggesting a different new path to be taken, but one not altogether alien to socialist sensibilities – the relationship of the reformist tradition and that of the new socialist approach could be described as symbiotic.[102]

With regard to undertaking and the burial services, the impact of the IfK was even less visible, and allowed for more influence by individual specialists. It exerted most direct influence by consultation on specific matters with individual cities' burial services. For this indirect and often informal influence, communication with the regional *Leitbetrieb* (leading concern) was the pivotal tool of coordination. From 1964 every region of the GDR had a designated leading burial service, often in the regional administrative centre, which had to fulfil the role of a model: it served as a testing ground for the introduction of new schemes and assisting in the planning of the regional burial needs. A short summary of the role of the *Leitbetrieb VEB (k) Gartengestaltung Rostock* for the region of Rostock indicated, in that peculiar official GDR wording, the significant tasks for these leading concerns in unifying an industry traditionally fractured:

> The *Leitbetrieb*, in cooperation with the governmental institutions, has to solve the following tasks:
> 1. Devising and creating perspective planning for the municipal cemetery and burial services in the region of Rostock.
> 2. Support of the regional council, department for local utilities [ÖVW] in examining structural questions and in the district organization with regard to cemetery and burial services, or the area of gardens, parks and burial services respectively.
> 3. In 1965 the *Leitbetrieb* will conduct conferences on the problems of gardens and parks and cemeteries and burials.
> 4. In order to improve the perspective planning for the companies and institutions of the *VEB (k) Gartengestaltung Rostock*, in cooperation with the *Institut für Kommunalwirtschaft*, is developing the necessary reference numbers for production planning.
> 5. In the region covered by the *Leitbetrieb* an inter-institutional competition [A socialist mechanism to introduce market competition – basically a comparison of reference numbers with regard to effectiveness] will be conducted between the individual companies and institutions. In conjunction with the monthly analysis, an exchange of experiences will be conducted.
> ...
> 9. The *Leitbetrieb* will conduct consultations on specialist matters in the individual cities to provide better technical assistance.[103]

The *Leitbetrieb* was an essential institution within the socialist economic framework, since it bolstered the process of centralization and was an indispensable aid in establishing perspective planning (*Perspektivplan*) for the coming years. The perspective plan was a statistical forecast of the services needed, allowing the burial service to project future demands, and determine the numbers for the production of coffins in advance. It also served as a fiscal planning and costing tool, making sure that the expenses were covered and that the councils knew if they were expected to pay subsidies or receive profits. Moreover, the *Leitbetrieb* offered the party and government a foothold from which they could begin to control, administer and centralize the whole sector, even if the sector within the region was highly fragmented. The ultimate aim was to establish a uniform level of socialist municipal services. The concept of a regional umbrella institution, as foreshadowed by the centralization of the coffin manufacture in Greifswald, was thus applied to the whole burial services.

The idea behind the *Leitbetrieb* was to follow the socialist 'ideal' of leading from the front, and by example. Hence another key task for the *Leitbetrieb* and its management was to advise the smaller burial services in the region, as well as to liaise with the IfK. The *Leitbetrieb* became the initiator – a fact demonstrated by the sheer number of files the *VEB Bestattungseinrichtungen* Dresden produced. This established an effective way to influence the activities of the smaller burial services in the surrounding towns, thereby propagating secular funerals. It shared this role with the Academies for Socialist Management (*Akademien für Sozialistische Wirtschaftsführung*). Both institutions operated on a regional level and offered help to those organising secular funerals. Furthermore, it allowed them to press their own agenda and join together, as the IfK ran regular meetings and conferences so ideas could be exchanged and common problems, such as the increasing labour shortage, could be reported. In effect this opened a channel through which the municipal services could lobby for the alleviation of common problems – such as the archetypical labour shortage for the maintenance of cemeteries and the digging of graves.[104]

The mechanism of the *Leitbetrieb* worked well within the limitations of the system, as the example of the standardization of coffin manufacture underlines. The *VEB Vereinigte Holzindustrie Finsterwalde* formed the *Leitbetrieb* for the entire coffin manufacturing industry. In this role it organized a meeting of the other major coffin producing firms in September 1968. During that meeting the standardization of measures for the four new main types of coffin was the principal point of discussion: coffin production was centred on the production of groups E (coffins for inhumation), F (coffins for cremation), ET (caskets for representative purposes) and EK (coffins for children). Within each category there were still different shapes and sizes. As this was the first attempt to standardize and reduce the overall number of types of coffins that would require future monitoring:

The currently produced types of coffin and varieties of design have been taken into the catalogue, without substantial reduction. This production program is far too extensive for efficient mass production. The main task of the production-sub-group 'coffins' will, therefore, be to effect a substantial reduction of the types, while bearing in mind the need for modern design – that is easy to produce, in order to be able to close existing gaps in supply. While doing this, care has to be taken that the pricing levels in the individual territories are not changed. The *Leitbetrieb* of the production-group 'coffins' asks all producers of coffins and burial institutions for energetic cooperation and support in the achievement of this comprehensive objective.[105]

While no significant reduction had been achieved, the coffin catalogue still listed thirty-two different types in a number of different sizes with the option for a number of decorations. The direction was clear.[106] A single institution could be given a leading role rendering the simplification of production and design more manageable while it might also help to keep prices low; it could, however, also entail what was characteristic for the East German economy in general: lack of quality, insufficient supply and inflexibility. A source describing the coffin question in the region of Dresden from February 1989 encapsulates this condition:

Despite many suggestions and complaints from companies and petitions from the population, the quality is still not satisfactory … The main defects and causes are:
1. The use of different decorations (differences in the shades of colour between the lower and upper part as well as of the decoration itself).
2. The use of wood that is too wet (the coffins became mouldy, after a short time – white layer).
3. The lower beams [giving stability] give too little security (only 2 beams instead of 3 or 4).
4. By using cardboard-laminate and by stapling individual pieces, the staples are, partly, shot through [and visible].
5. There is no closure between the lower and upper half … from the side one can look into [the coffin].
6. Using cardboard-laminate for cremation damages the cremation furnaces …
   …
8. The edges of the coffins and the shot-in staples are visible to everybody. No border is glued on top.
   …
In 1987 it was not possible to reject coffins, because otherwise burials could not take place.[107]

The last point brought a grave consequence, because it meant that every coffin that was delivered had to be used, regardless of its state and stability. This was one reason why the overall state of the burial services was widely perceived as deficient. Shortcuts and the substitution of materials in short supply, such as wood, plagued some parts of the coffin industry, resulting in numerous complaints and incidents like coffins covered in mould or hastily painted, as well as thick black smog emanating from crematoria.[108] Furthermore, the insistence on keeping prices for funerals down, curtailing any investment in the infrastructure, aggravated the situation even further. Refurbishments, such as painting ceremonial rooms, were kept to a bare minimum. Until 1989 the prices for funerals in Berlin, for example, remained at the same level as they had been in 1936. The fee charged for a simple grave plot (*Erdreihenstelle*) was as little as 15 Marks, while a small funeral, with coffin, flowers, funeral ceremony, etc., would cost around 600 Marks.[109] The government had frozen prices for burial plots at a pre-war level, but retained vast regional price discrepancies. In the long term this cause the income from the burial service to fail to cover the immediate costs, let alone the upkeep of the cemeteries or investment in better infrastructure. This issue was further aggravated by an increase in cremation and burials in *Urnengemeinschaftsanlagen*, both forms of burial which were subsidized in order to induce their propagation.[110] This induced a culture of neglect, in which supply of machinery and personnel was inadequate. The wave of publications from the IfK could do nothing to overcome this underlying problem of increasing dilapidation.

The example of a petition in Dresden vividly exemplifies this culture of dereliction. On 16 October 1979, Petra H., aged 25, was to be cremated in Dresden-Tolkewitz. The family was appalled with the organization of the funeral and the sister of the deceased wrote in a petition to the local administration:

> For the farewell we were led into a room; there the flowers were taken from me, against my will. I wanted to throw them on the coffin [before it was transported to the cremation oven] – that was not possible! The coffin stood undecorated in front of a dirty tiled wall. Visible numbers had been scrawled in chalk on the coffin.
>
> At that time – five minutes before the ceremony – a 'Herr' appeared, and tried to explain to my father that he was the speaker … How can such a speaker [without prior discussion] understand the deep pain of the bereaved and in his speech pay the deceased the last respect? Is this only about being paid – or better still – the receiving of 25.00 Marks? We declined his speech … When the coffin was brought into the ceremony hall, we were all overwhelmed by great indignation despite our deep grief. The coffin and the pedestal were basically naked. Not even 10 per cent of the flowers were there. Where are the beautiful orchids and chrysanthemums? There are no technical reasons nor is there a lack of space![111]

This describes a catastrophic funeral, a funeral that left the bereaved aghast, but it does not stand alone. Much depended on the individual speaker, the cemetery staff and the local organization, but complaints were numerous – good service often required extra payments. While a basic rate of 20 Mark, plus 10 Mark for extras, was the official rate for a speaker, speakers in Berlin in the 1980s charged about 100 Mark – more than three times the listed price.[112]

Besides the reality of the *Mangelwirtschaft* (an economy of bottlenecks) it was also the ambiguous role assigned to the burial service within society and especially in the politics of the GDR that caused this situation regarding burials. Whilst it was politically unpalatable to increase the price for funerals (and there was little inclination to spend more than necessary on this sector of the economy), the burial services were expected to fulfil their role in advocating and advancing socialist culture (especially if they were *Leitbetriebe*) as well as providing vital services in celebration of the achievement of former party members.[113] East Berlin in this regard presented a great problem to the city council and the Party, as in the capital of the GDR, private undertakers operated alongside the VEB, but both of them worked in a decentralized and often highly disorganized system unsuitable for a city of that size. A concept for the restructuring of the Berlin burial services written in 1971 stresses this contradiction and reveals the distance between ambition and reality:

> In order to stabilize the situation of the cemetery and burial system in Berlin and for a future development according to plan, centralization, concentration, specialization and amalgamation are indispensable. This process can only be realized step by step and requires uniform management of the cemetery system. The effect of these measures consists in particular of fulfilling the main tasks of the cemetery and burial system, to guarantee in the long term a hygienically impeccable, dignified and punctual [within the stipulated period] burial of the deceased in conjunction with a reduction in societal expenditure and an increase of cemetery and burial culture. The existing and deteriorating precarious situation regarding the realization of burial duties does not allow for any alternative to the immediate concentration of existing funds and capacities under an uniform administration of the whole process by the capital.[114]

This describes the ambition of the GDR, to merge the successful propagation of a political ideology, via the spread of a 'decent' (*würdige*) secular funeral, with the constrained economic framework. This was to be done through centralization, concentration, specialization and amalgamation; these four trends were added to or supplemented by the other major forces (such as professionalization, individualization, sanitation, regulation, rationalization) that had shaped the emergence of the modern sepulchral culture.

On a personal level the encounter with a death is generally infrequent, while on a national level it poses a vast organizational task, especially in a planned economy. Centralization, then, should be understood as the reaction of the modern state to the necessity of coordinating, regulating and also influencing the task of disposing of a substantial number of corpses per year. Similarly concentration is the result of the logical progression of rationalization, the desire to execute a rather complex task more efficiently. The urban environment in particular, through its population density and general complexity, aids both these developments, warranting centralized management and bureaucracy as well as allowing for an approach that exploits the greater frequency of death, the shorter distances, and makes efficiency gains through, for example, the widespread use of cremation over the more labour-intensive inhumation. Cremation, when seen as a technological solution to mass disposal, hints at the third process at work here: specialization, since both concentration and centralization necessitate the training of experts (leading to the rise of technocrats and professionals) and specialized processes (cremation or the research into a biodegradable urn). Amalgamation, while primarily a socialist term, does apply outside the socialist paradigm (as merger and acquisition), when given a slightly different slant – as in achieving synergies and gaining market shares.[115]

Skilling described similarities in the influences that interest groups could exert over the political process in industrialized countries, be it in West and East. The similarities went even further: a stark divide between East and West did not even entirely apply to the systems of disposal. Centralization, concentration, specialization and amalgamation can be observed as common and transnational processes in the modernization of systems of disposal within all industrialized countries, thereby adding a further illustration, as well as dimension, to the theory of convergence. There have certainly been differences in how these challenges have been interpreted, mainly according to the political and economic condition, but also the prevailing zeitgeist and fashion. All of the abovementioned trends are born (such as the need for increased sanitation, better regulation and a higher degree of rationalization) out of the nature of the modern state, economy and society (while psychological repression, it might be argued, arises out of the growing 'remoteness' of humans from death and dying and increasing isolation and individualization of society). Ultimately this means that a complex matrix of influences has shaped the collective and individual relationship to death and sepulchral culture in the East and the West. At the same time it explains why both the West and the East saw the rise of modern funeral direction even more clearly. Thus, the whole ambition of a socialist burial service – promoting a socialist sepulchral culture – can only be described as a paradox: since trying to advocate an idea did not sit well with financial constraint. Yet it is exactly this paradox that defined socialist sepulchral culture: the attempt to achieve a high-minded ideological ideal, a decent level of service and mass dissemination of standardized procedures on a very tight budget.

After the change of the leadership of the SED in 1971, this situation became even more tense, as Erich Honecker advocated the unity of economy and society (*Einheit der Wirtschaft und Gesellschaft*) and certain subjects such as private ownership of small businesses became even more ideologically charged. For example, those whose companies had managed to avoid being turned into or amalgamated with VEBs or PHGs faced further pressure. Additional ministries became involved in organising the ever more complex elements of the ideal socialist burial service. In 1975 the IfK published a brochure that could be best described as a handbook for socialist funeral direction. This catalogue enumerates, structures, and describes how a socialist burial service should organize the full spectrum of funeral preparations, arguing that 'the minimal program of burial services cannot only include the transportation of the body. The aim has to be to take full responsibility from the next-of-kin for the organization of all events in the case of a death'.[116] A burial service with such a remit clearly transcended mere undertaking; it had expanded its responsibilities and offered socialist funeral direction. This is underlined by the fact that the pamphlet goes on to address such topics as the optimal density of outlets in different sized cities and town, give advice on accessibility in rural areas and provide tables delineating organizational responsibility for all the different tasks within a funeral service and rituals.[117] However, the scope of the idealized socialist funeral direction goes beyond the provision of a service; the educational (Agit/Prop) role of the funeral services is evident. The brochure's closing pages reveal the purpose of the all-encompassing service, since they exclusively address the political question of secular funerals and the increase in cremation rates. The intention is clear: only a good burial service is capable of organising attractive secular funerals and advocating that most socialist of burials: cremation with subsequent secular burial in an *Urnengemeinschaft*.[118] This did not mark the end of the normative pressure. Some suggestions for the change of customs and habits to be encouraged follow clearly a materialist agenda, most strikingly for example, the explicit rule to conduct the last farewell separated from the coffin by a glass wall.[119] The argument of improved hygiene only obscures at least a partial ideological desire for a change in custom. There were similar suggestions, all of which are explicable only by a mixture of ideology and additionally a marked reluctance to psychologically deal with death – or what Bernd Cornelius, former director of the cemeteries of East Berlin, has called 'the lack of relationship to death' within the GDR.[120]

The importance of the Catalogue of Burial Services (*Katalog des Bestattungsleistungen*) should not be underestimated, since it gives an insight into the patchiness of socialist burial services. The publication preceded the first comprehensive analysis of the whole spectrum of the sepulchral culture undertaken by the government in 1976. The Ministry for Regional Industries and Food Production summarized statistics, trends and other findings, in order to provide other ministries, specifically the Minister for the Interior and the Minister for Health, with an overview. It found that the wide-ranging services offered were taken up unevenly, mainly depending on the location:

> It is clearly apparent that the services are conducted to a large extent on the premise of the burial institutions, but that the organizations providing the other services are predominately concerned with the transportation of corpses and urns. The performance of burials in smaller towns and municipalities without burial institutions is largely organized by citizens themselves. This ultimately leads to many citizens turning to the church authorities in this matter.[121]

Rural and urban areas, concerning funeral rituals and undertaking provision, have tended, at least in the modern era, to be very different. In the face of radical modernization, urban areas have been in the vanguard. For instance cremation in the last decades of the nineteenth century was predominately an urban phenomenon. Under socialism, with its emphasis on the transformation of the social and economic base, one might have assumed a certain tendency to 'modernize' rural areas too.[122] However, sepulchral culture, unlike agriculture, was not forcibly altered; the countryside in the GDR remained the stronghold of the church. This had its implications for the development of sepulchral culture, since most rural cemeteries were church cemeteries, and left the state with the problem of advancing a social agenda without the support of a strong organizational framework, in this case the local cemetery administration. Consequently, this disparity between urban and rural availability and acceptance of socialist funeral direction was to be expected, in particular within a system in which specific social change was propagated mainly by the IfK with the assistance of *Leitbetriebe* and its employees, most of whom worked on the large urban cemeteries, not the small rural church cemeteries.

The official explanation, as expressed in the 1976 analysis, criticized as so often before the sporadic nature of legislation and administrative control, blaming a general lack of stringency for the multitude of problems that persisted. Ultimately this led to the decision to tackle the lack of a coherent framework by assembling a group of specialists from different ministries, institutions and the IfK, in order to agree a new legal foundation. This legislation then would finally supersede all previous laws. November 1977 was fixed as the deadline for the enterprise and that deadline passed by without a result. The group debated for more than three years, until it finally prepared a draft for the *Ministerrat* in 1980.[123] That the matter of disposal still had very low priority for the central government should not be surprising. It is remarkable that the legal framework singularly lacked any radical social or political agenda. Most regulations resemble those passed in the West, with very few noteworthy exceptions.[124] First, Paragraph 6 (3) legislated that those who were buried on behalf of the state, mostly in cases where there was no family, were to be cremated, with the obvious exception of suspicious cases (when the cause of death could not be determined, the police were called in and criminal investigation procedures took over), or if the deceased had not left instructions to the opposite. This reveals the state's tendency to propagate cremation and cost-efficiency solutions, especially as the ashes were to be buried in a *Gemeinschaftsanlage*. Secondly, paragraph 10 gave ultimate jurisdiction over all cemeteries, including church-owned ones, to the local councils, which had to approve any changes and any rules that governed the cemetery. Thirdly, the convention for implementation (*Erste Durchführungsbestimmung*) explicitly allowed the burial of ashes with or without an urn and even the scattering of ashes. This rule deviated significantly from the rules of other European countries and, like the ban on any construction of mausoleums or vaults, shows a clear socialist agenda. Fourthly, there was in paragraph 7 the explicit requirement to use a glass wall to prevent any direct contact with the corpse when conducting the 'last farewell'. The introduction of these regulations meant the end of thirty-five years of often piecemeal legal provisions. Nonetheless, it did not mark a revolution; it only enshrined the legal framework arrived at over the years through an incremental socialist reorganization of disposal within the GDR.

The organization of the disposal of the dead did not change greatly after 1980, except that the condition of many burial services and the equipment used became even more dilapidated.[125] The crematoria were aging, since most ovens were built in the 1920s and 1930s, and only unavoidable repairs were considered.[126] Based on the analysis of complaints made in Dresden, the number of incidents resulting from mistakes (often arising out of alcohol consumption), incompetence, rudeness (mostly arising out of indifference), or any combination of the three, increased substantially between 1980 and 1989.[127] Standards regarding the organization of funerals remained quite low.[128] In a number of cases, cemeteries were no longer able to offer anything except cremation. As there was nobody to dig a grave, members of the family had to fulfil that task themselves if they insisted on inhumation.[129] The work for burial services and on cemeteries was physically as well as psychologically challenging. It was neither prestigious nor well paid, and there was little by way of perquisites. The burial services therefore remained chronically understaffed, the percentage of staff near retirement was high, and the existing personnel was often under-qualified.[130] Nevertheless, a job in the sector of disposal also entailed employment away from the rest of society, and the freedom that came with working in a neglected niche of the economy:

> In the GDR it was not only alcoholics and people with little education who worked with the dead, as one generally imagines, but also dropouts from the system. That is where many 'bridged' the time until their application for an exit visa was approved, since their situation meant they were unlikely to find employment in many other companies. Others wanted to work as independent artists or authors. A contract with the cemetery for two days a week was enough to count as being in regular employment, and spared them the accusation of asocial behaviour, which was punishable in the GDR.[131]

With reunification came the sudden end of the socialist organization of disposal in East Germany. The re-privatization of many funeral services and the establishment of new companies marked the end of a process that had begun in May 1945. In 1989/90, as in 1945 but on a much smaller scale, there was no upheaval, no disruption; continuity of service and the phasing into capitalism accompanied the political transition. One might argue that the previous socialist paradigm of 'normality' in the burial services and in the cemeteries of the GDR was gradually overlaid by the new paradigm of the post-reunification sepulchral culture – a paradigm dominated by the relaxation of rules and restrictions, and sometimes breath-taking diversification that would have been previously unthinkable.[132]

Forcing changes to sepulchral culture tended to be slow, measured and often restricted – with a tendency to be reverted once the pressure subsided (see for example Joseph II's enlightened cemetery reform). These changes were subject to numerous influences and restrictions, be they deficient funds, the lack of political will to challenge the role of the church, or merely the stubborn persistence of old values and ideas about what constituted a 'proper' funeral. It is this continuum that also explains to a certain degree the slow emergence of a socialist organization of disposal. While it actually hindered its ultimate imposition on the whole of the nation, the fact that change was persistently, albeit not with excess of force, propagated meant that slowly changes did occur. These changes were in

Figure 2.1 The changing nature of German cemeteries due to the reuse of burial plots.

turn aided by processes that turned the GDR into a modern urbanized industrial country. It is axiomatic that society has to dispose of its deceased, and as such certain basic forces exert their influence on the minimum requirement for a 'decent' disposal, except in times of catastrophe. Complex systems of disposal, and with them funeral direction, became essential in the modern urban environment in order to organize the disposal of the deceased on behalf of the family. This led to one truly revolutionary innovation in East Germany after 1945, in nature if not in scope: the transformation of the municipal burial services (modelled on those of the 1920s) into a modern socialist form of funeral direction. The rise of a socialist counterpart to the capitalist funeral director, offering a comparable package of bespoke services (from collection of the corpse to pension application), shows surprising similarities between the social developments and attitudes towards death and disposal between East and West. Even if the services offered were limited to the inhabitants of the larger East German cities and their quality was sometimes appalling, that should not prevent one from acknowledging the existence of similarities. Nevertheless, the prevalence of political and ideological factors in establishing these services should not be forgotten: the state of the services reflected socialist ideals – and thus reflected on socialist society.[133] This becomes even clearer when looking at what may be described as the ideals of the socialist cemetery.

Notes

1. S. Radder, '8. Mai 1945 – 60 Jahre Kriegsende – Bevölkerungszahlen aus den Jahren 1945 bis 1947', *Statistische Monatschrift – Berliner Statistik*, 5 (2005), 146.
2. A. Confino, 'Dissonance, Normality and the Historical Method – Why Did Some Germans Think of Tourism after May 8, 1945?', in R. Bessel and D. Schumann (eds), *Life after Death – Approaches to a Cultural and Social History of Europe During the 1940s and 1950s* (Cambridge: Cambridge University Press, 2003).
3. While I criticise the concept of the 'Zero Hour' at the level of the whole society, I am acutely aware of the significance on the personal level.
4. The idea of a continuum of routine is not necessarily limited to the mundane. Hermann Glaser's reference to continuity and discontinuity in regard to the Berlin Philharmonic Orchestra, giving a last concert under Hitler's rule on 15 April 1945 (Beethoven and Wagner) and the first concert after the surrender on the 26 May 1945 (Mendelssohn, Mozart and Tchaikovsky) hints at how profound the struggle between routine and change can be, considering the swiftness of the return of high culture at a time of disorder, suffering and enormously high death rates. See: H. Glaser, '1945 – Cultural Beginnings: Continuity and Discontinuity', in R. Pommerin (ed.), *Culture in the Federal Republic of Germany, 1945–1995* (Oxford and Washington: Berg, 1996), 19; R. Steininger, *Deutsche Geschichte seit 1945 – Darstellung und Dokumente, Vol. 1, 1945–1947* (Frankfurt: Fischer, 1996), 65–71; R. Bessel, *Nazism and War* (London: Weidenfeld and Nicolson, 2004), 153–67.
5. R. Bessel, *Germany 1945: From War to Peace* (London: Simon and Schuster, 2009).
6. *Statistisches Jahrbuch 1955 der DDR* (Berlin: Staatsverlag der DDR, 1956), 53.
7. R. Overmans, 'Die Toten des Zweiten Weltkriegs in Deutschland – Bilanz der Forschung unter besonderer Berücksichtigung der Wehrmachts- und Vertreibungsverluste', in W. Michalka (ed.), *Der Zweite Weltkrieg: Analysen, Grundzüge, Forschungsbilanz* (Munich: Piper, 1989); R. Overmans, *Deutsche Militärische Verluste im Zweiten Weltkrieg* (Munich: R. Oldenbourg, 2004).
8. Near collapse in Dresden in April 1945. See: Jörg Friedrich, *Der Brand – Deutschland im Bombenkrieg 1940–1945* (Berlin: Propyläen, 2002), 431; R. Behring, 'Das Kriegsende 1945', in C. Vollhals (ed.), *Sachsen in der NS-Zeit* (Leipzig: G. Kiepenheuer, 2002), 227.
9. G. Pritchard, *The Making of the GDR 1945–1952* (Manchester and New York: Manchester University Press, 2000), 2–3.
10. BLHA Potsdam, Rep. 211 MfG, No. 1126, f. 3 VS: *Aktenvermerk,* 6 August 1945.
11. Ibid.
12. StA Dresden, Rep. 9.1.14, No. 812: *Jahresbericht des KWU – Bestattung,* 20 May 1950.
13. BLHA Potsdam, Rep. 211 MfG, No. 1126, f. 3 RS: *Aktenvermerk,* 6 August 1945.
14. A. Camus, *The Collected Fiction of Albert Camus*, trans. Stuart Gilbert (London: Hamish Hamilton, 1960).
15. There is no accounting for likely fluctuations (due to proximity to Berlin) in the number of inhabitants between 1944 and 1945. The exhumations were commonplace in Germany between 1945 and 1950s because temporary mass graves for bombing victims were often opened in order to give as many as bodies as possible their own grave.
16. Fischer, *Vom Gottesacker zum Krematorium*, 116. There is remarkably little literature on cremation during the two World Wars.
17. 'In 1946 the cremation oven was reopened. With this the whole process of disposal for the city of Dresden was greatly eased', StA Dresden, Rep. 9.1.14, No. 812: *Jahresbericht des KWU – Bestattung,* 20 May 1950.
18. It has been estimated that 110,000 trees were cut down in order to provide some kind of fuel. See also Steininger, *Deutsche Geschichte seit 1945*, 66–67.
19. See LA Berlin, C Rep. 110, No. 1068.
20. See the work coordinated by Leeds University: B. Niven (ed.), *Germans as Victims. Remembering the Past in Contemporary Germany* (London: Palgrave, 2006) and H. Schmitz (ed.), *A Nation*

of Victims? Representations of German Wartime Suffering from 1945 to the Present* (Amsterdam and New York: Rodopi, 2007); as well as R. Moeller, *War Stories: The Search for a Usable Past in the Federal Republic of Germany* (Berkeley: University of California Press, 2001).

21. 'But at night, the rats sleep', in W. Borchert, *Draußen vor der Tür und andere ausgewählte Erzählungen* (Frankfurt: Suhrkamp, 1982).

22. Confino, 'Dissonance, Normality and the Historical Method', in Bessel and Schumann (eds), *Life After Death*, 326.

23. See: LA Berlin, C Rep. 110, No. 1068: *Das Bestattungswesen im neuen Berlin*, undated but 1945, 1.

24. See: LA Berlin, C Rep. 109, No. 1070.

25. E. Fischer and K. Bärbig, *Die Sozialisierung des Bestattungswesens – Veröffentlichung der sächsischen Landesstelle für Gemeinwirtschaft* (Dresden: v. Zahn and Jaensch, 1921), particularly 5–9, 49–58.

26. In 1925 the cities of Weimar, Freiburg, Heidelberg and Giesen were among the cities that had municipalized their undertaking services, and Bielefeld, Heilbronn and Lübeck were seriously considering the issue.

27. Fischer and Bärbig, *Die Sozialisierung des Bestattungswesens*, 32.

28. Pritchard, *The Making of the GDR*, 2.

29. 'Yes, we sadly have too many undertakers in Berlin, considering that in specialist circles the opinion is held that there should be 50,000 or 60,000 inhabitants to one undertaker. This would mean that with 80 to 100 undertakers Berlin should be sufficiently covered. In Berlin we, however, have double that, namely circa 200 undertakers with 220 outlets. The profession is therefore largely oversubscribed … Since today it is still difficult to envisage which dimension and how many inhabitants the new Berlin will have, once cannot determine the future number of undertakers. Without doubt, however is that considering the above: even the number of 80 [undertakers] is far too high', LA Berlin, C Rep. 110, No. 1068: *Das Bestattungswesen im neuen Berlin*, 2.

30. The charge of 'profiteering' and prevention of deriving unwarranted economic gains out the misery of the bereaved has always been an issue of discussion, and to this day remains a constant problem when talking to undertakers about their public perception, as the anthropologist has stressed in her study of that occupation. See G. Schiller, *Der organisierte Tod – Beobachtungen zum modernen Bestattungswesen* (Düsseldorf: Fachverlag des deutschen Bestattungsgewerbes, 1991); Fischer, *Wie wir unter die Erde*, 127–30; G. Schiller, *Bestattungsunternehmen*, available at <http://memopolis.uni-regensburg.de/lekt…texte/tod_und_gesellschaft/shiller.html> (accessed 10 March 2003).

31. LA Berlin, C Rep. 110, No. 1068: *Das Bestattungswesen im neuen Berlin*, 3.

32. LA Berlin, C Rep. 110, No. 1068: *Ergänzungen zu meinen Ausführungen über: Das Bestattungswesen im neuen Berlin*, 2 July 1945.

33. 'The burial departments are only established to address the question, if the deceased should receive his individual coffin (danger of contagious diseases) or a rental coffin' (*Die Bestattungsämter waren lediglich dazu eingesetzt [die Frage] zu klären, inwieweit der Verstorben einen eigenen Sarg (Seuchengefahr) oder einen Leihsarg erhalten sollte*), LA Berlin, C Rep. 110, No. 1068, 16: Letter, *Hauptamt für Planung – Grünplanung an Finanzabteilung*, 24 October 1946.

34. LA Berlin, C Rep. 110, No. 1068: *Hauptamt für Grünplanung und Gartenbau an Direktion des Bestattungsamtes München*, 17 December 1947.

35. NWSA Detmold, D 106 Detmold, No. 2152.

36. This is further underlined by the disbanding of a number of communalized undertaking services under the local government of the Nazis after 1939.

37. 'The Reich may, via legislation, establish principles for: … (5) system of disposal of the dead [*Bestattungswesen*]', H. Mosler, *Verfassung des Deutschen Reichs vom 11. August 1919* (Stuttgart: Reclam, 1972), 9.

38. I would argue it is really a reference back to the *Erfurter Programm* of the SPD and that hints at a long tradition of parts of the party that saw a profit-orientated undertaking industry as amoral and profiteering from loss and grief.

39. LHSA Magdeburg, Rep. K2 Ministerpräsident, No. 695, Film 175, f. 132 RS: *Kommunalabteilung K I, Halle/Saale*, 15 May 1946.

40. S. Creuzberger, *Die sowjetische Besatzungsmacht und das politische System der SBZ* (Weimar: Böhlau, 1996), 53–93, in particular 60–68.

41. 'Verordnung über die wirtschaftliche Betätigung der Gemeinden und Kreise (Kommunalwirtschaftsverordnung) vom November 24, 1948', *Zentralverordnungsblatt*, Jahrgang 1948, 558–60.

42. See Creuzberger, *Die sowjetische Besatzungsmacht*, 124–66.

43. StA Greifswald, Rep. 7.9., No. 260: *Vorgänge KWU*.

44. U. Mählert, *Kleine Geschichte der DDR* (Munich: C.H. Beck, 1999), 24.

45. See Fischer and Bärbig, *Die Sozialisierung des Bestattungswesens*.

46. Mortality had returned to pre-war levels and that the crematoria had been repaired as early as 1946, thus easing the problem of limited cemetery capacity. StA Dresden, Rep. 9.1.14, No. 812: *Jahresbericht KWU – Bestattung*, 20 May 1950.

47. Creuzberger, *Die sowjetische Besatzungsmacht*, 173–75.

48. Mähnert, *Kleine Geschichte der DDR*, 56–69.

49. R. Jessen, 'Partei, Staat und "Bündnispartner": Die Herrschaftsmechanismen der SED-Diktatur', in M. Judt (ed.), *DDR-Geschichte in Dokumenten: Beschlüsse, Berichte, interne Materialien und Alltagszeugnisse* (Berlin: C.H. Links, 1997), 27–53, in particular 10.

50. 'Verordnung über die Organisation der volkseigenen örtlichen Industrie und er kommunalen Einrichtungen', 22 February 1951, *Gesetzblatt der Deutschen Demokratischen Republik*, No. 25, Berlin 28. Februar 1951, 143.

51. See: *Beschluss der II. Parteikonferenz, 9.–12. Juni 1952*. See also Judt, *DDR Geschichte in Dokumenten*, 52–53.

52. VLA Greifswald, Rep. 200 2.1, No. 1, 18: *Vorlesung des Genossen Willi Barth an der Parteihochschule "Karl Marx" am 21. Oktober 1952*, 3.

53. 'Propagation' in this context is used to mean the organized popularization and promotion of ideas through means of agitation, propaganda, regulations and incentives.

54. StA Greifswald, VA 1390: *Zuarbeit zum Informationsbericht für die Komplexkontrolle*, 15 March 1988.

55. MHLA Schwerin, Rep. 6.11-11 MdI, No. 561, 32–33: *Auszugsweise Abschrift des Verbesserungsvorschlages 17 AT 39 177 – Kuhn – Umgestaltung des Bestattungswesens. Variante I.*

56. MHLA Schwerin, Rep. 6.11-11 MdI, No. 561, 34: *Auszugsweise Abschrift des Verbesserungsvorschlages 17 AT 39 177 – Kuhn – Umgestaltung des Bestattungswesens. Variante II.*

57. For all details mentioned below see: MHLA Schwerin, Rep. 6.11-11 MdI, No. 561, 44–46: *Bericht über die Dienstreise vom 25. bis 28. Februar 1952 nach Altenburg betr. Erfahrungsaustausch über Friedhofsangelegenheiten.*

58. This drive for efficiency is also very evident in the changes in the sepulchral cultures of Western Europe and the US from 1930 onwards and especially after 1950. For example it was one factor that gave rise to the widespread introduction of lawn cemeteries. They required far less manpower for maintenance yet the orderliness and conformity suited reformist ideas about cemetery design. See: Julie Rugg, 'Lawn Cemeteries: The Emergence of a New Landscape of Death', *Urban History* 33:2 (2006), 213–33. See also the files of ZISW (Zentralinstitut für sozialistische Wirtschaftsführung beim ZK der SED), especially SAPMO-BA Berlin, DY 30, No. 26343.

59. MHLA Schwerin, Rep. 6.11-11 MdI, No. 561, 44–46.

60. The GDR chief ideologist Kurt Hager, for example, remarked that death is a challenge for the Marxist-Leninist Philosophy: K. Hager, *Philosophie and Politik* (Berlin: Dietz, 1979). Also

Kay Blumenthal-Barby: 'A lot still remains to be done in order to instill in the public, as well as in the medical staff, an attitude towards dying and death that is based upon rationality and objectivity': Blumenthal-Barby, *Betreuung Sterbender*, 18.

61. A good example is provided by the Victorian fashions shaping funerals. See Curl, *Celebration of Death*, 204–18.

62. In Mecklenburg the following VEB Stadtwirtschaft incorporating burial services were founded: Schwerin 1952 (VEB Grünanlagen was separated in 1965), Wittenberge 1952, Parchim 1964, Hagenow 1965, Ludwigslust 1967, Güstrow 1969.

63. To understand how much the word 'desire' fits, see any account of the 1953 campaign with the codename 'Aktion Rose', that enforced the nationalization, in certain cases by means of threats, extortion and blackmail, of many properties along the coast of the Baltic Sea. See F. Werkentin, *Politische Strafjustiz in der Ära Ulbricht – Vom bekennenden Terror zur verdeckten Repression* (Berlin: C.H. Links, 1997).

64. SSA Chemnitz, BT and RdB, Abt. Örtliche Wirtschaft; see also M. Fetscher, *Die Reorganisation von Eigentumsrechten mittelständischer Unternehmen in Ostdeutschland*, PhD thesis, Universität Konstanz 2000, 31–33.

65. StA Greifswald, Rep. 7.9., No. 298.

66. The aptly named 'Plan for the Provision of the 1000 items for Everyday Life' was one reaction by the regional governments to overcome some of these shortages that for many characterized life in the GDR. For a quaint view see: B. Deja-Lölhöffel, *Unbekannter Nachtbar DDR* (Arau and Stuttgart: AT Verlag, 1987), 18–27; 119–25.

67. Especially as, increasingly, more craftsmen retired without a successor: J. Nawrodsi, 'Der Not gehorchend… – Handwerk in der DDR', *Die Zeit*, 20 August 1976.

68. StA Dresden, Rep. 9.1.13, No. 737: *VEB Bestattungs- und Friedhofswesen Leipzig: Vorschläge für Regelung der Sargfrage*, 30 September 1960. The use of MDF and laminated wood proved extremely corrosive when these coffins were used in crematoria, thus they were not used for cremation. Neither did they decompose well, which also posed problems when graves were reopened for re-use.

69. BA Berlin, DO 4 Kirchenfragen, No. 2162: *Das Bestattungs- und Friedhofswesen in der DDR*, 4.

70. LA Berlin, C Rep. 115, No. 220: *Letter Magistrat von Groß-Berlin Abt. Kommunale Wirtschaft an Abt. Land- und Forstwirtschaft*, 5 August 1958, 1.

71. LA Berlin, C Rep. 104, No. 607: *Magistratsvorlage No. 60/71 zur Beschlußfassung für die Sitzung am 17. März 1971*.

72. StA Dresden, Rep. 9.1.14, No. 204: *Zusammenstellung von vereinheitlichen Definitionen zu Begriffen des Friedhofs- und Bestattungswesens der DDR mit dem Ziel der Ergänzung der einheitlichen Definitionen für Planung, Rechnungsführung und Statistik Teil 5 Stadt- und Gemeindewirtschaft, IfK*, 15 December 1971, 4.

73. The importance of the service provided, in accordance with a statement of Walter Ulbricht, is highlighted by a letter indicating the developments in Dresden since the late 1950s: StA Dresden, RdS, I/18/70: *Schreiben vom 16. März 1964*.

74. 'At the beginning of the 60s the enlargement and refinement of the sector providing services to the population was ever more pressing. Especially with regard to the burial services a situation existed that required change since character and quantity no longer suited societal development', quoted in P. Frenz, *Die historische und gesellschaftliche Entwicklung des Bestattungswesens unter besonderer Berücksichtigung der aktuellen Situation in der DDR*, PhD thesis University of Halle-Wittenberg, 1979, 158.

75. G. Howarth, *Last Rites – The Work of the Modern Funeral Direction* (Amityville: Baywood Pub., 1996); R. Bourgeois, 'De croque-mort à entrepreneur des pomper funèbres: La Martinme Funeral Directors' Association et la montée du professionalisme au début du 20e siècle', *Acadiensis (Fredericton)*, 31 (2002), 97–128.

76. For a short summary of the history of the undertaker see: Fischer, *Wie wir unter die Erde kommen*, 117–27.

77. Gender here is very interesting; until 2003 women were clearly in the minority. In Germany that has changed with about half of available apprenticeships being taken up by women. For an insight and further statistics see: 'Frauenpower: Ist "sie" der bessere Bestatter?', *Bestattung – Fachzeitschrift des VdZB*, 24 June 2010.

78. 'Attaining the different welfare payments and services offered in the case of death often exceeds the physical ability of the usually elderly bereaved. A well organised burial service provider has, if the citizen gives the instruction, therefore, to be able, for an appropriate fee, to attain these'. IfK, *Katalog der Dienstleistungen im Bestattungswesen* (Dresden: IfK, 1975), 13.

79. This was a hypothesis which incidentally was shared by Mao and was at least partly responsible for his support in favour of the Cultural Revolution. H.G. Skilling and F. Griffiths (eds), *Interest Groups in Soviet Policy* (Princeton: Princeton University Press, 1971), 5–17.

80. Corey Ross points out the danger of this view of the GDR: Ross, *The East German Dictatorship*, 36.

81. J. Redlin, *Gegenwärtige großstädtische Bestattungsriten – eine empirische Untersuchung in der Hauptstadt der DDR*, Belegarbeit im Fach Ethnologie Humboldt Universität, 1985, 7.

82. Redlin, *Gegenwärtige großstädtische Bestattungsriten*, 6–7. Her thesis puts emphasis that the Berlin burial service trace back their roots to the *Gemeinnützigen Bestattungs-GmbH* founded in the 1920s, just because it used first eight, later three, of this institution's locations.

83. BA Berlin, DO 4 Kirchenfragen, No. 2162: *Das Bestattungs- und Friedhofswesen in der DDR*, 6.

84. Ibid., 1. [NB: on the limitation to urban location: socialist sepulchral reform is very much limited to where it can operate efficiently.]

85. 'Of course this marginal field cannot be moved so much into the foreground that other responsibilities of our Republic suffer. But based on my experience in the field of the burial and cemetery system, I saw it as my duty to inform the central committee of our Party about the current condition [implies negative situation].' BAB, DO4 Kirchenfragen, No. 2162: *Das Bestattungs- und Friedhofswesen in der DDR*, 13.

86. Only in the mid 1980s could Jane Redlin write: 'All companies in the burial service industry and, with the exception of the church owned cemeteries, all cemeteries are subject to the control of the Ministry for Regional Industry and the Food Industry (*Ministerium für bezirksgeleitete Industrie und Lebensmittelindustrie*)'. The ministry did not really exercise this control, but detailed research is hampered by the fact that most files have been rendered inaccessible because of fungal growth. Redlin, *Gegenwärtige großstädtische Bestattungsriten*, 3.

87. Jugendweihe was the socialist rite of passage at the age of fourteen representing the equivalent to Protestant confirmation.

88. B. Hallberg, *Die Jugendweihe – Zur Deutschen Jugendweihetradition* (Göttingen: Vandenhoeck and Ruprecht, 1979).

89. LSA Merseburg, RdB Halle, No. 3800, 43–48: *Protokoll Treffen mit Staatssekretär Eggerath*, 8 July 1957.

90. MLHA Schwerin, Rep. 7.1-1, RdB Schwerin, 1. Überlieferungschicht, No. 3995 b: *Vorwort zum Bericht der Arbeitsgruppe für weltliche Bestattung im Bezirk Schwerin*.

91. See the chapters on internal normalization in: M. Fulbrook (ed.), *Power and Society in the GDR, 1961–1979 – The 'Normalisation of Rule'* (Oxford and New York: Berghahn, 2009), 181–320; P. Major, *Behind the Berlin Wall: East Germany and the Frontiers of Power* (Oxford: Oxford University Press, 2010).

92. Happe, 'Die Sozialistische Reform der Friedhofs- und Bestattungskultur in der DDR', in Sörries (ed.), *Vom Reichsausschuß zur Arbeitsgemeinschaft Friedhof und Denkmal*, 185–212; and in the same volume, Hoffjan, 'Existierte eine spezifische realsozialistische Friedhofgestaltung in der DDR', 171–84.

93. R. Sörries, 'Kontroverse um Sozialistische Friedhofskultur' Friedhof und Denkmal, 41:1 (1996), 11; Schelenz and Meinel, '"Sozialistische" Friedhofskultur in der DDR?', 12–15.

94. R. Sörries, 'Studienfahrt durch die Oberlausitz', *Friedhof und Denkmal*, 41:1 (1996), 12.

95. H. Skilling, 'Interest Groups and Communist Politics', *World Politics*, 18:3 (1966), 435–51.

96. Sörries, 'Kontroverse um Sozialistische Friedhofskultur', 11.

97. 'Every two years the institution should clothe, or pay a clothing fee to, its employees. Grey or anthracite coloured are to be treated with preference, while black clothing are no longer propagated (*propagiert*)', IfK, *Katalog der Bestattungsdienstleistungen*, 13–14.

98. Happe, 'Die Sozialistische Reform', in Sörries, *Vom Reichsausschuß zur Arbeitsgemeinschaft Friedhof und Denkmal*, 185–86.

99. The perspective plan for the *Textiltreinigungsleistung* for the region of Gera was memorably classified in red as a confidential document (*Vertrauliche Dienstsache*). For the empty phrase argument: 'The publication [Gestaltung unserer Friedhöfe (1963)] was, like all publications of state institutions, interspersed party political phrases' (Schelenz and Meinel, '"Sozialistische" Friedhofskultur in der DDR?', 14).

100. The journal was aptly titled 'Informationen aus der Praxis für die Praxis'.

101. IfK, *Gestaltung unsere Friedhöfe* (Berlin: Staatsverlag der DDR, 1963).

102. Schelenz and Meinel, '"Sozialistische" Friedhofskultur in der DDR', 13–14.

103. VLA Greifswald, Rep. 200 4.3.1, No. 1, 8: *Arbeitsplan des Leitbetriebes VEB (K) Gartengestaltung Rostock für den Bereich Gartengestaltung, Friedhöfe und Bestattungswesen im Bezirk Rostock*, 19 November 1964.

104. This labour shortage affected both municipal as well as church cemeteries. EZA Berlin, Rep. 101, No. 2565: *Friedhofsfehlbeträge*, 30 October 1976.

105. StA Dresden, Rep. 9.1.14, No. 381: *Typenkatalog Särge, 20. December 1968*, 2–3stre.

106. By 1989 the regional coffin production plan for Dresden only lists six types (the major two types representing 88.7 per cent of the whole production). StA Dresden, Rep. 9.1.14, No. 131: *Sargbilanz Fertigsärge – Ullersdor*, 1989.

107. StA Dresden, Rep. 9.1.14, No. 131: *Zur Sargsituation im Bezirk Dresden*, 27 February 1989, 2.

108. StA Dresden, Rep. 9.1.14, No. 288 and No. 289: *Eingabeanalysen*.

109. Geißler, 'Unter der Erde der DDR', in Michel and Spengler, *Todesbilder*, 81; after 1989 the same service cost about quadruple that amount.

110. 'The development of our disposal services has the aim to increase the percentage of cremations', StA Dresden, Rep. 9.1.14, No. 761: *Planung und Verrechnung von preisgebunden Subventionen und Abgaben*, 31 March 1976.

111. StA Dresden, Rep. 9.1.14, No. 288: *Eingabe*, 6 September 1979.

112. Geißler, 'Unter der Erde der DDR', in Michel and Spengler, *Todesbilder*, 82.

113. As decided by the Commission for the dignified burial of distinguished Party veterans (*Kommission zur würdigen Beisetzung von verdienten Parteiveteranen*). For example: SSA Leipzig, Bezirksleitung Leipzig, IV E-2/10/589: *Bericht der Kommission für verdiente Parteimitglieder*, 1984, 16–17.

114. LA Berlin, C Rep. 104, No. 607: *Konzeption zur Stabilisierung der Lage im Berliner Friedhofs- und Bestattungswesen durch Stadtrat Reutter*, 22 February 1971, 2.

115. In a number of countries there has been a growth of large market shares with regard to funeral directing, such as the Co-operative Funeral Homes in Britain which conducted 87,000 funerals (in 1996 14 per cent of a market worth £800m per year). The British market share of Co-op Funerals subsequently rose, and the last time it was calculated in 2006 it was 21.91 per cent. For the United States (conservatively estimated to be an annual $16 billion market) there have been a string of mergers and acquisitions by mainly three large companies SCI (Service Cooperation International), Loewen Group, Stewart Enterprises, all of which rely heavily on synergetic effects, gains in efficiency and price rises to maintain a high profit margin (25 per cent). These companies have also extended their influence abroad, acquiring significant market shares; for instance one fourth of all funerals in Australia are conducted by SCI. This has lead, as Jessica Mitford predicted in 1963, to an increase of costs. Some suggest for Australia that there was as much as a 40 per cent rise in the cost of an average funeral

between 1996 and 2002. For an introduction see: J. Mitford, *The American Way of Death – Revisited* (London: Virago, 1998); 'The Business of Bereavement: An Expensive Way to Go', *The Economist*, 4 January 1997; M. Barnett and S. Rodriguez, 'Death goes Global: An Examination of Foreign Direct Investment in the Death Care Industry' (unpublished paper, 2003); F. Schulz, 'The Disappearing Gravestone: Changes in the Modern German Sepulchral Landscape', in M. Aaron, *Envisaging Death: Dying and Visual Culture* (Newcastle: Cambridge Scholars, 2013).

116. IfK, *Katalog der Dienstleistungen im Bestattungswesen*, 1–2.

117. The details sometimes touch the ludicrous, e.g., the helpful hints to the extent that the waiting room should have 10–15 chairs.

118. 'Great attention is to be given to the high-quality conduct of secular funerals.' (*Große Aufmerksamkeit ist der qualitativ hochwertigen Durchführung weltlicher Trauerfeiern zu widmen.*) In: IfK, *Katalog der Dienstleistungen im Bestattungswesen*, 10.

119. 'The farewell from the deceased … should be conducted so that the bereaved can see the coffin through a plane of glass ("behind glass") … With regard to new constructions this is an absolute necessity', IfK, *Katalog der Dienstleistungen im Bestattungswesen*, 12.

120. '*Die Leute in der DDR hatten kein Verhältnis zum Tod*', Geißler, 'Unter der Erde der DDR', in Michel and Spengler, *Todesbilder*, 82.

121. BA Berlin, DO1 34.0, No. 48678: *Analyse des Friedhofs- und Bestattungswesens der DDR (1976)*, 4.

122. A. Humm, *Auf dem Weg zum Sozialistischen Dorf? – Zum Wandel der dörflichen Lebenswelt in der DDR und der Bundesrepublik Deutschland 1952–1969* (Göttingen: Vandenhoeck and Ruprecht, 1999), 307–22.

123. The files concerned with many of the burial services and especially the deliberations for the 1980 *MRB* (*Ministeratsbeschuß*) were kept by the Ministry for Regional Industries, but most of the files concerning this ministry are inaccessible due to fungal infestation. One has therefore to rely on other sources to reconstruct the course of events.

124. 'Verordnung über das Bestattungs- und Friedhofswesen vom 17. April 1980 / Erste und Zweite Durchführungsbestimmung', *Gesetzblatt der Deutschen Demokratischen Republik*, Teil I, No. 18, 26. Juni 1980, 159–64; see also J. Gaedke, 'Friedhofs- und Bestattungsrecht in der DDR', *Deutsche Friedhofskultur – Zeitschrift für das gesamte Friedhofswesen*, 71 (1981), 274.

125. 'With the continued existence of the GDR the archival materials report states of emergency with regard to the disposal of the dead in form of the lack of coffins, the lack of manpower for the digging and caring for the graves, as well as missing resources for the extension or construction of cemeteries' (*In den Archivmaterialien wird mit zunehmender Dauer der DDR über Bestattungsnotstände in Form von Sargmangel, fehlenden Kräften für den Erdaushub und die Pflege der Gräber sowie fehlender Ressourcen für die Erweiterung beziehungsweise Neuanlage von Friedhöfen berichtet*), Happe, 'Die sozialistische Reform', in Sörries, *Vom Reichsausschuß zur Arbeitsgemeinschaft Friedhof und Denkmal*, 194.

126. MLHA Schwerin, RdB Schwerin, Abt. ÖVW, No. 36354: *Bericht über Zustand der Krematorien im den Nordbezirken*, 1978.

127. But also earlier: the 1971 report on the situation of undertaking in Berlin emphasised that an ageing and declining workforce did not allow for any alternative to the process of concentration, inasmuch as the system might otherwise collapse altogether. LA Berlin, C Rep. 104, No. 607, 2.

128. StA Dresden, Rep. 9.1.14, No. 299: *Eingabeanalysen 1980–1989*. I use Dresden as a particular example, because I have found there the most comprehensive archival material.

129. IfK, '*Analyse des Friedhofs- und Bestattungswesens mit Schlußfolgerungen und Vorschlägen zur Lösung der bestehender Probleme*' (Dresden: IfK, 1976), 8.

130. By the late 1970s fifty per cent of all eulogies in Rostock were held by two elderly gentlemen.

131. Geißler, 'Unter der Erde der DDR', in Michel, *Todesbilder*, 87.

132. Much physical evidence of the socialist cemetery culture has already been irretrievably lost

owing to the reconstruction measures hurryingly executed after 1990. On the other hand the diversification can be seen in the number of options that are available. By 2005 Bielefeld cemeteries (in the West) offered nearly a dozen different possibilities, including 'urn-skyscrapers', anonymous graves and a new ash scattering field, and that despite one of the lowest rates of cremation – highlighting the fundamental change after 1989. See <http://www.bielefeld.de/de/un/fried/gub/> (accessed 4 August 2005).

133. M. Kramer (ed.), *Erarbeitungen von Vorschlägen und Normativen zur Erhöhung des Dienstleistungsniveaus im Bestattungswesens* (Dresden: IfK, 1974), 3.

Chapter 3

RESTING PLACES? CEMETERIES IN THE GDR

Whereas the previous chapter focused on the organization and administration of disposal, this one looks at the location of disposal. This has artificially separated two very closely linked institutions: the burial service provider and the cemetery. The former offers an array of services and the organizational framework needed for a funeral, whilst the latter generally furnishes the space where the funeral is conducted, the resting place, and increasingly the regular maintenance of the burial site.[1] This separation is necessary in order to give cemeteries and undertaking and their respective roles in the socialist sepulchral culture the individual space they deserve. Yet in Germany we see another important link: in the role and relationship of the church to both these institutions and to the state in the form of local and central government. The entangled nature of cemetery ownership has already appeared as a feature of East German sepulchral culture, for instance the burial service of Dresden needed to negotiate specific times of access with the churches in order to carry out its tasks. Moreover, the statistic that 70 per cent of all cemeteries remained church-owned could easily be used as key evidence that *de facto* it is hard to speak of any such thing as a socialist cemetery culture. This figure is beyond doubt and even if it is brought into some perspective by describing the proportion of church-owned burial space rather than absolute numbers of (sometimes very small) cemeteries, one is still left with the fact that around 60 per cent of all cemetery space of the GDR was ecclesiastic property.[2] However, these figures despite their *prima facie* strength do not reflect the real complexity of the role of cemeteries in aiding or hindering the emergence of a socialist sepulchral culture, this complexity can be seen by the example of the region of Leipzig as provided in Table 3.1.

Notes for this section begin on page 117.

Table 3.1: Cemeteries and their ownership in the region of Leipzig circa 1960.

District	Number of all Cemeteries	Church Cemeteries	Municipal Cemeteries
Altenburg	46	42	4
Borna	51	39	12
Schmölln	37	32	5
Geithain	38	38	–
Torgau	58	48	10
Eilenburg	42	32	10
Delitzsch	43	40	3
Wurzen	42	35	7
Oschatz	43	27	16
Grimma	46	43	3
Döbeln	38	36	2
Leipzig-Land	69	60	9
Leipzig-Stadt	25	20	5
Overall	*578*	*492*	*86*

(Data: SSA Leipzig, RdB Leipzig, No. 20679)

When reporting on an excursion of members of the *Arbeitsgemeinschaft Friedhof und Denkmal* (AFD) made in 1995 to visit East German cemeteries, Reiner Sörries, then the director of the AFD, came to the conclusion that there had been a pronounced ideological and political component of the IfK guidelines for cemetery design.[3] Two East German members of AFD objected the publication of this view:

> The design regulations and guidelines during the GDR, whether on municipal or church level, were conceived autonomously by cemetery specialists, not on the behest of governmental institutions and supervisory bodies, but certainly with reference to earlier guidelines (Reichsausschuß Friedhof und Denkmal). In those cemeteries where they [the regulations] became practice, this was always dependant on the persuasion of the local employees [at the cemetery].[4]

This argument, culminating in the dismissal of the idea that there was a socialist sepulchral culture, contradicts much of the archival evidence. Their argument to a degree reflects the local perspective derived from the experience of the day-to-day operation of cemeteries in the GDR. The two authors, hence, rightfully emphasize the fact that 60 per cent of the cemetery space of the GDR was church-owned and thus not subject to direct means of state control. Like Sörries, they point to the significance of the historical precedent of reform (while they do not stress the comfortable compatibility of reformist ideas with socialist ideals) and they correctly identify and stress the role of individuals' initiative in the success of reforms. However, their argument disregards the wider perspective of disposal in a planned socialist economy, and the crucial role played by cemeteries therein; they neglect the changes and shifts in sepulchral culture that occurred over nearly half a century; and they, at least partially, overlook the interactions of politics and ideology with their particular field of expertise. The issue of cemetery administration and cemetery design in the GDR was much more intricate.

Cemeteries are an integral part of the wider organization of disposal, and thus have traditionally been regulated by various governmental and religious agencies, especially in complex modern societies. The official East German definition of the cemetery in 1971 acknowledged this explicitly, when it, in that distinct technical East German style, stressed the functionality and, strangely, if not portentously, the impermanence of cemeteries:

Cemetery

An open space of a locality (village/town/city) set aside within the framework of urban planning for the sole purpose of the hygienic disposal of the dead and honouring their memory through burial in grave plots; it includes functionally necessary cemetery buildings for the organization of the conduct of funerals and certain facilities for upkeep and maintenance until the dissolution of the cemetery; it is the people's property or church property and is administered by municipal or church cemetery departments, on instruction of the legal owner.[5]

The key points encapsulated in this definition were the result of a long process of specialization and accumulation of technical expertise by those in charge of cemetery administration (independent of the ownership of the cemeteries). From at least the middle of the nineteenth century, the organization of the disposal of the dead in Germany, beginning with the urban centres, became a municipal responsibility. After the growth of the cities and hygienic considerations had forced the cemeteries outside of the city walls, the explosion of the urban population created the demand for new large cemeteries.[6] The churches declared these cemeteries sacred ground and sanctified the new cemetery chapels, but the land was civic property – managed by civil servants on behalf of the public. The city or town owned these new cemeteries and thus acquired the power to regulate activities taking place on its property. Two further processes underlie this transition. First, the linguistic shift from the word *Gottesacker*) or *Kirchhof* (the equivalent of churchyard) to the term *Friedhof* (as in, enclosed yard) – a shift that markedly removed, at least in a linguistic sense, reference to the churches.[7] Secondly, this secularization was reflected in a more physical sense by the rise of the municipal mortuary, the *Leichenhalle*. The mortuary became the cornerstone of modern German sepulchral culture; it became the place to which the dead were removed, the place where relatives could see their loved ones for the last time, and the place from which the final journey of the corpse began. The municipal mortuary with the adjacent chapel/ceremony room (*Feierhalle*) epitomizes the most decisive sepulchral shift of the twentieth century; with the advent of refrigeration, and owing to hygienic considerations, the dead were no longer laid out on their deathbeds, but quickly removed to the mortuary. The first municipal mortuaries were built in the big cities. Famous amongst these is the mortuary of the

Figure 3.1 Chapel/Ceremonial Hall at a local cemetery on the outskirts of Leipzig. The dual purpose of the room is apparent. By bringing in a cross the priest/pastor can transform it into a chapel.

Viennese *Zentralfriedhof*. However, in rural areas, where the sparse population did not justify the opening of new municipal cemeteries, change arrived later. As a result, many rural cemeteries in Germany have a mortuary made not from sandstone or bricks, but concrete, glass brick and breezeblocks. The cemetery space in the countryside remained in general sufficient, so the existing cemeteries remained in the hands of the churches. However, even in church cemeteries, municipal authorities often built the mortuaries, making for a difficult legal situations.

Whilst in the church province of Saxony this meant that Protestant cemeteries were actually in the possession of the central church administration, in most other areas cemeteries were the possession of the local parish and centrally administered by the burial office of the regional church. Moreover, it is noteworthy that from 1933, the creation of new church cemeteries or the extension of existing ones was no longer permitted. Where the Nazi state had begun to assert its authority by using the control measures of planning permissions, this policy continued in East Germany as no new church cemeteries were opened.[8]

This dual church–municipality ownership of cemeteries and the tendency of the state to extend its authority generated an unacknowledged contestation that shaped the history of cemeteries in the GDR.[9] The historical ideal of the freedom of church property was to clash with the idea of the sovereignty of the socialist state. Moreover, the Potsdam conference (July/August 1945) and the subsequent accords – settling the immediate future of occupied Germany – specifically granted churches and church property special protection from state interference. As early as 1946, facing the first attempts to municipalize church cemeteries in the church province of Anhalt, and basing his prophetic interpretation on the recent experience of Nazism (and its attempts to infiltrate, curtail and misuse church institutions), *Kreisoberpfarrer* (district superintendent) Max Weyhe urged his superiors in the *Landeskirche*[10] to resist even initial discussions about the municipalization of church cemeteries on two counts, the practical and the philosophical:

> The cemeteries are locations of Christian preaching in both the chapels as well as at the gravesides. This, however, does not only take place through the spoken word, but also through the form of the gravestones (cross) and through their inscriptions. That the freedom of both these components is ensured more fully when the parish is the owner, than when it is owned by the municipality, which depend on the ruling political party-constellations in their administrative principles and measures, does not require explanation. The parties come and go. The church remains.[11]

Pastor Weyhe was not so much speculating as basing his assumptions on historical precedents. The Protestant Churches had just experienced a period of explicit politicization of religious life. Furthermore, the ability to influence cultural practice and the design of cemetery and memorials – through standards, regulation and control – had proved to be an effective tool when employed by those seeking to advance the ideals of the cemetery reform movement in conjunction with governmental agencies.[12] The rigid regulation of the *Waldfriedhof* in Munich, imposed by Hans Grässel, indicates the potential scope of these measures. Pastor Wehye's explicit reference to inscriptions and crosses as outward expressions of Christianity that could easily be prohibited by changing cemetery regulations underlines this. Hence the suspicion that similar measures employed in a far more politicized environment could undermine the standing, strength and general role of Christianity in sepulchral culture was justified.

The political situation of the churches in the aftermath of the war, and especially in the face of the Soviet occupation of East Germany, was bound to become tense. There were a whole set of practical as well as ideological reasons for, at best, a strained relationship between church and state. At worst, this had the potential for an outright struggle in which the state would try to impose its views and policies. Materialism, the very basis of Marxist-Leninist thought, derives one of its origins and a fair share of its intellectual attraction from the initial critique of religion.[13] It interpreted religion as a tool of control as well as solace in an alienated world.[14] Communist thought stands, thus, in contrast to religion and its organized forms, because it envisages an enlightened socialist society in which there is ideally no need (and no room) for religion. On a practical level the churches provided a basis from which systematically to challenge the state, its policies and, possibly more importantly, its general ideology.

Nonetheless, in Germany there was no vehement and direct clash between state and church; on the contrary the period between 1945 and 1990 was characterized by subtle variations in the relationship between the *Sozialistische Einheitspartei Deutschlands* (SED) and the Churches. Lenin had taken up Engels's original warning against the folly of forbidding religion as such.[15] The situation is best described as a state of toleration and attempting to remove religious activity as far as possible from the public sphere, i.e., following Lenin's famous dictum of tolerating religion as a private affair. Hence, for both the Catholic as well as the Protestant churches it was obvious that in the Soviet zone they had to operate within a setting that was not friendly towards organized religious institutions. Moreover, as the political trends and the future of East Germany were becoming clearer in the summer of 1946, especially in the context of the pending autumn local elections, the tensions began to grow. This explains the initial deliberations over municipalization of church cemeteries, which represented places of religious connotations amidst a widely secularized state – and as such potential bulwarks of the 'reaction'. Moreover, the Soviet military administration (*Sowjetische Militäradministration in Deutschland* or SMAD) and the SED became increasingly sceptical of the political intentions of the churches, fearing 'reactionary' interference. When, in April 1946, Otto Dibelius, the influential 'conservative' Protestant bishop of Berlin-Brandenburg, urged the clergy to participate actively in political life, the propaganda department of the SMAD (under the leadership of politic officer colonel S.I. Tjul'panov) became concerned.[16] Consequently he framed the main aim of Soviet propaganda as being to support the 'progressive' elements of the clergy under the leadership of Dibelius's deputy, the superintendent of Berlin and later bishop of Greifswald, Friedrich-Wilhelm Krummacher. His role as a conduit between Party and Church was important, since it offered the SED insight into, and gave direct means of influence on, an element of the Protestant Church.[17] The SMAD made a conscious decision to concentrate on the Protestant Church, thereby establishing a pattern that would prevail over the entire lifespan of communist rule. The decision to focus on the Protestant Church had a number of motivations: the Protestants represented 85 per cent of the population, and as such was the more powerful institution of the two main churches. Moreover, its decentralized regional structure and progressive tendencies marked a difference from the strict hierarchy and dogmatic stance of the Catholic Church. A 'progressive' element in the church, such as that headed by Krummacher, could achieve more within the Protestant framework of confederated *Landeskirchen*. Lastly, it was presumed that the Protestant Church had a general historical propensity of having a closer relationship to the state.[18]

The SMAD and the 'progressive' elements of the Protestant Church did not want a direct confrontation. The ultimate ideal would have been the integration of the Protestant Church from the inside and thus to isolate the Catholic Church. There was of course a strong reason for this in the fact that any form of communist rule was not securely established; the SED and its SMAD advisors feared, drawing upon the Soviet experience, that any persecution and repression would only strengthen those who already saw themselves as Christians and the conservative opposition towards the changes that would come with socialist rule. A stout voice of dissent could be ill afforded, and if signs of it occurred they were noted and acted upon if possible.[19] Consequently, at first an attempt was made to incorporate the Protestant Church in the anti-fascist and 'democratic reconstruction', and the initial idea to municipalize church cemeteries was dropped as contravening existing legal restrictions.[20] Whilst the SMAD was keen on the integration, the SED was far less enthusiastic. Creuzberger shows that the entire policy of the party's relation to the churches and the moderate course was dictated by the political advisor of the SMAD.[21] Under direct Soviet influence, SED policy papers articulated inclusiveness; thus being a church member was not an obstacle to joining the SED. The propaganda unit of the SMAD was keen on including and employing progressive elements of the Protestant Church and especially pastors in an effort to win the elections, and it retrospectively judged that strategy to have been successful.[22]

This explains why, in the initial period, church activities were not systematically curtailed, and it explains why despite the beginning of the municipalization of burial services in certain cities, there were no steps taken to municipalize the large church cemeteries. Furthermore, the articles on religious freedom in the East German Constitution of 1949, which are reminiscent of those in the Weimar Constitution and which explicitly reiterated the guarantees given to the churches in the Potsdam accords, bear witness to this initial toleration and constructive engagement.[23] The constitutional acknowledgement of religious freedom and of the legal status of the churches remained at the centre of nearly all policies concerned with church matters: an outright legal ban of the churches was not seen as an option. This provided a clear legal constraint on what could be done. With the *de jure* separation into two Germanies in 1949 and Stalinization of the SED, the attitude towards the Churches was to undergo a drastic transformation.

Protestant Church leaders' accusation of manipulation and fraud in the election of May 1949 for the first East German parliament served as a trigger for open repression: church newspapers were suspended, church services disrupted, and certain members of the clergy harassed and even arrested. This climate fostered the emergence of a clear 'them and us' confrontation that reminded many church activists of the conduct of the Protestant Church in the Third Reich. By early 1950, the Church was increasingly alarmed by what the historian Gerald Besier has called a divergence from the path of democracy (*'Abweichen von der Demokratie'*). The Protestant leadership decided to deal with this matter in the nationwide Easter Address, but this was forbidden.[24] With the SED taking control of all the levels of government immediately after the foundation of the GDR in 1949, the tendency to compromise dramatically decreased. The state had clearly changed tack and insisted vehemently on an outright recognition of its political supremacy.

Nevertheless, most of this only served as a prelude to the more systematic challenge of the church that began with the socialist reorganization of the entire system of government and the disbanding of the *Länder* in 1952. The ideological and organizational screws were tightened as the state tried very hard to construct a 'real existing' socialist state. This meant that aspects of everyday life increasingly came under governmental scrutiny.[25] The Party reacted fiercely against any influence that the churches, especially the Protestant Church, tried to assert over politics, youth and education. The state disbanded the church youth organization, curtailed church-run hospitals, or repeatedly flagged up a ban of any religious instruction in schools and on school (state owned) property.[26] The Party's attitude was vividly encapsulated in Otto Grotewohl's statement that the church had to be regarded as the only legal stronghold of 'reaction':

> *We have to understand, that the church is the only legal basis of the enemy of the working-class.* The tolerance hitherto shown should no longer prevail. If there is sufficient evidence, one should act.[27]

By 1952 there can be very little doubt that, owing to the prevailing ideological interpretation of religion, in the long term the only aim of the state and party was to force churches gradually to the margins of society by overcoming their spiritual significance, undermining their traditional roles and authority and limiting their spheres of influence without causing too much political damage and resistance. In short, the aim at the time was to 'purge' the church from society, and to establish Ulbricht's aspiration for a society *'ohne Türme'* (without bell towers).

Cemeteries provide a case study in the church–state relationship in the GDR. The underlying assumption was that the ideal of a socialist society demanded secularization, on an ideological as well as practical level. This meant, on a practical level, restricting the influence and significance of the churches with regard to the disposal of the dead. Written in 1946 as a response by the Department of Church Questions (*Kirchenfragen*) in the province of Sachsen-Anhalt to the proposals made by the local government department, an official position paper pointed clearly in this direction, yet enumerated the difficulties of enforced secularization.[28] Consequently, it stressed that the proposed changes to the ownership of cemeteries and the churches' role in burial culture not only clashed with a number of legal restrictions and obstacles but also faced a number of practical difficulties. These ranged from how to value the real estate (given the unstable economic conditions of 1946 and the question of classification – i.e., should cemetery land be valued as farmland) to legal difficulties in the transferral of ownership in the cases of jointly owned cemeteries (it had been common practice for the local government to build mortuaries on church-owned property or to extend cemetery space in conjunction with the local parish). In addition, there was the central issue of resistance by all religious entities when faced with the loss of control over traditional burial sites, the religious ritual and rite of passage:

> The churches will resist on principle a general regulation of the organization of disposal on a worldly basis, as the process of the disposal of the dead is seen in Christian teachings as a holy act, subject to by a specific rite. To change this rite, which is regulated in different ways in individual areas and in individual parishes and is established by funeral regulations, would mean changing an element of Christian religious practice. It is beyond doubt that the churches, protected by the Potsdam Accords, would resist such change with all their might.[29]

This official analysis underlined that there was very little chance for imminent radical change, leaving only the gradual extension of control over the organization of undertaking and funeral direction as a viable alternative. Nevertheless, a second process – the attempt to gain decisive 'control' of the cemeteries – ran in parallel. Interpretations of this idea of 'control' differed, as did the number of potential means of its attainment. They ranged from a radical confiscation of church cemeteries, to the offer to exchange ownership of cemeteries for agricultural land or money (often needed desperately for repairs), or the minimalist solution of 'merely' imposing increased jurisdiction. This last measure meant that local councils or regional governments passed restrictive legislation necessitating their express consent for any ordinance concerning local cemeteries owned by the local parishes and insisting on equality between rituals (making it illegal for pastors to ban socialist flags when conducting socialist funerals on church cemeteries on the basis of religious freedom).[30] Hence regulated access and freedom to conduct secular rituals on church property formed the minimal aspiration in the face of legal obstacles and the threat of political resistance.

However, the reaction of the churches to these deliberations in 1946 reveals more. The Department of Church Questions, in its role of a liaison between government and the churches, had approached the higher church administrations to comment in principle on the question of cemetery ownership. The very consideration of such measures threatened the church, and indeed the discussion of the proposal provoked several very outspoken responses by the individual churches.

The Catholic Church was adamant. The Catholic Archbishop of Magdeburg gave a very short and decisive rejection:

> Our church cemeteries are the property of the Catholic parishes. A 'transfer of these into the property of the councils', as it is hinted at in the current text, would have no legal basis and would constitute an arbitrary intervention in church assets. We express our emphatic and categorical objection to this intention. In any event this question does not stand in the foreground of interest.[31]

The intention was clear: this open and direct rebuttal, with reference to the arbitrary legal nature of the position and its moral implications, sought to close down discussion from the outset. Moreover, the timing was poor; the Archbishop's last phrase alludes to the political nature of the suggested changes. In May 1946, just twelve months after the end of the war and the end of Nazi oppression, with considerable need for reconstruction, there were many more pressing needs than a substantial reform of cemetery ownership. This leaves little doubt that the Catholic Church saw a political motivation behind these measures.

The reaction of the Protestant Church was more varied, reflecting its more diverse organization. The highest Protestant administration did not simply assert the illegality of the scheme but contested it in legal terms and on the basis of its logic. First, it referred back to the fact that many cemeteries had been in church possession since the Middle Ages. Secondly, it stressed that 'churchyards' logically had to remain in the hands of the 'church'. Thirdly, it noted that even losing cemeteries, 'which had usually in recent times been established by parishes away from the church and which used up considerable means, without generating, in the countryside, appropriate income, would cause widespread concern in our parishes and for our parishioners'.[32] This marks a different approach, that of trying to argue a case, rather than outright rejection. The general tenor of this source from 1946 is emblematic of the exchanges between the state and the Protestant Church. The less strident, more bureaucratic language – the more decentralized nature when compared to the Catholic Church – created an interpretative latitude and thus the expectation on the part of state officials that the resistance of the Protestant Church would be more easily overcome:

> In the entire cemetery organization, especially in terms of the burial of the dead, inner values of mind and piety are currently so intertwined in such a way that one should not, *if possible*, interfere with these or undertake any changes in this area, at least in the current time of need when the population is suffering enough from the destruction of countless external and internal goods [as in properties]. As the greater majority of the community members hold fast to a church funeral, it is expedient, indeed emphatically recommended, that the cemeteries remain in the possession of the churches. We, therefore, emphatically wish to distance ourselves from the plan for a change in the organization of disposal, especially in form of changing church cemeteries into municipal property.
>
> Should the circumstances arise we would otherwise have to draw attention to the fact that according to the Potsdam Accords religious institutions are be respected.[33]

This represents in essence the same message that the Catholic Church sent, an unequivocal 'no', in this case strengthened by the reference to the Potsdam accords.

The files of the President of the Province of Saxony contain internal consultation papers of the Protestant Church. Amongst them are two very strikingly different comments. First, *Kreisoberpfarrer* Max Weyhe, the author of the prophetic document above, saw only one possible motive. The decision to dispossess the churches of their cemeteries, even if vaguely disguised behind the pretence of standardization and the economic requirements of reconstruction, stemmed only from political deliberations – what he damningly termed *gleichmachende Vereinheitlichung*:

> The plan of a new regulation of the cemetery and disposal system certainly did not arise from church interest, but from internal political ones. Perhaps a cultural concern played a role (care for the cemeteries, preservation of old gravestones, uniform design of the greenery, levelling of old cemeteries in order to create People's Parks, etc.). Nevertheless in the near future this cultural concern would have no impact, because of a lack of funding. This leaves only political interest as worthy of consideration, i.e., the interest in establishing a levelling consolidation (*gleichmachende Vereinheitlichung*).[34]

The last phrase was a conscious reference to National-Socialist *Gleichschaltung* (inadequately translated as coordination), and Weyhe's tone confirms that he, like so many others, was clearly aware of the dangers that the SED and its proposed policy posed. Most comments received from parishes by the *Konsistorium* (the central administration of a Protestant church province) reflect this rather categorical point of view, even if they expressed themselves less eloquently.[35] However, there are also a number of replies that were more or less insistent on the principle of ownership of the cemeteries. Some of these, one might suspect, came from those elements within the church that the state classified as more 'progressive', others adopted such positions on analytical grounds. The *Kreisoberpfarrer* of Dessau, for instance, distinguished between three different cases: a) the traditional churchyard cemetery (*Kirchhof*) with the graves around the church, where great problems would arise if the church were surrounded by land not owned by the Church or if the building itself were state-owned; b) separate cemeteries completely in Church possession (*Gottesacker*) where no problems would arise if communalized; c) a mixed ownership cemetery, owned partly by the municipality and partly by the Church, where, in the eyes of the *Kreisoberpfarrer*, municipalization would be desirable if certain conditions safeguarding access and freedom of ritual would be met.[36] This is representative of a second set of replies, from those who were willing to yield, or at least to compromise, if certain safeguards were granted. Their reservations were diverse, but in general they focused on the freedom to conduct church rituals free from interference and they envisaged some form of financial compensation. Nonetheless, the initial reaction of both major churches can be justly described as resolutely opposed to a change of ownership of cemeteries.

This, in conjunction with the decision to incorporate the Protestant Church into the 'democratic reconstruction', meant that the ownership of very few church cemeteries changed; there were only a few such cases, in which specific contracts were made between the local councils and the parishes regulating the further rights of the church with regard to the cemetery. Altogether, the comprehensive reform envisaged with regard to the cemeteries did not take place for a number of reasons. One reason has to be the initial resistance by the Protestant and Catholic church administrations and the political risk of a reform against outspoken opposition at a time of intense political and ideological struggle. Another was the fact that there was a multiplicity of regulations, ordinances and other statutes that been issued over more than a century, resulting in a fragmentation of the legal framework that was difficult to overcome without sweeping reforms. Moreover, there was an inability as well as a certain unwillingness of ministries to tackle the legal issues of disposal that for such a long time had been outside the remit of the central government.[37] As with burial regulation, the ordinances, legislation and rules for cemeteries were mostly regional and local and the everyday operation of church cemeteries governed by parish charters. Standardized (i.e., national) legal compulsion had existed only with regard to the fundamental problems of disposal, such as health and safety rules, legal requirements for cremation and the traditional *Friedhofszwang* – the legal requirement that burials could only be conducted (even when urns were concerned) on designated cemeteries (public, church and private), and not on private estates, unless the area had been surveyed, tested for its geomorphological and legal suitability, and officially approved as suitable.[38]

In June 1949 that fragmentation began to have real consequences. The FRG had been founded in May 1949 and the unity of Germany was broken. Institutions needed to know which legal framework was still valid, and which was not. In June 1949 the state governments in the Soviet zone issued guidelines, in effect declaring much of the legislation of the Reich to be valid for the immediate future in order to have a valid legal framework. The departments of health stressed that the regulations with regard to sepulchral issues passed in the 1930s remained the standard.[39] The question of a new legislative framework for burials and cemeteries would have to be addressed at a later stage. Even the influence exerted through the *Reichsausschuß* (the voluntary reformist committee of those in charge of cemeteries within the German Reich, founded in 1934) continued, namely its model guidelines of 1937. They still served as the basis for the ordinances of municipal cemeteries in the Soviet zone.[40]

Church cemeteries were subject only to the legal regulations on safety, planning and hygiene, not directly to any governmental edicts issued by ministries. For some, this heterogeneity signalled the Party and state administration's lack of control. This unevenness persisted and individual officials asked for it to be addressed time and again over the coming decades. Those who advocated tighter legislation and greater control presented their argument on two lines: a rational one and an ideological one. The former was that undertaking services and cemeteries were essential functions that had to be performed effectively in the complex environment of the modern state and society. Both formed a part of the core (together with hospitals and public control mechanism) of modern public hygiene. Their functioning at an appropriate level was essential for the maintenance of a high standard of sanitation. The second, ideological, case was that cemeteries played an important cultural role in the commemoration of the dead (*Totengedenken*). While the general commemoration of the dead is by no means comparable to the prominence of the cult of the fallen soldier or other forms of *Totenkult* (of victims of accidents or other tragic losses), the way a nation provides for the commemoration of its dead collectively as well as individually should not be absent as an indicator of a government's operational efficiency.[41] The cemetery has performed a key role in this commemoration, not only on the national days of remembrance such as All Soul's Day, but in the everyday visits to the graves of loved ones. In 1959 Dr Krüger, a lecturer of administrative law at the University of Leipzig, wrote a proposal to the Central Committee on the importance of controlling undertaking and cemeteries. The report explained why control of cemeteries was essential for the socialist state:

> The construction and maintenance of cemeteries is a sovereign task of the municipalities, i.e., of the state apparatus. They constitute hygienic establishments since they facilitate the elimination of the health risks arising from unburied corpses. At the same time the cult of death, deeply rooted in our people, is conducted in the cemetery. This ethical task, viewed as a cultural expression, should not be underestimated.[42]

In short, it advocated the line taken by many within the Party that any cultural activity in general should ultimately be under some form of state control. In this context the disposal of the dead was obviously too important a task to leave, at least to such a substantial degree, in the hands of a non-governmental institution that was, crudely put, perceived as a rival to the Party and threat to 'stability'.[43]

However, even strong views and position papers like these, spelling out what were by no means radically new positions, had very little immediate effect. There was without doubt an awareness of the issue as a whole, but the government reacted sluggishly to various suggestions made by individuals like Dr Krüger or local and regional (*Bezirk*) party secretaries. As *Staatssekretär* Eggebrath was to do later, these individuals were reacting to local problems (such as a controversy about a secular funeral in a church cemetery). The debate about communalization, however, had initially arisen from deliberations within the city and provincial administration in Magdeburg in 1946. The immediate results were meagre and, due to the determinacy by the churches, not much was achieved. Nevertheless, the Department for Local Affairs in Magdeburg and the Magdeburg City Council began to serve as points of coordination, organizing an exchange of ideas in the effort to reorganize undertaking and to unify the administrative control over all cemeteries in the hands of the local government. A letter from the Schwerin Council to the Magdeburg City Council with the intention of promoting a forum for ideas summarizes the complexity of the problem as seen in the summer of 1951. It refers to the legal and organizational entanglements, but also throws light on the reasons for the lack of actual reform:

> The suggestion you made to transfer these cemeteries into the administration of the municipalities is to be commended. Such a ruling can only, in the opinion of the Ministry of the Interior [of the state of Anhalt], be effected by the government of the German Democratic Republic under consideration to our current political situation. A banning of the services of private undertakers would have to be carried out by the government of the German Democratic Republic. The Ministry of the Interior is, however, of the opinion that such a ban cannot be carried out at the present time. We commend, above all, the suggestion to create a uniform structure for the administration of cemeteries. The Ministry of Interior is of the opinion that the administration of cemeteries should be incorporated into the Ministry of Health.[44]

Alongside the central political concerns of the expropriation of church property, the key problem was that no single ministry was in overall charge of organizing and coordinating the disposal of the dead. Any given aspect of this matter could involve: a) the Ministry of the Interior (because of policing matters), b) the Ministry of Health (because of regulatory issues), c) the Ministry of Finance, d) the Secretariat for Church Questions, e) and diverse ministries for industry, such as the Ministry for Regionally Administered Industries (*Bezirksgeleitete Industrie*), Light Industry (*Leichtindustrie*), or the Ministry for Wood Consuming Industry (*Ministerium der Holzverarbeitenden Industrie*). In addition, any panel would also comprise members of local funeral services to provide expert opinion (and later also members of the IfK). So, like the issue of burial services, any deliberations on the reform of the cemeteries consequently required inter-ministerial dialogue that needed to be coordinated. This function was mainly facilitated by the Ministry of the Interior, but in the early 1950s there were very few signs of immediate large-scale action. It seems the Ministry was put in charge because it dealt with relations with the churches (and the administration of alternative socialist rituals).

After the Soviet repression of the revolt of 17 June 1953, the Party's grip on power was tightened. On 14 March 1954 the *Politbüro* made two essential decisions in religious matters. First, it decided not to challenge the legal position of the churches within the constitutional framework or to limit their constitutional rights, despite the deepening ideological gulf – especially the detestation of 'non-progressive elements'. Secondly, it opted to broaden and strengthen the ideological struggle through anti-religious propaganda and to tighten the legal framework within which the churches existed. One immediate result was a surge in the publication of materialist treatises, especially by the Party-owned *Dietz Verlag*, accusing the church of dodging the scientific challenges made by advances by the Soviets such as the launch of Sputnik. Of far greater magnitude was the decision also to challenge the churches with more practical strategy through the introduction of alternative socialist rituals in 1955. The state-sponsored secular rituals (as opposed to the long tradition of atheist rituals sponsored by Freethinkers and other groups) marks a significant shift in policy from reactive and legal measures to active attempts to 'modernize' and secularize socialist society.[45] In 1956, the Party decided to erect further practical obstacles. It organized masses of members leaving the churches (*Massenkirchenaustritte*), discontinued the collection of tithes on behalf of the churches, and began to cut drastically subsidies and money for building work and repairs. This had direct ramifications for church cemeteries in the GDR, as the parishes suffered from chronic underfunding, which was reflected in the condition of the cemeteries. Combined with shortages of materials and labour, the constant dearth of funds meant that church cemeteries would progressively deteriorate over time.[46]

In September 1956 the EKD (Head Organization of the Protestant Church in the whole of Germany until 1969) began to encounter another obstacle. In Saxony local planning authorities declined permission for five different church cemetery extensions.[47] As a result of a complaint from the Protestant Church of Saxony, the EKD sent a request to all regional churches in the East to report problems with extending or opening new church cemeteries. When replies from the other churches revealed that this problem did not only persist in Saxony and that in the Church Province of Anhalt the church was barred from buying any land, it became clear that the Protestant Church's autonomy was being challenged in yet another field.[48] With mounting pressure on the church hierarchy – with regard to church youth groups, confirmation, or religious instruction on school premises – the non-conformity of the Protestant Church began to become a genuine opposition.[49]

The infamous case of *Propst* (provost) Otto Maercker of Pampow near Schwerin showed how the SED used a considerable propaganda machinery to force the Protestant Church into a decidedly defensive stance.[50] Nineteen-year-old Edeltraut Andersson had died of tuberculosis and Otto Maercker, the local pastor, in accordance with church regulations, denied her a Christian burial in the church cemetery, because the family had deliberately chosen to send the daughter to receive the *Jugendweihe* instead of confirmation. This scenario was not unique, but the SED used the very emotional case for a public propaganda campaign. Otto Maercker was arrested, charged with rabble-rousing propaganda (*Hetze*) and in December 1957 tried and sentenced to two and a half years in prison. Simultaneously, similar cases were publicized and the emotional press campaign orchestrated by the SED and Erich Mielke (who had succeeded Ernst Wollweber as head of the *Staatssicherheit* in November 1957) increased the pressure on the 'reactionary' Church. The Maercker case resulted in a fairly famous show trial, one neglected aspect of which was that it highlighted the nature of the control the churches had over their cemeteries. Late in 1957, the *Staatssekretär für Kirchenfragen*, Werner Eggerath – who was instrumental in the attempts to split the Protestant Church – sent drafts of a decree and of a completely new standard regulation for cemeteries (*Musterfriedhofsordnung*) directly to Karl Maron, the Minister of the Interior, with the request to check and to promulgate them.[51]

Eggerath explicitly referred to the Maercker case as his rationale, especially the matter of unlimited access to church property. This letter did not elicit an urgent response. On the contrary, a handwritten note scribbled on the letter and dated 10 February 1958, makes it clear that the issue was not deemed pressing and that it needed further discussion. However, from 1958, things began to be discussed and ultimately to change.

In many ways 1958 was to become an important year. In addition to the climax of anti-church legislation and measures, concerted effort by the central government began to address the question of cemeteries and disposal.[52] The real change came at first from a lower level of government as a result of a specific problem of denied access. When secular alternatives to church ceremonies were introduced they provoked local resistance. The regional churches and parishes, exercising their legal rights as the owners of the property, tried (as they had done in the past) to prevent secular or even socialist rites from being practised on their property.[53] This, evidently, led to heated exchanges. When in October 1955 one of the directors of the local *VEB Granitwerke Häslich* in Saxony took part in a funeral ceremony for a co-worker, he, contrary to his usual habits, finished his remarks laying down a wreath with an atheist statement:

> 'There is nothing else in the world except for the progression of life towards death, for there is no resurrection and no reunion for the deceased.' After this sentence, that mocks all preachings of our faith, I, as the incumbent pastor, shouted at him: 'I forbid you to use such words in this place.' Since he nonetheless continued to speak I showed my protest by leaving the churchyard. At the end of his speech I once more stepped up to the graveside and said ... 'I hereby forbid you in the Lord's name ever to speak again on this churchyard and to utter such obvious blasphemy; I have enough witnesses here!' Upon which he answered: 'I thank you.'[54]

This specific case provided little more than anti-religious propaganda. A legal expert of the regional church determined that there was no legal basis to challenge the banning of such graveside outbursts. However, when some cases resulted in protest, the regional governments began to insist upon exercising the right to conduct secular rituals on church property without any limitations on the language or decorations (such as red flags or socialist insignia). Moreover, the issue of financial discrimination prompted debate: for example, church cemeteries tended to charge non-church members more than church members – in extreme cases up to five times the standard fee for a parish member.

An insistence in the small town of Wriszen near Eberswalde further highlights the politicization of burial and cemeteries in the aftermath of the introduction of the *Jugendweihe*. The context in this case of the rural small town where cemeteries typically were church property is significant. The secretary of the local committee for the *Jugendweihe*, who by 1959 was also responsible for the organization of other socialist and secular rituals, wrote directly to the Central Committee in Berlin to complain about the problem of church discrimination:

It will not only be the case here that very great difficulties arise with regard to socialist funerals, because the cemeteries in the villages are the property of the churches. From this arises the paradoxical situation that the non-religious part of the population is forced to contact the church in order to arrange for the use of the mortuary and to purchase a grave plot.

The church extensively exploits its monopoly in this field and demands from the non-members a multiple of the fees demanded of its parishioners. Here in our community it is 200 per cent; that means for a grave plot for two one has to pay between 360 to 500 DM. [Roughly a month's salary for a skilled worker]

This consideration plays a role in our canvassing for the *Jugendweihe*, when the question is repeatedly posed: 'Yes, but what about later, when it comes to the funeral.'[55]

The complaint continues with suggestions as to how to remove the exploitation of the monopoly and asks for an explanation for why that had not yet been done. The author suggests the church should be banned from charging discriminatory fees, that the legal status of the church cemetery should be altered, or simply that a municipal alternative could be constructed and thus the local monopoly broken. However, the letter's conclusion is most revealing, as it illustrates vividly why the socialist reshaping of sepulchral culture was extremely difficult and slow; as the disposal of the dead had been – at least in Germany – a very parochial issue with many idiosyncrasies and oddities:

As experience shows, this path of development [the construction of a municipal cemetery and mortuary] could take much time. The municipal cemetery in our community is situated behind the churchyard, and is colloquially referred to as 'the pauper's cemetery', [and] actually looks accordingly and thus does not offer any competition to the very pretty churchyard. Because of this, all non-religious citizens return to the bosom of the church, i.e., via the church mortuary into the churchyard.[56]

On a larger scale, in some regions, for example in Rostock and Karl-Marx-Stadt in 1958, and in Dresden in 1960, similar problems resulted in the assertion of the supremacy of the state and the legal imposition of anti-discriminatory rules.[57] The statutes that were passed in effect followed the basic suggestions discussed since 1946 without assuming state ownership of the cemeteries as such. The property rights remained unchanged, while the scope and ability of the parishes to issue bylaws were heavily curtailed. Two legal arguments served as justification: the first was the equality principle, namely that all citizens had the same rights; the second was the duty inherent in the ownership of property (*Eigentum verpflichtet*) and that any use of it must not conflict with the public good. The district of Rostock passed a statute in February 1958, which was very typical:

In order to avoid undignified occasions during the funerals of citizens, as well as to assure an orderly and dignified disposal, the regional council has decided, based upon Article 6, Paragraph 2, and [Article] 24, Paragraph 1 of the Constitution of the GDR.
1. The system of disposal and the administration of cemeteries are the responsibility of the council of the municipalities. The district councils exercise the control thereof.

2. In cemeteries all those persons are usually [leaving a legal loophole for Jewish Cemeteries] to be buried who upon their death had their place of residence or who lived in the district of the particular cemetery, regardless of their ideological or religious beliefs, or the political affiliation of the deceased or the bereaved.

3. Mortuaries, chapels and other cemetery buildings and equipment have to be made equally available and under the same conditions to all citizens.

4. No discriminatory differences are to be made in the burial. Grave plots are to be allocated in the usual fashion, independent of the ideological standpoint [*Weltanschauung*] or religious affiliation of the deceased.

5. The liturgy of the funeral, as well as the choice of the speaker is to be decided by the bereaved or their representative, or respectively by any other designated person. The same applies to the design of gravestones. Legal restrictions and the ideology of the working-class are not to be contravened.

6. The price for the grave plot has to be calculated on the basis of the service provided, independent of the ideological standpoint and religious beliefs held by the deceased.

7. The construction of new cemeteries, as well as the closure or the extension of existing [cemeteries] necessitates the approval of the district council. Prior to approval, the district council has to consult the concerned municipalities.

8. Contravening Sections in cemetery regulations are repealed.[58]

The practical consequences, as highlighted in the preamble, were that it became illegal for the church to deny non-church members a plot in the local cemetery, to discriminate against non-parish members by imposing higher tariffs, or obstruct secular funeral rituals on church property. On the back of 'anti-discriminatory' proposals the state had established a legal precedent, albeit a minor one. While the statute did not interfere with (details and) practical aspects, such as the prescribed length of the resting periods of bodies or the individual design rules of each cemetery for permissible gravestones, it imposed significant principles of supervision and legislation that could override local regulations. Moreover, these eight points established, at least for the Rostock region, a level of administrative control over all cemeteries, independent of their ownership, and placed the ultimate power of intervention firmly in the hands of the district governments. This step reduced the authority of the individual parishes to that of consultative bodies. This meant that two essential prerequisites – the inclusion of church cemeteries within the remit of legislation and the shift of responsibility from the local councils to higher levels of government – had been established to permit the state's endeavour to influence sepulchral culture according to its ideological stance.

When, on 22 February 1959, in its second meeting, the Committee for Burial Services in the GDR (*Arbeitskreis Bestattungswesen in der DDR*) urged the formation of the Central Committee for Design and Organization of Cemeteries in the GDR (*Zentraler Arbeitskreis für die Friedhofsgestaltung der DDR*), it was a clear sign that the idea of a specifically socialist cemetery design and burial culture was gaining momentum.

> Coordinated work of all four groups [municipal and church cemeteries, garden architects and garden designers, as well as sculptors and stonemasons) is therefore necessary to bring into alignment, in a socialist sense, all parallel and contravening efforts and to guarantee a uniform development in the GDR. This is all the more necessary since an interested and central entity in charge of specialist questions in the field does not exist.[59]

The last sentence emphatically decries the lack of a central body in charge of this specific field, a sign that specialists were getting weary of administrative inertia. In this light it is not surprising that the meeting also decided to propose the complete redrafting of the existing guidelines for design and planning as well as a new standard regulation for cemeteries. In general this was a clear indication that a characteristic East German cemetery culture was about to be conceived. The small circle of interested specialists had found a forum in which to exchange ideas and to stipulate, in the specifically socialist practice of consultation, socialist concepts and suggestions to be addressed within the administration. It was this form of consultation that aided the formation of a view that was not politically driven but the result of local personnel. As in many other specialized fields of governmental activity, where the specifics of some technical issues required a great deal of specialist input, disposal and cemetery design were the domain of highly skilled experts. Therefore the suggestions, recommendations and deliberations of these committees often became the basis for subsequent administrative decisions and guidelines.

It did not take long for the Protestant Church to react to the rumours of pending change. The *Generalsuperintendent* of Berlin in April 1959 wrote directly to the *Staatssekretär* for Church Questions to state the Church's point of view. The tone of the communication is ambiguous; most is clearly courteous about the fact that the consultation of the churches in the process was planned, and while a there was some grovelling, there were also implied threats. The introduction observed that around 70 per cent of the cemeteries and 60 per cent of the overall cemetery area of the GDR was in the ownership of the Protestant Church, a point made to underline that the Church's cooperation would be indispensable.[60] This attitude seems to reflect the attempt to find a *modus vivendi* with the state. This was a process which had begun in Thuringia under the orchestration of Bishop Moritz Mitzenheim, who was the first regional church leader to abandon resistance to the *Jugendweihe* in 1959.[61] Altogether, this argument seems to be supported by a catalogue of wishes and suggestions by the Church administration; a mood of compromise, mixed with a sense of foreboding, ran through the many points separated into its three subsections. The first restates the argument that the status quo with regard to the ownership issue was not to be changed. Ownership rights would remain with the Church, while the Church would have to consult the local authorities on a number of issues and would concede on the issue of celebrating secular and socialist burials on church property throughout the whole Republic without any form of discrimination, as long as the financial basis of recouping the costs of maintaining the cemeteries was not curtailed to the disadvantage of the already weakened finances of the Church.[62] The second set of positions reveals a very much more defensive stance. They were clearly intended to prevent a further tightening of the ideological net around the exercise of traditional church rituals. There was a free choice of ritual in all cemeteries and subject to the wishes of the bereaved. Additionally, the Church emphasized its right to use freely the cross and gravestone inscriptions to demonstrate religious affiliation.[63] In retrospect, and in the light of the physical evidence, some of the fears seem exaggerated, but in the climate of the late 1950s the fears seemed justified.

The last section returns to the perennial ethical problem of the power of shaping the design and layout of cemeteries from above by means of regulation and restriction. Ever since the rise of the reform movement, that system of influencing public taste had been criticized as either constituting a benign aesthetic tyranny or a malignant unrepresentative dictatorship as well as the imposition of taste by a technocratic minority without public involvement.[64] However, in this case the difficulty was redoubled. The Protestant Church was broadly in favour of advancing towards an aesthetical ideal in which the cemetery fused with the surrounding landscape, but clearly feared that excessive powers could be misused as means of political oppression. In that case, they could function as a kind of stumbling block obstructing the plans and designs of those not sharing the same ideological point of view:

> The churches welcome all suitable measures that are aimed at achieving a dignified design of cemeteries. They are, however, of the opinion that this cannot be achieved through regulation, bans and complicated systems of approval, but rather through patient and constructive educational work.[65]

The fears implied in this argument were amplified by historical events. With the building of the Berlin wall, many issues and fears voiced by the pastors who spoke out against the initial suggestions of giving up the ownership of the cemeteries in the province of Anhalt (1946) appeared ever larger. However, after the initial shock, it became clear that for the Protestant Church as well as for the Catholic Church hard times might lay ahead, and leading figures in the Protestant churches, chief amongst them the 'progressive' bishop Albrecht Schönherr, began to press for an arrangement with the state. Under such influences the Protestant church hierarchy decided to choose, or rather was forced to choose, the narrow path between acquiescence and opposition. This state of compromise in a certain regard was reflected in the legal state of the church cemeteries. Their role was not further challenged by the administration; by the mid 1960s municipalization was no longer a viable option because it would interfere with the political balance that had been achieved. The *modus vivendi* arrived at was very much along the lines suggested by the *Generalsuperintendent* of Berlin. Furthermore, they were mainly established not through the central government of the GDR, but through a number of regional councils that passed legislation akin to the precedent set in Rostock or Dresden.

Regional councils had established the precedent, not the Ministry of the Interior, and that meant that the evolution of the cemetery culture of the GDR was in future to come from local initiatives and individuals, not from above and by party decree. Similarly, with regard to burial services the IfK was to assume a pivotal role in coordinating such initiatives. Key personnel were taken on from the two committees concerned with the organization of cemeteries and burial services before 1962.[66] Karl Thomas swiftly became one of its key members. In June 1962 he was the representative presenting the institute's arguments to the Secretariat for Church Matters, arguing that:

> [T]he development in the future [as predicted] does not allow for a segregation between municipal and church cemeteries. Church cemeteries will on principle not be extended in their size, only municipal cemeteries will be expanded or new ones established. The decision on these questions rests with the representatives of executive power. Therefore, in accordance with this, all basic regulations for the cemetery and disposal system in the German Democratic Republic have to be formulated uniformly for municipal and church cemeteries.[67]

This idea became the basis for the new *Musterfriedhofsordnung* worked on by the IfK and, amongst others, the Christian Democratic Union (CDU) as a party

Figure 3.2 Ceremonial hall at the *Inselfriedhof* Eisenhüttenstadt. It shows typical socialist functional architecture with its clear intention to provide service in the form of a local florist (on the right).

more closely linked with the Protestant Church. It is significant that the suggested *Musterfriedhofsordnung* first written by the CDU in 1962 did not differ much from that of the IfK.[68] This too suggests that the Protestant Church had resigned itself to the fact that equality between religious and secular rites in every cemetery was the most it could achieve under the prevailing conditions.[69] That resignation was greatly aided by the often very good relationship between church and local government. Thus, when the *Inselfriedhof* of Eisenhüttenstadt was planned and built in 1969/1970 both local church representatives were consulted and asked if they had any specific wishes to be considered in the planning process.[70]

However, the officials of the IfK did not merely wish to administer the status quo, so they kept up pressure for change. Only a year after its foundation, in 1962, the IfK published the first material on cemetery organization and design. Taking the political situation and political priorities into account, this clearly indicated that determined individuals were at work. The IfK was relatively autonomous, inasmuch as the party line set a broad framework, but within that there was some space to manoeuvre. Moreover, as no ministry was in overall charge, there was simply no other institution that interfered in the minutiae of policy making. Therefore, as so often in the history of reform of cemetery design, one is forced to observe the importance of the individual. A small number of specialists can shape an entire area of aesthetics, either setting examples or via the more restrictive measure of ordinances or even legislation. Most ground-breaking reforms of German sepulchral culture would have been unthinkable without the convictions of individuals such as Hans Grässel, Karl Thomas or of a small group of like-minded people willing to advance their ideals often without much regard for the prevailing popular opinion that favoured plaster cast ornaments and leaf gold inscriptions. In effect the IfK employees, like those of the AFD, were exercising what Marcus Bohl rightly calls power without discourse.[71] From 1962 onwards the IfK followed the precedent of the *Waldfriedhof* in Munich. There one man's vision had become the guiding principle in the fight against contemporary 'excesses'. However, Grässel's regulations only represented the beginning of a reform movement that culminated in the first publication of the *Reichsausschuß* in 1927 with the title 'The Graves and Cemeteries of the Present'. As Marcus Bohl rightly observes, the list of authors gives a representative snapshot of the driving forces behind the inter-war reform movement.[72] Moreover, in the introduction Stephan Hirzel referred to the antinomy between '*Volksgemeinschaft*' and 'individuality', a contrast of ideals which he saw as a threat that had to be opposed. This rejection of individuality was axiomatic and German cemetery design would henceforth be governed by the ideals of order, integration (into nature) and simplicity.[73]

Hence the original German cemetery reform movement can be criticized as, at most, an undemocratic aesthetic revolution from above, and at least as an exceptionally successful exercise in social and cultural engineering by a small elite of specialists, technocrats and administrators. Few members of the public are aware that even today German cemeteries are largely the result of a clear cultural and ideological heritage – a heritage that actually reflects very little true public taste and aesthetics but mainly that epochal phrase by Grässel: '*Schon Ordnung ist Schönheit*' (Order itself is already beauty). Due to the ordinances and regulations, all gravestones, even bespoke ones, have had to follow a more or less rigid set of prescribed measurements and design guidelines. This marks another key similarity between the sepulchral culture of East and West Germany; the ideological heritage of the AFD and the IfK was, at least at first, dominated by the rejection of the pre-reformist pomp that was often perceived as being ridden with class distinctions and an overindulgent individualism that characterized capitalism.[74]

All this is evident in the publications of the IfK. Even the title of the key text *Gestaltung unserer Friedhöfe* (Design of our Cemeteries), published in October 1963, hints at the underlying asumptions: the creation of cemeteries in line with the ideal of both the community and socialist society.[75] This was also the occasion on which Karl Thomas outlined the specific cultural role of cemeteries within the social and historic fabric of the GDR:

> This demand for the exertion of influence on the comprehensive improvement of cultural standards in many cemeteries directly corresponds with the tasks that our state has set to itself owing to the changed circumstances of production, and as an obvious duty in the construction (*Aufbau*) of a socialist society, for the continued furtherance of culture in all areas of life.[76]

In this view cemeteries were seen as institutions of culture, not unlike theatres or cinemas, and thus as a means to reflect and to bring about or assist change in the prevailing values of society. The construction of a socialist society in the eyes of party intellectuals such as Kurt Hager necessitated the construction of a socialist culture, not merely a change in the economic circumstances and the ownership of the means of production.[77] This hints at the scope and intention of some of the initial work of the IfK. It especially regarded the new socialist design of cemeteries as a break with a capitalist culture and advocated it accordingly:

> In the capitalist age cemeteries have increasingly become objects of extortion by profiteers and a hotbed of false representation. Inhumation, in a family or freely chosen grave became the choice of disposal of the ruling class, the allocated grave plot in the row of graves the symbol of the exploited stratum. The blueprints of cemeteries with their representative axes, the family vaults and behind those the fields of graves in rows for the poorer classes are characteristic of this period. The signs of cultural decay in the second half of the nineteenth century did not stop outside the cemetery [gate].[78]

Since it was exactly in that period when most major urban cemeteries, as well as many medium and small municipal cemeteries in Germany were built, this task was to represent an enormous challenge.[79] Furthermore, socialist rhetoric permeates the quotation; the sentiment expressed, especially in the last sentence, is nonetheless reminiscence of Hirzel's argument that cemeteries should underline community, as they are collective spaces. Barbara Happe revealingly stresses that cemetery reforms were driven by a mentality reminiscent of enlightened absolutism and quotes Richard Frey's aphorism of 1924: 'To create something important, the individual has to subjugate her/himself to the whole'.[80] Furthermore, some elements of this view are not without their parallel in other countries; overindulgence in pomp and especially a severe critique of the commercialization of undertaking has an extensive tradition in many Western countries (for example with the advocacy of anonymous burial in Scandinavia or the Netherlands).[81] Besides the clear references to historical materialism, it is fair to argue that much what the IfK envisaged for the future was inherited from the reform tradition. The IfK did not therefore advocate vastly different design guidelines when compared to the AFD. For example, there is a clear return to the basics such as the integration of the cemetery into the landscape; the discouragement of parks with tree-lined main axes; the incorporation of hills and other natural features; arguing staunchly against terraces and unnatural landscaping. And most importantly grave fields should be dominated by similar shapes of gravestones in order to underline a non-oppressive uniformity. The industrially produced broad stone (*Breitformatstein*), with its 100 to 150 cm width and low, often shaped or cut out, height, which was already seen as the scourge of the modern cemetery in the 1920s, was heavily attacked by both institutions.

Figure 3.3 A *Breitformatstein*. Despite the efforts of over fifty years it proved to be popular and remains so.

In short, given the maxim of 'order itself is beauty', the IfK viewed the wishes of the individual and the expression of individuality as secondary to the creation of the public space:

> In our socialist order of society the cemetery has for first time become the burial site for all elements of society, without any privileging of an individual. Every citizen has the right to be buried according to his/her needs (free choice of the family plot or an individual grave plot); in the cemetery – as a public institution – he/she, however, also has a duty towards society, to accept the respective order or to subjugate him/herself to the regulations of individual grave fields.[82]

This highlights one distinct characteristic of East German cemetery design after 1962: freedom of choice as long as it did not infringe on the dictum of uniformity or the need for efficient design. The arguments brought forward by the reform movement were thus easily adapted to suit and be integrated into the framework of the regime's discourse. That development hinged significantly on the legitimacy of the discourse that cemeteries were public spaces, making it necessary, one might even argue, imperative, that individuals follow the rules set by those in authority. In the context of socialist thought, since the cemetery was a public space, interference with the choices of the individual was in this context not only seen as legitimate but in some cases it was acknowledged as indispensable in order to establish the homogenous design that was desired. Moreover, the boundary between interference and restriction of choice became ever more blurred. Homogeneity of design was to become the hallmark of the ideal socialist cemetery.

The IfK went so far as to clearly demarcate the difference between the public and the private, and in doing so the cemetery was designated a public space, not the site of personal commemoration. This resulted in a very stark differentiation that was potentially at odds with the needs and wishes of the bereaved. Nonetheless, the IfK officials framed their view of the role of the cemetery and the individual in that landscape bluntly:

> Within the apartment every individual can arrange for this [the commemoration of the dead] as he/she sees fit. The neighbourhood of the cemeteries and the public space, however, necessitate appropriate restraint. They cannot be impaired by dissenting personal views. Just as in the community of the living certain requirements to fit in have to be taken as a matter of course with regard to the conduct in public, so similarly certain requirements govern the integration of gravestones in the public domain, which draw attention to themselves through their particular statements.[83]

These rules not only concerned the choice of gravestone (its design, inscription, height or material), but they addressed the wider question of what kind of private commemoration was sanctioned in public. The IfK implicitly made it clear that there was a distinct separation between the public and the private. In the cemetery, as a public space, the commemoration was to underline, and celebrate, as was the design, one overarching aspect above anything else: *Gemeinschaft* (community) through coherence. This decision was to create a substantial measure of potential tension between the two spheres.

This lack of consideration for the needs of the individual quickly becomes apparent in the more technical language that sets out the three guiding principles to this form of cemetery design earlier in the same booklet:

> The different forms of disposal should not be isolated from each other, but could be included in a 'community of graves'. As different as the design of such a community of graves might be, based upon the natural conditions or different uses of materials (stone or plants), something should unite them:
>
> 1. [A] meaningful integration of the individual grave fields into the general concept of the cemetery design and conceptual coordination within the grave fields. In doing so there should on principle be no isolation or separation of grave fields from each other, if this does not appear necessary for reasons of space;
>
> 2. Subjection of individual wishes to the overall design of the grave field and support of the communal appearance through gravestones coordinated in measurement, form and material; no fundamental separation of freely chosen family plots and single grave plots; planting only within the framework decreed for the particular grave field; whenever possible level grave plots and avoiding vertical paths between graves (lengthwise to the grave); avoidance of concrete settings (of the plot), grave gravel and similar things; avoidance of head-to-head plots and other systems of order that disturb the communal.
>
> 3. A community of graves can emphasize the communal especially through the placement of an artistically meretricious memorial that has the right proportion to the grave field. This necessitates, however, a stronger restraint or possibly sacrifice of individual gravestones.[84]

This set of basic rules was geared to achieve the most coherent impression of community, i.e., no physical or optical separation, arrangement in horizontal lines, no elements of emphasis or visual disturbances and no alteration of the perspective within the natural landscape were allowed except when these came as a result of a central memorial serving the collective (i.e., the community as a whole). Moreover, the last point already contained the embryonic idea of what later would become the most archetypical socialist form of burial, enshrining the idea of a socialist community of the dead: the anonymous communal internment of urns (*Urnengemeinschaft*).

Nevertheless, the creation of a sense of community was not to lead to creating a scourge of dull sameness (as opposed to the aim of positive uniformity); it has to be understood that IfK officials made a clear distinction between a sense of community achieved through order and uniformity and bland, relentless repetition of identical forms (driven by the application of Fordist principles). Uniformity in the understanding of cemetery designers required a specific design framework that reflected the competing needs, and resulting tensions between personal wishes (in this case explicitly mentioned!), economic efficiency and design:

> It should not be the case that there are only a few forms and materials as well as methods of sculpting left, that are then endlessly repeated. That would constitute torturous monotony

Figure 3.4 Urn burial field in Wismar.

and a levelling that would contravene the justified wishes of the bereaved for an individual treatment of their deceased. The personal relationship (to the gravestone and grave plot) should certainly be retained … Basic types must be used, in which new findings combine with well-established forms and sizes. If these standard forms, with their appropriate variations, accommodate the specific nature of the raw materials, they will guarantee an economic and efficient application.[85]

The goal was, as the illustration indicates, to create a harmonious overall appearance, in which the individual gravestone contributed to the great scheme. The ideal field of graves, in the eyes of the IfK, was a well-balanced entity avoiding the overuse of plants, stones, or other design elements, and trying as far as possible to integrate the cemetery into the existing landscape.[86] This ideal underlined the emphasis on the recreational function that green areas played within the *Raumplanung* of the GDR (special planning). The examples of Hoyeswerda, with its integration of the cemetery into the fir tree forest, of Wismar with its exemplary (if monotonous) use of space, or of the homogeneity of Dresden-Tolkewitz, illustrate the different ways these guidelines were interpreted. However, other cemeteries, such as Halle-Neustadt or Eisenhüttenstadt, show that these design principles were sometimes sacrificed in favour of simpler maintenance or due to restrictions given by the terrain.

Reforming cemeteries along these lines was not a straightforward undertaking. A number of problems prevented the immediate realization of these prescriptions.

With new cemeteries, or newly opened areas, the changes were simple, but cemeteries are like organic entities: they mature over a long period, as new graves are added and old ones are levelled and replaced by new graves reflecting more recent tastes. Radical alterations to existing fields and plots posed legal as well as practical problems. The minutiae were often beyond the comprehension of non-specialists, and radical plans necessitated the provision of practical advice for the administrators of smaller cemeteries. The favoured method, therefore, that came to dominate many East German cemeteries was the *Durchgrünung* (harmonization by using shrubs throughout the cemetery). It allowed for a minimum of intrusive measures with a maximum effect on appearance:

> In new fields one should consistently apply the new design concept. If it is, however, necessary to continue to design existing fields then additional gravesites and gravestones – in consideration of the local conditions – should also be designed in accordance with up-to-date conceptions. One has to consider that during a usage period of between twenty to thirty years, in fields and in cemeteries, in which a rolling use takes place, a large number of the grave plots are reused. If we start now to advance the design of gravesites the overall picture will change in the course of time … The cemetery administration, alongside making long-term improvements, must try to change the current condition as fast as possible. Most of the time there are grave plots in grave fields that are no longer cared for and that give a dilapidated impression. After being raised to the ground, these plots are the starting point of a harmonization through greenery … It is imperative even in old grave fields that one has to attempt to get rid of the charmless [*lieblos*] gravel areas … Demarcations, even concrete covers of graves, if a removal is not possible, can be covered by bushes or ivy within a very short time … The hideous backs of broad gravestones can within a few years be masked through the planting of a shrub behind them … If every opportunity is used in these older fields to plant uniting greenery you will soon see an improved appearance.[87]

The harmonization by using greenery was a specifically East German method, as it was efficient, cheap and allowed for relatively swift early results.

Furthermore, it was based on the idea of integrating the cemetery within the surrounding environment, an idea that had previously led to the concept of the cemetery integrated into a forest (generic *Waldfriedhof*). This concept of harmony with the landscape persists within the realm of cemetery design. Similarly, patina on gravestones (the formation of algae and moss) was actively encouraged and not seen as a sign of lack of care, but as a sign that stone and nature were growing together.[88] On numerous occasions the cemetery administrations banned the protection of plants and bulbs planted on the grave against the frost and snow with the branches of fir trees (*Tannenreisig*), since it was seen as unaesthetic (*unschön*), unnatural and as a custom that precipitated the proliferation of plants that were simply not hardy enough. Yet it was precisely thoughts such as these, insisting on certain types of plants for their hardiness not their decorative value, which went against the popular taste. A pretty grave plot, an orderly cemetery, and a clean gravestone were often regarded as matters of personal pride;

a dirty gravestone or a neglected grave, on the other hand, especially in rural areas, was often seen as sending a clear message that one did not care for that particular member of the family. In contrast, graves which had nobody to tend them because the family had left were often cared for by everybody as a matter of course.[89] Complaints about neglect and this strategy of letting nature take its course even made it into the papers:

> Besides the problem of fir tree cuttings the director of the *VEB Bestattungseinrichtungen* and the chairman of the working-group and his deputies have hopefully taken notice of other things when they visited the cemeteries. I have to say a large part of our cemeteries in the city area are uncared for. An attractive and clean environment should also include well-tended cemeteries. You could, for example, start with using evergreens on the gravesites that you look after [paid for by subscription]. In the past these gravesites largely offered a sad sight.[90]

Public tastes can be greatly at odds with the opinion of experts and the rules. This simple observation was not underestimated by the IfK. Conventional, conservative and traditional attitudes towards (contrived) change in the sepulchral culture were to be overcome by the application of what in GDR German, was wonderfully entitled '*Geschmackumbildungsprozess*' (the process of the reformation of taste).[91] As with regard to the burial services, the socialist idea of emulation was taken up once more. In this didactic concept the *Leitfriedhof* (leading cemetery, compare *Leitbetrieb*) played a central role. Its task was to popularize the new socialist design of cemeteries by serving partly or in whole as a model, thereby confronting the public with an actual example of how the new cemetery fields would look. As in the 1920s, when this idea was used for the first time in Nuremberg, it was thought that over time taste could be affected by the existence of a positive example:

> Model grave fields [*Mustergrabfelder*] should be constructed on all *Leitfriedhöfen* of the region and in all cemeteries in cities; they should be based on the concept of communal appearance and the subjugation of the individual. There is, for example, the possibility of designing these *Mustergrabfelder* as unused fields. It would, however, be better and more economical to show *Mustergrabfelder* in which burials take place.[92]

The IfK did not want to rely solely on the imposition of guidelines via the medium of ordinances, but also believed in the ability to shape tastes over the long term. Furthermore, that process was also much more economically viable. Like burial services, cemeteries had to operate within very limited resources. The outline of the new ideal socialist cemetery, generally very idealistic in tone and ambition, already contained paragraphs on the practicalities of increasing the levels of efficiency in order ultimately to achieve some form of economic sustainability of the municipal cemeteries within the troubled GDR economy. In general the prescribed aesthetics did not conflict with these aims. The rejection of vertical paths through grave fields is a good example of the compatibility of

Figure 3.5 Typical GDR grid-system.

the two prerequisites. In conjunction with avoiding the head-to-head arrangement that dominated many church cemeteries, the typical GDR grid-system (*Rastersystem*) was born – creating that impression of 'seas of stone' that can overwhelm the observer in certain East German cemeteries.

As a design feature, with its rows of 1.30 m by 2.80 m burial plots that included an 80 cm path at the bottom of each plot, it proved both easier to maintain and allowed for the preferred aesthetic arrangement in uniform rows.

However, as the physical evidence indicates it also reflects a greater turn towards more economic considerations, as its prime characteristic was an increase in the efficiency of cemetery maintenance. This marked the beginning of a clearer shift in the design paradigm. In 1969 the IfK had named three key targets with regard to cemeteries: a) the reduction of investment in new or in the extension of existing cemeteries by increasing the rate of cremation, b) the concentration of investment in cemeteries in areas with dense settlement and the closure of small cemeteries, c) the introduction of new forms of burial such as *Urnengemeinschaftsanlagen* and *Aschestreuwiesen* (ash scattering fields).[93] All of these, but especially the introduction and propagation of new forms of burial, were predominately driven by a desire to increase efficiency. The formula to calculate the specific space required for cemetery sizes in different cities as worked out by the IfK shows a very different area required per inhabitant depending on the choice of disposal. In cities with a low rate of cremation and a high rate of inhumation between three to five square metres had to be set aside for each

Figure 3.6 Typical uniformity of a GDR cemetery created by the interaction of regulations and economics.

inhabitant, while for cities with a high rate of cremation that figure could be reduced to between 1.8 and 2.5 square metres.[94]

This represented a significant impact upon the requirements to expand existing cemeteries. Furthermore, by using an anonymous communal area for the internment of urns (UGA) this figure could be cut to between a mere quarter and a half square metre. The task to unite both economic efficiency and ideological aspects in the socialist reconstruction of cemeteries was to prove difficult, especially under the increasing economic constraints of the East German economy and the chronic lack of manpower in areas such as burial services and cemeteries. This meant that increasingly the ideological side was neglected when it clashed with the reality of economic constraints.

The IfK played a key role in the formulation of the new *Musterfriedhofsordnung* of 1967, and the accompanying model work regulation (*Musterarbeitsordnung*) of 1973.[95] However, a Ministry of the Interior's analysis, written in 1975, stressed the restrictions imposed by local and economic factors:

> The majority of cemetery space consists of grave fields for inhumation on the old design with costly fields of single plots.
>
> However, in recent years, activities were increasingly developed to integrate suitable cemeteries into the system of urban green spaces through new methods of design and equipment, and to thereby create burial sites with the character of parks. In recent times it has been possible in a number of cemeteries (Eisenhüttenstadt, Jena, Neubrandenburg) to come closer to this aim by erecting benches, small sculptures, fountains, etc. The

UGAs in Karl-Marx-Stadt, Halle, Erfurt, Leipzig und Dresden, Jena und Görlitz serve a similar function. The same is true for the construction of modern grave fields in Cottbus, Frankfurt/Oder, Leipzig, Eisenhüttenstadt und Halle. The newly established Waldfriedhof Schwerin deserves a special mention. The lack of personnel for cemetery work, however, has proved hindering in this regard. Reasons for this can be found in the poor provision of technology and in the insufficient willingness to take a job in this field.[96]

With the exception of Eisenhüttenstadt and Görlitz, the examples of improvements refer to changes in large urban cemeteries (mostly in the more densely populated southern regions of the GDR); this highlights the fact that East German cemetery reform was predominately urban. For most rural cemeteries, even if they were municipal ones, the investments appeared to have been too high in relation to the potential benefit (as measured by the population concerned). The example of the new *Waldfriedhof* in Schwerin (1975) is a good example of the publicity that large scale projects created. A quintessential socialist cemetery was built as a prototype, with a concrete celebration hall, socialist statues and murals and a park-like arrangement. A wide long open space, along a natural dell, divided the two parts of the cemetery, while the fields of both parts were arranged in the typical grid-system. The individual fields were separate but visually held together to form a unity. Altogether, it still strikes the visitor as an enormous open public space, in which some graves look rather forlorn. Schwerin stands as evidence that the socialist administration favoured the grand gesture. Municipal rural cemeteries, unless they were in areas with dense industry (e.g., Schwarze Pumpe), like most church cemeteries, remained largely untouched by the aesthetic revolution – at least directly. Indirectly, mainly owing to the limited supply of standardized gravestones, there was a process of uniformity by default. The outcome of this is still evident in the vast quantities of 'high format' gravestones (*Hochformatsteine*) that dominate many cemeteries.

Since church cemeteries were not extended, one can surmise that both bureaucrats and by extension the Party thought that gradual and evolutionary change would suffice, or that there remained very little ideological concern. Both views are supported by the lack of real changes to the existing legal framework governing the East German burial services and cemeteries after 1968. The last change by the *Ministeratsbeschuß* of April 1980 merely codified most changes made earlier.[97] The focus of attention had shifted to two other areas of sepulchral culture: the expansion of cremation (inseparably linked with the advent of the *Urnengemeinschaftsanlagen*) and the propagation of secular rituals. What remained as the key force for change was the inclination towards achieving a higher degree of efficiency and the need for economy. Wilfried Scherzer, head of the department for cemeteries at the IfK in the 1970s, put it bluntly when addressing a Swedish delegation:

> We are developing new forms of disposal and aim to keep the required cemetery space as small as possible. Our financial potential is low. It is already the case today that an area the size of a football pitch has to feed three people.[98]

From the 1960s onwards both cemeteries and burials services became part of the service economy in the GDR as well as in the West (i.e., the FRG). However, there was just one fundamental difference, as in the West this led to the commercialization of funeral direction and cemetery operation. In the GDR, with its state-run economy, and its conviction that disposal was a *Hoheitsaufgabe* (sovereign task) of the state, this resulted in the development of an ever more efficient means of disposal – with all the problems such an approach entailed.[99] The *Südfriedhof* of Leipzig, extending over 74 hectares, was the largest cemetery of the GDR. When in the mid 1970s it was to be redeveloped, the planning of that project, despite being couched in ideological considerations, gave a clear rationale for redevelopment:

> The importance of this green space is indicated by the fact that here, as in many other cities, the cemetery is a site of burial for the dead as well as a site for contemplation and relaxation for the living …
>
> The starting point for the reconstruction of the *Südfriedhof* Leipzig was the dearth of further areas for burials. At the same time there was a desire to make the cemetery design better as a whole, in order to create the preconditions for efficient maintenance. Both considerations were closely linked with the rise in cremation rates and the concomitant need for unified and delineated areas for the new form of disposal UGA.[100]

The result was an integration of architecturally significant memorials into a landscape that otherwise reflected GDR principles of design, such as the grid-system, anonymous communal areas for the internment of urns and the socialist field of honour along the great avenue leading from the main entrance to the crematorium. These features combine the truly 'socialist' elements in the changing complexion of the East German cemetery after 1945. The characteristic features of the urban East German cemetery were the advocacy of economic efficiency in cemetery design, the propagation of cremation, the introduction of the anonymous communal area for the internment of urns and the celebration of the socialist elite by that distinct feature of the *Leitfriedhof* of any *Bezirksstadt* (regional capital), the field of honour (*Ehrenfeld*).

The two last features stand in starkest contrast to one another.[101] The communitarian urn field, devoid of signs of individuality, and the field of honour, celebrating the achievements of high-ranking party veterans, are not easily reconciled, as a commission found when setting up a field of honour for the region of Erfurt. Several interest groups in the socialist state advocated that their deceased should be treated differently from the rest of society. The NVA (the East German army) stressed their worthiness for a special field for their dead; in similar fashion the organization of those persecuted by the Nazis (VdN) insisted on a specific field and memorial to honour its dead members. In the end, the commission found that each decision has to be made by the regional Party Secretariat, and that nobody should be exhumed in order to be placed in the field of honour.[102] Only the specific paradoxes of GDR ideology could generate such contrast: while insisting on a 'community of the dead', only the regime's logic could reconcile the rejection of individuality with the celebration of particular individuals in a secular socialist pantheon.

It is, however, possible that in our cemeteries special communal areas, for example, graves for outstanding citizens, are created at especially chosen points of the cemetery, and in which citizens are buried who earned special merits in the construction of our society. These commemorative and burial sites form a central point in the cemeteries for the living generation and thus should be designed artistically. Communal expression can be especially emphasized here.[103]

Notes

1. The separation is also artificial because in a number of German cities (in East and West) the burial service has been fused with the municipal cemetery administration as a result of the municipalization taking place throughout the twentieth century; moreover it overlooks the fact that maintenance of graves through a system of yearly subscription has become a major service offered by some urban cemeteries.

2. These two figures are often quoted, but seem to come from only one source: BA Berlin, DO 4, Kirchenfragen No. 2162: *Anlage zu Brief Generalsuperintendent von Berlin Sprengel II an Staatssekretär für Kirchenfragen*, 13 April 1959, 1.

3. Sörries, 'Kontroverse um Sozialistische Friedhofskultur', 11.

4. Schelenz and Meinel, '"Sozialistische" Friedhofskultur in der DDR?', 15.

5. StA Dresden, Rep. 9.1.14, No. 204: *Zusammenstellung von vereinheitlichen Definitionen zu Begriffen des Friedhofs- und Bestattungswesens der DDR mit dem Ziel der Ergänzung der einheitlichen Definitionen für Planung, Rechnungsführung und Statistik Teil 5 Stadt- und Gemeindewirtschaft*, H, Kluge, IfK, 15 December 1971, 28.

6. The naming of most German city cemeteries hints at this process. These large new cemeteries are frequently called the central cemetery (*Zentralfriedhof*), despite the fact that they were generally built at the periphery of the cities. This peripheral location is reflected in the second category of names that dominate the urban cemetery, *Westfriedhof, Nordfriedhof*, which refer to the general location relative to the city centre, followed by names that describe the landscape *Heidefriedhof, Sennefriedhof,* or *Waldfriedhof.*

7. In British English there is a similar shift from the term churchyard to the word cemetery; according to the OED it has a specific connotation of a public area owned by the town or city. Moreover, the word cemetery is derived from the late Latin term *coemeterium* meaning dormitory. The etymology of the German term is much more difficult as it is argued that there are a number of Germanic concepts, plus the reinterpretation of the term in direction of the German word Frieden (peace) as in peace of the soul; while these words are related, there is a distinct difference between the original meaning (as in the word *umfriedet*) and the contemporary connotation.

8. BA Berlin, DO 4 Kirchenfragen, No. 2162: *Das Bestattungs- und Friedhofswesen in der DDR*, 4.

9. In the *Bezirk* Leipzig, for example, the decision that new church cemeteries were not to be allowed had real consequences, as in the region the mining of coal lead to the resettlement of a number of villages, inclusive of cemeteries. In the question of new church cemeteries the local government checked with Berlin if it should allow the planning of new cemeteries, and was instructed that it would be against policy. SSA Leipzig, BT/RdB Leipzig, No. 21420.

10. The organization of the Protestant Church in Germany is, owing to historical reasons, very complicated. The Protestant Church is based upon regional churches (*Landeskirche*) that sometimes exist within the borders of the former principalities, and sometimes along more modern dividing lines (i.e., *Länder* or Provinces). These *Landeskirchen* have districts and sub-districts in order to provide some decentralized organization. All these generally meet in the form of elected councils (synods) and debate issues and elect members for the next level of council.

11. LHSA Magdeburg, Rep. K2 Ministerpräsident, No. 695, Film 175, f. 147 (VS): *Kreisoberpfarrer Max Weyhe an Evangelischen Landeskirchenrat Dessau*, 16 June 1946.

12. M. Bohl, 'Die Ethik der Nützlichkeit – Nützlichkeit der Ethik. Intentionen, Strategien, und Interessen der Friedhofsreformbewegung und deren Auswirkungen auf heutige Diskurse', in Sörries (ed.), *Vom Reichsausschuß zur Arbeitsgemeinschaft Friedhof und Denkmal*, 115.

13. V. Kieran, 'Religion', in T. Bottomore (ed.), *A Dictionary of Marxist Thought* (Second Edition) (Oxford: Blackwell, 1991), 465–68.

14. It is essential to encapsulate both dominant aphoristic views of religion existent in Marxist-Leninist thought in the attempt to understand the tension between communism and religion: The famous Leninist dictum of 'Religion as Opium for the People' – with its superimposed quality deriving out of the Russian context of the Orthodox state church – as opposed to Marx's original view of 'Religion as Opium of the People'– with its origins in an analysis of religion as a 'sigh of the oppressed creature'. See also D. McLellan, *Marx* (London: Fontana, 1986), 31.

15. Kieran, 'Religion', in Bottomore (ed.), *A Dictionary of Marxist Thought*, 467.

16. Creuzberger, *Die sowjetische Besatzungsmacht*, 76–77.

17. He had been a trusted member of the national committee for a free Germany (NKFD) – the Moscow based group that became the nucleus for the East German elite – additionally between 1946 and 1954 he had worked as an informant for the Soviet secret police (NKVD). See: Creuzberger, *Die sowjetische Besatzungsmacht*, 78; G. Besier, *Der SED-Staat und die Kirchen – Der Weg in die Anpassung* (Munich: C. Bertelsmann, 1993), 25–26.

18. The political council of the SMAD Vladimir Semënov also stressed the significance of church support in the success of any party. See: Creuzberger, *Die sowjetische Besatzungsmacht*, 78–79 and footnote 193.

19. E. Neubert, 'Kirchenpolitik', in Judt (ed.), *DDR – Geschichte in Dokumenten*, 364–65; VPKA Bericht über Äußerung Superintendent Gerboth (Sangerhausen): 'We have experienced once before that one man wanted to usurp all the power, but even the Third Reich has passed, only the Lord is eternal', LHSA Magdeburg, Rep. K2 Ministerpräsident, No. 3885, Film 471, f. 290.

20. S. Wolle, *Die heile Welt der Diktatur – Alltag und Herrschaft in der DDR 1971–1989* (Berlin: Ch. Links, 1998), 248.

21. Creuzberger, *Die sowjetische Besatzungsmacht*, 80.

22. Ibid., 84.

23. See: Article 41 to 48, Constitution of 1949. § 1 of Article 43 is exactly the same as that used in the Weimar constitution: 'There is no state church. The freedom to form religious communities is to be protected.' Moreover, it also asserts the church's status as a legal person (*Körperschaft des öffentlichen Rechtes*). See *Gesetzblatt der DDR*, 1949, 5–16.

24. Besier, *Der SED-Staat und die Kirchen*, 69. A report from the Chief of the *Volkspolizei* in Sachsen-Anhalt underlines the socialist understanding of the role of the church in its projected society: 'The Protestant Church is duty-bound to recognize the constitution and like every citizen, to comply with it, to support the tasks that the National Front has set itself, and to view these as the wider mission of the German People … The content of the letter was permeated with Western-imperialistic agitation against the German Democratic Republic and its constitution with the purpose of causing a rift in the National Front of the population fighting for the unity of Germany … The unconditional commitment of the Protestant Church and its dignitaries to the constitution of the GDR is to be striven towards, as is their exertion of

influence in favour of the peace movement, the National Economic Plan, and the struggle of the German people in the National Front for the unity of Germany.' LHSA Magdeburg, K2 Ministerpräsident, No. 3885, Film 471, f. 287, *Brief von Paulsen an Innenminister,* 15 April 1950.

25. The attempts to exert pressure were manifold and often started in the small things, for example in Magdeburg in a campaign to force pastors not to exceed twenty minutes for every funeral. AKS Magdeburg, No. 903 d: *Zeitüberschreitungen bei Trauerfeiern,* 6 March 1952.

26. S. Wolle, *Die heile Welt der Diktatur,* 249.

27. 'The rivalry is not merely of a theological nature, it concerns reality.' THSA Weimar, BPA Erfurt, B II/2/14-001: *Bericht über die am 17.-18.11.1952 in Berlin stattgefundene Arbeitsbesprechung der Referenten für Kirchenfragen.*

28. LHSA Magdeburg, Rep. K2 Ministerpräsident, No. 695, Film 175, ff. 137–38: *Brief Abteilung Kirchenfragen and Kommunalabteilung K I , Halle/Saale,* 23 May 1946.

29. LHSA Magdeburg, Rep. K2 Ministerpräsident, No. 695, Film 175, f. 138.

30. LHSA Magdeburg, Rep. K2 Ministerpräsident, No. 695, Film 175, ff. 416–17, *EKD: Mitnahme von Parteifahnen bei Beerdigungen auf kirchlichen Friedhöfen,* 29 May 1949.

31. LHSA Magdeburg, Rep. K2 Ministerpräsident, No. 695, Film 175, f. 139: *Erzbischöfliches Kommissariat an Präsidenten der Provinz Sachsen,* 13 June 1946.

32. LHSA Magdeburg, Rep. K2 Ministerpräsident No. 695, Film 175, f. 140: *Evangelisches Konsistorium der Provinz Sachsen an Präsidenten der Provinz Sachsen,* 19 June 1946.

33. LHSA Magdeburg, Rep. K2 Ministerpräsident No. 695, Film 175, f. 141.

34. LHSA Magdeburg, Rep. K2 Ministerpräsident, No. 695, Film 175, f. 147 (VS): *Brief Kreisoberpfarrer Max Weyhe an Evangelischen Landeskirchenrat,* 16 June 1946.

35. 'The plan of the province seems to be only the first step in a measure, arising from a minority which is not intended to promote the advancement of the church.' LHSA Magdeburg, K2 Ministerpräsident, No. 695, Film 175, f. 150: *Evg. Pfarramt St. Georg, Plötzkau an Evg. Landeskirchenrat für Anhalt,* 16 June 1946; also LHSA Magdeburg, K2 Ministerpräsident, No. 695, Film 175, ff. 141–63.

36. LHSA Magdeburg, K2 Ministerpräsident, No. 695, Film 175, ff. 141–42: *Brief Kreisoberpfarrer zu Dessau an Landeskircherat für Anhalt,* 5 June 1946.

37. BA Berlin, DO 1 MdI, 34.0, No. 48678.

38. In Saxon-Anhalt in 1949, as well as the other provinces that had been part of Prussia, for example, the practicalities of burials were regulated by the *Erlass* of 20 January 1892 – *M9127 GI GII GIII,* published in the *Ministerial Blatt für Medizinische Angelegenheiten,* 32; augmented by the *Runderlass of the Reichs- und Preussische Ministeriums des Inneren and the Preussische Ministerium für kirchliche Angelegenheiten* vom 18.1.1937, *RMBL .i.V. No. 4,* 114. Also in 1934 the *Reichsfeuerbestattungsgesetz* and an accompanying *Musterbetriebsordnung* had set a standard, *RMBL,* 380 / 519.

39. LHSA Magdeburg, 2 Ministerpräsident, No. 695, Film 175, ff. 408–9: *Brief Landesgesundheitsamt an Räte der kreisfreien Städte und Landkreise,* 10 June 1949.

40. The term *Musterfriedhofsordnung* suggests the very character of these regulations within the highly localized German system. This regulation was a set of rules, suggested by an advisory body, urging all those institutions with legal remits over cemeteries to adopt these in order to establish a uniform legal framework.

41. While the quote above does not distinguish between the commemoration of the dead (*Totengedenken*) and the cult of the dead (*Totenkult*) it seems that in the context of a specific historical discussion a separation of terms is necessary, especially since this thesis omits the issue of the cult of the dead in the GDR.

42. BA Berlin, DO 4 Kirchenfragen, No. 2162: *Das Bestattungs- und Friedhofswesen in der DDR,* 3.

43. 'Lenin teaches us that a reduction in the effort to carry a socialist consciousness into the working-class movement is equal to leaving ground to enemy forces that they can use, in

order to drag the working-class movement on to the path of bourgeois Trade Unionism or on to the path of the ideology of parsons (Lenin Band V Seite 398)', MLHA Schwerin, Rep. 7.1-1, RdB Schwerin, 1. Überlieferungschicht, No. 3995 b: *Rechenschaftsbericht 1959 (Rednerkollektiv)*, 1.

44. MLHA Schwerin, Rep. 6.11-11 MdI (1946–1952), No. 1791, 26: *Schreiben an den Rat der Stadt Magdeburg, Abt. Garten- und Friedhofswesen*, 8 December 1951.

45. LSA Merseburg, RdB Halle, No. 3800, 43–48: *Protokoll Treffen mit Staatssekretär Eggerath*, 8 July 1957.

46. 'Many cemeteries in the GDR, presumably most, are under church administration … During our visit we saw, and that very briefly, only one of these parish cemeteries, the one in Altenburg, which was in a rather neglected state. It can be assumed that the cemeteries of the parishes elsewhere are also looked after badly, because the lack of personnel would be felt even more strongly there': in N. Grufman and S. Ingemark, *Feuerbestattung und Friedhofswesen in der DDR – Schwedische Feuerbestatter berichten* (Berlin: Volks-Feuerbestattung e.V., 1972), 4.

47. LKA Dresden Bestand 2, No. 34100, p. 33 a/b: *Schwierigkeiten bei der Erweiterung bestehender und der Errichung neuer kirchlicher Friedhöfe*, 20 September 1956.

48. 'This autonomy is only guaranteed, if the church can built and administer its own cemeteries': EZA Berlin, ZA 5109/02, No. 104/1216: *EKD Kirchenkanzlei an die leitenden Verwaltungsbehörden der östlichen Gliedkirchen*, 20 September 1956, 1.

49. In February 1956 three children from the orphanage of Lohme drowned in a frozen lake. As this occurred during the initial process of introducing secular rituals, it was decided by the local authority, because the state was the guardian of the three, to bury them with a secular ritual, despite the protestations and indignation of the local people. The local pastor wrote: 'The religious participants of the funeral characterized it as dreary, while the wife of a policemen declared that in future she would scrimp to pay church tax, about which her husband grumbled, so that her next of kin would be buried by the church. The takings of the subsequent street collection (of church taxes) around Lohme was better than the previous one': EZA Berlin, 4/716, 636: *Brief Ev Pfarramt Dobbin/Rg. an Ev. Konsistorium Greifswald*, 19 April 1956.

50. A good summary and selection of materials of the case can be found in G. Diederich, B. Schäfer and J. Ohlemacher, *Jugendweihe in der DDR – Geschichte und politische Bedeutung aus christlicher Sicht* (Schwerin: Landeszentrale für politische Bildung Mecklenburg-Vorpommern, 1998).

51. BA Berlin, DO 4, Kirchenfragen, No. 2162: *Brief Staatssekretär für Kirchenfragen W. Eggerath an H. Maron, MdI*, 25 October 1957.

52. 'Hence cemeteries are cultural sites the care of which, but no less their artistic standing, is put into the caring hands of both the individual and also of the state.' This already highlights the beginning of a shift away towards the dominance of the collective importance of cemeteries. A. Kortüm, 'Ordnung oder Uniformität', *Mitteldeutsche Neuste Nachrichten*, No. 274, 27 November 1958.

53. For some cases in 1949 see LHSA Magdeburg, Rep. K2 Ministerpräsident, No. 7696, Film 175.

54. LKA Dresden, Bestand 2, No. 34232, f. 10a: *Abschrift Ev. Pfarramt Eischheim an Ev. Landeskirchenamt Sachsen*, 3 October 1955.

55. BA Berlin, DO 4, Kirchenfragen, No. 2162: *Ortsausschuß für Jugendweihe Wriszen an das ZK der SED*, 31 July 1959. Similar deliberation with regard to paying church tax for the future service of a Christian burial still play an important role in Germany, especially in rural areas.

56. BA Berlin, DO 4, Kirchenfragen, No. 2162: *Ortsausschuß für Jugendweihe Wriszen an das ZK der SED*, 31 July 1959.

57. BA Berlin, DO 1 MdI, 34.0, No. 48678: *Brief Dr. Wange, Ministerium für Bezirksgeleitete Industrie an Generaloberst Dickel, Ministerium des Inneren*, 4 November 1976, Anlage 1,

8. Details on Rostock see below; Karl-Marx-Stadt: Beschluß des BT vom 20. März 1958; Dresden: Beschluß des BT vom 19. Februar 1960. For the church reaction in Saxony see: LKA Dresden, Bestand 2, No. 3404, Band 1, 43–44.

58. VLA Greifswald, Rep. 200 7.1, No. 189, ff. 3–4: *Beschluß No. 16–4./58 über die Regelung des Friedhofswesens im Bez. Rostock*, 15 February 1958.

59. BA Berlin, DO 4, Kirchenfragen, No. 2162: *Arbeitsentschließung, Arbeitskreis Bestattungswesen in der DDR, Cottbus*, 21 February 1958, 2.

60. BA Berlin, DO 4, Kirchenfragen, No. 2162: *Anlage zu Brief Generalsuperintendent von Berlin Sprengel II an Staatssekretär für Kirchenfragen*, 13 April 1959, 1.

61. In the specific case of Thuringia, the role of OKR Lotz, who worked as an informant for the Stasi and who had significant influence on Mitzenheim, should not be underestimated. G. Besier, 'The German Democratic Republic and the State Churches, 1958–1989', *Journal of Ecclesiastical History*, 50:3 (1999), 530.

62. BA Berlin, DO 4, Kirchenfragen, No. 2162: *Anlage zu Brief Generalsuperintendent von Berlin Sprengel II an Staatssekretär für Kirchenfragen*, 13 April 1959, 1–2.

63. Ibid.

64. Bohl, 'Die Ethik der Nützlichkeit', in Sörries (ed.), *Vom Reichsauschuß zur Arbeitsgemeinschaft Friedhof und Denkmal*, 122–25.

65. BA Berlin, DO 4, No. 2162: *Anlage zu Brief Generalsuperintendent von Berlin Sprengel II an Staatssekretär für Kirchenfragen*, 13 April 1959, 2.

66. Happe, 'Sozialistische Reform der Friedhofs- und Bestattungskultur der DDR', 186.

67. BA Berlin, DO 4, No. 863: *Aktenvermerk über eine Beratung zum Friedhofs- und Bestattungswesen am 5. Juni 1962*, 2–3.

68. BA Berlin, DO 4, No. 863: *Aktenvermerk* 24 July 1962.

69. The official view of the IfK had not changed in 1972, it had only become more assertive: 'In future the Church will administer its property according to the guidelines that are in place here': in W. Scherzer, in Grufman and Ingemark, *Feuerbestattung und Friedhofswesen in der DDR*, 9.

70. StA Eisenhüttenstadt, Sig. S 77: H. Bräuer, *Die Ersten Drei Jahrzehnte der Ev. Friedenskirchengemeinde Eisenhüttenstadt –Erinnerungen*, 404.

71. Bohl, 'Die Ethik der Nützlichkeit', in Sörries (ed.), *Vom Reichsauschuß zur Arbeitsgemeinschaft Friedhof und Denkmal*, 123.

72. The authors were members of the industry, high civil servants, members of church administration, or academics: Prof. Kurt Groß, Direktor der Staatlichen Akademie für Kunstgewerbe; Stadtbaurat Paul Wolf; Gartenbaudirektor Johann Erbe; Regierungsbaudirektor Waldo Wenzel; K. Siegrist, Bürgermeister i.R. and Syndikus des Verbandes Deutscher Granitwerke; Dr Ing S. Hirzel (ed.). As quoted by Bohl, *Ethik der Nützlichkeit*, in Sörries (ed.), *Vom Reichsauschuß zur Arbeitsgemeinschaft Friedhof und Denkmal*, 130. While the official IfK personnel was not so eclectic in origin, the wider circle of people consulted was very comparable in breadth. It did not exclude members of the church administration specifically in charge of the church cemeteries, neither did it exclude representatives of the guild of stonemasons. This openness to expert or technical debate explains why certain critiques of the state of GDR cemeteries made it sometimes into official publications (if not policy papers), such as the IfK newsletter, *Aus der Praxis für die Praxis*.

73. Bohl, 'Ethik der Nützlichkeit', in Sörries (ed.), *Vom Reichsauschuß zur Arbeitsgemeinschaft Friedhof und Denkmal*, 116.

74. 'Despite their disparate aims and ideals, their shared [AFD and IfK] starting point was the critique of the forms of sepulchral expression of the *Gründerzeit* [the era following the foundation of the German Empire after 1871], that were perceived to be pompous, artificial and excessive'; in Happe, 'Der Sozialistische Reform', in Sörries (ed.), *Vom Reichsausschuß zur Arbeitsgemeinschaft Friedhof und Denkmal*, 185; Or as the key IfK text so very vividly phrased it: 'Kitsch is untruth, it is hypocrisy [N.B.: the connotation of the word 'hypocrisy' in this

context refers back to the 'Ethik des Nützlichen'], it is inappropriate and alien to the material, kitsch is a form of excessive individualism.' IfK, *Gestaltung unserer Friedhöfe*, 60.

75. The previous publication by the provisionary committee was called fittingly: *Cemetery: Thoughts for All* (*Friedhof: Gedanken für Alle*).

76. IfK, *Gestaltung unserer Friedhöfe*, 6.

77. See for example the developments as traced by A. Port, *Conflict and Stability in the German Democratic Republic* (New York: Cambridge University Press, 2007). The 1960s saw change, but the most interesting crystallization comes with the rise of Kurt Hager from 1958. As a key source see: K. Hager, *Zu Fragen der Kulturpolitik der SED – Referat auf der Sechsten Tagung des Zentralkomitees der SED* (Berlin: Dietz Verlag, 1972).

78. IfK, *Gestaltung unserer Friedhöfe*, 22.

79. The same challenge of modernization was faced by many West German municipalities after 1945 in treading the narrow path between conservation of the overall impression of the park and landscape cemetery and the demands of changing attitudes of the modern and more democratic society intend on more equality in design twinned with the introduction of machinery, rationalization and the mantra of functionality. In short, they too were forced by the development of what Sloane so rightly termed: the advent of entrepreneurial efficiency. D. Sloane, *The Last Great Necessity – Cemeteries in American History* (Baltimore: Johns Hopkins University Press, 1991), xxiii.

80. 'Um Bedeutsames zu erzielen, muß sich das Einzelne dem Ganzen unterordnen': in Happe, 'Der Sozialistische Reform', in Sörries (ed.), *Vom Reichsauschuß zur Arbeitsgemeinschaft Friedhof und Denkmal*, 193.

81. Julie Rugg, writing from a British perspective, is more open in her definition of cemetery space and fully acknowledges the rights of the individual and the crucial role of the cemetery as a site of contemplation and remembrance. The latter use seemed often forgotten in the German discourses. Rugg, 'Defining the place of burial', 259–75; G. Stuut-Rothkegel, 'Friedhofskultur in den Niederlanden', *Friedhofskultur*, 91 (2001), 26.

82. IfK, *Gestaltung unserer Friedhöfe*, 22.

83. Ibid., 39.

84. Ibid., 23–25.

85. Ibid., 40.

86. Hoffjan, 'Friedhofsgestaltung in der DDR', 176.

87. IfK, *Gestaltung unserer Friedhöfe*, 35–36.

88. Hoffjan, 'Existierte eine spezifische realsozialistische Friedhofgestaltung in der DDR', in Sörries (ed.), *Vom Reichsauschuß zur Arbeitsgemeinschaft Friedhof und Denkmal*, 177.

89. About five years after the unification I visited friends in a small village called Trebnitz, on the train line between Berlin-Lichtenfelde and Frankfurt/Oder. The cemetery was untouched by much reconstruction and was a small village cemetery in the sandy soil of the *Oderbruch*. There was little lawn and most paths were raked sand. I walked across the cemetery out of curiosity. Just before leaving an elderly lady approached me and pointing to a number of rakes hanging from the lower branch of a tree said: 'You would get rid of your shoes before you entered the living room!' She pointed to my footsteps that had destroyed the neatly raked lines.

90. StA Dresden, Rep. 9.1.14, No. 130: *Leserbrief an die Sächsiche Zeitung*, 14 March 1989.

91. Hoffjan, 'Existierte eine spezifische realsozialistische Friedhofgestaltung in der DDR', in Sörries (ed.), *Vom Reichsauschuß zur Arbeitsgemeinschaft Friedhof und Denkmal*, 174.

92. IfK, *Gestaltung unserer Friedhöfe*, 25.

93. IfK Archiv, Sig. 20 A, 20B: 12/69, *Zweckmäßige Formen der Organisation und Methoden der Planung stadtwirtschaftlicher Leistungen nach Versorgungsarten bei rationellem Einsatz der modernen Technik und Anwendung des Neuen ökonomischen Systems, 2 Teile*, 166, as quoted in Happe, 'Die Sozialistische Reform', in Sörries (ed.), *Vom Reichsauschuß zur Arbeitsgemeinschaft Friedhof und Denkmal*, 186.

94. StA Dresden, Rep. 9.1.14, No. 204, 33.

95. BA Berlin, DO 1 MdI, 34.0, No. 48678: *Analyse des Friedhofs- und Bestattungswesens der DDR (1975)*, 1.

96. Ibid., 3.

97. 'Verordnung über das Bestattungs- und Friedhofswesen vom 17. April 1980 / Erste und Zweite Durchführungsbestimmung', *Gesetzblatt der Deutschen Demokratischen Republik*, Teil I, No. 18, 26. Juni 1980, 159–64. Especially § 2 section 5 and 6.

98. Grufman and Ingemark, *Feuerbestattung und Friedhofswesen in der DDR*, 8.

99. Happe, 'Die Sozialistische Reform', in Sörries (ed.), *Vom Reichsausschuß zur Arbeitsgemeinschaft Friedhof und Denkmal*, 188 and note 12.

100. IfK, *Rekonstruktion des Südfriedhofes Leipzig* (Dresden: IfK, 1978), 24.

101. See for example the scathing comment: 'Of all the European capitals, with 225 Berlin has the most cemeteries. Together they occupy 1.5 per cent of the entire area of the city. All this supports the starting hypothesis that the elitist element of the German people occupies much space even beyond their death': in H. Höge, 'Ehrengräber für die Elite', *taz*, No. 7257, 14 January 2004, 15.

102. THSA Weimar, BT Erfurt, Abt. Parteiorgane, No. 3347: *Ausarbeitung einer Ordnung über die Belegung von Ehrengrabfeldern auf dem Hauptfriedhof Erfurt*, 30 November 1973, 2.

103. IfK, *Gestaltung unserer Friedhöfe*, 22.

Chapter 4

BURNING BODIES
CREMATION IN THE GDR

Enemies of cremation often assert illogical claims, that are in no way true. Cremation is hygienic, aesthetic, reverent, it constitutes a cultural progress in the field of undertaking.[1]

When the corpse of the poet Shelley was washed ashore after a shipwreck in 1822, his friend Lord Byron arranged for it to be burned on a pyre – akin to the Indian custom. Whilst this act did not send ripples through the fabric of European burial culture, let alone rip it apart, it did set a powerful and inspirational precedent. The idea of cremating humans has been around for a considerable time; Sir Thomas Browne's treatise of 1658 (subsequent to the finding of an ancient urn) or the legalization of cremation in the wake of the French Revolution are examples of this.[2] The act of cremation and its reception resound with scientific, historical, political and literary references. These range from a simple act of rebellion (whether against religious values or bourgeois aesthetics) to a romantic attempt to reconnect with an idealized past, full of images of Viking warriors cremated in their longboats. Though all these references reveal the motives, intentions and justifications of those who have promoted cremation, they can nonetheless only be regarded as secondary. The radiant effigy of progress towers over them all.

The ideal of enlightening sepulchral culture by promoting cremation has been pivotal in all cremationist movements, independent of their political or social standpoints. Even National-Socialist cremationists, while drawing upon romanticized historical precedents, actually tried to strive towards a 'new' culture which was merely *labelled* (very much in the marketing) as *völkisch*. For them, as well as for the freethinkers, whether liberal or proletarian in persuasion, the bottom line was a desire to change an 'outmoded' tradition, in other words to achieve cultural progress. Therefore, cremationist thought, especially in the first half of the twentieth century, has to be regarded as an individual (or collective) expression of modernism – at least in the broadest interpretation of cremation. The choice of cremation as 'the' form of disposal, besides adhering to changes in sepulchral fashion, thus became a conscious statement of an affiliation to a cause or ideology.[3] Until at least 1945, most of those who had chosen to have their corpses cremated, with the exception of cremation as a means for the disposal of paupers, had done so in the knowledge that they were moving a new agenda forward.[4] A glance at the different forms of urn graves that were built around the turn of the twentieth century underlines this argument. Prevailing trends in gravestone design, such as oversized black marble urns framing family grave plots or name plaques with the gilded symbol of the *Flamenschale* (flaming dish) on the walls of community graves of the freethinkers, were expressive attempts to demonstrate public support for this 'progressive' form of disposal. Such gravestones were more than mere ornaments or status symbols. They were, in fact, a means to popularize the concept of cremation. Like the growing number of publications and pamphlets published on the subject in the first half of the twentieth century, the gravestone played a central role in representing the idea of cremation to the German public. The frankness of many publications (e.g., explicit descriptions of rotting bodies) underlines the moral superiority felt by the cremationist movement when advocating their progressive ideals and practice.

From the 1920s, however, local governments and, after 1945, state governments increasingly replaced associations and individuals as the driving force behind the propagation of cremation. Originally officials of the local government, and later sections of the administration acting in their professional capacity, became the principal agents for change.[5] Individuals were still important in lobbying for the promotion of cremation, but in general a professional consensus had been reached that cremation represented an efficient and necessary form of disposal, integral in many ways to the modern urban environment.[6] Thus, cremation was to be fairly widely labelled as the 'modern form of disposal'.[7] This marked a distinct shift in the nature of the propagation of cremation. The focal point of change had shifted from the individual's conscious choice, based upon a host of beliefs, to the application and provision of incentives, information and regulations through the agencies of the state. The roots of this process lay in the closer involvement of the state – or more precisely a limited number of specialists or technocrats – in the organization of disposal. For the GDR this, in conjunction with the ideologically tempting proposition of establishing or at least steering towards new traditions and customs (in short, cultural engineering), made for a very potent combination. Despite substantial investments and running costs there was not only the lure of form and functionality but also of efficiency. This was a tempting combination not only for the GDR, but also many other countries, in the second half of the twentieth century.

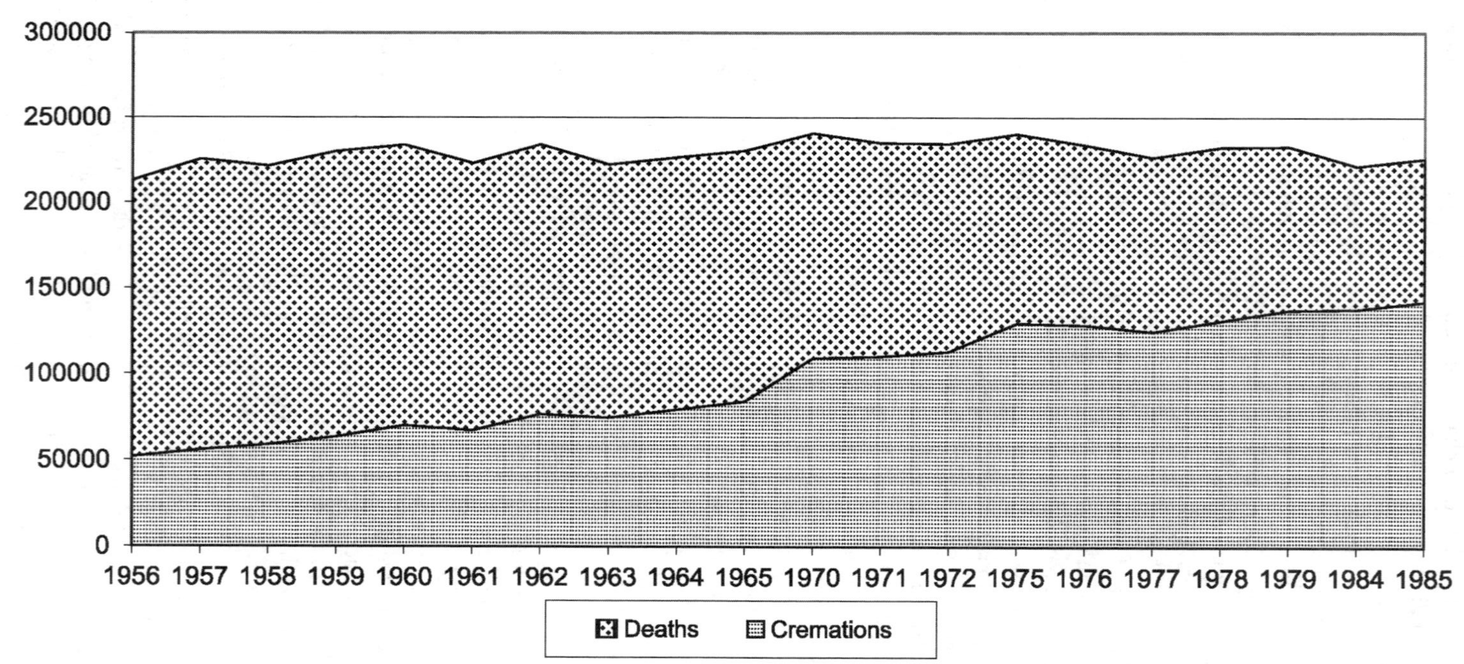

300000
250000
200000
150000
100000
50000
0
1956 1957 1958 1959 1960 1961 1962 1963 1964 1965 1970 1971 1972 1975 1976 1977 1978 1979 1984 1985
Deaths
Cremations

	1956	1957	1958	1959	1960	1961	1962	1963	1964	1965
Number of Cremations in the GDR	51,897	55,854	58,891	63,497	70,064	67,212	76,715	74,688	79,436	84,289
Number of Deaths in the GDR	212,676	225,179	221,113	229,898	233,759	222,739	233,995	222,001	226,191	230,254
Cremation Rate (in per cent)	24.4%	24.8%	25.6%	27.2%	30.0%	30.2%	32.8%	33.6%	35.1%	36.6%

	1970	1971	1972	1975	1976	1977	1978	1979	1984	1985
Number of Cremations in the GDR	109,370	110,385	113,251	129,857	128,852	125,033	131,357	137,571	138,197	142,637
Number of Deaths in the GDR	240,821	234,953	234,425	240,389	233,733	226,233	232,332	232,742	221,161	225,536
Cremation Rate (in per cent)	45.4%	47.0%	48.3%	54.0%	55.1%	55.3%	56.5%	59.1%	62.5%	63.2%

Graph 4.1 The graph and the related table show the development of the number of cremations in the GDR in comparison with the number of deaths, and the table shows the calculated cremation rates for the periods 1956–1965, 1970–1972, 1975–1979, 1984–1985. The data that could be collected do not allow for a continuous timeline.

(Data: Numbers of cremations assembled from all available sources within the archives, mainly from the reports of the individual crematoria and IfK sources. The deaths are from the *Statistische Jahrbücher der DDR*)

In 1961, when East German cremation personnel met to exchange ideas and experiences, the burial service of the city of Altenburg presented a list which enumerated the common misconceptions about cremation to be 'eradicated' in order increase its popularity:

> Those uninformed and sceptical about cremation can persuade themselves at a guided tour of a crematorium:
> 1) that only one deceased alone can be cremated in the (cremation) chamber
> 2) that the deceased is not burned in an open fire
> 3) that the coffin is cremated
> 4) that the deceased does not twist and sit up during the cremation
> 5) that the ashes cannot be interchanged.[8]

This list does not appear exceptional – in so far as it catalogues the (still) commonly voiced fears and concerns (such as the myth of corpses banging at the oven doors, flames eating away at the body, and the very German issue of institutional coffin pilfering). Yet the list does mark a distinct shift in paradigm given its absolute pragmatism. In the past arguments for cremation had been based either on an intellectual level addressing rational concerns (i.e., hygiene) or on philosophical/ideological lines (i.e., as an expression of enlightened and modern thought). In contrast, the main thrust was now to thwart commonly held superstitions. The suggestion of guided tours of crematoria and redecoration of the premises indicate the expansion of the intended target audience. These East German technocrats felt duty bound to familiarize the whole of society with the concept of cremation. Demystification played an important role – cremation needed to be popularized and promoted. It is this policy of state-sponsored propagation of cremation throughout the whole GDR that marks the true difference between East and West German sepulchral culture, rather than merely the advancement of specific forms of design, the organization of cemeteries, or varied changes in the rate of secular rituals. What set the GDR apart from many, though not all, Western countries was an appreciably higher overall cremation rate, which was achieved as a result of the systematic propagation of cremation as the preferred form of disposal. The rise of cremation to the dominant form of disposal in the GDR was founded in a number of processes. With the decline of individual affiliation to cremation societies and the rise of the propagation of cremation, broader factors became important. Cremation rates thus reflect, to very high degree, local social and cultural attitudes, history and to a certain degree religious affiliations.[9] Uniform developments throughout entire countries, or even regions, are therefore very rare. Protestant or urban areas, for example, traditionally have a more rapidly rising cremation rate, and Catholic or rural areas have generally lagged behind. A major factor has been the proximity to the crematoria: cities with a crematorium tend to have a higher rate of cremation than cities without. Despite all these qualifications, and despite further factors to be discussed below, the statistics from the small town of Zörbig, situated in the triangle between Dessau, Halle and Leipzig, offer a glimpse of general trends both in the rise and fall of

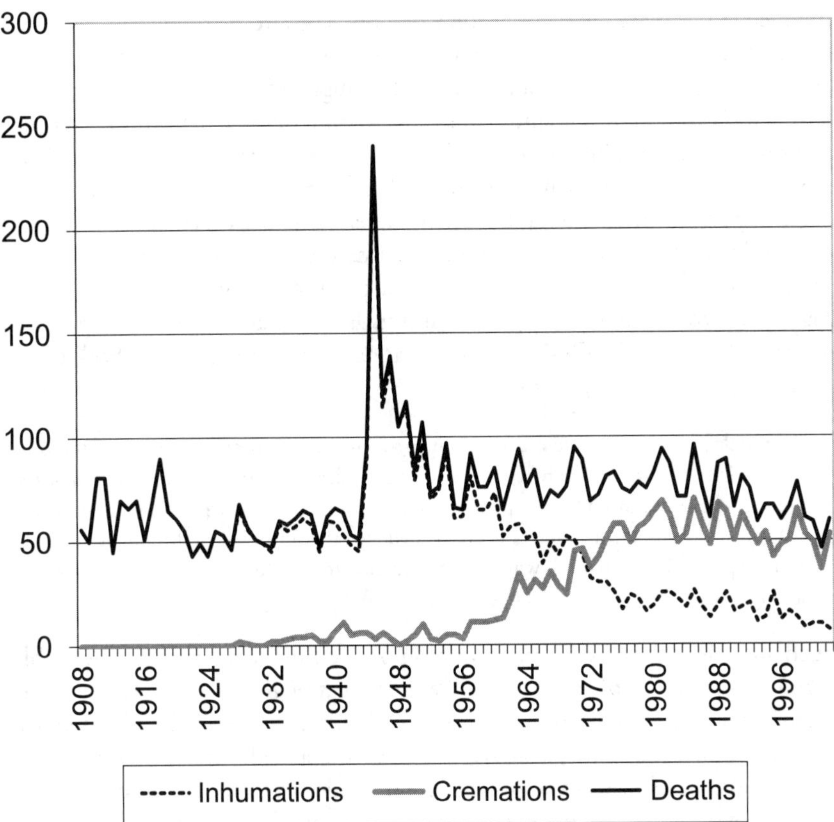

Graph 4.2 Deaths, cremations and inhumations in the town of Zörbig, between April 1908 and 2002.

(Data: *Heimatmuseum* Zörbig)

death rates and in the choice of disposal. Whilst one small town cannot be seen as being statistically representative, the graph neatly reflects the general trends that resulted from the propagation of cremation in the GDR.

This is especially true for the overall post-war development, when, after an initial recovery from the aftermath of the war, the death rate fell gradually and then stabilized with a slight tendency to decline. In the middle of the 1950s, the number of cremations grew, while the number of inhumations began to fall rather sharply. Parity was reached in 1971/72. Thereafter, cremation was established as the predominant choice, with a ratio of at least three to one.

The cremationist lobby within the GDR saw East Germany as the motherland of modern cremation. Whilst the entire cremationist movement has to be seen as being truly pan-European and transnational in character, there was the perception that certain key advances in the cremationist agenda of furthering cremation were German in origin.[10] This argument centres around, amongst other things, the Siemens furnace (with its feature of non-exposure of the corpse to direct flame), Feuerbachian secularism and exceptionally high rates of cremation, with 70 per cent and more in certain cities in Thuringia. However, the principal line of reasoning was more straightforward: the first modern crematorium was operating in Gotha by 1878, even though the first crematorium was built in Milan (1867). Historical materialism as an ideological framework added to the force of the argument. It is striking how many references to archaeological finds and medieval history are to be found in East German source material. In 1979, when the director of the Potsdam cemetery (acting as the coordinator for the region: *Bezirksleitbetrieb*) delivered a speech outlining sepulchral changes of the previous thirty years within the GDR, his examination of cremation looked back to the archaeology of bronze age settlers:

> Richer clans begin to make a distinction between their dead and the mass of the other deceased. In the Bronze Age this trend becomes even clearer. With the *Linienbandkeramikern* cremation can be proven for this period. Besides inhumation the first urn burials have been identified at Arnstadt. From this it can be deduced that in this period inhumation began to be replaced by cremation, which then remained the predominant form of disposal for a long time.[11]

Such historical references were common and dominated many of the public arguments in favour of cremation. Like the thanatological debates, the academic examinations and publications on sepulchral culture were filled with references to anthropology and archaeology. In his very detailed and fascinating work, Peter Frenz developed an argument from modern India (stressing the point that the pyre is often both a means for the disposal of the body and the resting/dispersal place of the ashes, thus offering certain parallels to the scattering of cremains), via fifteenth-century France and the renaissance of classic thought to nineteenth-century German thought, and twentieth-century advances in the technical aspects of cremation.[12] Like the authors of most other similar works, Frenz relied on the historical background as the essential basis for an argument in favour of cremation and the introduction of socialist funeral rites.[13] In general, therefore, the progressive quality of these two ideas were contrasted with a less enlightened past. The rediscovery of cremation was celebrated as a sign of human progress and a stand against the conservative forces (i.e., religion):

> In about 800 AD [789] Charlemagne forbade cremation as a heathen custom and violently eradicated it with the justification 'alive or dead the Christian belongs to the Church'. In this worldview of the Middle Ages there was no space left for cremation ... For this reason the site of burials was placed around the church and the rites of disposal that had been connected with nature were changed ... Cremation, completely forgotten, was reintroduced in a hard struggle against the reaction, through theoretical justifications and conscious acts of enlightenment by progressive individuals that caused a change in public consciousness.[14]

Such were the philosophical and ideological roots of the socialist understanding of cremation. In contrast to the design of cemeteries, cremation was embedded within the ideological framework of socialism. An introductory speech delivered to a conference of secular funeral orators in the region of Potsdam encapsulates the essence that underpinned the two (distinctly different) thought processes that dominated policies on cremation within the GDR:

> It is known to all that with the development of the productive forces, with the growing influence of the revolutionary working-class, a fundamental change occurred in the cultural sphere, leading to the overcoming of ancient and traditional views and customs.
>
> We as socialists advocate cremation as a form [of disposals] that concurs with our ethical ideas about the disposal of human corpses.[15]

The socialist roots of cremation are to be found in the people's cremation societies (such as the one for Greater Berlin, established in 1913 – *Volks-Feuerbestattungsverein von Groß-Berlin*) and the proletarian freethinker movements.[16] Moreover, strong socialist precedents were set by occasions such as the cremation of August Bebel in August 1913. After 1949, the East German state could thus easily claim to be the 'rightful' successor to a proletarian tradition. In addition, that the Catholic Church only re-legalized cremation in 1963 strengthened the ideological case – especially in times of the repeated spells of anti-church agitation in the 1950s and 1960s.

However, the propagation of cremation in the GDR was not straightforward considering that the political system did not resist taking a radical stance. The propagation of cremation after 1945 was initially rather slow. As in the case of cemeteries, the initial focus was on re-establishing services, i.e., repairing cremation ovens and coping with the large number of corpses. It was the major cities that relied on cremation as a means to deal with the rising death toll of 1945. Dresden stands as a famous example; the number of corpses was so great that the administration had to resort to mass burning on the *Altmarkt* in the centre of the city and on its outskirts.[17] In addition, Norbert Fischer argues that the chimneys and furnaces of the concentration and death camps also left a metaphorical dark cloud behind.[18] However, despite the initial lethargy in the propagation of cremation there is one clear trend: cremation continued to be popular in the areas that hitherto had seen high cremation rates. In short, the war did not fundamentally change the perception of cremation. For example, in his study of the GDR Peter Frenz addressed the implications of Auschwitz on cremation in just a single, short paragraph.[19] He further argued that one should also not overlook the discrediting effect of such negative associations with cremation, with the burning of heretics as a further example. Frenz then turned swiftly to an exploration of the many economic advantages. Thereby, he mirrored reality – cremation had come of age: it might be tainted, but not truly discredited. This is mainly because cremation could be justified in persuasive terms that allowed an attractive alternative in the context of the needs of modern industrialized societies.[20] The true attractions of cremation, however, were undoubtedly found in the realm of rational thinking, or as Peter Frenz so succinctly put it: 'The economic advantages of cremation appear pretty obvious'.[21]

However, it took until 1955 for cremation to take a central role in the planning of various specialists, as well as of local and regional officials concerned with a working system of disposal. There is not a single specific date, and no specific governmental decision, that can be pinpointed in retrospect. Not even the IfK was sure what initiated the rising cremation rates. Karl Thomas, a leading official and author of most of the IfK's reports on burial and disposal, had to refer to a broad set of causes when formulating the first major forecast of the cemetery and burial complex:

> Since about 1955 the idea of cremation has increasingly been publicized to the population through progressive cemetery administrations and managements of crematoria, local [party] organs and advanced church administrations, which has thus lead to a more rapid rise in cremations.[22]

He stresses that no *Politbüro* decision in favour of cremation was taken, no ministerial directive was given to explain this rise; on the contrary, individual institutions had begun independently to work towards the same aim. Comprehensive and reliable data regarding the entire nation are only available from 1955 onwards; however, there can be no doubt that real progress was only made thereafter. The reason why cremation became an increasingly popular choice was the intersection of two especially strong forces.

First, there was the correlation between the ideological struggle and the increased popularity of cremation. The latter was in part the consequence of the increasing banality of cremation: a familiarization with cremation as a possible 'proper' alternative to inhumation. One should not underestimate the importance of precedent. Positive examples of 'decent' funerals and 'proper' graves using cremation rather inhumation was often pivotal. Political decision further aided the challenge to the sepulchral status quo. The systematic challenge of the traditional role of the church in society began in earnest, with the introduction of the *Jugendweihe*, and continued through the propagation of secular alternatives for all important church rituals. The idea of propagating cremation, especially given its partially secular tradition, fitted into this process. This prompted an almost tangible element of ideological motivation into the propagation of cremation.[23] The collection of cremation data on a national level from 1955, and the initial rises between 1956 and 1960, reveal the interest the government showed in secular alternatives. However, the ideological aspects should not be exaggerated. It is equally telling that it was initially local, regional and district governments that actively supported cremation, and that it was not until after 1962 that any officials at the central ministerial levels showed any sustained interest in this matter. The large-scale analysis of how secular rituals had spread throughout the GDR best exemplifies this. *Staatssekretär* Grünstein in the Ministry of the Interior during the 1960s commissioned this survey, but it included only occasional references to cremation.

Secondly, individual agency played a significant role through the small number of experts responsible for various local burial services or crematoria, who were well placed to push the initial propagation of cremation in the lower levels of government.[24] With the creation of the VEBs, considerable managerial freedom could be exercised; the burial service director could press for certain measures with respect to services, thereby influencing the attractiveness of particular options. A 1958 survey, conducted by the *Arbeitskreis Bestattungswesen*, found large variations in prices throughout the country. The fee charged for a cremation varied from 84.50 Mark in Rostock to a mere 15.27 Mark in Erfurt; burial of the ashes in Eberswalde was charged at 12.00 Mark while in Mühlhausen it cost 1.50 Mark.[25] Price variations affected the degree to which cremation was common practice from place to place, and equally burial costs also varied to a similar degree. The opening and closing of an allocated grave (*Reihengrab*) cost 40.00 Mark in Werdau (near Zwickau) but only 5.00 Mark in Wittenberge (northwest of Berlin). It is no coincidence that this corresponded to the respective cremation rates. Helmut Kluge, director of the burial service and crematorium in Jena (which had a very high cremation rate and low prices), pointed this out:

> Cremation in the north is well below the average; in the south it is above the average; this can without doubt be explained by the high fees for cremation.[26]

Moreover, the fact that these differences were noticed, discussed and tackled, reveals that by 1955, a nucleus of experts had begun to communicate, meet and interact. Out of their ranks would emerge the personnel for the IfK, giving the institution a specific outlook right from its formation.[27] Thus the seed of organizational coordination was planted and would soon come to fruition with the establishment of the IfK in 1962. The central ministerial administration initially showed little interest in the details of the infrastructure for socialist burial services, but practitioners were beginning to make the case for cremation.[28]

The degree to which ideological considerations played a role is, and is likely to remain, debatable. However, comparison reveals that an increase in cremation rates is by no means unique to East Germany, as even Jane Redlin, in her 1985 study at the Humboldt University in East Berlin pointed out:

> The turn to cremation [as a primary choice of disposal], which primarily had economic and hygienic reasons, is a development that has affected the GDR, but also the European capitalistic states.[29]

Indeed, these other European countries, such as Sweden, Denmark and Czechoslovakia saw a similar or, in the case of Great Britain, an even higher growth in the cremation rate during the period between 1956 and 1967.

The UK actually achieved a higher annual growth rate (2.0 per cent) than the GDR (1.4 per cent). Switzerland and Norway lagged behind, whilst in West Germany and many other countries cremation grew steadily but much more slowly. The five countries with the highest growth rates, Sweden, Denmark, Czechoslovakia (ČSSR), Britain and the GDR, share a number of common denominators: a) cremation was perceived (albeit to varying degrees and for

Table 4.1: Comparison of cremation rates and yearly growth rates in various European countries, 1956, 1960, 1963, 1967, compared with 1997.

	Cremation Rate for 1956	Cremation Rate for 1960	Cremation Rate for 1964	Cremation Rate for 1967	Cremation Rate for 1997	Annual growth rate 1956–1960	Annual growth rate 1960–1964	Annual growth rate 1964–1967	Annual Average 1956–1967
Great Britain	26.3	34.7	43.2	48.6	72.2	2.1	2.1	1.5	2.0
GDR	24.4	29.8	35.1	39.6	69.8**	1.4	1.3	1.5	1.4
Denmark	25.9	30.0	33.6	36.1	71.3	1.0	0.9	0.8	0.9
Sweden	22.2	26.6	31.1	35.0	67.5	1.1	1.1	1.3	1.2
Czechoslovakia	16.0	24.2	32.4	34.0	76.2*	2.1	2.0	0.5	1.6
Switzerland	21.7	23.8	26.3	29.6	67.3	0.5	0.6	1.1	0.7
Norway	18.2	19.8	21.3	23.9	31.0	0.4	0.4	0.9	0.5
FRG	9.9	10.4	11.2	12.0	30.2***	0.1	0.2	0.3	0.2
Netherlands	3.0	4.0	5.8	8.2	47.8	0.2	0.4	0.8	0.5
Austria	5.6	6.1	6.7	7.7	17.6	0.1	0.2	0.3	0.2
Finland	3.8	4.5	4.3	5.1	22.4	0.2	0.0	0.3	0.1
France	0.2	0.2	0.2	–	13.7	–	–	–	–

*   = Czech Republic

** = Eastern states without Berlin, also 1996 and 1998 were both over 73.0 %, so not an entirely representative outlier

*** = Western states with Berlin

(Data: BA Berlin, DO4, No. 892, p. 16; Cremation Society of Great Britain Figures on International Cremation; Press release of Deutscher Städtetag)

different reasons) as a force for progress and modernity and thus could secure some form of political support (Sweden serves as an example with its strong social democratic government and the country's commitment to equality); b) cremation was embraced as a force to overcome tradition or solve the fallout of the death of tradition after 1945, in order to address the growing problems of disposal in terms of space and costs (both private and public) in urbanizing countries with declining family ties; c) cremation rates differed enormously in the countryside (less than 50 per cent, regularly far less) and in urban areas (up to 90 per cent). All other countries with an accelerating growth in cremation (such as Norway, Switzerland, Austria, the Netherlands, FRG), as well as very recent examples such as France (1980 onwards), experienced similar sets of problems and developments.[30] The East German cremation rate is, therefore, not unique. After 1945, burial space in many European countries threatened to become scarce (at least in projections). Traditional rules and customs, such as long periods in which the graves are not disturbed (resting periods), still dominated sepulchral cultures; however, these were ultimately not compatible with the fact that urbanization dominated the European landscape. With the exception of Japan, with its high cremation rate of about 95 per cent, cremation has always been more of an urban phenomenon, since the limits of the traditional system of disposal are reached much more swiftly in an urban environment with its higher population density and its limited space.[31] Moreover, social factors play an crucial role in what the sociologist Klaus Feldmann calls the 'revolution of death', a consequence of the fact that the average life expectancy is still increasing while close family or community ties are in decline. This adds to the attractiveness of cremation as it leaves a number of options open as to what to do with the cremains – and urn burials do not necessitate a lot of care afterwards.[32]

The 1960s saw a real upsurge of activity with regard to cremation in many European countries. For East Germany and the ČSSR, this is explained easily by the fact that these were socialist states with planned economies and strong central governments under strict party control with a particular interest in advancing cremation because of its perceived socialist (secular) tradition. However, the list of countries with strong growth rates includes three democratic countries – Britain, Sweden and Denmark. What united all these countries were governments not reluctant to engage in an exercise of cultural and social engineering. The three non-communist countries invested substantially in cremation, and undertook a large expansion of cremation capabilities.

Sixty per cent of British crematoria and fifty-five per cent of Swedish crematoria were built after 1950. Furthermore, there were policies enacted explicitly to aid cremation, so that in 1967 the number of cremations exceeded the number of burials for the first time in British history.[33] With regard to the Britain, evidence cited in the eighth report of the Select Committee on Environment, Transport and Regional Affairs in 2001 actually goes so far as to say that further promotion would be difficult because of the high rates already achieved and that free choice of the disposal method had in some places been limited.[34]

Table 4.2: Development of cremation rates between 1956 and 1964 in selected European countries. Construction of European crematoria between 1950 and 1969 and proportion of new crematoria in selected European countries.

	Cremation Rate in 1956 (%)	Cremation Rate in 1964 (%)	Number of Crematoria (1964)
GDR	24.4	35.1	53
Great Britain	26.3	43.2	182
Denmark	25.9	33.6	27
Czechoslovakia	16.0	32.4	14
Sweden	22.2	31.1	61
Switzerland	21.7	26.3	24
Norway	18.2	21.3	30
FRG	9.9	11.2	63

	Crematoria built until 1949	Crematoria built between 1950 and 1959	Crematoria built between 1960 and 1969	Proportion of Crematoria built after 1950 (in per cent)
GDR	53	–	1	2
FRG	60	3	5	12
Czechoslovakia	13	1	1	13
Denmark	20	4	8	37
Sweden	29	15	21	55
Great Britain	82	49	73	60
Netherlands	1	1	3	80

(Data: Karl Thomas in an internal IfK report in 1968, as quoted in Frenz, *Entwicklung des Bestattungswesen*, 151–2)

This expansion of cremation capacity in the Western European countries compares to a single new crematorium built in the GDR and to two in the ČSSR.[35] Moreover, the East German one was a small crematorium in the town of Schmalkalden, in the region of Suhl (in Thuringia) – the only region to have a crematorium in nearly every district. In Schmaldkalden's first year of operation only 519 bodies were cremated, which amounted to less than half of one per cent of all the cremations conducted in the GDR in 1970. While the GDR did not expand its cremation capability, in the 1980s especially it did undertake rebuilding efforts and renovated a number of cremation ovens in order to be able to deal with the rising number of cremations. The growing cremation rate was largely achieved by longer operating hours and more shifts, leading to increasing complaints about smoke emissions and other environmental issues from those living in the vicinity of busy crematoria.[36] The lack of expansion and investment was a direct result of the very specific socialist motivation for the propagation of cremation. That peculiar mixture of political, rational and economic considerations is best summed up in the governmental language of Karl Thomas's definition that was used in a paper outlining his projection on the development of cremation in the GDR after 1970:

> The development of cremation in the GDR is the manifestation of an aesthetically irreproachable [faultless], hygienically expedient and economically desirable form of disposal that is appropriate to the progress of socialism.[37]

With the formation of the IfK in 1962, cremation had moved up the agenda.[38] Most statistical material that can be found with regard to cremation and in most communications within the administration had its origins in requests or suggestions made by officials of the IfK. A good example can be found in some of the projections: Table 4.3 shows such a projection made early in 1976. These projections show the ambition of the IfK. The IfK tried to coordinate the attempts and schemes that emerged in different cities between 1956 and 1962 and helped to work out technical guidelines and calculations for the most economic usage of crematoria. This became increasingly important as any crematorium has a ceiling on the number of cremations it can deal with, and small crematoria have to store bodies in order to be certain of an entire day's work.[39]

Besides the technical and economic details of organizing cremation, the IfK had to deal with the everyday reality of the state of most cemeteries and burial services. The propagation of cremation was instrumental in the attempt to overcome the shortfalls of the system:

> Difficulties arise with regard to inhumations to an ever larger extent through the lack of personnel, spaces and the decreasing willingness to aid neighbours in excavating graves in smaller villages. The 'Inhumation' form of disposal must therefore, be widely replaced by the 'Cremation' form of disposal. For the period of the prognosis, it is thus essential actively to exert influence on the population through explanation, stimulation and, amongst other means, through prices and the fostering of farewell ceremonies of a high cultural standard. In 1980 an average cremation rate of 65 per cent should be achieved in the GDR, and consequently the rate of inhumation should be reduced to 35 per cent.[40]

The technical detail of this internal document (and it is worth pointing out that the report was classified [*Vertrauliche Dienstsache*] and that only sixty-five copies were distributed) stated the basic aim, the means and ways very plainly. Cremation was the way forward, not only in the sense of progress, but also in order to avoid an anticipated breakdown of the system of disposal. The annual growth target was two per cent, and that was, as the above statistics show, rather ambitious, considering that over the previous twelve years only a 1.4 per cent annual growth rate had been achieved. Moreover, it would have signified a considerable increase in the number of cremations. In 1966, 86,000 bodies (38.1 per cent of deaths) were cremated. The two per cent growth target would have meant 161,400 cremations in 1980. This increase would have been unevenly

Table 4.3: Northern regions of the GDR and their crematoria projections for the second half of the 1980s compared with the reality of 1974/75.

Region	Crematorium	Estimated Number of Deaths	Expected Cremations per annum	Desired Cremation Rate (%)	Number of Cremations in 1975	Cremation Rate in 1974 (%)
Rostock	*Rostock*	6,200	5,600	90.32	1,815	29.2
	Stralsund	2,900	2,400	82.75	To be built	
	Greifswald	2,900	2,400	82.75	1,360	
Schwerin	*Schwerin*	6,400	5,600	87.5	1,590	16.7
	Wittenberge	4,150	3,600	86.75	To be built	
Neubrandenburg	*Neubrandenburg*	4,800	4,200	87.5	To be built	5.2
	Prenzlau	3,800	3,400	89.47	To be built	
Potsdam	*Potsdam*	5,900	5,300	89.83	1,430	24.2
	Brandenburg	3,600	3,200	88.89	1,340	
	Fürstenberg, Oranienburg, Neuruppin	3,100	2,600	83.87	450	
Frankfurt/Oder	*Frankfurt*	4,000	3,500	87.5	600	17.5
	Eberswalde	4,800	4,000	83.34	To be built	
Cottbus	*Cottbus, Forst*	5,200	3,200	92.31	2,480	30.1
			1,600			
	Senftenberg	4,400	4,000	90.91	To be built	
Magdeburg	*Magdeburg*	6,600	6,200	93.94	5,450	38.9
	Stendal, Gardel.	3,400	3,000	88.24	To be built	

(Data: MLHA Schwerin, RdB Schwerin, Abt. ÖVW, No. 36364; merged with own data)

distributed, with the south having to achieve an 80 per cent cremation rate as compared to the north which had set 35 per cent as its aim – owing to the different base levels of cremation. Even on a practical level this represented an enormous task, especially considering the lack of investment and the difficulty of fostering real and sustained political will to address the challenges that had to be surmounted to establish a unified socialist sepulchral culture. Moreover, beyond the organizational problems lurked the murky waters of human nature – it proved very difficult to plan for the idiosyncrasies of human whim. Ultimately Karl Thomas's forecasts were merely the archetypical musings of a technocrat (*Gedankenspiel*) speculating about the fruits of rationalization and centralization (in which the *Leitbetrieb*, led by enlightened efficiency, had taken over the day-to-day coordination for the entire region) which would culminate in the smooth operation of a finely tuned organization, leaving curiously little space for the caprices of human nature:

> Cremations will be carried out in centres of disposal with crematoria, and the size of their catchment areas will be exactly determined in accordance with economic principles ... A transport organization, administered centrally from the centre of disposal, will coordinate the prompt transport from the location of death to the nearest ceremony hall and will conduct collective transports from these branches to the crematorium ... [T]ransports of individual [corpses] from flats will have become rare, since the developed health and social system will on principle look after the ill and old citizens in clinics, hospitals and care homes. This will therefore create a network of optimal locations of modern crematoria of a uniform technical specification in the GDR. Cremation is the duty of society, the citizen will no longer incur any costs for disposal.[41]

A doubling of cremations in a mere fourteen years, leading to a fully integrated socialist system of disposal of the dead, was sustainable only if a new infrastructure was built, and for this, there were two alternative scenarios.

The first was to establish an optimized network of crematoria, as envisaged above – with catchment areas of 20 km in the south and 50 km in the north – thus securing economically viable transport costs, leading to a centrally administered efficient entity (see below). The second was clearly based on the experiences of the region of Suhl. It suggested a small crematorium (in combination with a ceremonial hall) in each district town, thus not only creating many fairly small units but also avoiding any shortages in cremation capacities and still allowing for the possible future transition towards the first scenario (once all problems had been removed and the large-scale model could work even more efficiently). Shortages were expected when cremation rates rose to their projected levels, since most East German cremation ovens in 1968 were still on a pre-1930s technical level.[42] Karl Thomas, therefore, urged for the construction of a number of new crematoria, but to no avail.

This hints at the fact that outside the IfK the reality was very different. With the intensive spending on the military, border and state security and the relative decline of the GDR economy, the cremations per crematoria increased

Table 4.4: Overview of twenty-five years in the development of the number of cremations taking place in the regions.

Regions	Number of Cremations in 1960	Number of Cremations in 1985	Increase (1960=100)	Total Number of Deaths in 1985	Cremation Rate in 1985 based on raw data calculation (in %)	Cremation Rate in 1985 (according to 1986 IfK Report)
Rostock	1,226	4,799	391	10,021	47.89	43.3
Schwerin	705	2,391	339	7,693	31.08	28.3
Neubrandenburg	–	–	–	7,400		16.3
Potsdam	1,387	4,667	336	14,504	32.18	31.4
Frankfurt/Oder	184	900	489	8,595	10.47	25.4
Cottbus	676	3,063	453	10,999	27.85	49.5
Magdeburg	2,479	6,710	271	17,259	38.88	53.8
Northern Regions	6,657	22,530	338	76,471	33.08	38.1
Halle	7,471	19,148	255	25,007	76.57	70.8
Erfurt	7,333	13,079	189	16,404	79.73	75.9
Gera	5,026	7,459	148	9,894	75.39	89.9
Suhl	3,087	6,636	215	7,490	88.60	88.5
Dresden	9,529	20,047	210	25,513	78.58	71.2
Leipzig	9,837	18,389	187	19,889	92.36	77.5
Karl-Marx-Stadt	11,394	20,809	182	29,812	69.80	71.5
Southern Regions	53,677	105,567	198	134,009	78.77	74.4
East Berlin	9,730	14,540	149	14,882	97.70 (~80%)	74.9
GDR	*70,064*	*142,637*	*205*	*225,362*	*63.30*	*63.0*

NB: Raw regional cremation figures do not take account of overlapping catchment areas for crematoria servicing border areas (see example of Neubrandenburg and Gera). The IfK data are more accurate as in many cases they take the origin of the corpse into account. The error margin is stated as +/- 0.2. Therefore, the last right hand column represents the best picture of cremation in the GDR in the 1980s.

(Data: BLHA Potsdam, Rep 601, No. 34043, and *Statistisches Jahrbuch* der DDR 1986, merged with own data)

significantly but the number of operational ovens actually fell as there was not enough money earmarked for anything except essential repairs.[43] The most striking development was the increase in high-capacity crematoria with more than 3,000 cremations per annum, tripling their number by 1980. (See Tables 4.3 and 4.4.) While the cremation rate did not rise as sharply as predicted, the annual growth rate remained high. This is even more astonishing considering that the network of crematoria remained largely unchanged. In 1990, cremations were conducted in fifty out of the fifty-one locations where cremations had been conducted in 1940 (as well as in one new location). This points to the enormous strain which the increase of cremation rates had put upon an overstretched, understaffed and technologically outmoded system of disposal, reflecting once more the often bleak reality of disposal in the GDR.

Many of the ideas in Karl Thomas's analysis reflected a fascination with the precedent set by the ČSSR in nationalizing and streamlining its sepulchral culture in a socialist way.[44] Thomas, and the aforementioned Kluge, were members of the small number of specialists who attended a semi-official cremationist conference on 28 April 1962. The official report notes not only that cremation in the ČSSR, and especially its propagation through the national cremation society (with 500,000 members out of a population of 12 million), received all the necessary backing of governmental agencies, but also the radical nature of the changes that had taken place:

> In 1958 the Communist Party of the ČSSR decided in a resolution on the cultural revolution that all burial services and cemeteries had to be merged with the state-run concerns. Due to this, all ceremonial halls were changed [from chapels] and their interior modernized [that is secularized] … The number of orators who speak at funerals from a progressive perspective was strengthened. With these measures a large success was achieved. At the moment 80 per cent of all ceremonies in Prague are conducted by secular orators who originally only covered 12 per cent.[45]

This report mentioned the idea of scattering ashes for the first time, eighteen years before the 1980 changes in the burial laws made it a legal possibility. Most Czech delegates commented on a certain lack of hygienic storage for the corpses and the very difficult working conditions within the crematoria they had visited. More revealing is the return journey that was made in November 1965, when a German delegation inspected Czech crematoria and wrote a 35-page report, revealing their admiration for the extent of the change that had occurred since 1958:

> All cemeteries and burial services are the property of the people. Apart from the Jewish cemeteries, there are no religious cemeteries anymore. Through this the administration of the cemeteries, prices and fees, the conduct of ceremonies and the services for the population are regulated in a uniform fashion throughout the entire country. Only in Prague, as the capital, are there a few special regulations, because of the partially increased requirements. The production of coffins for the entire Republic has been concentrated in

two People's owned companies … The municipal cemetery and burial administration are administered through the political councils of the cities … Following a governmental resolution, the central administration has developed an action plan to achieve a rapid increase in the rate of cremation … Through the construction of seven crematoria by 1970, the construction of numerous ceremony halls and mortuaries funded with money by the state as well as through initiative of the population to help the increase of the cremation rate, in conjunction with further education [enlightenment, as in propagation of cremation] the space required for cemeteries could be reduced, the number of workers lowered, and the cost per burial cut.[46]

The enumeration of all these decisions (plus a number of highly specialized matters) casts into sharp relief the lack of determination shown in the GDR. In East Germany local government did not take over all cemeteries and burial services; prices were frozen, but not standardized, coffin production was notoriously decentralized and often relied on artisan production to make up the full planned quota. Central government did not take any authoritarian decisions concerning cremation or sepulchral culture as a whole. Furthermore, supplementary investment on any larger scale looked unlikely and, in general, and in contrast to the ČSSR, was only made available in an ad-hoc fashion. The success of reforms in the ČSSR must have been nonetheless frustratingly comprehensive for the delegates of the IfK (see Table 4.5). Although one must note that in Slovakia some aspects lagged behind – not a single crematorium was built there.

The simple observation that in 1965, Prague, with its population of just over a million, already had a cremation rate of about 80 per cent, highlights this point. Similarly, it was noted that in Prague the required area of cemetery space per corpse had been reduced to a mere 0.8 m^2 compared to an average of between 3 and 5 m^2 in the GDR. Therefore, many of the conclusions – even those dealing with very technical aspects, such as the modernization of cremation oven technology – bemoaned the fact that changes of comparable scope were impossible or impractical in the GDR due to its existing legal framework. Regarding the question of the campaign in favour of cremation, the authors went even further, coming close to outright criticism of central governmental organs:

> The governmental program for the advancement of cremation in the ČSSR represents for us the largest known exertion of influence by a state with a high economic value. The disinterest of the governmental organs of the GDR in at least increasing cremations leads inevitably to ever new weaknesses in the disposal of corpses, worsens the personnel situation and necessitates the development of new areas for cemeteries, often using agricultural land. The governmental program of the ČSSR should therefore be used as the basis of a fundamental discussion between the appropriate central governmental agencies of the GDR.[47]

In short, the example set by the ČSSR was the socialist technocrats' dream of how to organize, control and influence the change from a capitalist to a socialist sepulchral culture – and the last sentence reflects the lack of any political or ministerial direction forthcoming from the government of the GDR. Change on the

Table 4.5: Comparison of ČSSR and GDR rates of cremation, as given in IfK documentation.

Year	Cremations in CSSR	% of Deaths	Cremations in GDR	% of Deaths
1955	18,311	14.49	51,797	24.4
1956	20.166	15.96	51,897	–
1957	22,799	16.95	55,854	–
1958	24,240	19.26	58,891	26.6
1959	28,021	21.35	63,497	27.7
1960	30,402	24.23	70,064	29.8
1961	33,191	26.26	67,212	30.8
1962	39,191	28.2	76,715	32.8
1963	40,382	30.38	74,688	34.3
1964	43,513	32.37	79,436	34.3

(Data: StA Dresden, Rep. 9.1.14, No. 205, merged with own data)

scale envisaged, affecting the burial organization of an entire nation, ultimately hinged on political will. In the ČSSR this political will existed and was exercised; in the GDR it did not. The inability to marginalize the church, the fact that burial organization had traditionally been a question of local jurisdiction and governance, real economic constraints and the absurdities of economic planning, as well as a general apathy towards sepulchral change and innovation meant that reforms were enacted but ultimately remained extraordinary fragmented.

The prime example for this must be the introduction of the scattering of the ashes after 1980, which resulted in the construction of two ash scattering fields in the entire GDR, of which only the one in Rostock became operational; the second, in Zittau, remained unopened. The scattering of the ashes in the German context represented a very stark contrast to the traditional treatment of cremains.[48]

Before 1985 in both East and West Germany the law necessitated an entombment of the ashes. Unlike in many other countries, the ashes could not be handled by the bereaved. However, in 1985 the council for the city of Rostock decreed that it would be lawful to scatter cremains in a designated area, breaking for the first time with this persisting German tradition. Despite scattering being the cheapest form of disposal, in the next four years only seventy-six cremains were actually scattered and of these a number were paid for by the state, indicating that its introduction had little uptake.[49] Nonetheless, the fact that by 1985 a local council took this step indicates the fragmentation of and the strains on the sepulchral culture of the GDR.

In the 1970s, concern to emulate the approach of the ČSSR government, the increasingly alarmist comments in reports that the whole burial system could collapse, and the advice of the IfK did not lead to the proposed construction work of new crematoria, and nor did the demand for comprehensive reform yield swift results.[50] When it became clear that large scale reforms and large

Figure 4.1 The socialist design of *Neuer Friedhof* Rostock.

investments were not pending, despite the bleak picture of disruptions in the disposal of the dead within an acceptable timeframe and the lack of capacity on the cemeteries, the IfK returned to the organization of details. The IfK abandoned the mission of political transformation and returned to the traditional path of cemetery and burial reform in Germany: embracing local regulation to effect the gradual 'education' of public taste and the creation of showcase examples. The local burial service and its regional *Leitbetrieb* became the main instrument in the popularization of cremation. The organizational emphasis was laid upon to the need to reduce costs and prices for all services. The intention was to create a 'composite price' (*Komplexpreis*) per cremation, covering everything from coffin to ceremony and urn, while for burials all items were to be charged separately. Besides recovering the 'true' costs of burials, the stimulation of cremation via financial incentives, was a major element in these thoughts:

> The prices for cremation are to be fixed so that they have a stimulating effect on the propagation of cremation: e.g., a uniform price for transport in the catchment area of a crematorium [i.e., not charged per km], and if necessary through balancing prices through subsidises by the local councils when higher costs are incurred (transports in the northern regions, currently uneconomic cremation in small crematoria).[51]

Costs and savings dominated the discussion, as future efficiencies, especially in the form of the reduction of burial space per corpse, became the mainstay of any argument (see Table 5.2).

In 1971, a Swedish delegation travelled to the GDR to study the East German cremation system. Wilfried Scherzer, then head of the department for cemeteries and burial services at the IfK, welcomed them and made it unmistakably clear that attention had turned to the maximization of cremation: 'We are developing new burial forms and aim to keep the cemeteries space as small as possible.'[52] The proposal to charge for a resting place according to its actual size in square metres was clearly intended to persuade the public to choose cremation. Urn burials, *Urnengemeinschaftsanlagen* (UGAs), or the scattering of ashes, would thus have been made the three most financially attractive forms of burial.[53] In Jena, a standard urn burial plot cost 100 Mark while a place in the *Urnengemeinschaftsanlage* cost 10 Mark. Moreover, most UGAs offered longer or even unlimited resting periods (such as in Karl-Marx-Stadt/Chemnitz), while some cemeteries had the resting period for inhumations cut to as little as fifteen years.[54] The dominant rationale was the drive to maximize efficiency with regard to disposal and maintenance costs. This caused the Swedish delegation to summarize:

> As is generally known, one can also learn from mistakes, and in our view there are also enough errors as well as shortcomings in the GDR. We, for example, see it as an error if in the GDR one becomes rigidly committed to reduce repeatedly the size of cemeteries. This aim is to be achieved through a progressive increase in the rate of cremations. In principle we have little to object. We think it is appropriate if cremation is propagated, inasmuch as the lowering of the cost of disposals aids both the municipalities and the bereaved. We Swedes support cremation, but we cannot accept it if someone who insists on an inhumation must consider himself as old-fashioned and backward; while on the other hand it is considered acceptable – with regard to so-called UGAs – to offer unlimited periods of use and constant plot care with floral decoration.[55]

This external analysis highlights the policy towards cremation as advocated by the IfK. It rightly identifies the main motivation for the policy as the fascination with the reduction of burial space per head. However, the reduction of cemetery space cannot be classified as primarily a socialist ideal. It should be understood as an expression of a managerial or economic or even technocratic preoccupation with space and, to a degree, efficiency. Cremation was the means to achieve that aim of the reduction in cemetery space. Nevertheless, the Swedish delegation also rightly points to the problem inherent in the IfK's cremationist agenda in this fashion: the problem of convincing more and more people to choose cremation without referring to alienation or inducements such as the promise not to reuse the UGAs.

The local burial services were consequently left with the task of convincing those seeking their services to choose cremation. The 1979 second edition of the documentation '*Dienstleistung im Bestattungswesen*' (services in the burial services) makes this unmistakably clear. There are a number of illustrations highlighting certain techniques to suggest the preferable options for disposal, such as hanging pictures of *Urnengemeinschaftsanlagen* (UGAs) in the office where the burial was arranged (*gezielte Sichtwerbung*), or an open advertisement

Table 4.6: Comparison of capacity development of East German crematoria, 1960–1978.

Cremations per annum	1960	1975	1978	1985
up to 500	17	5	2	2
500–1,500	24	20	17	17
up to 1,500	41	25	19	19
1,500–3,000	8	15	20	16
over 3,000	4	11	10	15
over 1,500	12	26	30	31
overall	53	51	49	50*

NB: 1,200–1,500 cremations guarantee an economic operation of a small two-oven crematorium.

* = classification problem with regard to Pößneck/Saalfeld

(Data: MLHA, RdB Schwerin, Abt. ÖVW, No. 36364, merged with own data)

showing the current number of cremations in the form of a chart. Moreover, in many burial service offices, pamphlets and other material in favour of cremation were available and were used to convince those who had no firm idea about what to choose. The *VEB Gartengestaltung* Rostock went further still. It developed a clear set of guidelines with a set of question for its office staff dealing with the bereaved. The introduction to the guidelines is very clear about the aim and less clear about its parameters:

> Through targeted questioning, and whilst taking into account the stated wishes of those responsible for paying the funeral [*Bestattungspflichtigen*], the choice of the form of disposal is to be taken in favour of cremation.[56]

Consequently, the suggested opening lines for the interview tackled how to ask the most important question:

> You will, of course, have already decided on the form of disposal? We recommend to you the *modern* form of cremation which is most frequently asked for in Rostock [71.2 per cent in 1977] and which has a number of advantages (If necessary point to the placard 'Development of Cremation in Rostock' hanging in the waiting room).[57]

Cremation was thus associated with modernity, in contrast to the 'superseded' choice of burial. In combination with the suggestive and 'inspirational' graphic representation of the growth of cremation in Rostock on display in the waiting room, this constituted a clear attempt to influence the choice of the bereaved. The IfK adaptation of the Rostock model went even further, as the burial service employee became the advocate for cremation. The document insists that:

> The person conducting the conversation has to be able to elucidate convincingly the advantages of cremation (knowledge of the technological process is a precondition).[58]

Table 4.7: Example of individual district cremation rates in the southern region of Dresden.

Districts	Deaths 1981	Cremations 1981	Cremation Rate 1981 (in %)	Cremation Rate 1970 (in %)	*Rise per year in %*
Bautzen	1,832	809	44.1	26.0	*1.6*
Bischofswerda	1,078	627	58.2	31.0	*2.5*
Dippoldiswalde	685	301	43.9	32.4	*1.0*
Dresden (Land)	1,832	1,152	62.9	41,8	*1.9*
Freital	1,502	1,100	73.2	51.6	*2.0*
Görlitz (Land)	486	209	43.0	26.3	*1.5*
Großenhain	583	204	35.0	29.4	*0.5*
Kamenz	855	461	53.9	25.0	*2.6*
Löbau	1,550	1,023	66.0	47.2	*1.7*
Meißen	1,819	1,368	75.2	64.0	*1.0*
Niesky	554	166	30.0	16.3	*1.2*
Pirna	1,798	1,215	67.6	39.9	*2.5*
Riesa	1,293	907	70.1	49.0	*1.9*
Sebnitz	790	491	62.2	37.5	*2.2*
Zittau	1,592	1,220	76.6	62.3	*1.3*
Dresden (Stadt)	7,596	5,627	74.1	60.0	*1.3*
Görlitz (Stadt)	1,293	1,078	83.3	74.8	*0.8*
Entire Region	27,138	17,958	66.2	n/a	n/a

(Source: StA Dresden 9.1.14 No. 373)

The propagation of cremation moved away from subsidies to direct influence via the funeral service provider. Expertise on the benefits of cremation and techniques to dispel the most common misconceptions became essential for this task. The role of the individual employee who had to balance advising the bereaved against the promotion of cremation is extremely difficult to judge. Some cities paid a very small bonus, of between 0.10 to 0.50 Mark, for each cremation, an interesting case of using incentives, albeit minute ones, in a socialist economy.[59] Nevertheless, the fact that such a script of questions was devised, and then published, by the IfK, underlines the role of this means of propagation. The fact that Rostock, as a northern city, had such a high cremation rate in 1977 reveals, at least to a degree, the importance of the individual burial service as an agent of cremationism. (See Graph 4.3.)

This reaffirms that the general picture of how cremation developed between 1945 and 1990 is complex since it depended on many predominately local factors (compare the variations in Tables 4.7 and 4.8 respectively). The most obvious, yet central, observation is that cremation rates rose substantially despite the lack of political direction. By 1989 cremation had become by far the most common form of disposal in the GDR. Estimates generally vary, as reliable figures do not seem to exist for the last four years of the GDR.[60] Nevertheless, it

Table 4.8: Example of the individual district cremation rates in the northern region of Schwerin.

Districts	Deaths 1976	Cremations 1976	% Cremation 1976	Deaths 1977	Cremations 1977	% Cremation 1977
Schwerin-Stadt	1194	512	59.6	1157	714	61.7
Bützow	356	n/a	n/a	410	n/a	n/a
Gadebusch	320	31	9.7	324	28	8.6
Güstrow	942	139	14.8	898	155	17.3
Hagenow	964	75	7.8	975	66	6.7
Ludwigslust	893	100	11.2	817	103	12.6
Lübz	483	23	4.8	534	41	7.7
Parchim	519	55	10.6	449	33	7.3
Perleberg	1199	227	18.9	1157	199	17.2
Schwerin-Land	448	56	12.5	431	64	14.8
Sternberg	317	21	6.6	316	17	5.4
Entire Region	7635	1439	18.8	7470	1420	19.0

(Source: MLHA, RdB Schwerin, Abt. ÖVW, No. 36364)

is safe to assume that for about two-thirds of all deaths, cremation was chosen as the form of disposal. This stands in contrast to the figure for West Germany of around the 28 per cent mark. The GDR had achieved a high level of cremation, overcoming more than the West the regional particularism of its sepulchral culture. This, however, has misled some scholars who seem to take cremation rates as indicators for standard countrywide pattern.

In some instances in the GDR, there was not even choice as to which form of disposal was possible, since there was nobody to dig a grave. Distinct regional variations have to be the analytical point of departure. According to the 1985 figures, the last complete set available, these might be summarized as follows: Firstly, there is a north–south divide. The southern regions had a much higher rate of cremation (78.8 per cent) than the northern regions (33.1 per cent), and both were close to their 1980 target level. Several factors account for this latitudinal fault line. The south not only had the higher population and the greater number of crematoria, but could also lay claim being the traditional heartland of German cremation.

Moreover, the north saw a disproportionate influx of refugees, mainly from the lands east of the Oder-Neiße (with a strong sense of tradition). It also had a much lower urbanization and lacked a regular distribution of urban centres on the scale of Dresden or Leipzig.[61] Secondly, Berlin does not fit easily into the

Table 4.9: Distribution of cremation comparing north and south of the GDR in 1967.

Regions	Number of Crematorium	Cremations in %	Area covered by each Crematorium in km²	Cremations per Crematorium
Rostock	2	19.1	3,538	880
Schwerin	1	13.4	8,673	998
Neubrandenburg	–	–	–	–
Potsdam	3	12.3	4,188	613
Frankfurt/Oder	1	3.2	7,187	276
Cottbus	1	11.3	8,261	1,190
Magdeburg	1	17.7	11,527	3,196
7 Northern Regions	9	12.2	–	1,029
Halle	7	44.8	1,253	1,551
Erfurt	10	56.7	732	887
Gera	5	62.6	798	1,176
Suhl	8	58.3	485	489
Dresden	4	46.1	1,685	3,074
Leipzig	3	58.4	1,654	4,090
Karl-Marx-Stadt	6	50.9	1,003	2,499
7 Southern Regions	43	51.8	–	1,606
Berlin	1	64.0	403	11,012
GDR	53	39.5	–	1,685

(Data: Karl Thomas in an internal IfK report in 1968, as quoted in Frenz, *Entwicklung des Bestattungswesen*, 153)

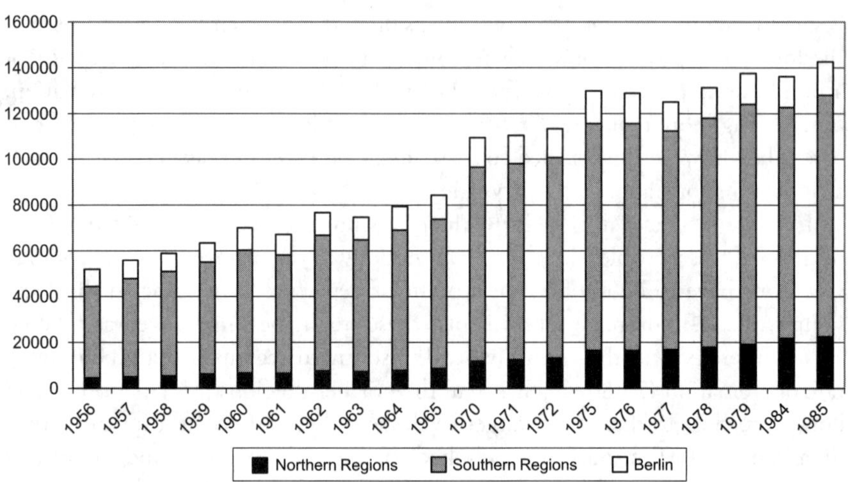

Graph 4.3 Regional distribution of the number of cremations in the GDR, 1956–1965, 1970–1972, 1975–1979, 1984–1985. The data do not allow for a continuous timeline.

(Data: see explanation, Graph 4.1)

north–south divide, having a high cremation rate, but the statistics suffer from certain abnormalities. The crematorium *Baumschulenweg* did not statistically discriminate between Berliners and those who were transported from outside the city. Furthermore, Potsdam and Teltow took some of Berlin's dead for cremation. A conservative estimate is that the cremation rate in Berlin was somewhere around 80 per cent, with the likelihood that it might have been even higher.[62] Thirdly, the north–south divide fails to capture highly significant regional and sub-regional variations.

Within the northern and southern regions, the general rates differed a lot from district to district. Table 4.8 and Table 4.10 vividly demonstrate the differences within each region.[63] Most striking is the observation that northern cities could have quite substantial cremation rates – more than 60 per cent. However, most rural districts in the north, like Lübz, showed a very low cremation rate indeed. Others, such as Bützow, registered cremations only on very rare occasions. Sadly, it is extremely difficult to find enough data to paint a detailed picture of cremation at such a local level. However, even in the south, especially in rural Catholic areas such as the Eichsfeld, or in special areas such as Niesky with a high Wend population (an ethnic minority with a conservative burial tradition), one finds that cremation rates remained well below the regional mean. In both cases, the propagation of cremation encountered the same inhibiting forces which the cremation movement had encountered in the decades before 1945. Independent of who or which institution had been advancing the ideal of cremation, the ultimate challenge had been to convince those making the decision on the form of disposal of the merits of cremation.

Table 4.10: Growth of cremations in the 25-year period between 1960 and 1985 in all GDR crematoria. In twenty crematoria new record levels of cremations were reached in 1985. Potsdam and Halle (3 months) had to close for some time in 1985.

Region	Crematorium	Growth of cremations until 1985 (1960=100)
Rostock	*Rostock*	305
	Greifswald	560
Schwerin	*Schwerin*	339
Potsdam	*Potsdam*	368*
	Brandenburg	281
	Fürstenberg	910
Frankfurt/Oder	*Frankfurt*	489
Cottbus	*Forst*	453
Magdeburg	*Magdeburg*	271
Halle	*Halle*	287*
	Bernburg	308
	Dessau	196
	Eisleben	256 **
	Quedlinburg	330
	Weißenfels	397
Erfurt	*Erfurt*	176
	Apolda	167
	Arnstadt	156
	Eisenach	153
	Gotha	143
	Langensalza	228
	Mühlhausen	169
	Nordhausen	279
	Sondershausen	366
	Weimar	182
Gera	*Gera*	114
	Jena	188
	Pößneck	123
	Saalfeld	398
Suhl	*Suhl*	169
	Eisfeld	130
	Hildburghausen	429
	Ilmenau	169
	Lauscha	145
	Meiningen	216
	Bad Salzungen	196
	Schmalkalden	148***
	Sonneberg	179
Dresden	*Dresden*	191
	Görlitz	181
	Meißen	282
	Zittau	244

Table 4.10: (continued).

Region	Crematorium	Growth of cremations until 1985 (1960=100)
Leipzig	*Leipzig*	151
	Altenburg	234
	Döbeln	344
Karl-Marx-Stadt	*Karl-Marx-Stadt*	207
	Plauen	155
	Reichenbach	325
	Zwickau	213
Berlin	*Berlin-Treptow*	149

*   comparison with 1984, not 1985

**   1965=100

*** 1970=100

(Data: BHSA Potsdam, Rep 601, No. 34043)

Ultimately, the propagation of cremation has left a lasting legacy. While initially after the unification cremation rates dropped substantially (e.g., to 54.7 per cent in 1993), they then rose very quickly to new heights. There is evidence that this decline mainly had technical causes: most East German cremation ovens need to be urgently replaced or repaired. In 1999, the five East German Länder together had a cremation rate of 75.3 per cent – a rate that meant that out of 160,988 corpses, a mere 39,784 were buried.[64] This leaves, in conclusion, two seemingly contradictory observations to be balanced: that the propagation of cremation lacked persistent and countrywide political commitment, especially when compared to the scope of change in the ČSSR; but that nonetheless the propagation of cremation had its successes, culminating in a high cremation rate, albeit with appreciable regional differences.

The propagation of a form of disposal to such an extent, especially without sustained and decisive interference by central governmental or party figures, highlights that sepulchral culture in Germany, be it East or West (where crema-tion rates were also highly regionally differentiated), remained primarily a local matter. In the GDR, the advancement of cremation as the preferred means of disposal operated on a local, district, or regional level. In the absence of a more coercive legal framework and the investments it advocated, the IfK, as the example of Rostock illustrates, functioned as a forum facilitating interaction and the exchange of ideas between those operating burial services and the crematoria. Ideological considerations can be found, but in the end, as any close study of the files of the *VEB Bestattungseinrichtungen Dresden* demonstrates, economic considerations dominated the day-to-day operation of these services. Amongst the tightening fiscal parameters and growing shortages of labour, the expan-sion of cremation was the best way to cut expenditure, as was the introduction of *Urnengemeinschaftsanlagen* (UGAs). Both were, at least to a certain extent, expressions of turning towards an industrial (i.e., efficient) process to help overcome the strains of organizing the task of disposing the dead of a modern society in an acceptable manner. This explains both the apparent discrepancy between the reality of socialist sepulchral culture (including the often astonishing utopianism put forth by some publications) on the one hand, and the managerialist practice on the other. One of the most striking examples is quoted by Barbara Happe at the beginning of an essay on the *Urnengemeinschaftsanlage*:

> Perhaps the task of cemetery reform will first be fulfilled when we again have a cemetery without graves as a form of 'Grove of Death' [*Totenhain*] in the middle of our settlements.[65]

Bold visions such as this these might not reveal the potential of Marxist-materialist sepulchral reform, but they do reveal an ideal. The reality looked quite different. Ideological coherence played an important role in making cremation attractive as a socialist form of disposal, but here as elsewhere the day-to-day operation was governed by more mundane thoughts and limitations. The propagation of cremation within the socialist framework of the GDR certainly changed East German sepulchral culture. It influenced and helped the formation of novel rituals and shaped new elements in cemetery design, but it did not do so to the radical degree that it aspired to or that has been portrayed after 1990. The main reason for this can be found in the observation that the organization of systems of disposal that do not operate within a free market economy (i.e., that are entirely driven by the balance between the wishes of customers and the creation of profit, and even those still have a marked propensity towards cremation) have tended to become the realm of technocratic agents, more often than not setting their own agenda.[66] In the GDR, it seems fair to argue, this agenda was the orderly disposal of the dead; due to its planned economy, this already represented first and foremost a dramatic organizational challenge in which cremation proved the most efficient solution. The fact that it could easily be fitted into a framework of socialist ideals was merely secondary. In addition, there is a deeper factor that is difficult to quantify. This factor is best described as the persistence of the 'long durée' in the form of German particularism having a tangible impact on patterns of everyday life regarding practice, beliefs and customs.[67]

Notes

1. StA Greifswald, Rep. 7.9., No. 287: *Arbeitskreis Friedhof- und Bestattungswesen, Niederschrift über den Erfahrungsaustausch für Heizer*, 22 September 1961, 3.
2. Prothero, *Purified by Fire*, 9.

3. One of the most striking examples of this politicization can be found in the May 1933 edition of the *Zentralblatt für Feuerbestattung*, in which the President of the *Großdeutschen Verband der Feuerbestattungsvereine* wrote an editorial titled: *Der Großdeutsche Verband und Deutschlands Erwachen*, followed by a number of ideologically charged articles. THSA Weimar, Thüringischen Ministeriums des Inneren, E 1551.

4. The most common exceptions can be found in areas such as Gotha or Jena, where one finds exceptionally high rates of cremation as early as 1910; this suggests that in those places the choice of cremation as a means of disposal was less an expression of an individual agenda and more the result of an agenda that saw the widespread promotion of cremation as a move towards progress.

5. What Julie Rugg describes as the appropriation of elements of death rituals by an elite: 'The theme of the ownership and management of the corpse in the twentieth century can be interpreted in terms of a Foucauldian appropriation of the body by the professional elite. The elite defined a set of exclusionary activities around the corpse, undermining traditional practice and introducing ostensibly "technical" and specialized tasks that in turn defined the professional status of the elite actors': Rugg, 'Lawn Cemeteries', 226; see also: G. Howarth, 'Undertakers', in G. Howarth and O. Leaman (eds), *Encyclopaedia of Death and Dying* (London: Routledge, 2001).

6. This becomes very clear reading the literature of city planning (*Städtebau*) from 1910 onwards. It is also clearly reflected in the documents that refer to the construction of new crematoria after 1920. StA Bielefeld, Akte FW 152–54 (*Krematorium Sennefriedhof Vol. I – III*); N. Fischer, 'Die Einführung der modernen Feuerbestattung im späten 19. Jahrhundert', in AFD (ed.), *Die Geschichte der Friedhöfe*, 151–58.

7. For the GDR see: StA Rostock, Rep. 2.2.8, No. 12: *Befragungsschema, Anlage F/B 2-77*, 1.

8. StA Greifswald, Rep. 7.9., No. 287: *Arbeitskreis Friedhof- und Bestattungswesen, Niederschrift über den Erfahrungsaustausch für Heizer*, 22 September 1961, 3.

9. One needs to be careful not to overstate the importance of religious affiliation where cremation is concerned. The factors are difficult to generalize: two of the lowest cremation rates are not found in south German cities, but in Krefeld and in Bielefeld, both with fairly long-established crematoria but different religious affiliations – while the former is largely Catholic, the latter city is largely Protestant. Nonetheless cremation rates in both cities were as low as 23.3 per cent and 27.4 per cent respectively (1999). Thus the two cities have a cremation rate well below the West German average of 31.8 per cent (overall national average of 40.1 per cent, East German average: 75.3 per cent). See: Deutsche Städtetag, *Presseinformation*, 17 May 2001, available at <http://www.bestatter.de/dh/04/feuerbestattung_99.html> (accessed 10 June 2003).

10. The main argument is that a multitude of groundbreaking decisions and developments took place chiefly in Italy, France, Britain and especially Germany, before it spread to other European countries (especially Protestant countries such as Denmark, Sweden and later of course to the USSR and Czechoslovakia) and to the United States. There, German publications and immigrants were instrumental in setting up cremationist movements in the US. See: Prothero, *Purified by Fire*, 138.

11. BLHA Potsdam, Rep. 401, RdB Potsdam, No. 21780: *Eröffnungsrede zum Erfahrungsaustausch*, ca. 1979, 5.

12. For example: P. Frenz, *Die historische und gesellschaftliche Entwicklung des Bestattungswesen unter der Berücksichtigung der aktuellen Situation in der DDR*, PhD Thesis Martin-Luther-Universität Halle-Wittenberg, 1979, 57–70.

13. 'We can establish that the choice of the forms of disposal reflects the prevailing level of the development of human society and often depends on the mystic and religious belief, which in different cultures and religions were, and still are, essentially determined by death, by the meaning of life and by the continuation of life after death': BLHA Potsdam, Rep. 401, RdB Potsdam, No. 21780: *Eröffnungsrede zum Erfahrungsaustausch*, ca. 1979, 8.

14. BLHA Potsdam, Rep. 401, RdB Potsdam, No. 21780: *Eröffnungsrede zum Erfahrungsaustausch*, ca. 1979, 6–7. Despite the naturalness of decomposition, the naturalness of cremation is a factor that is often used as an argument in favour of cremation. Presumably, naturalness here is seen in a historical rather than a biological light.
15. BLHA Potsdam, Rep. 401, RdB, No. 21780, *Eröffnungsrede zur Rednerweiterbildung*, ca. 1976, 11.
16. J.-C. Kaiser, *Arbeiterbewegung und Religionskritik – Proletarische Freidenkerverbände in Kaiserreich und Weimarer Republik* (Stuttgart: Klett-Cotta, 1981).
17. Friedrich, *Der Brand*, 431; Behring, 'Das Kriegsende', in Vollhals (ed.), *Sachsen in der NS-Zeit*, 227.
18. For a brief description see: Fischer, *Vom Gottesacker zum Krematorium*, 125–28. Fischer makes a case for the use of cremation under National Socialism, as the ultimate expression of a '*Technologisierung*' of death, while omitting many of its implications for post-war policy and attitudes. The radical change in the architecture of crematoria built after 1945 and the general tendency, throughout Europe, to return, at least publicly, to traditional nineteenth-century rationales with regard to cremation – with their clear emphasis on aesthetic, economic and hygienic advantages – suggest a rather larger trauma. One of the few references to Auschwitz can actually be found in the exchanges between East German and Czech cremation specialists, in which it is noted that the legacy was making the propagation of cremation very difficult: see BA Berlin, DO 4, No. 891: *Bericht über Erfahrungsaustausch mit der Delegation von Freuden der Feuerbestattung aus der ČSSR und Vertretern einiger Krematorien der DDR*, 3. For a European perspective of the architecture of crematoria see: '*Friedhöfe-Krematorien*', in *AW – Architektur und Wettbewerbe*, No. 192, December 2002.
19. Frenz, *Entwicklung des Bestattungswesen*, 67–68.
20. Once more, this is reflected in the architecture of many crematoria. Beginning in the 1920s, their style was increasingly inspired by industrial buildings – the chimney no longer being entirely hidden. Ultimately, in the (re-)construction of crematoria in recent years, such as in Halle, Kassel or Chemnitz, stainless steel chimneys have become highly visible signifiers of crematoria's technological angle. In Kassel (2001) this is amplified by the installation of lights that at night suggest a flickering of fire coming from within the building.
21. Frenz, *Entwicklung des Bestattungswesen*, 68.
22. BA Berlin, DO 4, No. 892: *Prognose für die Entwicklung des Friedhofs- und Bestattungswesens*, 10 April 1969, 15.
23. 'The development of cremation was first fostered by the trade unions, who deliberately resisted church dogmas. But in recent decades [cremation] has been left to itself': BA Berlin, DO 4, No. 892: *Prognose*, 10 April 1969, 15.
24. Altenburg, and the role of its director in the *Arbeitsgruppe Friedhof- und Bestattungswesen*, is a good example of how individual ideas can serve as an example to be emulated.
25. VLA Geifswald, Rep. 200, 7.1, No. 189, f. 28: *Protokoll über die 3. Arbeitstagung vom 11.–14. Juni 1958*, 2. In 1960 the average monthly income of a worker was 555 Mark, see *Statistische Jahrbuch der DDR 1989* – Lohnentwicklung.
26. VLA Greifswald, Rep. 200, 7.1, No. 189, f. 29: *Protokoll*, 3.
27. Helmut Kluge went on to publish a number of papers for the IfK, such as the seventh chapter of: IfK, *Gestaltung unserer Friedhöfe*.
28. 'In the initial years the neglect of the cemetery and burial service through the institutions of state was typical for the GDR': Groschopp, 'Weltliche Trauerkultur in der DDR', 109.
29. Redlin, J., *Gegenwärtige großstädtische Bestattungsriten – eine empirische Untersuchung in der Hauptstadt der DDR* (Belegarbeit im Fach Ethnologie Humboldt Universität, 1985), 14.
30. For a modern analogy, see developments in France post 1980 in C. Behrens, 'Kremation im internationalen Kontext und am Beispiel Frankreichs', *Ohlsdorf – Zeitschrift für Trauerkultur*, 83:4 (2003).
31. The burial acts of 1846 and 1850, being direct answers to the shortcomings of the disposal system in times of crises, are good example of urban areas being at the forefront of sepulchral

change. Compare this also to the growth of cremation in urban China and Hong Kong: for example early indications of the potential scope in F. Lisowski, 'The Practice of Cremation in China', *Eastern Horizon*, 19:6 (1980), 21–24.

32. K. Feldmann, *Sterben und Tod – Sozialwissenschaftliche Theorien und Forschungsergebnisse* (Opladen: Leske + Budrich, 1997), 47.

33. 'The two countries referred to [UK and ČSSR] present above all through state controlled measures (construction of crematoria, pricing) a far stronger increase [of cremations]…': BA Berlin, DO 4, No. 892: *Prognose*, 10.04.1969, 16. See also P. Jupp, 'Cremation or Burial? Contemporary Choice in City and Village', in D. Clark (ed.), *Sociology of Death: Theory, Culture, Practise* (Oxford: Blackwell, 1995), 169–97.

34. 'The growth of cremation in the UK has meant that existing cemeteries have continued to be available to the diminishing number of people who wished to use them. It was suggested to us that further promotion of cremation as an option for the disposal of the dead would be the best means of avoiding the problem of the availability of space for burial. We do not agree, however, that further promotion of cremation is desirable. Indeed, it is doubtful whether it is even possible. Current trends indicate a levelling-out of cremation rates in recent years at around 72 per cent. Witnesses argued that it was difficult to see what more could be done to promote cremation as an option. Dr Tony Walter, an author and reader in sociology at the University of Reading, told us "Cremation has been actively promoted in Britain for over 100 years and active promotion has been continuing throughout that 100 years. If you look at the graph it was going up throughout the middle of the century and then it has tapered off. I am not quite sure what extra propaganda in favour of cremation one could produce." It seems likely that there will always be a significant minority who will wish to be buried. To pressure the bereaved into considering cremation instead of burial would be to deny them the choice to which we believe they are entitled.' See HMSO, *Select Committee on Environment, Transport and Regional Affairs, Eighth Report (2001)*, section 14–16: available at <http://www.parliament. the-stationery-office.co.uk/pa/cm200001/cmselect/cmenvtra/91/9102.htm> (accessed 10 June 2004).

35. 'Because of a lack of guidance by the state, repairs [Reconstructions in GDR German] and building new crematoria was left in the hands of the local administration': Redlin, *Gegenwärtige großstädtische Bestattungsriten*, 14.

36. The optimum capacity for the Crematorium Baumschulenweg was 11,250, but in 1970 it already had to cope with 12,600 cremations. This, according to one report, resulted in a higher possibility of breakdowns. LA Berlin, C Rep. 104, No. 607: *Magistratsvorlage No. 60/71 – Konzeption zur Stabilisierung der Lage im Berliner Friedhofs- und Bestattungswesen*, 22 February 1971, 2.

37. BA Berlin, DO 4, No. 892: *Prognose*, 10 April 1969, 15.

38. The 1963 edition of the IfK's design manual for cemetery devotes three pages to the propagation of cremation and UGAs, chiefly on the basis of economic reasons. See: IfK, *Gestaltung unserer Friedhöfe*, 74–77.

39. The standard measure for a crematorium with three ovens; two in use one in reserve or repair: two shifts (operating time: 06.00–22.00, Mon–Fri) 30 cremations per day (+8 Saturday), 158 per week, max. 7,900 a year; or 3 shifts (24 hours): 48 cremations per day (+12 Saturday), 252 per week, max. 12,600 per year. In 1980 Dresden had reached 44 cremations per day, in two shifts, amounting to 10,656: StA Dresden, Rep. 9.1.14, No. 373.

40. BA Berlin, DO 4, No. 892: *Prognose*, 10 April 1969, 15.

41. Ibid., 20.

42. 'While a number of the crematoria still operate with coal and coke without sanitary equipment [i.e., filters], and inadequate heating possibilities for staff and visitors, oil and gas powered or electric ovens have become a matter of course in the most advanced countries (UK, Japan, Sweden, US), or rather fully mechanical ovens will become operational (ČSSR, USSR). The GDR-type until now deemed efficient in operation and handling … thus can be described as

obsolete also in comparison with socialist countries': BA Berlin, DO 4, No. 892: *Prognose*, 10 April 1969, 22–23.

43. See for example documentation of repairs in: StA Dresden, Rep. 9.1.14, No. 373.

44. The very first reference to Czech material with regard to sepulchral culture that I found was a 1960 translation of material on Czech secular ceremonies and their organization.

45. BA Berlin, DO 4, No. 891: *Bericht über Erfahrungsaustausch mit der Delegation von Freuden der Feuerbestattung aus der ČSSR und Vertretern einiger Krematorien der DDR*, 2.

46. StA Dresden, Rep. 9.1.14, No. 205: *Bericht über die Studienergebnisse der Delegation des IfK in die CSSR*, 9–10.

47. StA Dresden, Rep. 9.1.14, No. 205: *Bericht über die Studienergebnisse*, 31.

48. 'Trends in der Feuerbestattung', *Das Bestattungsgewerbe*, No. 9, 1986, 345.

49. StA Dresden, Rep. 9.1.14, No. 137: *Rednerweiterbildung – Vortrag Herr Kramer*, 1 November 1989.

50. 'As was unambiguously stated in the prognosis for the Development of Cemetery and Burial Services, 1968/69, cremation alone allows for the orderly disposal of all deceased': K. Thomas, IfK Archiv, Sig 44, 30, as quoted in Happe, 'Die Sozialistische Reform', in Sörries (ed.), *Vom Reichsausschuß zur Arbeitsgemeinschaft Friedhof und Denkmal*, 194–95.

51. BA Berlin, DO 4, No. 892: *Prognose*, 10 April 1969, 36.

52. Grufman and Ingemark, *Feuerbestattung und Friedhofswesen in der DDR*, 8.

53. 'Furthermore, cremation is an economically advantageous form of disposal, since cremation requires much less space and since it necessitates less expenditure of human labour in order to prepare the burial site. In the design of cemeteries, we are aiming therefore for urn fields and anonymous mass urn fields': BLHA Potsdam, Rep. 401, RdB, No. 21780: *Eröffnungsrede zur Rednerweiterbildung*, ca. 1976, 11.

54. There had been some disquiet about this decision, but ultimately very few complaints can be found. In many ways this seems to represent a parallel to the very prescriptive West German cemetery ordinances and state laws that have insisted on the entombment of cremains. Both were taken as given, in short rules that warranted very little comment, and receiving any widespread criticism only as late as 2003. See for example the 2 February 2004 ruling of: VGH Neustadt an der Weinstrasse, 1K 2258/03.NW.

55. Grufman and Ingemark, *Feuerbestattung und Friedhofswesen in der DDR*, 3–4.

56. StA Rostock, Rep. 2.2.8, No. 12: *Befragungsschema, Anlage F/B 2-77*, 1; or quoted with minor alterations in IfK, *Dienstleistungen im Bestattungswesen* (Dresden: IfK, 1979), 51. See StA Dresden, Rep. 9.1.14, No. 1828.

57. StA Rostock, Rep. 2.2.8, No. 12: *Befragungsschema, Anlage F/B 2-77*, 1.

58. IfK, *Dienstleistungen im Bestattungswesen*, 51.

59. See for example: R. Schwarz, 'Aktive Einflußnahme in Leipzig – Wettbewerb zur Steigerung der Feuerbestattung', *Informationen aus der Praxis für die Praxis*, No. 3–4 (1970), 30.

60. Equally there are no reliable post-reunification figures for the new Länder until 1993.

61. A very good explanation for the distinct differences between the north and the south is given in another of Karl Thomas' analysis: 'Besides the unbalanced distribution of crematoria and size of available cemetery space which is in general still adequate, the cause for the lagging behind [of the northern regions] is attributable to the traditional beliefs of the population. Aside from this, the economic repercussions of cremation on the burial services do still play an important role, inasmuch as the macroeconomic [as in Volkswirtschaft] gains in efficiency are much higher for cremation than those for inhumation, but in the case of rising rates of cremation the individual burial service has to deal with falling revenues. The advantages of cremation outnumber the disadvantages (considerable savings in the space needed, utterly minimal need for personnel for disposal and cemetery services, and the most advantageous form of disposal with regard to municipal hygiene), but in general they cannot be offset by the considerable transport costs that are incurred through the transportation of individual corpses to the crematorium.' In MLHA Schwerin, RdB Schwerin, Abt. ÖVW, No. 36364, K. Thomas, *Analyse der Krematorien in den Nordbezirken der DDR*, 15 September, 1976, 2.

62. The last reliable figure is 74.9 per cent for 1985. For 1991 the cremation rate for the unified Berlin was 71.7 per cent, in 2002 it was 75.8 per cent. *Pressemitteilung 210/03 vom 18.9.2003*, Statistisches Landesamt Berlin.
63. These district figures tend to be the most reliable figures that are available, if they can be found. Unlike the figures of the crematoria they included only those who had lived in the district.
64. Deutsche Städtetag, *Presseinformation*, 17 May 2001.
65. H. Keller, 'Möglichkeiten zur Ermittlung des Friedhofsflächenbedarf', Belegarbeit Humboldt Universität Berlin, Sektion Pflanzenproduktion, Abteilung Freiflächengestaltung Dessau, 40, as quoted in Happe, 'Die sozialistische Reform', in Sörries (ed.), *Vom Reichsauschuß zur Arbeitsgemeinschaft Friedhof und Denkmal*, 185.
66. It is telling that many countries with high cremation rates have at least locally such closed systems of disposal, for example Sweden – Stockholm or Switzerland – Bern, while on the other hand the US, one of the most unregulated markets for funeral services, had for the longest time a very low cremation rate.
67. The best example that I encountered is the custom on many Baltic coast cemeteries to incorporate benches on the grave plots. To the best of my knowledge this was a custom that seems to have migrated westwards with the influx of Eastern refugees after 1945.

Chapter 5

THE COMMUNAL BURIAL OF ASHES
'NEW' SPACES FOR DISPOSAL

With few exceptions the German cemetery before 1870 had been a space dominated by individual and family graves. The subsequent experience of social change caused by industrialization and urbanization, as well as by the major conflicts in the twentieth century, was accompanied by a number of transformations in the cemetery landscape. Many cemeteries, especially urban ones, saw a transition in the use of space. This shift was not away from the private as such, defined by the predominant functions of burial and the tribute of friends and family, but it was overlaid with a perceptible increase in public commemoration.[1] Large park-like landscaped cemeteries were increasingly adopted as the locations for diverse sites of commemoration. The maps that are displayed near the main entrances of any larger German cemeteries testify to the proliferation of commemorative spaces. These spaces, normally prominently located (near the entrance, in the middle, or beside the main paths), are dedicated to a specific subject group, such as the many different victims of warfare, political upheaval, or National Socialism.[2] These places, like the socialist fields of honour, differ in their nature from the surrounding graves (and the traditional churchyard), since they were created as spaces bearing witness to losses that assumed significance beyond the personal sphere. The personal sphere is of course not excluded, but these spaces were designed primarily to facilitate public acts of commemoration and foster collectivism – as most clearly indicated by the provision of space for ceremonies.[3] In this regard they share some similarities with another space, namely that of mass burial sites such as the *Urnengemeinschaftsanlage* (anonymous communal area for the internment of urns, or UGA).[4] Not only is the UGA regularly highlighted on the same cemetery maps as a distinct space apart from the traditional family and individual grave plots, but both the UGA and these other communal spaces often wrestle with similar problems such as sacrosanctity and how they, in contemporary society, address the issue of commemoration.[5]

The layout of the *Hauptfriedhof* of Sondershausen, which was opened in 1889 and extends over an area of just under four hectares, can stand as a typical example for the relationship between these spaces in many East German cemeteries. Down the tree-lined main avenue that extends all the way from the main entrance and past the crematorium (opened in 1930), and past the 1970s ceremonial hall on the left, there is the heroes' grove (*Ehrenhain*) for the victims of war and behind it the well-tended lawns of the UGA. It is not only in its location that the UGA in Sondershausen is quite representative. The design too follows convention. Lawn areas covering the buried urns are framed by surrounding trees and shrubbery, paths separate different fields and to the side is a paved area for ceremonies. There are also designated areas for laying down wreaths or placing flowers. Nearer to the main path stand a number of benches for those seeking contemplation or rest. As a space for burial this represents the antithesis to the conventional burial plot. This became even clearer when in 1993 a central memorial was installed. Most UGAs had a central memorial. The smaller ones were often inscribed with the term '*Urnengemeinschaft*'.

The larger UGAs had specifically commissioned sculptures, either abstract or artistic – such as a bronze snake spouting water into a stone basin – to underline the communality of the space and following a number of design guidelines.[6] However, the central memorial as a feature underlined the special status of the UGA, especially in contrast to the normal burial plots. The official IfK definition of an *Urnengemeinschaftsanlage* underlines both its special location as well as its defining characteristics, but the definition also hints at the reason why the concept of anonymous mass burials of urns was to acquire such a prominent role within the sepulchral culture of the GDR:

> Special burial site situated in an urn field (*Urnenfeld*) or in a special grave field in a favoured position, emphasized through representative garden design, designated for the communal burial of larger numbers of urns (16–25 urns per m²) with a central memorial.
> Characteristics and Conditions:
> Burial of urns with or without a communal ceremony, but no individual burials.
> The precise position of the urn is not known to the bereaved, names do not appear on the memorials.
> Laying down of wreaths by the bereaved is always possible on the designated areas.
> Removal of urns is not possible, the reuse of the sites is not recommended.[7]

This definition describes the idealized version of the UGA, but crucially it stresses the prominent location and the representative design that were to mark the role of the UGA in the GDR.

By 1985 around one hundred and forty UGAs had been opened in cemeteries throughout the GDR.[8] One year later the first ash-scattering field (*Aschestreuwiese*)

Figure 5.1 A smaller UGA in Halle/Saale.

became operational in Rostock.[9] Additionally, there was another rare form of burial in some cities, the anonymous and communal burial of cremains without an urn or any holding vessel in an *Aschengemeinschaftsanlage*. All these developments, even though the latter two remained rare, indicate that 'new' forms of disposal had evolved. Karl Thomas, one of the leading IfK officials, had, amongst others, called for their introduction and subsequent propagation as early as the 1960s on the grounds of reducing cemetery space and labour costs.[10] All three more radical forms of disposal – in the sense of breaking with convention – became the cornerstones of Thomas's prognosis of the future challenges and the potential crisis of the sepulchral culture of the GDR:

> If the ashes are buried [collectively] the cemetery space needed for burial is reduced by circa 66 per cent. Accordingly all efforts to introduce new forms of disposal, such as *Urnengemeinschaftsanlagen* and the scattering of ashes – as they are also generally promoted in capitalist countries – should be further promoted in order to solve the problem of disposal.[11]

The rise in the number of UGAs, therefore, coincided with cremation becoming the predominant choice for disposal throughout the early 1970s. This emphasizes the point that UGAs were not meant as a new form of disposal to be introduced in every cemetery – UGAs only make economic sense when a minimum of twenty burials a year could be sustained (thereby making UGAs rare in rural cemeteries).[12] They were part of an attempt to create a centralized system of disposal that largely utilized cremation and the UGA as the most efficient means to dispose of ashes.[13] Consequently, Karl Thomas, in a second position paper of 1970, was positively alarmist about the impending strains on the system of disposal, and again the anonymous communal area for the internment of urns or UGA was the foremost solution advocated by the IfK.[14] The introduction of the model cemetery regulation (1967) and the model work regulation (1973) played a significant role, as their adoption by the municipal cemeteries and burial services added impetus and professional clout to the dissemination of collective forms of burial.[15] When it came to the *Gemeinschaftsanlage*, the authors of the 1980 edition of the main IfK publication on cemetery design rightly pointed to the importance of regulations in influencing future developments and the clear dominance of cremation in most urban centres:

> In these regulations space is also given to the new developments in our cemetery spaces. *Urnengemeinschaftsanlagen* and other collective forms of burial are emphasized and their promotion deliberately prioritized … There is no doubt that in future the overall appearance of the municipal cemeteries will be ever more marked by the presence of urn graves, *Urnengemeinschaftsanlagen* and other similar forms of burial that are closely linked with cremation.[16]

This analysis is essentially correct, and while the figure of 140 UGAs might appear low given that there were 7,565 municipalities and about ten thousand cemeteries in the GDR, *Urnengemeinschaftsanlagen* not only occupied prominent positions in these 140 cemeteries, they were also used for a very significant overall number of burials. Since most UGAs were established in urban cemeteries, and thus served large communities with higher cremation rates, the number of buried urns was often considerable. For example, by 1989 around 40,000 urns alone were buried in one of the largest UGAs on the *Heidefriedhof* in Dresden.[17] Moreover, by 1993 the full capacity of fifty thousand urns had been reached (despite the initial post-reunification slump in the cremation rate). The site was closed and a new UGA opened.[18] Dresden in many ways was an exception, as not all UGAs were that large, but one can safely assume that most sites were designed for more than ten thousand urns and for long periods over which burials could take place (generally more than twenty years).[19] By the 1980s most experts considered the ideal, but an ultimately achievable one, to be for any UGA to absorb about 50 per cent of all cremations (thus catering for about 30–35 per cent of all burials).[20] The southern cities of the GDR, with their strong tradition of cremation and their municipal burial services providing free burials, saw even higher rates of adoption than this target. In some cities burial in a UGA became by far the most common form of burial. In Plauen, for example, 71 per cent of all burials took place in a UGA, while it was 61 per cent in Weida, and 55 per cent in Erfurt and Altenburg. Chemnitz, Jena and Zwickau achieved a rate of 40 per cent, which, in combination with orthodox urn burial, must have made it the most common form of burial, while Dresden with a rate of 39 per cent was close behind.

In the north, rates did not exceed 30 per cent; Stralsund had one of the highest rates with 29 per cent. Other cities such as Frankfurt/Oder (23 per cent), Rostock (22 per cent), Greifswald (21 per cent) and Wismar (17 per cent) all remained beneath the 30 per cent threshold.[21] The organization of the burial service and general acceptance of cremation played a crucial role. Dresden and Altenburg, for example, served as models for how to municipalize burial services, and Jena was one of the first cities to achieve a cremation rate of over 90 per cent. However, there is also another factor: this specific form of burial, like cremation, required time to lay down its own traditions and to take root. The first UGA of the city of Jena (famous for its very high cremation rate) had been established in 1966 and in the first five years attracted 750 burials in special cardboard urns.[22] By 1971 only about 10 per cent of burials in Jena were conducted in the UGA. This hints very strongly at the resistance against anonymous burials despite a high rate of cremation. It thus reveals that a more thorough introduction of this form of disposal required a different set of factors.

The *Urnengemeinschaftsanlage* of the *Neue Friedhof* Karl-Marx-Stadt (Chemnitz) underlines this point poignantly, inasmuch as it was one of the largest cities, with over 300,000 inhabitants that had introduced free funerals for its citizens in the 1920s – most of which had then been cremations.[23] Moreover, in the early 1930s anonymous urn grave fields had existed in Chemnitz, and a second one in Leipzig, which means that these were some of the oldest modern anonymous communal graves in Germany. Therefore, in Karl-Marx-Stadt a high cremation rate and a tradition of anonymous burial combined with policies of the cemetery administration to make UGAs attractive. That conjuncture allowed for a swifter introduction and is also clearly reflected in the radical appearance of the UGA. The communal grave space occupies a considerable area in the northwestern corner of the cemetery and has some unique features. The whole site is divided into strips of land, which are intersected by narrow rows of bushes which separate different sections. These intersections separate the different years in which the deaths occurred, so, for example, the first section covers the years from 1948 to 1953. After 1956 (coinciding with stronger anti-church propaganda), each section – roughly the same size – covers one year, each similarly sized signed to a particular year, with additional markings for each month, engraved in the first row of concrete slabs that form the area that is provided for mourners to place flowers or wreaths. This offers the public a timeline to locate their dead.

Before 1990 there was no central memorial. All that marked the rows of grass areas were black flat headstones (*Kissensteine*) inscribed with the phrase *Urnengemeinschaftsgrab* (communal urn grave) and the respective year.

The first German UGA had been built in the cemetery of Magdeburg in December 1925, and proved so popular that a second one was opened there in July 1930. Unlike the identical above-ground urn cemeteries (*Aschegrabanlagen*) of Hamburg-Ohlsdorf, Jena, or Dresden-Tolkewitz that were built in the 1920s and had been inspired by an architecture that was seeking uniformity and order, the Magdeburg site, besides burying urns underground, omitted all references to

Figure 5.2 The UGA Chemnitz, with the timeline built in. The inscribed stones can be seen under the bushes and, embedded in the pavement, the month.

Figure 5.3 Chemnitz UGA marker that denotes the year of burial.

names and dates in favour of a central memorial. In order further to differentiate it from the *Aschegrabanlagen*, the site was referred to as an *Urnenhain* (a phrase used here despite its real meaning of 'urn grove' because it suggested an enclosure). The freethinkers, who had initiated its construction and bestowed it with the official title, decided on the portentous: *Neue Deutsche Bestattungsklasse* (new German burial class).[24] This term made a radical break with the convention of a specific and marked grave plot. Most surprisingly, even for its advocates, it proved popular, not least because it embraced modernity, efficiency and, most importantly, the ideal of communality.[25] Furthermore, it did so at a time when the memories of the mass graves and anonymous graves of the Great War were very vivid.[26]

For those attempting to steer sepulchral culture, such as the IfK and individual cemetery administrations, the UGA represented the same ideal as it had to the freethinkers, and this led to its increased propagation during the 1970s. Moreover, the UGA began to serve as the embodiment of the merger of economic efficiency and progressive socialist thought. The opening of the first UGA in the northern city of Rostock in 1977 offers an ideal backdrop against which these specific motivations can be studied.

> The citizens of our city should be able to commemorate their dead in well-tended and harmonious surroundings. On the other hand they should also recognize that individualistic tendencies adopted from the capitalist past are alien to our socialist society, and that those [tendencies] are being counteracted through suitable measures.[27]

This argument preceded the introduction in the extensive documentation that suggests a need to sway the local political will. The two key policies to overcome the 'capitalist' character of sepulchral culture were the campaign for cremation and the propagation of the communal burial of the cremains.[28]

Previously, similar charges of 'individualistic tendencies' had been expressed in relation to hierarchical and thus capitalist features of cemeteries. Whilst uniformity, for example in plot layout and gravestone design, was seen as a suitable remedy in the short term, the UGA represented the long-term solution. The idea of an anonymous communal burial site for urns rejected not only extreme expression of individual identity but of individuality *per se*. This thus helped in the process that, according to the East German psychiatrist Gabriele Brunnemann, laid the foundations of the Marxist reaction to death:

> For this foundation [high level of social provision] has been laid in our country. Through the accumulation of quantities a new quality of 'man' could develop here. Because in a socialist system man no longer needs to be the enemy of the other for economic reasons (profit) …
>
> For based on the economic foundation of our society we can nurture our second side, to be 'good and show solidarity', and from that gain security, which counters anxiety.[29]

The UGA thus serves as a vehicle to foster some of this solidarity and security (as in *Geborgenheit*) in the form of a community of bereaved and deceased.[30]

Figure 5.4 The first Urnengemeinschaftsanlage *Westfriedhof* Rostock. The inscription reads: 'What would life be without death, it would lose its uniqueness and its preciousness.'

Moreover, it extends to bereavement and commemoration by taking the Marxist-Leninist interpretation of death to its logical conclusion.[31] If death is only imbued with any meaning by an accomplished life, then commemoration only gains any meaning if the accomplishments of life are collectively appreciated.[32] Furthermore, if one cannot argue that there is no afterlife, then one solution is to incorporate the dead, since in the strictest socialist interpretation, it is mainly through the community (of the dead and the living) that the dead are truly honoured:

> Communality, even in the time of bereavement, the collective honouring of the dead, and their commemoration independent of all religious affiliations or *Weltanschauung*, are expressions of our socialist society. Burial in an *Urnengemeinschaftsanlage* is such a form of disposal that emphasizes the communal.[33]

Consequently, only a collective commemoration after burial in a communal burial site constitutes the ideal socialist sepulchral culture.

However, anonymous burials have by no means been limited to socialist countries (such as Czechoslovakia). West Germany, the Scandinavian countries (e.g., Copenhagen, 80 per cent), the Netherlands and Britain also had a growing tradition of anonymous and communal grave fields (as well as ash scattering,

Figure 5.5 The second UGA in Rostock, with its enigmatic central memorial, representing one of the trends in the GDR central memorial of UGAs.

mainly due to their liberal tradition and lack of legislation on what can be done with the dead).[34] Towards the end of the twentieth century anonymous burial has found increased acceptance as a means of avoiding the placement of any burden (financial or temporal for the tending graves) on one's family after one's death, or as a conscious act negating a materialist world.[35]

Nonetheless, despite the impression conveyed by the rigid definition of the UGA quoted above, there were stark variations in the degree of anonymity really achieved. The reason for this can be found in the municipal rules governing UGAs, and especially the greater variety of ceremonies during which the urns were buried.[36] Some cities ruled that ceremonies had to be conducted in such a way that the exact location of the urn should not be revealed to those attending the funeral. This precluded any individual ceremony ending with the urn being lowered into the UGA in the presence of the attending guests. In Chemnitz, the funeral took place in the ceremonial hall, and finally an employee of the crematorium (*Urnenbeisetzer*) would step up and ceremoniously remove the urn, carrying it down the main aisle. It was then buried before the assembled friends and family walked over to the UGA in order to say their final farewells. Alternatively, there was the option of a communal ceremony (*Urnengemeinschaftsfeier*). This specific form of ceremony was unique to the GDR and accorded with the concept of collectively shared grief and anonymity. It required a waiting period until a specified number of urns had been buried, and only then was a ceremony organized that would honour all the deceased collectively.[37] In this case, after an official ceremony (rather than a personalized one) in the largest ceremonial hall, all attending people would walk to the UGA and lay down their wreaths and collectively remember the dead, while the urns had been buried beforehand.

Not all cities offered such communal ceremonies; for example Berlin had no provision of this kind.[38] What was offered was a choice of ceremonies according to the number of people attending. In most cases all ceremonies ended with a committal ritual for the urn (in the same way as in the case of Charlotte Ulbricht). The reason for this can be found in the way the IfK advised burial services to determine the specifics of the ceremonial while considering tradition, local peculiarities, and the local infrastructure, and to adapt accordingly.[39] In Rostock, therefore, the official guidelines specifically stressed the similarities with the traditional funeral ceremony, arguing that the only difference was that instead of a coffin an urn were used.[40] As one option, many cemeteries, like Rostock, offered a burial without a ceremony (*Beisetzungshandlung ohne Feier*), which is a misleading phrase as its main feature was the exclusion of a personal eulogy. Otherwise even this urn burial ceremony, exclusively used for UGAs, still included many elements that linked it clearly to the traditional funeral ceremony liturgy:

> When the funeral guests have taken their seats, for 5 to 10 minutes gentle music will be piped in via sound engineering. After a moment of silence the urn burial specialist (*Urnenbeisetzer*) enters the ceremonial hall, bows towards the urn and then, turning to the guests, says:
>
> 'We honour the deceased through a minute of silence. I ask you to stand up.' …
>
> Thereafter the urn burial specialist takes … the urn from the pedestal and says:
>
> 'We now go to the final resting place of the deceased.' …
>
> [He] takes the urn. While showing it to the family, he says:
>
> 'According to the laws of our state and the custom of our peoples we commit the urn to home soil [*Heimaterde*].' …
>
> The next-of-kin have the option of saying a final word. Sand or flowers to scatter should be provided when wished for by the bereaved.[41]

Such ceremonies full of familiar elements certainly helped to establish UGAs in places that had had little experience of anonymous burials before. However, such ceremonies meant that family members were aware where exactly the ashes of their loved ones had been buried. Consequently, in many UGAs in East Germany flowers were regularly placed to mark an exact spot.[42] This meant that the cemetery administration had to remove flowers and place them in the designated area.

The spectrum of anonymity achieved in the GDR was therefore broad. Nevertheless, all UGAs built in the GDR shared one common characteristic: they positively embraced the idea of namelessness. The names of the dead, and here the UGA shares a characteristic with mass graves (unknown soldiers as well as pauper's graves), were absent. Other reference points such as the exact

Figure 5.6 A working UGA in Chemnitz; the majority of burials of the city have taken place on this site.

or approximate location might be known, but the names of others who are also buried there are not, unless through human contact in the ceremony, or at the graveside. This might represent the most decisive step towards new sepulchral culture, one that in the GDR embraced the idea of the socialist collective and was advanced by certain measures:

> Even if the process of re-modelling mankind from 'the I to the We', that is, to collective thinking and acting, is developing according to the laws of socialism, then the dynamic of this process is still influenced by conscious changes to the framework of the [social] environment.[43]

The propagation of cremation and the UGA according to this reasoning was thus a conscious attempt to alter a social environment for a specific ideological purpose. Barbara Happe argues that precisely this was at the heart of the radical cemetery reform of the GDR. Its aim was to overcome traditional forms of commemoration by stressing the 'we', in this ideological motivation for the propagation of UGAs – and thus, as a logical conclusion, banning the 'I' to those areas of the cemetery that had not been modernized.[44] On the surface, there seems to be much direct evidence that this collectivization created tensions:

> Since there had already been a suggestion in 1969 to create an [anonymous] urn grave field … but which was never realized, initially the same location was considered, the one which

had previously been suggested, directly across from the 'special cemetery for Socialists'. The subsequent extension of the *Ehrenhain* … and the direct comparison between the *Ehrenhain*, with its flat headstones and engraved names, and the *Gemeinschaftsanlage*, without gravestones or engraved names, makes this location no longer feasible.[45]

Socialist society was not free of contradictions, and this made for such stark contrasts at times. Further tensions regarding UGAs were hinted at in the introductory IfK definition, with the reference that a removal of urns was not possible. This specific rule pre-empted any change of mind in families after the funeral had taken place. One encounters today much physical evidence of these tensions at many UGAs, for example in the guise of flowers specifically positioned in order to mark the site of burial (which also contravene the many signs that admonish: '*Burial Site. Do not enter!*').

When a Swedish delegation visited Leipzig in 1971 they commented on this habit, and that there was little that could be done to prevent this from happening.[46] Other more poignant acts of re-establishing individuality can also be observed, for example in the form of vases that have name and dates inscribed on them, and that serve as surrogate grave stones. All these acts reveal the limited achievements of the UGAs' ideological goals of reducing expressions of individuality and of economy through homogeneity.

Furthermore, these acts of reassertion, for want of a better word, in conjunction with local official decisions to conduct ceremonies that deliberately revealed

Figure 5.7 Warning signs against entering a UGA: 'Attention Burial Site. Do not enter!'

Figure 5.8 Some cemeteries have given up the fight to keep the UGAs in a pristine and anonymous state: relatives use the space to commemorate.

the exact location of the specific urn, suggests that in the establishment of UGAs ideology was secondary to cost.

The economic side of the argument was fairly straightforward: between 16 and 25 urns could be buried per square metre of the burial area of a UGA. When one factors in such necessities as walkways, flower holders and ceremonial space, one arrives at the urban planning figure used for UGAs graves of between 0.25 to 0.5 square metres per person. This compares favourably with all other forms of disposal, except for the scattering of ashes. It was this motivation that is reflected in the model calculation such as the one shown in Table 5.1. The macroeconomic (*volkswirtschaftliche*) element is evident in the desire to reduce the overall space of cemeteries, as the tables below indicate.[47]

Other local documents go further and stress microeconomic (*betrieb-swirtschaftliche*) benefits relevant to the specific case and cemetery. In Rostock, to return to the best documented example, the UGA was to offer space for the burial of 15,696 urns (which was thought to be enough space to last until 2008). The authors then contrasted the costs of burial in the UGA and normal urn burials (it explicitly excluded the 30 per cent of burials that were inhumations). While the UGA would occupy an area of 1,320 m², conventional urn burials would occupy an area of 23,544 m² in total. Furthermore, the land and the construction of the UGA would cost 96,500 Mark compared with 659,565 Mark for 15,696 urn burial plots. Therefore the reduction in costs would be 563,068 Mark or 35.50

Table 5.1: Projected change in the use of UGAs in an urban environment with a 70 per forty-year period correlated to the required cemetery space.

Year of Plan	Conventional Urn Burials (%)	Burials in a UGA (%)	Required Cemetery Space in m^2 per Inhabitant
5	70	–	3.12
10	60	10	2.93
15	50	20	2.74
20	40	30	2.55
25	30	40	2.36
30	20	50	2.17
35	10	60	1.98
40	–	70	1.79

(Source: Happe, 'Die sozialistische Reform', in Sörries (ed.), *Vom Reichsauschuß zur Arbeitsgemeinschaft Friedhof und Denkmal*, 197)

Table 5.2: Comparison of the space required per planned burial plot. The net space required would be higher, as it included a proportion of the space needed to utilize the burial space, i.e., pathways and other technical space.

Family grave 2 plots (free choice of location)	10.2 m^2
Freely chosen grave plot	5.1 m^2
Allocated burial plot within the grid system	3.4 m^2
Freely chosen urn burial plot capable of holding up to 5 urns	2.5 m^2
Allocated urn burial plot within grid system capable of holding up to 3 urns	1.7 m^2
UGA per urn	0.08–0.2 m^2
Scattering of ash (per person)	0.04 m^2

(Source, IfK, Thomas, 1968, BA Berlin, DO 4, No. 892)

Mark for every single urn.[48] There were additional savings when it came to the funerals, memorials and care of the cemetery and even higher savings if more people could ultimately be persuaded to opt for burials in UGAs. In Jena, five smaller UGAs had cost 5,000 Mark and saved 145,000 Mark in investments.[49] Such figures and model calculations can be encountered on a regular basis. Most municipal burial services and nearly all church cemeteries operated with a chronic lack of revenues and with fixed prices that often did not even cover the costs incurred.[50] Measures that achieved some relief were thus seen in a positive light, making the proposition of promoting communal forms of burial extremely tempting. This might even explain why by 1985 the church even offered its own guidelines on UGAs that were to be built in church cemeteries.[51]

Financial constraints and the desire to achieve greater efficiency not only occurred in the later years of the GDR, as another example highlights. Between 1959 and 1964 there was an anonymous urn garden behind the crematorium in Leipzig, and in that period it had been customary to plant a rose above every urn buried. In 1964 that idea, however, was dropped and the urns were covered with turf, because care for the roses was simply too labour-intensive and could only done manually. Thereafter Leipzig established a normal UGA. Conversely, the burial services had to make the choice of UGA as attractive as they could. This was mainly achieved by pricing UGA funerals accordingly. In Rostock the burial services suggested a one-off fee of 15 Mark for a disposal in the UGA, which included 5 Mark as a basic usage fee, 5 Mark for the funeral ceremony and 5 Mark for care and decoration of the UGA. Before the UGA was opened it was raised to 25 Mark. Yet the price still compared favourably to the cheapest alternative form of urn burial for which the Rostock burial services charged 220 Mark. Costs for any other form of burial, especially inhumation, were much higher. In Leipzig, for example, the usage fee alone for a traditional family grave plot was 1,800 Mark in 1971.[52] When one compares these tariffs, it becomes even clearer how important pricing proved in shaping developments in the sepulchral culture.

Such pricing policies, the frequency of detailed calculations of economic savings, and the constant references to the reduction of the cemetery space stand in stark contrast vividly with the predominately ideological case in favour of the *Urnengemeinschaftsanlage*. In the introduction of the handbook for UGA design, for example, the following statement can be found:

> To reduce the cemetery space with the help of *Urnengemeinschaftsanlagen*, is not, however, the prime objective, but to create, in every single instance, sites that are appealing in design and culture [sic], and that are appropriate to the area provided.[53]

It is no coincidence that references to culture and, by association, the ideological agenda are more frequent in the context of the question of how to design UGA sites. The latter focus allowed authors to concentrate attention on the public dimension of sepulchral culture, rather than its technical and economic angle. In other words such statements were primarily meant to strengthen the case for creating 'appropriate' UGAs that in turn reflected the ideals of socialist society, while they left the calculations of economic savings to appear elsewhere – i.e., the domain of officials, administrators and experts.

Additionally, designing appropriate UGAs was a task which did not always prove simple, especially if one considers the numerous examples of UGAs that were criticized even within the professional circles of the GDR. Manfred Kramer eloquently sketched the design framework that should govern any creation of a UGA:

> The space should emanate tranquillity, dignity and harmony. It is formed through the allocation of flat and horizontal design elements (burial area, paths, lawns) with vertical design elements (trees, bushes, walls, memorials).
> Aims of the design are: …
> – restraint in the use of colour and form in design elements,
> – restraint in the use of stone and concrete …

– restraint in the use of extensive garden design elements …

The *Urnengemeinschaftsanlage* is a grave field of a special kind, but not an object of presentation, just as the cemetery as a whole should not be one. Essential elements [of the *Urnengemeinschaftsanlage*] should be governed by appropriate proportions to the whole and always subordinated to the thought of communality [as in *Gemeinschaft*].[54]

That ideal was not always realized when compared to some of the actual sites, most famously Rudolf Sitte's gigantic brown ceramic sculpture of a heart on the heavily criticized UGA on the *Heidefriedhof* Dresden.

These design guidelines did not always govern the process of opening a UGA. In 1980 the master stonemason Günther Bollenbach published a rare and explicit critique in the IfK magazine. In this he explicitly castigated the motives for constructing large UGAs:

In most of the previous attempts to design such grave fields, it was regrettably mostly economic aspects that stood to the fore. In those cases, societal, cultural, ethical and aesthetic points of view were pushed into the background.[55]

Bollenbach, after going into great detail on the design elements that he did not consider appropriate – which he defined as any collective memorial of a UGA that if put into an alternative context outside a cemetery would not look out of place (e.g., fountains with bronze cast ornaments that could be placed in any

Figure 5.9 Ceramic heart on the *Heidefriedhof* UGA in Dresden. This site was closed once it reached 55,000 urns.

Figure 5.10 Inscription of the *Heidefriedhof* UGA: 'Whatever good we have bestowed upon you – Shall be your command to honour life'.

decorative context) – stressing that any central memorial should address aspects of communality and bereavement. Moreover, he demanded that the creation of meaningful burial sites should not be governed by economic considerations.[56] Such a passionate defence of the UGA stressed the tensions between the idealism and the reality inherent in much of the sepulchral culture of the GDR.

Barbara Happe, in her work on the *Urnengemeinschaftsanlage*, comes to the conclusion that the aim of the cemetery reform in the GDR was to make a radical break from traditional forms of commemoration, especially those tainted by association with the capitalist system. For the same reason she interprets the economic thrift in design and execution as a sign to break with concepts of 'bourgeois representation'.[57] This conclusion might, on first glance, be sustainable if one considers the existence of the one hundred and forty *Urnengemeinschaftsanlagen* as well as the doubtlessly radical views expressed in many of the IfK policy papers.[58] However, in the light of more detailed evidence on how individual municipal burial services tried to propagate UGAs by adapting the ceremony designs one is forced to consider whether the UGAs were such a radical innovation. They were certainly sepulchral spaces that broke with conventional and traditional ideas of appropriate disposal, mainly by leaving the deceased unnamed, but this step happened in the context of a violent century that had seen many forms of collective commemoration.[59] Furthermore, the particular considerations that motivated the individual cemetery administrations, and which are reflected in the specific policies and economic considerations, played a crucial role in popularizing the UGA as an alternative form of burial. But the success of the UGA reveals deeper connections with the economic imperatives of both the purveyors and consumers of burial services, since these groups jointly reacted to changes in the demographics (i.e., smaller families, more singles and ageing) and the underlying patterns of economic development (such as low wages and hardship). In this light the UGA might represent a rare occasion when the economic imperatives of consumers and suppliers actually converged. This does not mean that there was not a genuine demand for anonymous burials. The example of other countries underlines a general trend: during the twentieth century the technical and scientific attitude towards the dead human corpse is reflected in the ascent of a minimalist approach to disposal (cremation and anonymous burial).

However, UGAs in the context of the GDR also represent a 'peculiar marriage' of high cremation rates, achieved by forms of propagation and owing to economic contraints, with a desire to reduce further cemetery space and curtail cemetery maintenance. Cremation was not, therefore, as Barbara Happe argues, a prerequisite to the establishment of UGAs, but more a cause (in the sense that large numbers of cremations made the economy of scale with regard to UGAs ever more attractive).[60] The research into developing a biodegradable plastic urn (also used later in the burial of Charlotte Ulbricht) in the 1980s underlines the supremacy of economic considerations, since it allowed for the easier reuse of burial space.[61] Like cremation, the concept of anonymity and communal commemoration could easily be linked with the socialist ideal of a collective sepulchral culture and this aided its advance within the political framework of the GDR. Yet ultimately its ideological appropriateness remained of secondary importance. It is precisely for that reason that after detailed calculations the authors of the Rostock report returned, in their conclusion, to the other less tangible, not to say tenuous, outcomes of establishing the first UGA in Rostock:

> – By creating the first *Urnengemeinschaftsanlage* a real need of the population of Rostock is being fulfilled.
> – At the same time a further step is being taken to advance cemetery culture in accordance with the new requirements that confront the modern cemetery of today.
> – The cultural-political value that is created by re-valuing the cemetery as a cultural and commemorative site increases the entire value of such a site.[62]

In many ways the cemetery was indeed re-evaluated in the second half of the twentieth century, and for East Germany the UGA was one part in this process that increasingly made cemeteries sites of collective commemoration. Nevertheless, the concept of communal burial proved to be attractive, especially in its more diverse and more flexible manifestations. Since the reunification many new UGAs have been built. Some have continued the tradition of anonymous urn burials, but others have rejected the element of anonymity. The names of all those buried on the site are inscribed on the central memorial or on memorial plaques.

Figure 5.11 A contemporary communal urn burial, but without the anonymity as everybody's name is inscribed in the stones.

Collective forms of burial have spread across the whole of Germany, because they are based on a response to demographics, a rejection of the rigid reformist tradition inherent in the rules governing much of German sepulchral culture and also because it is less of a break with the burial traditions of a clearly identifiable grave.[63]

Notes

1. See the introduction to: R. Koselleck and M. Jeismann (eds), *Der Politische Totenkult – Kriegerdenkmäler in der Moderne* (Munich: W. Fink, 1994), 13–17.

2. To a lesser degree industrialization also reverberates in this change, as cemeteries have fields dedicated to the victims of large industrial accidents – an area lacking research. For an introduction to shifts in the political nature of commemoration see: U. Jeggle, 'In stolzer Trauer – Umgangsformen mit dem Kriegstod während des 2. Weltkriegs', *Tübinger Beiträge zur Volkskultur*, 1986, 242–59. See also: LHSA Magdeburg, P13, SED-Bezirksleitung Magdeburg, No. 22810: *Dokumentation VdN-Ehrenhain Westfriedhof*, 1971.

3. 'The grove of honour (*Ehrenhain*) embodies a living cultivation of tradition and enables funerals, commemorative celebrations and honouring to be conducted in an appropriate setting': KA Weimarer Land, Apolda, RdK Apolda, No. 3476: *Gestaltungskonzeption für die Vorbereitung und Einrichtung eines "Ehrenhaines" auf dem Friedhof der Stadt Apolda*, 5 August 1987, 1.

4. See: A. Assmann, *Erinnerungsräume – Formen und Wandlungen des kulturellen Gedächtnisses* (Munich: C.H. Beck, 1999), 11–15.

5. In a number of East German cemeteries I have encountered signs that read 'Caution, Graves: Do not Enter!' There are few areas in the cemeteries of this world that require a sign to stop the casual visitor from stumbling over graves. However, having dispensed with markers such as gravestones and in extreme cases any form of central memorial, some *Urnengemeinschaftsanlagen* need this protective measure. In this light, signs like these, however, cannot merely be regarded as 'keep-off-the-grass' warnings; they are a deliberate attempt to make up for a lack of inherent sacrosanctity. This is especially the case considering that sanctity is mainly defined by the juxtaposition to the profane and vice versa. See: M. Eliade, *The Sacred and the Profane – The Nature of Religion* (New York: Harper and Row, 1961).

6. One of the earliest references: IfK, *Gestaltung unserer Friedhöfe*, 22.

7. StA Dresden, Rep. 9.1.14, No. 204: *Zusammenstellung von vereinheitlichen Definitionen zu Begriffen des Friedhofs- und Bestattungswesens der DDR mit dem Ziel der Ergänzung der einheitlichen Definitionen für Planung, Rechnungsführung und Statistik Teil 5 Stadt- und Gemeindewirtschaft*, H. Kluge, *IfK*, 15 December 1971, 38. Original has no punctuation.

8. M. Kramer (ed.), *Planung, Gestaltung und Pflege von Urnengemeinschaftsanlagen* (Dresden: IfK, 1985), 7.

9. An internal inquiry of all Protestant Churches reveals that the scattering of ashes was not seen as a very dramatic prospect nor perceived as a threat to the church. EZA Berlin, Rep. 101, No. 2567: *Aschestreuwiesen auf Friedhöfen*, 12 April 1982.

10. A number of pamphlets were used in different cities that introduced citizens to the *UGA* and its advantages. Additionally placards and small exhibitions were used to popularize the new form of disposal. StA Rostock, Rep. 2.2.8, No. 10: *Maßnahmeplan zur Eröffnung und Inbetriebnahme der ersten Urnengemeinschaftsanlage der Stadt Rostock*, 23 November 1978.

11. BA Berlin, DO 4, No. 892: *Prognose für die Entwicklung des Friedhofs- und Bestattungswesens*, 10 April 1969, 11.

12. M. Kramer (ed.), *Planung, Gestaltung und Pflege von Urnengemeinschaftsanlagen* (Dresden: IfK, 1985), 25; 'The wish for an Urnengemeinschaftsanlage should be fulfilled. In doing so, however, the projected usage should be decisive, since a very slow use can end in interest subsiding fast': StA Dresden, Rep. 9.1.14, No. 825: *Umgestaltung Ländlicher Friedhöfe*, 36.

13. BA Berlin, DO 4, No. 892: *Prognose für die Entwicklung des Friedhofs- und Bestattungswesens*, 10 April 1969, 10.

14. IfK Archiv, Sig. 22: *Voraussetzungen zur Erhöhung der Feuerbestattung (K. Thomas)*, 108, in Happe, 'Die sozialistische Reform', in Sörries (ed.), *Vom Reichsausschuß zur Arbeitsgemeinschaft Friedhof und Denkmal*, 194–95.

15. Autorenkollektiv, *Der Friedhof: Gestaltung und Pflege* (IfK: Dresden, 1980), 8.

16. Ibid., 9.

17. Happe, 'Die sozialistische Reform', in Sörries (ed.), *Vom Reichsauschuß zur Arbeitsgemeinschaft Friedhof und Denkmal*, 203.

18. In 1992 it had been decided that the site was already too oversized and cumbersome, and that such a large UGA was no longer seen as appropriate to the times [*unzeitgemäß*]. StA Dresden, Rep. 9.1.14, No. 644, *Anschreiben*, 14 July 1992.

19. The first larger UGA in Leipzig had been planned for 20,000 urns. StA Dresden, Rep. 9.1.14, No. 825: *Umgestaltung Städtischer Friedhöfe – Am Beispiel Leipzig*, 50.

20. StA Dresden, Rep. 9.1.14, No. 137: *Rednerweiterbildung*, 1 November 1989.

21. Despite an extensive search I could not locate any comprehensive contemporary statistics. Barbara Happe does not offer any dates for these rates, but they might reflect trends towards the end of the 1980s. Happe, 'Die Nachkriegsentwicklung der Friedhofe in beiden deutschen Staaten', 223.

22. Grufman and Ingemark, *Feuerbestattung und Friedhofswesen in der DDR*, 10–11.

23. StA Schwerin, Abt. MF, No. 82: *Die Unentgeltliche Totenbestattung in Sachsen*, 3.

24. Krenzke, *Magdeburger Friedhöfe und Begräbnisstätten*, 101–2.

25. See the idea of *Aschebeete* and the rejection of anachronistic ideas with regard to urn burials in: J. Hempelmann, *Die Praxis der Friedhofsgärtnerei, Anlage, Verwaltung und Instandhaltung von Friedhöfen und Gräbern* (Berlin: Parey, 1927), 53–67.

26. The same experience also facilitated a further development that of the privatization of commemorating the individual through personal shrines. A development that would be interesting to study in regard to the GDR and those buried in UGAs.

27. StA Rostock, Rep. 2.2.8, No. 10: *Dokumentation über die erste Urnengemeinschaftsanlage der Stadt Rostock*, 5 May 1977, 2.

28. 'The version of a ceremony with the urn with subsequent burial of the urns has to be popularized with regard to those organising the funeral through the burial department': StA Rostock, Rep. 2.2.8, No. 12: *Richtline F/B 2-77*, 4 August 1977, 6.

29. G. Brunnemann, *Zur Betreuung Hinterbliebener – Trauer und Trauerstörungen unter besonderer Berücksichtigung von Patienten- und Therapeutenverhalten*, PhD, Akademie zur Ärztlichen Fortbildung in der DDR, Berlin (circa 1985), 13.

30. Especially in the sense of one quotation of Albert Einstein quite commonly used at the end of eulogies. 'We morals are thus immortal, where we toiled collectively on collective works' (*So sind wir Sterblichen darin unsterblich, wo wir an gemeinsamen Werken gemeinsam schufen*). See for example: StA Dresden, Rep. 9.1.14, No. 126: *Abschrift Trauerfeier für Hilde H.*, 30 August 1979, 6.

31. Anonymity, in this context, represents a cure from individual tendencies and an embracing of the collective reflecting the fifth Principle of Socialist Ethics and Morals (1958): 'Thou shalt act in the spirit of mutual support and comradely cooperation during the construction of socialism, respect the collective, and take its criticisms to heart'; as translated and discussed in J. Rodden, *Repainting the Little Red Schoolhouse: A History of Eastern German Education, 1945-1995* (New York: Oxford University Press, 2002) p. 108. SSA Chemnitz, RdB Karl-Marx-Stadt, Abt. Inneres, Personalwesen, No. 47109: *Methodisches Material für Namensweihen, Sozialistische Feiern bei Eheschließungen, Trauerfeiern sozialistischen Inhalts*, 28.

32. 'Individual demise may be collectively annulled. Posterity (which, after all, is by definition more lasting than the ego's own life), is that site where the hope, if not certainty, of the ego's immortality, or at least the ego's longer-than-life existence, can be invested': 'On Bidding for Collective Immortality', in Z. Bauman, *Mortality, Immortality and Other Life Strategies* (Cambridge: Polity Press, 1992), 51. The secularized form of All Souls Day (*Totensonntag*) is a wonderful example of this: that Sunday saw the collective celebration of all dead in *Totengedächtnisfeiern* (Celebrations of the Memory of the Dead). See StA Dresden, Rep 9.1.14, No. 189; LA Berlin, C Rep. 115, No. 215.

33. StA Rostock, Rep. 2.2.8, No. 10: *Dokumentation über die erste Urnengemeinschaftsanlage der Stadt Rostock*, 5 May 1977, 6.

34. In Flensburg 43 per cent of burials were anonymous, in Lübeck and Travemünde the rate was at 42 per cent, only insignificantly lower; the larger cities of Kiel, Bremen and Hamburg all have a rate of over 25 per cent. In the cities on the banks of the river Ruhr and Rhine levels reached about 10 per cent in 1998. Further to the south the rate quickly declined. See B. Happe, 'Zur Lage der anonymen Bestattung in Deutschland – eine Umfrage bei kommunalen und kirchlichen Friedhofsverwaltern', *Friedhof und Denkmal*, 43:2 (1998), 39–54.

35. This is a very broad topic that underlies a lot of the contemporary developments, such as the natural death movement and other forms of commemoration. For an introduction see: M. Venne, 'Anonym Bestatten – Digital Gedenken', *Friedhof und Denkmal*, 44:1 (1999), 17–34; B. Happe, 'Veränderungen in der sepulkralen Kultur am Ende des 20. Jahrhunderts, *Friedhof und Denkmal*, 45:2 (2000), 9–20; and S. Lichtensteiger (ed.), *Last Minute – Ein Buch zu Sterben und Tod* (Baden: hier + jetzt, 1999). For an excellent case study arguing clearly against the negative views of UGSs also see: T. Sørensen, 'The Presence of the Dead: Cemeteries, Cremation and the Staging of Non-place', *Journal of Social Archaeology*, 9:1 (2009), 110–35.

36. This has even been the subject of technical research. StA Dresden, Rep. 9.1.14, No. 102: *Ablaufplanung verschiedener Bestattungsformen*, 9–16.

37. StA Dresden, Rep. 9.1.14, No. 204: *Zusammenstellung von vereinheitlichen Definitionen zu Begriffen des Friedhofs- und Bestattungswesens der DDR*, 15 December 1971, 18. The most extreme case in the GDR was the UGA in Plauen, where burials were only carried out about twice a year, normally when around 250 urns had been collected.

38. Redlin, *Gegenwärtige großstädtische Bestattungsriten – eine empirische Untersuchung in der Hauptstadt der DDR*, Belegarbeit im Fach Ethnologie Humboldt Universität (1985), 18.

39. Kramer (ed.), *Urnengemeinschaftsanlagen*, 27.

40. StA Rostock, Rep. 2.2.8, No. 12: *Richtline F/B 2–77*, 4 August 1977, 7.

41. StA Rostock, Rep. 2.2.8, No. 10: *Dokumentation über die erste Urnengemeinschaftsanlage der Stadt Rostock*, 5 May 1977, 12.

42. However, the same problem can be found in the West, where cemetery administration has also removed these flowers swiftly.

43. StA Rostock, Rep. 2.2.8, No. 10: *Dokumentation über die erste Urnengemeinschaftsanlage der Stadt Rostock*, 5 May 1977, 6.

44. Happe, 'Die sozialistische Reform', in Sörries (ed.), *Vom Reichsausschuß zur Arbeitsgemeinschaft Friedhof und Denkmal*, 205.

45. StA Rostock, Rep. 2.2.8, No. 10: *Dokumentation über die erste Urnengemeinschaftsanlage der Stadt Rostock*, 5 May 1977, 7.

46. Grufman and Ingemark, *Feuerbestattung und Friedhofswesen in der DDR*, 14.

47. See also: BA Berlin, DO 4, No. 892: *Prognose für die Entwicklung des Friedhofs- und Bestattungswesens*, 10 April 1969, 13.

48. StA Rostock, Rep. 2.2.8, No. 10: *Dokumentation über die erste Urnengemeinschaftsanlage der Stadt Rostock*, 5 May 1977, 14.

49. Grufman and Ingemark, *Feuerbestattung und Friedhofswesen in der DDR*, 11.

50. Exact figures for a section of the church province of Sachsen reveals that the church charged 12 Mark for each inhumation while it incurred costs of 43.50 Mark, and 6 Mark for every urn burial while the real costs were 9 Mark. No service provided actually recouped the real costs. For 1977 that added up to a loss of 84,083.13 Mark. EZA Berlin, Rep. 101, No. 2565, *Vergleich von Einzelleistungen beim KFA Leipzig 1977*.

51. EZA Berlin, ZA 5109/02, No. 101/5221: *Allgemeine Gestaltungshinweise für Urnengemeinschaft sanlagen auf kirchlichen Friedhöfen*, 10 January 1985.

52. Grufman and Ingemark, *Feuerbestattung und Friedhofswesen in der DDR*, 15.

53. Kramer (ed.), *Urnengemeinschaftsanlagen*, 7.

54. Ibid., 28–29.

55. G. Bollenbach, 'Gemeinschaftsanlagen – aber wie?', *Informationen aus der Praxis für die Praxis*, Jahrgang 1980, No. 1/2, 7. Also quoted in Happe, 'Die sozialistische Reform', in Sörries (ed.), *Vom Reichsauschuß zur Arbeitsgemeinschaft Friedhof und Denkmal*, 202.

56. Bollenbach, 'Gemeinschaftsanlagen', 21.

57. Happe, 'Die sozialistische Reform', in Sörries (ed.), *Vom Reichsauschuß zur Arbeitsgemeinschaft Friedhof und Denkmal*, 205–6.

58. For example Karl Thomas's plan of a heavily centralized burial system.

59. B. Schwartz, 'The Social Context of Commemoration – A Study in Collective Memory', *Social Forces*, 61:2 (1982), 374–402.

60. Happe, 'Die sozialistische Reform', in Sörries (ed.), *Vom Reichsauschuß zur Arbeitsgemeinschaft Friedhof und Denkmal*, 206.

61. The fact that the urn and the cremains no longer needed to be disturbed (before they had been buried in plastic urns that had to be dug out and disposed of – i.e., mixed with earth and re-buried) was the only non-economic advantage out of nine enumerated in favour of the bio-degradable urn. BA Berlin, DO 4, No. 892: *Angaben zur verrottbaren Fasergußurne und deren Verwendung*, 1984, 1.

62. StA Rostock, Rep. 2.2.8, No. 10: *Dokumentation über die erste Urnengemeinschaftsanlage der Stadt Rostock*, 5 May 1977, 15.

63. Nicole Sachmerda-Schulz is conducting a PhD research project at the University of Leipzig on this. For a summary see: N. Sachmerda-Schulz, 'Die *grüne Wiese* als Gottesacker? Eine religionssoziologische Studie zum Wandel der Bestattungsnormen und zur Normalisierung der Anonymbestattung', *Arbeitstitel – Forum für Leipziger Promovierende*, 3:1 (2011), 65–66.

Chapter 6

FUNERALS IN THE GDR
A DIVERSITY OF RITUALS

Completely on the quiet, the SED created an association of funeral orators, especially in the larger cities. They are trained in oratory skills at courses and receive their own mourning uniform [grey suits]. The introduction of the anti-Church graveside eulogy is the latest stage on the path to excluding the Church from the stage of public life.[1]

*T*his was the alarmist reaction of official West German counterpropaganda in 1958/59 to the orchestrated introduction of additional socialist rites and the most open anti-religious policies since 1951. This specific booklet was not merely targeted against secular funerals, but also socialist naming ceremonies (replacing the sacrament of baptism), socialist marriage ceremonies (as an alternative to the church ceremony) and above all the *Jugendweihe* (as the secularized version of confirmation). The vehement language of the document is born out of a period that saw the highest tension between state and church in the GDR as well as the strongest drive to propagate atheism by state-sponsored means. Yet despite secular funerals only coming to general popular attention in 1959 – unlike the drive to establish the *Jugendweihe*, which started in 1955 – the tradition of secular funerals in Germany is much older.[2] The first broader discussion of the issue resulted from two court cases in the mid 1920s that made it all the way to the *Reichskammergericht* (Imperial Supreme Court) in Leipzig. The question in these cases, as it was to be again in the 1950s in the GDR, was the thorny issue of whether laypeople (such as freethinkers) could deliver eulogies and officiate at atheist funerals on church property. The Weimar-era Supreme Court had decided that they could not do so against the express will of the parish or the

Table 6.1: National rates for the three socialist rituals.

	Socialist Naming Ceremonies (%)	Socialist Marriage Rituals (%)	Socialist Funerals (%)
1959	20.8	9.2	–
1960	–	–	–
1961	20.4	12.9	16.1
1962	18.2	8.6	16.5
1963	17.3	10.6	16.9

(Data: BA Berlin DO 1 MdI, 34.0, No. 26207)

cemetery regulations.[3] At municipal cemeteries, on the other hand, burial acts by lay speakers (*Laienbegräbnis*) had been permitted for some time. This demonstrates that the 'spectre' of secular funerals did not suddenly emerge in the 1950s. They merely became one further element in the SED's concerted effort to secularize everyday life.

Moreover, they were to play a long-term role in the decline in religious affiliation in East Germany over the second half of the twentieth century. The speed of this decline was one of the legacies of the rule of the SED. Secular funerals (and silent ones) as an index of religious affiliation and the state of religiosity in society have received wider scholarly attention.[4] However, there is also the issue if the choice of funeral really reflects the depth of religious affiliation. In addition, the problem that all this scholarship faces is considerable: the archival material available on secular funerals, while abundant, is also highly fragmented (see for example the limited data in Tables 6.1 and 6.2). This form of funeral ritual must also be placed in the wider context of other alternative rituals.

Table 6.2: The distribution of secular and religious ceremonies of all cremations that took place in the crematorium of the *Südfriedhof* of Leipzig 1951–1956. All figures in brackets are those in the original document, the other percentages are calculated.

	Number of Rituals	Rituals administered by Funeral Orators	Rituals administered by Clergy	Secular Ceremonies (in %)	Religious Ceremonies (in %)
1951	4,000	1,439	2,561	36.0 (36)	64.0 (64)
1952	4,377	1,599	2,778	36.5 (37)	63.5 (63)
1953	3,757	1,469	2,288	39.1 (40)	60.9 (60)
1954	4,853	2,143	2,710	44.2 (44)	55.8 (56)
1955	4,322	1,757	2,565	40.7 (40)	59.3 (60)
1956	4,990	1,929	3,061	38.7 (40)	61.3 (60)
1951–1956	*26,299*	*10,336*	*15,963*	*39.3 (40)*	*60.7 (60)*

(Data: SSA Leipzig, BT/RdB Leipzig, No. 20679)

Table 6.3: The distribution of secular and religious ceremonies of all inhumations that took place in the cemeteries of Leipzig 1951–1956. All figures in brackets are those given in the original document, the other percentages are calculated.

	Number of Rituals	Rituals administered by Funeral Orators	Rituals administered by Clergy	Secular Ceremonies (in %)	Religious Ceremonies (in %)
1951	1,976	225	1,751	11.4	88.6
1952	2,024	238	1,786	11.8	88.2
1953	2,179	257	1,922	11.8	88.2
1954	2,239	293	1,946	13.1	86.9
1955	2,237	301	1,936	13.5	86.5
1956	2,096	261	1,815*	12.5	86.5
1951–1956	12,751	1,575	11,156	12.4 (13)	87.6 (87)

* = inconsistency in the original.

(Data: SSA Leipzig, BT/RdB Leipzig, No. 20679)

Table 6.4: The distribution of secular and religious ceremonies of all inhumations that took place in the cemeteries of Sellerhausen and Kleinzschocher. These two places were working-class suburbs with very similar demographics and similar numbers of deaths. However, their developments with regard to the 1950s advance of secular funerals are diametrically opposed developments. All figures in brackets are those given in the original document, the other percentages are calculated.

	Sellerhausen		Kleinzschocher	
	Secular Ceremonies (in %)	Religious Ceremonies (in %)	Secular Ceremonies (in %)	Religious Ceremonies (in %)
1951	18.2 (20)	81.7 (80)	13.7 (14)	82.3 (86)
1952	19.8 (20)	80.2 (80)	16.3 (16)	83.7 (86)
1953	16.1 (16)	83.9 (84)	20.6 (20)	79.4 (80)
1954	15.8 (15)	84.2 (85)	20.7 (21)	79.3 (79)
1955	14.0 (14)	86.0 (86)	20.8 (21)	79.2 (79)
1956	10.3 (10)	89.7 (90)	22.4 (22)	77.6 (78)
1951–1956	15.6	84.4	19.1	80.3

(Data: SSA Leipzig, BT/RdB Leipzig, No. 20679)

Secularization is a process that affected both East and West Germany, and many parts of Western Europe. Klemens Richter is hence right when he contextualizes the development of the East German secular rituals within the gradual secularization of a modern industrialized society.[5] Detlef Pollack's work indicates that by 1990 only a quarter of the East German population were still members of the Protestant Church.[6] There is little doubt that secularization was far more pronounced in urban areas. For example in 1986 only 7 per cent of the population of East Berlin, and in its newer socialist quarters less than 3 per cent, remained members of the Protestant Church.[7] However, a strong secular trend can also be seen in the countryside. Antonia Maria Humm, in her study of the Thuringian village of Niederzimmern, indicates that to a certain extent the nationwide decline of church membership and participation in secular rites is echoed in the developments in rural areas. The number of those who participated actively in parish life was low and limited to about fifty, most of whom were farmers, but she also states that there remained a core understanding of the value of the church as a local institution.[8] The church was aware of this overall trend and accommodated those who wished for a religious funeral for their loved ones, even though the deceased individual had not been a Protestant as such:

> To an increasing degree Christians live together with others in marriage, with family, relatives, in friendship, who are not, or who are no longer, members of the church, or whose church rites are no longer active. While on the one hand Christians are no longer buried by the Church because the relatives reject this option, on the other hand, Christians specifically ask that their deceased, who do not have this right, be buried by the church …
>
> The church takes such questions for answers drawn from the Christian message, as well as the sorrow and the appeals of its parishioners seriously. It offers the bereaved a 'Church funeral in special circumstances' if, above and beyond the immediate context, a relationship can be identified between the bereaved and the Christian message.[9]

This reflects a fundamental change that had occurred with regard to religious ceremonies in the GDR, where the church accommodated (within reason) a changing society. The initial reaction was different in each *Landeskirche* (Protestant church administrative areas), with some pastors refusing to conduct burials of non-religious individuals.[10] However, generally the situation was simply settled and it became a constituent part of religious life in the GDR.

The historian confronts a dearth of sources capable of explaining the detailed development of secular rites in the GDR after 1965 because the Ministry for the Interior no longer collected data on a regular basis. That task was left to the regional administrations, which executed it with varying degrees of thoroughness.[11] From the patchwork of information, it is clear that the 1980s saw a wider uptake of secular funerals but, even then, most regions retained a significant urban–rural differentiation.

Detlef Pollack estimates that for the whole of East Germany by 1980 only 40 per cent of all deceased received a church funeral, and that this figure had dropped to 31 per cent by 1989).[12] This estimate backs up claims made by party officials. As an illustration, when in 1985 a number of regional officials met to discuss the success of secular ceremonies in the region of Neubrandenburg in June 1985 the conference closed with the remark:

Table 6.5: Rates of socialist/secular funerals in the individual districts of the region of Frankfurt/Oder.

District	Socialist funerals 1962 (in %)	Socialist funerals 1963 (in %)	Secular funerals 1980 (in %)	Secular funerals 1984 (in %)	Secular funerals 1988 (in %)
Angermünde	11.4	12.5	44.7	52.8	54.8
Beeskov	4.1	10.2	33.8	37.5	32.5
Bernau	19.6	22.2	39.2	47.2	41.8
Eberswalde	13.6	16.8	39.4	43.0	50.6
Freienwalde	8.3	7.4	31.5	33.8	43.5
Ehst./Land	12.4	7.8	31.1	33.5	40.1
Fürstenwalde	14.2	14.3	41.0	49.0	52.0
Seelow	11.5	10.2	33.5	40.0	50.1
Strausberg	30.3	23.9	43.6	48.0	61.7
Frankfurt/Oder	34.3	31.0	51.1	70.9	58.7
Eisenhüttenstadt	35.4	43.4	67.1	84.6	74.1
Schwedt	31.6	31.2	56.6	61.4	56.9
Overall Region	*17.5*	*18.2*	*41.8*	*44.6*	*52.5*

(Data: BLHA Potsdam, Rep. 601, No. 34043; BA Berlin, DO1 34.0, No. 26207)

Table 6.6: Rates of socialist/secular funerals in the region of Frankfurt/Oder for the years in which data were collected.

	1959	1960	1961	1962	1963	1980	1984	1988
Frankfurt/Oder	9.1	14.9	16.0	17.5	18.2	41.8	44.6	52.5

(Data: BLHA Potsdam, Rep. 601, No. 34043; BA Berlin, DO 1 MdI, 34.0, No. 26207)

> It has been confirmed that secular ceremonies, as a component of the socialist way of life, have become a need of our citizens and that secular ceremonies in the factories, in the cities and villages of our region are developing into a part of our spiritual-cultural life.[13]

This meant that the process begun in the 1950s had embedded itself firmly throughout the entire region, but the conference report also acknowledges that there was still plenty more to achieve for the bureaucrats in charge of administering ceremonies in the region, because of the uneven development. The rate for secular funerals in the Region of Neubrandenburg as a whole for 1964 was 10.2 per cent; by 1972 it had risen to 19.1 per cent and by 1975 it was estimated to be around 25 per cent (for the neighbouring region of Frankfurt see Tables 6.5 and 6.6). Yet this overall figure of a largely rural region compared to a rate of nearly 71 per cent for the city of Neubrandenburg (70.7 per cent).[14] By the 1980s in the larger cities, such as East Berlin, Halle, or Chemnitz, the drop had become more pronounced, with less than 20 per cent of the population choosing a religious funeral.[15] Across a whole region, the developments diverged. Table 6.7 shows this by showing the developments for the region of Frankfurt/Oder and shows the urban centre reached over 70 per cent, and remained at around a third in the more rural sections. However, the detailed data also reveal how important the presence of a municipal funeral service was for the propagation of secular rituals. As the secular funeral ritual replaced the traditional religious funeral, this trend was often lamented as a decline in sepulchral culture or 'de-ritualization' (*Entritualisierung*).[16]

This assertion of de-ritualization was correct as there was an increasing number of people who were buried without the presence of any mourners. However, this needs to be understood in the light of the emergence of five distinct forms of rituals in the GDR: the religious funeral conducted by a priest or pastor following a Christian liturgy; the socialist funeral for socialists and other 'deserving' individuals with a speech delivered by a high functionary; the secular funeral (*weltliche Bestattung*), mainly conducted by a secular funeral orator; the burial without a ceremony (*Beisetzungshandlung ohne Feier*), described below; and the silent funerals (*stille Feiern*), where the congregation merely witnesses the entombment of the body or urn. These last two varieties did not help in the collection of official statistics, a problem even more amplified by the loose application of terminology. Officials in the GDR used freely a host of terms such as 'secular funerals', '(secular) funerals with a socialist content' ([weltliche] *Bestattungen mit sozialistischem Inhalt*) and the propaganda euphemism 'dignified funerals' (*würdige Bestattung*) as well as sub-categories (such as 'socialist funerals' or 'funerals with atheistic content') near interchangeably. In addition, officials often included burial without a ceremony and silent funerals in their statistics of 'socialist funerals', despite the fact that at least the latter could be judged as a rejection of all forms of rituals involving the spoken word, not merely religious ones.[17] This categorical conflation can be extremely misleading since it blurs the boundaries between the distinct forms of ritual that emerged, inasmuch as socialist funerals were secular, but secular funerals, which often inadvertently included elements of socialist ideology, were not necessarily entirely socialist in character. Therefore the historian must differentiate more clearly between the three basic forms of ritual: socialist, secular and religious.

Socialist funeral rituals, that is, the burial of party members, socialist heroes and those seen as 'deserving', have their origins in the long tradition of ceremonies at the burial of socialist and proletarian leaders as well as other worthy dignitaries.[18] The state did not always follow the deceased's expressed will; Berthold Brecht, for one, wanted neither a public funeral nor a socialist state funeral. This tradition of 'pompous' occasions continued after the reunification: the burial of Lotte Ulbricht, for example, where private individuals organized a 'state funeral'. Volker Ackermann, in his study of state funerals as 'national celebrations of death' (*Nationale Totenfeiern*), to use his terminology, links the role of the state funeral in the GDR and especially their semiotics to the construction of feelings of national unity akin to those created by national memorial days (*Gedenktage*).[19]

Table 6.7: Development of secular funeral rates between 1980 and 1984 in the region of Frankfurt/Oder, in relationship to urbanity, municipal cemeteries, and the number of available secular orators. Additionally, the table illuminates the rate of secular funerals amongst those funerals organized through the municipal funeral services.

District	Number of hamlets, villages and towns	Overall number of cemeteries	Thereof municipal cemeteries	Overall cemetery space in hectares	Rate of secular funerals for all deaths 1980 (in %)	Rate of secular funerals for all deaths 1984 (in %)	Growth in 4 year period	Cremation rate in 1984 (* = only figures for 1983	Rate of secular funerals amongst the funerals organized through VEB in 1984	Orators FT	PT
Angermünde	64	73	32	56	44.7	52.8	8.1	4.4*	52.8	–	7
Beeskov	75	84	64	41	33.8	37.5	3.7	9.1	39.6	–	7
Bernau	38	45	19	229*	39.2	47.2	8	23.8	35.0	–	15
Eberswalde	37	55	33	48	39.4	43.0	3.6	21.4	53.7	1	4
Freienwalde	42	70	48	55	31.5	33.8	2.3	6.2*	43.4	1	9
Ehst./Land	33	43	40	20	31.1	33.5	2.4	17.1	33.5	–	3
Fürstenwalde	48	59	48	53	41.0	49.0	8	24.1	59.5	–	4
Seelow	59	79	47	68	33.5	40.0	6.5	7.8	48.5	–	1
Strausberg	39	53	19	56	43.6	48.0	4.4	22.6	93.2	–	11
Frankfurt/Oder	1	8	5	37	51.1	70.9	19.8	49.4	70.9	1	3
Eisenhüttenstadt	1	3	2	16	67.1	84.6	17.5	42.6	84.6	1	5
Schwedt	1	3	2	18	56.6	61.4	4.8	27.1*	61.4	1	4
Overall Region	438	575	359	697	41.8	44.6	2.8	23.1	64.6	5	73

NB: Lobetal and Ahrensfelde stand out with two extraordinarily large cemeteries that also served as war cemeteries

(Data: BLHA Potsdam, Rep.601, No. 34043.)

Table 6.8: Detailed account of funeral rituals in the region of Frankfurt/Oder for the year 1988. Unlike other material, the sources for this table differentiate between overall rates and the rates achieved solely by the municipal burial services in their funerals. It gives more detailed information on silent funerals that made inroads in the 1980s.

District	Funeral Orators		Overall Number of Burials in 1988	Secular Funerals	Religious Funerals	Silent Funerals	Rate of Secular Funerals (in %)	Rate of Religious Funerals (in %)	Rate of Silent Funerals (in %)	Cremation Rate	Rate of Secular Funerals amongst the Funerals organized through VEB
	FT	PT									
Angermünde	–	7	146	80	62	4	54.8	42.5	2.7	25.3	60.3
Beeskow	–	8	305	99	148	58	32.5	48.5	19.0	17.7	50.5
Bernau	–	7	828	346	429	53	41.8	51.8	6.4	28.0	50.1
Eberswalde	–	6	1,005	508	462	35	50.6	46.0	3.4	27.3	54.9
Freienwalde	1	8	460	200	255	5	43.5	55.4	1.1	9.8	58.1
Ehst./Land	–	3	162	65	90	7	40.1	55.6	4.3	25.9	–
Fürstenwalde	1	6	404	210	126	68	52.0	31.2	16.8	32.2	75.5
Seelow	1	3	437	219	218	–	50.1	49.9	–	11.0	50.5
Strausberg	–	14	845	521	292	32	61.7	34.6	3.7	31.7	90.6
Frankfurt/Oder	1	8	847	494	185	168	58.7	21.8	19.9	56.1	78.1
Eisenhüttenstadt	1	3	455	337	53	65	74.1	11.6	14.3	50.3	87.9
Schwedt	1	14	290	165	73	52	56.9	25.2	17.9	17.6	75.4
Overall Region	6	85	6,184	3,244	2,393	547	52.5	38.7	8.8	30.5	68.6

(Data: BLHA Potsdam, Rep. 601, No. 34043)

Nevertheless, the focus on political semiotics in this case overlooks the formative sway of these occasions in constituting social and cultural perceptions of alternative funeral rites in a secularizing society. This is not to say that these ceremonies were not taken seriously. On the contrary any closer look at the funeral of the president of the GDR, Wilhelm Pieck, or of the chairman of the councils of ministers, Otto Grotewohl, indicate a vast amount of planning, and most importantly, a detailed analysis on what to improve.[20] Both were in Ackermann's list of twenty-two state occasions, yet there were hundreds of occasions when dignitaries, functionaries and party veterans died.[21] These occasions were all celebrated in a most visible way at a regional and district level, utilizing the honorary spaces (*Ehrenhaine*) in the local cemeteries.

Moreover, they resembled, albeit in a scaled-down version, the larger state ceremonies, and were always reported in the local media.[22] In the district of Zossen, the district party administration noted:

> Examples of recent times underpin the fact that a dignified funeral for our comrades cannot be left entirely to the bereaved [next of kin], and that the funerals of old comrades of lengthy service are generally followed closely by the population and can be judged for their political value.[23]

The issue of the propagation of socialist ideals leads back to the question of how to set positive precedents that could be emulated. A more striking parallel in all

Figure 6.1 Special cemeteries for socialists in Potsdam.

these cases is the existence of the obligatory socialist guard of honour: six party members flanking the coffin or urn for a five minute interval in order to pay their last respects. This became a staple image in the newspaper coverage throughout the GDR, and was taken up in all socialist funerals, playing a similar function to the 'Song of the Little Trumpeter'.[24] Indeed most aspects of the socialist funeral followed a similarly schematic approach, often covered by a pre-existing pattern established by party organizations and parts of the administration. The plans of the Ministry for the Interior, for example, contain explicit details for everything from the exact dimension of the wreath sent by the minister – 120 cm in diameter – to the exact location of the urn in the ceremonial hall.[25] Nevertheless, the language and the staging of the official obituaries and eulogies proved even more influential than this regulation of paraphernalia, as one example shows:

> As the son of a worker's family he had belonged since early childhood to the socialist youth movement and became a member of the Party in 1928. From this point onwards the revolutionary battle determined the content of his life. Despite persecution and incarceration he unwaveringly continued the fight in the time of fascism. His loyalty to the party and his conviction that the working class would be victorious were unshakable. After the liberation through the glorious Soviet army our comrade ... participated in the activities from the very beginning. He devoted his entire strength and his years of experience in class warfare to the unity of the working class ... His personality and achievements found recognition in the bestowal of high governmental and social awards. We will always hold our comrade in respectful esteem. [26]

This was the official language in which the loss of Party comrades was framed, and excerpts of eulogies and speeches were often used in the obituaries and in the newspaper reports of the funerals themselves, as the Party released the texts to the papers.

However, the constant repetition of similar sentiments and language not only set a precedent and a tone for what the party elite considered 'appropriate', but actually informed many aspects of the secular funeral oratory ('secular funeral' in this context meaning the burial of non-Party members in non-religious rituals). Certain eulogies and ceremonies were selected to illustrate how to construct an 'appropriate' secular funeral oration. In Freidank's handbook for secular funerals, one finds as models eulogies for a creative arts teacher that showed her love for socialist drama, one for a leader of the Young Pioneers (*Pionierleiterin*), as well as Friedrich Ebert's speech at the grave of Otto Grotewohl, and Friedrich Engels's words at the grave of Karl Marx.[27] This combination of a state occasion, the burial of Marx, of a young party functionary, and of an active member of socialist society shows how the precedent set at socialist funerals informed the ritual and oratory at secular funerals. Moreover, this was a development that we can also find in other socialist countries.[28]

Another reason for the blurring of the lines between secular and socialist funerals has its origins in the Leninist-Marxist interpretation of death, and the ideological brief that secular funerals propagated in the GDR tended to carry.[29]

The internal paper for a commission to work on a handbook for secular funerals in the region of Schwerin clearly reveals this duty:

> One will have to draw attention to the fact that a new life has begun in our state of workers and farmers. Occupational and other accidents are not 'fate', but are caused by a failure to observe due care and occupational health measures. There are so many people who had to participate in or experience the two wars. Here the task is to point to our battle for peace and indicate the years lost. In particularly tragic circumstances, such as unnatural causes of death (accidents, suicides, etc.), one should list the causes truthfully, in a manner appropriate to the contexts. Conceptualized like this we will offer comfort to the bereaved and serve our social order in these circumstances.[30]

In this utilitarian view of a funeral ritual there is little space for sentimentality and in its inception it is clearly geared towards the 'new' socialist being. The model of a socialist human being who can subjugate him/herself and parts of his/her feelings to the greater good of society shows the similarities between the secular funeral ritual and the *Urnengemeinschaftsanlage* as tools to overcome 'bourgeois individualism'.[31] The meaning of this socialist interpretation of life and death can be glimpsed in the words of the favoured Russian author, Nicolai Ostrowski:

> The most precious [possession] that a man owns is his life. It is given to him only once, and he has to spend it in such a way that the pointlessly spent years do not plague him later, that the shame of an unworthy, insignificant past does not weigh upon him, so that dying he can say: 'My whole life, my whole strength have I dedicated to the most glorious thing in the world – to the struggle for the liberation of mankind.' And he must grab life's chances. Since a stupid illness or some tragic coincidence can put an abrupt end to life.[32]

This quote was frequently cited quickly to sketch the stance any socialist should take towards life and death. It was this embrace of a salvation from the meaninglessness of death through an accomplished and productive life that helped to shape the core of the secular funeral liturgy.[33] Party members could be celebrated for their work in the institutions, their fight against fascism, or their part in establishing the GDR. Ordinary citizens lacked these critical reference points; therefore their work and their life in relationship to the history of Germany became the nucleus around which the funeral speech tended to be moulded. This led to the emergence of a number of model speeches that helped the professional funeral orators to frame their funeral orations.[34] They tend to follow a familiar pattern. After addressing the audience and welcoming the bereaved by name, the orator turns to the coffin and typically begins with a recitation such as:

> All your paths are trodden
> All your tasks complete
> All your cares and
> Your pleasures are ended.
> If there is anything left to do, it is for others to do,
> You knew: The most valuable thing that humans possess is life.

> You are no longer alive, and that fills us with sorrow.
> We have cause to be sad.
> Who does not believe they still catch sight of you amidst the living.

Alternatively a host of poems, quotations and sayings were provided in the appendices of handbooks and other socialist material such as propaganda material or socialist literature. Thereafter, the speaker turned to the character of the deceased in order to alleviate grief by commemorating the positive:

> Always happy, always busy, diligent – a good husband, father or grandfather (delete as appropriate). Genuinely committed to the new, an honest comrade and friend, helpful and caring, this is what you were like. Now you (insert name) live no longer, but the image of memories of your life fill us with pride in this hour.

Here the hour of bereavement and loss has been transformed into a moment of contemplative reminiscence and of pride in the achievements of the individual. Most urban burial services provided their staff with short questionnaires to be given to the bereaved that were used to ascertain the relevant information for these speeches. Besides character traits and hobbies, party membership and honours bestowed, there was always a space for education and employment history. Those areas were the subject matter for the main body of the eulogy:

> The image of your life is the image of a worker's life. Born in a village, a pupil of the village school, herd boy on the estate. After his school years, an agricultural labourer, then a labourer in construction, those were the first stages of your life (appropriate material can be woven in here)
> Period as a soldier, the barracks, the First World War …
> October 1917
> October 1918
> You sat up and took notice, but the old life continued
> You had a happy marriage, which resulted in … children.
> Inflation, economic depression, unemployment, fascism, war …
> You lived in the shadows of the houses you built, but it is the greatness of builders and builders' hodmen that they build, and do not destroy.
> In 1946 the time had also come for him …
> You also wrote the history of those times
> And so please stand, and remember our dead [insert name] in silence and with respect.[35]

This example clearly shows the similarities between secular and socialist eulogies, which attempted to celebrate the individual's achievements in the context of the emergence of the East German state (or at least the official party interpretation of that history). Of course not all secular funerals were made up quite such a long catalogue of set pieces, but this example gives a striking demonstration of the rudimentary bearings that most speeches did navigate. The result was a fairly strict secular liturgy that all too often manifested itself in uniform speeches and rituals that used a fairly restricted vocabulary.[36]

This was further aggravated by the small pool of people from whom professional funeral speakers could be drawn: the guidelines insisted that speakers had to have a firm grounding in socialism, scientific atheism, good diction, and should not understand their services as a form of business.[37] These often turned out to be teachers (for example of Marxist-Leninist philosophy) who used this as part-time employment.[38] In Dresden and Berlin, there were examination boards (consisting of party officials, burial service directors and university professors), that assessed the candidates, after they had conducted a number of speeches under supervision.[39] The processes of training and evaluation indicate the costs that arose from the organization of secular funerals. It was not only this process and the vocational background which had a limiting effect on the pool of orators, but age too. In 1977, the average age of the thirty-two secular orators (seven of whom worked full time) that worked in the region of Dresden was 59.1 years, with the oldest orator 74 and the youngest 35.[40] This sometimes caused problems, as in the case of a 71-year-old orator in Dresden. A family complained about the content and delivery of the speech. But the report made after another similar day which had secretly been recorded by the supervisor simply noted that the four eulogies, between 10 and 14 minutes, that she had delivered before lunch were up to the required standard, albeit that they all had been 'relatively simple ceremonies (elderly people, natural causes of death, average attendance)'.[41]

Two alternatives to a normal secular funeral were offered in the form of funerals without an orator or a eulogy but with a small farewell ceremony, and in the more radical silent funeral. In the latter, the bereaved commemorated the deceased in silence and the remains were lowered into the grave without anybody officiating. According to one source silent ceremonies had reached a level of 20.8

Table 6.9: Relationship of numbers of orators, population per orator and the change between 1962 and 1963 in the individual districts of the region of Suhl.

Districts	Number of orators in 1963	Population per orator	1962 Number of socialist funerals (and in %)	1963 Number of socialist funerals (and in %)
Suhl	5	16,029	195 (**39.3**)	214 (**22.1**)
Meiningen	6	11,894	102 (**14.7**)	78 (**9.8**)
Schmalkalden	6	11,239	19 (**2.5**)	23 (**3.0**)
Sonneberg	11	5,864	53 (**7.7**)	57 (**7.1**)
Bad Salzungen	15	5,783	101 (**10.6**)	75 (**7.6**)
Hildburghausen	12	5,635	24 (**2.8**)	47 (**6.1**)
Ilmenau	14	4,881	138 (**17.7**)	203 (**24.1**)
Neuhaus	9	4,728	69 (**12.0**)	76 (**14.2**)
Entire Region	78	6,993	701 (**12.2**)	773 (**10.2**)

(Data: TSA Meiningen, SED BL Suhl, No. IV/A-2.14/694)

Table 6.10: Silent funerals in the region of Frankfurt/Oder. The data were collected for an IfK publication, but some of the data such as those for Bernau should be viewed with caution because of the way the data were compiled.

District	1980	1985	1986	1988
Angermünde	2	4	4	4
Beeskow	2	5	2	58
Bernau	80	70	70	53
Eberswalde	65	60	71	35
Freienwalde	9	6	5	5
Ehst./Land	–	–	–	7
Fürstenwalde	35	57	73	68
Seelow	–	–	1	–
Strausberg	–	22	–	32
Frankfurt/Oder	60	130	115	168
Eisenhüttenstadt	33	87	90	65
Schwedt	40	63	39	52
Entire Region	*326*	*504*	*470*	*547*

(Data: BLHA Potsdam, Rep. 601, No. 34043)

per cent throughout the entire GDR.[42] There is also some data for the region of Frankfurt for most years in the 1980s: Table 6.10 indicates a lesser level.

Generally, the rate at which all secular rituals were taken up is very difficult to gauge. In the early 1960s, the permanent secretary at the Ministry for the Interior, Grünstein, required the regions to report the rate of adoption of socialist ceremonials (the reports are assembled in Table 6.11. This data offers a very patchy picture. Leipzig, Halle and Dresden have the highest proportion of secular funerals, but even in these regions the variations between the districts are considerable. In Halle, for example, the highest rate for any district was 40.7 per cent in Hohenmölsen, but only 8.4 per cent in Nebra. Moreover, in the period from 1 January 1959 to 30 June 1964, 29,389 people (22.7 per cent) received a socialist funeral; 6,055 (4.7 per cent) received no funeral of any kind; but 93,497 or 72.6 per cent were buried by a pastor or a priest.[43] Other regions, such as Gera, saw a decline in socialist funerals over the same period, while the three most northern regions showed very little change. The entire data sets reported back to Berlin (plus the fact that statistics for secular funeral were only collected from 1959 onwards) indicate that initially more emphasis was put upon the naming ceremonies and marriage ceremonies.[44] This suggests that the ceremonies that generally directly involved younger people (compare the insistency on the *Jugendweihe*) were accorded higher importance. Furthermore, the naming ceremonies and marriage ceremonies could rely on the existing organization of the registry offices (aided by the cultural facilities of the larger combines).[45] Conversely, the administration of secular funerals required the establishment of a wider organizational structure and service arrangement.

Table 6.11: Findings of the Grünstein analysis, the developments of the three socialist rituals in the different regions of the GDR between 1958 and the first half of 1964 (here secular funerals).

Regions	1958	1959	1960	1961	1962	1963	1964*	Highest Rate in any District	Lowest Rate in any District
Rostock	–	–	–	–	11.2	11.4	11.7		
Schwerin	–		–	11.3	8.7	10.1	12.2	23.9	5.4
Neubrandenburg	–	–	–	–	–	8.6	–		
Potsdam	–	–	–	–	16.1	17.9	~ 18.0		4.0
Frankfurt/Oder		9.1	14.9	16.0	17.5	18.2	–	43.4	7.4
Cottbus	–		14.2	–	–	20.8	–	36.3	4.9
Magdeburg	–		–	27.1	19.2	16.9	–		
Halle	–	20.2 / 2.5	21.3 / 3.7	24.2 / 3.8	23.7 / 4.6	23.6 / 7.5	24.0 / 7.0	40.7	8.4
Erfurt	–	–	–	–	–	17.1	18.9		
Gera	–	–	–	21.6	19.2	17.2	12.8		
Suhl	–	–	–	–	12.2	11.6	12.8*	26.8	5.0
Dresden	–	–	–	–	–	22.4	25.2		4.1
Leipzig	–	–	–	30.1	30.0 / 9.5	29.6 / 9.1	31.2 / 12.0		
Karl-Marx-Stadt	–	–	–	–	–	18.9	–		
Berlin	–	–	–	–	–	14.6	16.1		

(Data: BA Berlin DO 1 MdI, 34.0, No. 26207)

The later successes in establishing a secular funeral liturgy were built upon the initial effort to establish secular funerals throughout the whole of the GDR in the 1950s and early 1960s. The data for the entire GDR (Table 6.1) actually shows that where socialist funerals were concerned there was hardly any increase made over the initial period, despite the fact that the central government promoted the introduction of secular alternatives over church sacraments. One answer to this problem of stagnating national levels is that root-and-branch reform was only made at the local level, as is supported by the distribution figures. These clearly indicate a greater unevenness in distribution than with cremation.

This kind of unevenness can only be explained when a whole number of factors are taken into account. More than the dissemination of cremation, the success of secular funerals relied on the influence of local individuals, who had to deliver funeral speeches that could bear comparison with the ceremonies of the local pastor or priest. This was difficult to achieve and explains why religious funeral rates in Eisenhüttenstadt, for example, remained virtually unchanged (see Graph 2.1). The role of the local party officials, the directors of the collectives (often asked to deliver funeral eulogies for workers), and church officials could be crucial in aiding or hindering the propagation of secular funerals, since they were the individuals who were often called upon to organize a funeral. Greater diversity of funeral practices was greatly facilitated because of the

Table 6.12: Rates of secular funerals in the individual districts of the region of Cottbus in 1960 and 1964.

District	Number of Socialist Funerals in 1960	Rate of Socialist Funerals in 1960 (%)	Rate of Socialist Funerals in 1964 (%)
Forst (Krematorium)	238	33.2	35.0
Cottbus-Stadt	240	26.1	28.3
Spremberg	155	24.4	30.7
Weißwasser	116	23.6	24.4
Guben	101	20.9	20.0
Hoyerswerda	118	14.8	20.4
Senftberg	211	14.3	26.6
Liebenwerda	104	14.0	9.5
Finsterwalde	76	9.2	24.4
Herzberg	35	9.1	7.1
Jessen	30	5.7	7.6
Lübben	23	5.3	4.1
Calau	16	2.7	13.5
Cottbus-Land	17	2.4	7.8
Luckau	8	1.4	3.8
Region	*1,488*	*14.2*	*19.1*
(comparison 1959)	*(975)*	*(9.3)*	

(Data: BLHA Potsdam, Rep. 801, RdB Cottbus, No. 25874)

absence of direct financial aid from the central government; this was left to the individual burial services, local councils and the larger industrial combines. The inference was that they should include any costs or subsidies in their budgets and thereby cover the economic burden of this policy.[46] In the same context, the question of creating an appropriate and stimulating infrastructure was often mentioned, but it too was ultimately left to local institutions.[47] Therefore, the organization and administration of secular funerals became the realm of mid-level bureaucracy and its sporadic actions. Some officials urged greater central organization, arguing that 230,000 deaths a year with between fifteen and twenty people attending equalled an audience of 3–4 million people going to funerals per year, an audience that could be won over.[48] The route sometimes taken was for greater coordination on a regional level, but in 1985 a delegate at meeting in Neubrandenburg was still asking for a more rigid organizational structure.[49]

One has, therefore, to conclude that what the overall development in the adoption rates of secular funeral discloses is the significance of the quality of service (handicapped by the economic and operational realities) in conjunction with the general role of the church in society (requiring a consideration for every 'special case'). In addition, there is the issue of critical mass, albeit difficult to define, inasmuch as at a certain level secular funerals became the commonly accepted form of disposal for anybody with no religious affiliation. This development was further aided in everyday life by the fact that the burial services would organize a secular funeral, but a church funeral needed to be organized privately with the pastor/priest. Nonetheless, funerals of whatever description have traditionally been rites of transition, independent of the underlying liturgy or ideological orientation. They should be understood as a step for coming to terms with death and as a ritualistic response to often unsettling effects of loss and bereavement. Traditionally religious belief motivated funeral practices, but in the GDR political and ideological motivations in conjunction with a changing society necessitated the creation of alternative rituals. This led at one extreme to complete silence – and even the rejection of the spoken word as a source of solace. This silence can be interpreted in two ways: as a clear rejection of the meaning of all rituals in the modern world or as the mere rejection of rituals laden with beliefs that did not reverberate with this minority of citizens of the GDR. On the other extreme what we see is the continued presence of the socialist ritual that we encountered in the case of Lotte Ulbricht. The middle path was the secular funeral. This had, as Jane Redlin already noted in 1982, only two substantial differences from a conventional religious funeral ceremony: a) the pastor had the duty of pastoral care to his congregation, whereas the obligation of the funeral orator ended with his speech; b) the pastor generally spoke about somebody s/he at least knew and to an audience that was familiar or at least he had got to know – which was a luxury that many secular orators did not have, since in Fordist fashion they delivered up to four eulogies before lunch only to continue in the afternoon.[50]

Notes

1. EZA Berlin, 4/563: *Pseudosakrale Staatsakte in der Sowjetzone – Bundesministerium für Gesamtdeutsche Fragen*, 9.
2. We already saw that in some places problems arose with regard to socialist funerals as early as 1955, but the general discussion of the topic evolved only after 1957/58. For the tradition of *Jugendweihe* see Hallberg, *Die Jugendweihe*.
3. THSA Weimar, Thüringischen Ministeriums des Inneren, Akten E 1545: *Hausfriedensbruch auf kirchlichen Friedhöfen*, 15 April 1928, 1–2.
4. See: Richter, 'Der Umgang mit Tod und Trauer', in Becker et al., *Im Angesicht des Todes*; Hermelink, 'Die weltliche Bestattung', 65–86; Franz, '"Alles hat am Ende sich gelohnt"', 190–211.
5. K. Richter, 'Der Umgang mit Tod und Trauer', in Becker et al. (eds), *Im Angesicht des Todes*, 231–32.
6. D. Pollack, 'Von Volkskirche zur Minderheitskirche – Zur Entwicklung von Religösität und Kirchlichkeit in der DDR', in H. Kaeble, J. Kocka and H. Zwahr (eds), *Sozialgeschichte der DDR* (Stuttgart: Klett-Cotta, 1994), 272.
7. D. Pollack, 'Von Volkskirche zur Minderheitskirche', in Kaeble et al. (eds), *Sozialgeschichte der DDR*, 277.
8. Humm, *Auf dem Weg zum sozialistischen Dorf?*, 294–300.
9. EZA Berlin, ZA 5109/02, No. 101/3377: *Handreichung zur kirchlichen" Bestattung in besonderen Fällen*, 1.
10. LKA Dresden, Bestand 1, No. 803, 180 and No. 806, f. 25: *Einspruch gegen die Entscheidung Der Landessynode in Sachen "Bestattung in besonderen Fällen"*, 1986.
11. In 1975 about 23 per cent of all funerals in the region of Potsdam had been secular. BLHA Potsdam, Rep. 401 RdB Potsdam, No. 21780, *Vortrag*, 1977, 7.
12. D. Pollack, *Kirche in der Organisationsgesellschaft* (Stuttgart: W. Kohlhammer, 1994), 387–88.
13. MLHA Schwerin, Z 77/90, RdB Neubrandenburg, Abt. Inneres, No. 867: *Schlusswort bezirkliche Arbeitsberatung weltliche Feiern*, 13 June 1985, 1.
14. By 1980 the regional figure had risen to 35.3 per cent. See: MLHA Schwerin, Z 77/90, RdB Neubrandenburg, Abt. Inneres, No. 426.
15. In Halle it had been 20 per cent in 1990, but the rate had dropped to 12.5 per cent in 1998, indicating that the trend continued well beyond the re-unification. See Hermelink, 'Die weltliche Bestattung', 66.
16. See for example: B. Happe, 'Entritualisierung der Bestattung in der DDR', in G. Braune and P. Fauser, *Lebensende – Kulturgeschichtlich-volkskundliche Aspekte von Sterben, Tod, Trauer, Bestattung* (Erfurt: Thüringer Hefte für Volkskunde, Band 8/9, 2003), 134–45.
17. See for example: BA Berlin, DO 1 MdI, 34.0, No. 26207: *Handschriftliche Berechnungen*, 1963.
18. This was an international phenomenon: A. Tucholakova and T. Turlakova, 'Rituale und Symbole bei den Bestattungen der Anführer der bulgarischen Arbeiterbewegung'; or P. Verbruggen, 'Alternatives for the Traditional Religious Rituals and Symbols in the Social Democracy of Ghent, 1870–1914'; or C. Collette, 'The International Faith: Rituals and Liturgies of the British Labour Movement Internationalism, 1918–1939', all in B. Unfried and C. Schindler (eds), *Riten, Mythen und Symbole – Die Arbeiterbewegung zwischen "Zivilreligion" und Volkskultur* (Leipzig: AVA, 1999), 273–83, 90–110, 112–134; see also P. Betts, 'When Cold Warriors Die: The State Funerals of Konrad Adenauer and Walter Ulbricht', in Confino, Betts and Schumann (eds), *Between Mass Death and Individual Loss*, 151–76.
19. V. Ackermann, *Nationale Totenfeiern in Deutschland – Von Wilhelm I. bis Franz Josef Strauß – Eine Studie zur politischen Semiotik* (Stuttgart: Klett-Cotta, 1990), 304.
20. BA Berlin, NY 4036, No. 30: *Stenographische Niederschrift der Beratung der Partei- und Regierungskommission zur Vorbereitung der Trauerfeierlichkeiten (Pieck)*, 8 September 1960; also

NY 4090, No. 700: *Vermerk über eine Besprechung zur Auswertung der Erfahrungen bei der Aufbahrung und Trauerfeier für Genossen Otto Grotewohl*, 26 October 1964. There a decision was made that the Central Committee should store a more ornate coffin that would befit a state funeral, and that fitted more securely the mode of transportation (a gun carriage) used in the *cortege*.

21. BA Berlin, DA 5 Staatsrat, No. 8824: *Protokollabteilung.*

22. For example the Mayor of Leipzig Dr Karl-Heinz Müller: SSA Leipzig, BT/RdB Leipzig, No. 10521; Werner Wittig in Magdeburg: BLHA Potsdam, Rep. 530, NL W. Wittig, No. 8464, or lesser known individuals such as Werner Riechers (the Assistant Mayor of Magdeburg): StA Magdeburg, Rep. 41, No. 1562.

23. BLHA Potsdam, Rep. 531, SED KL Zossen, No. 892: *Festlegung für eine würdige atheistische Bestattung der Mitglieder unserer Partei*, 8 April 1981, 2.

24. The selection of music as well as poems and recitations were other aspects influenced by the precedent set at socialist funerals. SSA Chemnitz, RdB Karl-Marx-Stadt, Abt. Inneres, Personalwesen, No. 47109: *Methodisches Material für Namensweihen, Sozialistische Feiern bei Eheschließungen, Trauerfeiern sozialistischen Inhalts*, 21–27.

25. BA Berlin, DO 1 MdI, 2.3, No. 51891, 62–84: *Hinweise für eine Bestattung.*

26. THSA Weimar, AR BL, No. 3347: *Nachruf*, 1–2. The same file also contains an unusually rich assortment of funeral speeches that all provide solid evidence of the uniformity of such speeches.

27. Freidank, *Alles hat am Ende sich gelohnt*, 12–30.

28. 'The funeral bureau president speaks about the deceased's life and offers sympathy to the bereaved. Relatives and friends also say a few words, interspersed with funeral music from a band. There is a minute's silence. A black-bordered state flag is lowered. The official announces: "A citizen of the USSR (names) has completed his life's journey. The motherland says farewell to its son. May fond memories of him remain eternally in our hearts."' A 1979 ceremony in Leningrad as described by C.A.P. Binns, 'The Changing Face of Power: Revolution and Accommodation in the Development of the Soviet Ceremonial System, Part II', *Man: Journal of the Royal Anthropological Institute*, 15:1 (1980), 180. See also: F. Prosenjak, 'Die Bewältigung der Todesproblematik im sozialistischen Begräbnis in Jugoslawien', *Liturgisches Jahrbuch*, 29:3 (1979), 143–56.

29. SSA Leipzig, BT/RdB Leipzig, No. 18554: *Die Aufgaben bei der Entwicklung der weltanschaulichen-atheistischen Propaganda im Bezirk Leipzig*, 23 January 1964, esp. 3–12.

30. MLHA Schwerin, Rep. 7.1-1, RdB Schwerin, 1. Überlieferungschicht, No. 3995 a: *Anleitung für die Durchführung von Bestattungsfeiern für die nichtkirchliche Bevölkerung*, 4.

31. 'Der einzelne Mensch ist nichts für sich, erst in der Gesellschaft vollendet sich sein Wirken. Er gibt und nimmt von der Gesellschaft und ist ihr unverbrüchlich verbunden': MLHA Schwerin, Rep. 7.1-1, RdB Schwerin, 1. Überlieferungschicht, No. 3995 a: *Anleitung für die Durchführung von Bestattungsfeiern für die nichtkirchliche Bevölkerung*, 4.

32. N. Ostrowski , *Wie der Stahl gehärtet wurde*, in SSA Chemnitz, RdB Karl-Marx-Stadt, Abt. Inneres, No. 47109; see also Freidank, *Alles hat am Ende sich gelohnt*, 4.

33. 'The funeral eulogy is a potent form of ideological influence and education': SSA Leipzig, BT/RdB Leipzig, No. 21195: *Rahmenprogramm Rednerausbildung*, 1977, 12.

34. The model speeches were either in published booklets: Freidank, *Alles hat am Ende sich gelohnt*, or circulated internally: SSA Chemnitz, BT/RdB Leipzig, No. 20679: *Die wir das Leben lieben! (Gedanken zur Gestaltung sozialistischer Feiern)*, 1961.

35. MLHA Schwerin, Z 77/90, RdB Neubrandenburg, Abt. Inneres, No. 900: *Beispiel einer Traueransprache, 1987/88*, 1–2. The same document also contains a standard speech for the funeral of a child aged 2–5 years. Marxist-Leninist materialist thought had particular problems in imbuing sense in the death of young children. As an issue, it is addressed in all manuals providing guidance on how to conduct secular funerals, but these have problems addressing the issue of grief or avoiding banality, not least because of the brevity of the life being commemo-

rated. Post-reunification one therefore sees a strong increase in the commemoration of deceased children in the form of names on gravestones, ornaments and the placement of toys, etc., on the grave. This can be read as another attempt to reclaim individuality in East German cemeteries.

36. For a detailed analysis, see Richter, 'Der Umgang mit Tod und Trauer', in Becker et al. (eds), *Im Angesicht des Todes*, 246–56.

37. In the wake of anti-church measures a list of fourteen preconditions was drawn up in the city of Leipzig in 1956 stressing these points explicitly; it was sent out to other burial services in an exchange of ideas: MLHA Schwerin, Rep. 7.1-1, RdB Schwerin, 1. Überlieferungschicht, No. 3995 a: *Grundsätzliche Bedingungen für die Zulassung von weltlichen, freigeistigen Sprechern*, 19 January 1956.

38. Orators were paid 20 Mark per speech by the bereaved and 10 Mark extra if the speech was discussed beforehand in person. In the 1980s many speakers requested up to 100 Mark extra as a 'tip'.

39. LA Berlin, C Rep. 115, No. 215: *Fragebogen und Prüfungsordnung für Redner*. StA Dresden: Rep. 9.1.14, No. 189: *Beurteilungskriterien für Bestattungsredner*, 2 September 1977.

40. StA Dresden, Rep. 9.1.14, No. 126.

41. StA Dresden: Rep. 9.1.14, No. 189: *Reklamation der Trauerrede Ursula B./Hospitation 31.2.1982*, 1. The same source also reveals that the normal monthly rate for a part-time orator in Dresden was seventy-five eulogies. This may further explain a certain monotonousness.

42. BA Berlin, DY 30/IV B 2/14/46, *Arbeitsgruppe Kirchenfragen am ZK der SED: O.Klohr/W. Kaul/K.Kurth, Über Wirkungsfelder und Wirksamkeit kirchlicher Institutionen in der DDR. Kirchenstudie 1981 (Rostock Warnemünde)*. See also: I. Lange, 'Von der Wiege bis zur Bahre: Zur Geschichte Sozialistischer Feiern zu Geburt, Ehe und Tod in der DDR', *Kulturnation: Online Journal für Kultur, Wissenschaft und Politik*, 27:1 (2004). The area of funeral rites of the GDR warrants further study, ideally utilizing oral history projects to unlock the many regional differences.

43. BA Berlin, DO 1 MdI, 34.0, No. 26207: *Berichterstattung Halle*, 9 November 1964, 4.

44. BLHA Potsdam, Rep. 801, RdB Cottbus, No. 25874: *Feiern aus Anlaß von Geburt, Eheschließung und Tod*, 6 March 1961, 6.

45. See discussion of proper decoration of these rooms. BLHA Potsdam, Rep. 601, No. 34043.

46. TSA Rudolstadt, RdB Gera, Rep. 2.2.2/20, No. 353: *Finanzierung der sozialistischen Feiern aus Anlaß von Geburt, Eheschließung und Tod*, 28 March 1962, 1–2.

47. BA Berlin, DO 1, No. 31200: *Informationen über eine Beratung beim ZK*, 8 July 1964.

48. BLHA Potsdam, Rep. 601, No. 34044: *Kriterien für die Gewinnung und den Einsatz weltlicher Bestattungsredner*, 23 May 1977, 1.

49. MLHA Schwerin, Z 77/90, RdB Neubrandenburg, Abt. Inneres, No. 867: *Schlusswort bezirkliche Arbeitsberatung weltliche Feiern*, 13 June 1985, 13.

50. Redlin, *Gegenwärtige großstädtische Bestattungsriten*, 21–22.

CONCLUSION

The gravestone had become a trading good, like cooking pots and shoe laces.[1]

Cemetery director Georg Hannig's words, written in 1925 for his profession's foremost trade journal, sought to warn against erosion of professionalism typified by the declining craftsmanship of gravestones and the appearance of cemeteries. Moreover, it served as a clear indictment of what Hannig saw as the prevalence of economic considerations in a profession that should not be determined by the profane motivation of profit. This one sentence, therefore, encapsulates a pervasive and deeply rooted cultural pessimism. Many in charge of aspects of German sepulchral culture since 1945 held similar views, regularly decrying the commercialization of disposal.[2] Moreover, this criticism posited that cemeteries were mirrors of the culture and identity of the nation (as well as of the region) and thus should remain, above all, an artistic (and spiritual) domain. The strength of this conviction can be surmised from Hannig's observations on the application of industrialized production methods to modern cemeteries:

> Where there had been artistically accomplished craftsmanship, there were now serrated edges left by the machine saw, the proliferating greenery replaced by mass-produced railings. In this manner our cemeteries took on an uniform character that no longer touched the heart. The songbirds avoided the location that had once been so familiar, and soon men did too, who shivered when confronted by the cold, bare stone … the cemeteries of the larger cities deteriorated to 'disposal sites'.[3]

These sentiments echo the arguments and fears that motivated the conservation movement (*Heimatschutz*) in the first place.[4] In particular there was the fear of the cemetery becoming an unnatural place full of ornaments and made up of clearly demarcated individualized gravesides. Yet the quotation also highlights a much larger issue. From the late nineteenth and throughout the twentieth century the cemetery became and remained a contested space. Not only did collective commemoration (and ideas of communality) infiltrate the design and function of cemetery space, so did the challenges of modernity. These pressures included the mass production of gravestones; professionalization of funeral direction and technologization of disposal (cremation); the 'correct' level of individuality to be permitted; the balance between individuality and communality in the context of population growth and concomitant in cemetery size; as well as general changes in aesthetics and social mores. The cemetery thus became a locus for reactions against the encroachment of modernity on customs and values. Ultimately cemeteries in Germany (and not only there) became heavily regulated public spaces, through efforts either to enshrine a status quo or to impose an official aesthetics – often fronted by forceful individuals such as Grässel – of tasteful or simply the *correct* design.[5] However, this entrenched contest between idealism and traditionalism formed the backdrop to a permanent process of transmutation in German cemeteries. It was also at odds with the pragmatics of undertaking, cemetery administration and gravestone production as services purveyed or as business enterprises. The aspirations, needs and requests of consumers as well as the essential question of profitability also have to be considered.[6] In addition, there are also the basic needs of those mourning. This many-sided conflict was rendered less intense by the particular nature of cemetery ownership in Germany. Unlike in Britain or the United States there were hardly any private alternatives, allowing cemeteries to operate unchallenged on the basis of a local monopoly, and funeral directors (if licensed) had to adhere to a whole host of regulations. This meant that a disdain for overt economic considerations as well as a strong idealistic view of how cemeteries should look and function permeated and characterized much of German sepulchral culture in the first half of the twentieth century, and beyond.[7]

These deeply embedded traditions and mentalities help to explain the nature of East German sepulchral culture and the fact that changes and reforms after 1945 were gradual, patchy, hampered by administrative inertia and so seldom drastic. Indeed, often the same personnel remained in charge of managing both the day-to-day routine as well as the wider thinking on how to bury the dead.[8] Moreover, change was gradual not because of, but despite, there being a heavily centralized political system and a predominately Protestant, largely urban population. One example will suffice: the incomplete municipalization of the undertaking business. In East Berlin, private companies numbered seventy-two after the war, in 1963 there remained eight, but, as in Leipzig, there were still independent undertakers not offering the rationalized choices provided by the municipal burial services of cities like Dresden or Rostock. In short, even towards the end of the GDR the two largest cities of the GDR had not seen full municipalization.[9] Furthermore, despite suggestions to the contrary, the church cemeteries were not municipalized, nor was the influence of church institutions over their cemeteries at any point severely curtailed. Instead local level *modi vivendi* were found. Regarding the propagation of cremation, socialist institutions had great difficulty overcoming both the traditional north–south and urban–rural divides in the popularity of cremation as a form of disposal.[10] Similar problems were encountered with the promotion of burial in an *Urnengemeinschaftsanlage* (UGA). The advance of socialist and secular rituals faced an even more complex set of pressures, often of a local nature (such as the availability and skill of orators and the sheer embeddedness of tradition), that eased or impeded their introduction, promotion and ultimately their acceptance as an alternative to the traditional Christian funeral.[11] In the context of such obstacles to 'socialist sepulchral culture', it is very surprising that several commentators have afforded such scant emphasis on these conflicting imperatives.[12]

This is not to suggest there was no socialist sepulchral culture.[13] However, this sepulchral culture possessed far less ideological or totalizing radicalism than has generally been suggested.[14] The desire for more radical change was there, just as it was in other social projects such as the provision of housing or welfare support for working women.[15] In the initial debate about the municipalization of church cemeteries, for example, the intention had been to remove church ownership of cemeteries altogether, but that failed to account for the political implications of enforcing such a policy against the resistance of large sections of the churches. To put this gradualness into context, Czechoslovakia was the only Soviet bloc country that conducted a comprehensive socialist reform of sepulchral culture. This was possible because the decision to do so in 1958 was swiftly enacted.[16] Consequently, the Czechoslovak precedent became the index of success for any socialist reform.[17] Compared to the ČSSR, the East German steps towards achieving similar results appear drawn out and ultimately incomplete, thus challenging any interpretation that elided the many nuances in East German sepulchral culture. Even with the establishment of the IfK (*Institut für Kommunalwirtschaft*) in 1962 as a central agency to steer developments and to facilitate deliberation of alternative models, change did not occur immediately. On the contrary it took until the late 1960s for a definition of (an East German) socialist sepulchral culture to be systematized. This underlines the crucial point that changes in sepulchral culture were evolutionary.

The work of the IfK in this context is important, as are the roles of individual specialists such as Karl Thomas, Wilfried Scherzer and Manfred Kramer.[18] It was under their leadership that plans and conceptions were drawn up, and policies for future implementation formulated. Some of these ideas, such as the complete restructuring of the network of crematoria, remained utopian, but they highlight the importance of the individual specialist (and the quasi-interest group they formed together) in preparing the basic policies underpinning the emergence of a socialist sepulchral culture. Countrywide implementation of the other ideas – such as breaking with the tradition of bourgeois cemetery design, the concentrated propagation of cremation and the introduction of more UGAs

– that informed actual practice, took time. The main reason for this was that, unlike in the ČSSR, the initiative did not come from above, in the form of a single decision or a set of legal restrictions. Legal obstacles such as the Potsdam Accords, resistance of the churches, internal normalization, administrative disorganization and apathy, as well as a general lack of sustained political interest by a ministry or party organization prevented this.[19] In contrast, change was slowly introduced through the regional *Leitbetriebe* (leading concerns) on the basis of communication and dissemination of 'best practice'.[20] The introduction of a socialist sepulchral culture, therefore, relied on individual initiative, since despite the convoluted rhetoric of a 'community of the working people' (*Gemeinschaft der Werktätigen*), the leading cadres and the directors of the *Leitbetriebe* could initiate and coordinate such practices.[21]

Vectors of reform from the middle layer of regional administrators downwards help to explain two hitherto neglected issues: a) the large discrepancies between the regions and districts of the GDR, since this approach specifically accounted for considerations of the economic and political reality of each burial service and each cemetery and relied on individual initiative; b) the comparability with other European countries, since this approach avoids a reliance on the concept of monolithic or centre-driven change, and actually limits the scope for reform to cities and towns as well as certain regions, resulting in a dynamic amalgamation of social, political and economic imperatives. The introduction of the *Leitbetrieb* as the principal agent of coordination (the concepts were provided by the IfK) swiftly revealed the primacy of microeconomic (*betriebswirtschaftliche*) considerations. Thus, a fifty-page report on the municipal burial services and cemeteries in the region of Rostock written in 1974 reads like a strategic investments review, concerned primarily with where to concentrate the limited resources. However, most striking is the language when the report addresses the question of cremation, inasmuch as it makes a clear *volte-face*:

> Since cremation is an aesthetically faultless and hygienically expedient form of disposing of the dead appropriate to the development of socialism, the emphasis when judging the necessity of a crematorium cannot rest on economic considerations.
>
> Nonetheless in that which follows a number of economic advantages of cremation shall be described.[22]

After this interjection, the report does not mention anything except economic advantages and considerations.

Detailed economic plans and precise costing characterized the everyday operation of burial services and cemeteries in the GDR. The burial service of Dresden, for example, calculated detailed costs, revenues and profits for every single item or service it provided.[23] Hence, in Dresden in 1956 the average profit per burial was 6.48 Mark, while additional services such as transportation or coffins had higher profit margins (up to 56.7 per cent). As with cooking pots and shoe laces, revenue needed to cover costs, because the regional government, and ultimately the central government, were not willing (and to a certain extend increasingly unable) to subsidize the burial services. The establishment of a socialist sepulchral culture lost out. This left the burial services and the local governments to have to deal with the financial burden of this duty. Fluctuations in the numbers of burials (something a planned economy found difficult to account for) rendered estimates of profitability uncertain.[24] The clearest example of this phenomenon is a letter by the permanent *Staatssekretär* Grünstein to all regional and district administrations telling them that they should not budget for socialist rituals, but that institutions and companies should finance them independently.[25] The churches, by contrast, had to rely on financial aid from the West in order to cover the deficits they incurred because their funerals included many more inhumations and were thus more labour-intensive.[26]

This is not to discount the relationship with ideology altogether: ideology played a role, but only when economics intruded. Cremation illustrates this symbiosis, inasmuch as cremation neatly fitted into the ideological framework, and given that one half of its historical development could easily be linked with socialism and socialist aesthetics. The propagation of other ideas was more costly, and needed to address the tastes, needs and aesthetics of the audience. Much was said about creating a suitable ambience for socialist or secular funerals, but that demanded considerable investment. Yet investment was rarely available, otherwise the widespread decay of ceremonial halls cannot be explained. In 1987, for instance, a report on the region of Dresden found that in every district ceremonial halls were in need of renovation. In one case the local hall only had twelve non-matching chairs which members of the community had donated, and in another the ceremonial hall was also used to store corpses and gardening machinery.[27] Moreover, the many constraints on sepulchral culture became ever more pressing. In 1969 Karl Thomas gave a number of practical reasons why inhumation had to be curbed, highlighting the problem of personnel shortages:

> Through the orientation towards cremation and urn burials the digging of graves for inhumations will be limited. The personnel situation at the other cemeteries (circa 2,000 municipalities …) has to be secured for the coming development:
> - A substantial number of the employees are already of pensionable age; that percentage will rise to about 50 per cent at the end of the prognosis [1980] …
> - People's aversion, especially among young people, against working at a cemetery is growing, especially since no material incentives can be offered.
>
> The only possibility to secure operation is seen in the concentrating of concerns into economic combines.[28]

Whilst this gives an insight into immediate and future difficulties of recruitment, the economic constraints and an aging personnel, the rationale indicates that concentration and with it the economies of scale became the solution to the economic pressures (such as in the plans for the more centralized organization of cremation). Furthermore, it is precisely these constraints which ultimately explain the dissonances between the manifold ideological declarations in primary sources pertaining to sepulchral culture and the all-informing economic algebra that clearly underpinned much of the GDR's sepulchral culture.

Consequently, a Swedish delegation concluded that the new standard regulation for cemeteries clearly reflected economic and hygienic deliberations (as the fundamental duty of disposal), and not ideological fervour:

> The new standard regulation for cemeteries in the GDR deals extensively with the hygienic and economic necessities and points of view that have to be considered in the administration and establishment of cemeteries. In that regard the regulations are not sentimental, but in general seem to respect the right to one's grave that in the past had been granted 'in perpetuity'.[29]

The last phrase seems to insinuate that the authors expected a socialist country to be less respectful, and more radical. The close scrutiny of the methods used to propagate the different elements of socialist sepulchral culture, however, indicates the range of subtle means of propagation – and even the use of incentives (albeit minute ones) for the personnel of the burial services. Pricing policy played a role, as did the personal interaction with staff in the burial services organizing funerals, reflecting the nature of government in the GDR after 1960 and its interaction with society. An analogy exists here with the inconspicuous yet authoritarian means such as the *Aussprache* (the 'constructive' discussion between party officials and individuals or families) used with regard to matters such as the *Jugendweihe* or requests to leave the GDR for the FRG.

Despite these very specific East German methods, the development of the GDR's sepulchral culture closely corresponded with that of Western Europe as a whole, since most European countries faced the same challenges, such as demographic change or lack of cemetery space. Indeed, cremation in the UK rose substantially more rapidly than in the GDR, from post-war levels of around 4 per cent to 71 per cent in 2000.[30] Similarly, more than 90 per cent of those who die in the city of Copenhagen are buried in anonymous communal urn graves.[31] General trends are even more revealing. From the 1960s onwards, in the GDR as well as in Western Europe, both cemeteries and burial services became firmly part of the service economy. Funeral directors replaced traditional undertakers in the West, a development that was mirrored in the emergence of the comprehensive burial services in the cities of East Germany. However, there was one fundamental difference: while in Western Europe this led to the commercialization of funeral direction and, to a lesser degree, of cemetery operation, in the GDR, with its state-run economy and its insistence that disposal was a sovereign task of the state, it led to an ever more 'efficient' means of disposal – with all the problems such an approach entailed.[32]

Cemeteries and *Urnengemeinschaftsanlagen* showed most drastically what this meant. On the one hand, resting periods (the time during which the grave is banned from re-use) were cut to sometimes less than fifteen years, and, on the other, the quest for efficiency led to an incessant reduction in the area needed per burial – culminating in the UGA and the scattering of ashes. In this respect East

German developments in the organization of death and disposal curiously resemble those of housing construction. Both had similar ideological and political motivations and suffered from insufficient investment due to the escalation of the *X-Bereich* budget (secret spending on the military, the state security apparatus, border protection, police and party). Consequently, both housing and cemeteries increasingly failed to reflect the ideal. Burial plots, like the newly built flats, became smaller the longer the GDR existed. The comparison of their respective shortcomings resonates in another way: the general underlying economic condition of the GDR. A 1975 report on the problems of the socialist 'way of life' acknowledges that modern economic reality even governs the cultural development of a socialist country:

> The precondition for the fulfilment of the material and cultural needs of men, for the realization of all aspects of the socialist way of life, is an efficient economy and continual economic growth on the basis of planned and proportional development. Ever increasing productivity of labour and the raising of the efficacy of economic efforts are the precondition for raising the additional revenue (*Mehrprodukt*) that can be reinvested in [the] socialist society, which can be used for the ever better meeting of the needs and to increase the well-being of the people.[33]

Considering Hartmut Zwahr's argument that the GDR's economy was never healthy, it becomes clear that the 227,000 annual deaths simply surpassed the regime's capabilities – at least unless it reduced costs wherever feasible.[34] This resulted in systemic shortages of qualified personnel, inadequate investment, machinery and crematoria in need of repair, as well as dilapidated cemeteries, which caused resentment and outrage:

> You certainly have yet not looked at the appearance of the resting place of our loved ones! It resembles a dumping site for rubble! Yesterday we once again had to observe that the last burial area [of the UGA] for May is covered only in weeds, and it is intended for humans, who have dedicated all their energy to the construction of our Republic![35]

A focus upon differences between the East and the West of Germany alone is, however, at best, misleading: it fits too easily into existing patterns of explanation, and seems persuasive because confirming the assumption that sepulchral culture develops differently under an authoritarian/totalitarian regime. Such a view overlooks the more challenging, complicated and contradictory reality of the GDR and its sepulchral culture, inasmuch as it was a culture that was and became, as in the West, very much dependent on local and regional idiosyncrasies and individuals' idea of what constituted a 'decent and appropriate' burial – but which also had to negotiate the economic realities. The considerable differentiation in the organization and scope of burial services, in cremation rates and the acceptance of UGAs or secular funeral rituals has made this distinctive point repeatedly. This demonstrates that it is crucial to study sepulchral culture holistically and not to concentrate merely on micro-narratives – the detail may deceive:

the early success of UGAs in some cities of the GDR (such as Plauen, Erfurt, Chemnitz or Dresden) stands in contrast to the relative obscurity of anonymous burials in most of the FRG, for example. The panorama painted here avoids preconceptions of how change came about. Thus, the church was not exclusively a bastion of traditionalism, as its acceptance of UGAs and the scattering of the ashes demonstrates. Moreover, rural areas were not always resistant to sepulchral change, as some rural areas had very high rates of secular funerals, once more disclosing the weight of local factors and influences.

In this light it is even more surprising that so much of the history of German sepulchral culture, besides cemetery design and funeral rites, has yet to be researched in any great detail. A systematic post-war history of the sepulchral culture in West Germany is missing, as is a history of cremation after 1945. Ultimately, the present work might help to open a little wider the door to a world beyond silence, a world of rituals, habits, customs, designs, ideas, ideology, economics, technocrats and funeral directors. That is to say the realm emanating from the inescapable certainty of death.

Death has to be confronted by both individuals and states. Zygmunt Bauman has expressed our troubled relationship:

> We all 'know' very well what death is; that is, until we are asked to give a precise account of what we know – to define death as we 'understand' it. Then the trouble starts. It transpires that it is ultimately impossible to define, through attempts to define it – to master it (albeit intellectually), to assign it its proper place and keep it there – will never stop. It is impossible to define death, as death stands for the final void, for that non-existence which, absurdly, gives existence to all being. Death is the absolute *other* of being, an *unimaginable* other, hovering beyond the reach of communication; whenever being speaks of that other, it finds itself speaking, through a negative metaphor, of itself.[36]

That negative metaphor is life – life as the definable other; as such, discussions of death will always be discussions of life.

Notes

1. Hannig, 'Alte und Neue Friedhofskunst', 47.
2. A wonderful example is a booklet published in the 1960s that incorporated identical views: H. Schäfer, *Die Friedhofsgestaltung* (Detmold: Lippischer Heimatbund, 1960), 9–11.
3. G. Hannig, 'Alte und Neue Friedhofskunst', 46.
4. T. Rohkrämer, *Eine andere Moderne – Zivilisationskritik, Natur und Technik in Deutschland 1880-1933* (Paderborn: Schönigh, 1999), 126–40. See also: W. Oberkrome, *Deutsche Heimat: nationale Konzeption und regionale Praxis von Naturschutz, Landschaftsgestaltung und Kulturpolitik in Westfalen-Lippe und Thüringen, 1900-1960* (Paderborn: Schöningh, 2004).

5. Similar trends can be seen in Austria, Switzerland and to a lesser degree in Britain and the United States. The overlapping elements between proponents of the cemetery reform movement itself and the conservation movement (*Heimatschutz*), especially with regard to architecture, were numerous. Cemetery regulations of the period indicate a great interest in preserving the regional character of many cemeteries by prescribing the use of certain locally quarried stone and banning 'false practises' such as the use of coloured gravel or too ornate designs for gravestones.

6. A famous example of the friction between regulations and public tastes is the use of plastic or textile flowers. Most German cemeteries to this day will remove these whenever they are left on graves.

7. Bohl, 'Die Ethik der Nützlichkeit', in Sörries (ed.), *Vom Reichsauschuß zur Arbeitsgemeinschaft Friedhof und Denkmal*, 115–32.

8. The original pamphlet published by a number of specialists in 1958 uses socialist language, but clearly continues the earlier tradition of the reform movement. See: Provisorischer Arbeitskreis für Friedhofsgestaltung, *Der Friedhof – Gedanken für Alle* (1958).

9. Redlin, *Gegenwärtige großstädtische Bestattungsriten*, 6–7.

10. BA Berlin, DO 4, No. 892: *Prognose für die Entwicklung des Friedhofs- und Bestattungswesens*, 10 April 1969.

11. The entire analysis instigated by the permanent secretary Grünstein in the Ministry of the Interior makes this clear. See: BA Berlin, DO 1 MdI, 34.0, No. 26207.

12. For example: Happe, 'Die sozialistische Reform', in Sörries (ed.), *Vom Reichsauschuß zur Arbeitsgemeinschaft Friedhof und Denkmal*,187–93, but also Hoffjan, 'Existierte eine spezifische realsozialistische Friedhofgestaltung in der DDR?', in same volume, 171.

13. Schelenz and Meinel, '"Sozialistische" Friedhofskultur in der DDR?', 12–15.

14. For example, while Barbara Happe acknowledges the length of the process, she argues that there was a fundamental and concentrated effort to align the sepulchral culture of the country with the political ideology. Happe, 'Die Nachkriegsentwicklung der Friedhöfe in beiden deutschen Staaten', 215.

15. D. Harsch, *Revenge of the Domestic: Women, the Family and Communism in the German Democratic Republic* (Princeton: Princeton University Press, 2007).

16. To my knowledge there is no detailed study of the 1958 sepulchral reform of Czechoslovakia.

17. For example in 1962 a number of officials exchanged ideas with counterparts in ČSSR, noting that cremation got enormous support and that the government in Czechoslovakia had also decided to curb the 'cult of the person' by allowing the scattering of ashes. BA Berlin, DO 4, No. 891: *Erfahrungsaustausch mit der Delegation von Freunden der Feuerbestattung aus der CSSR*, 20 April 1962, 1. See also: BA Berlin, DO 1 MdI, No. 7800: *Übersetzung des Materials des Institut für Aufklärung in Prag*, 29 June 1960.

18. BA Berlin, DO 4, No. 892: *Prognose für die Entwicklung des Friedhofs und Bestattungswesens*, 31 January 1969; Kramer (ed.), *Urnengemeinschaftsanlagen*, 7.

19. J. Madarász, 'Economic Politics and Company Culture: The Problem of Routinisation', in Fulbrook (ed.), *Power and Society in the GDR*, 52–75.

20. It is important to stress that the role of the exchange of impressions and experiences between different institutions (*Erfahrungsaustausch*) was central and when taken seriously very detailed. For example in 1987 a delegation of the burial service Dresden visited the district city Pirna to assess the local burial service the report notes amongst numerous points that the furniture of the burial service office was 'light and inviting' and that 'a sign announcing the purpose of the office should be moved from the shop window to the street'. StA Dresden, Rep. 9.1.14, No. 136: *Erfahrungsaustausch in Heidenau und Pirna*, 15 December 1987, 1.

21. StA Dresden; Rep. 9.1.14, No. 731: *Richtlinien über die Stellung, Aufgaben, und Arbeitsweise von Leitbetrieben auf dem Gebiet der stadtwirtschaftlichen Dienstleistungen*, 1971, 2–3. The costs for operating as a *Leitbetrieb* had to be covered by the revenue of the concern in question and not by governmental subsidies, further stretching their finances and personnel.

22. VLA Greifswald, Rep. 200, 2.2.2.1, No. 97: *Konzeption zu Entwicklung des Friedhofs- und Bestattungswesens im Bezirk Rostock für den Zeitraum 1975–1990*, 15 November 1974, 43.

23. For example: StA Dresden, Rep. 9.1.14, No. 230: *Gegenüberstellung Erlöse und Kosten 1956, 6 August 1958*; StA Greifswald, Rep. 7.4, No. 300: *Rechenschaftsbericht für das Geschäftsjahr 1962 des Greifswalder Bestattungsinstituts VEB (st)*, 27 February 1963. Dresden offers one of the most complete pictures with regard to internal accounting, whereas other remain within the companies that emerged after 1990 or have probably not been kept for such a long period.

24. StA Dresden, Rep. 9.1.14, No. 761: *Planung und Abrechnung von preisgebundenen Subvententionen und Abgaben*, 31 March 1976.

25. TSA Rudolstadt, RdB Gera, Rep. 2.2.2/20, No. 353: *Finanzierung der sozialistischen Feiern aus Anlaß von Geburt, Eheschließung und Tod*, 28 March 1962. In the 1980s there were some exceptions, but the burden was squarely put on the local level, as some decided to put aside a small reserve to stimulate secular funerals. For example, in 1987 in Bad Freienwalde, 3,200 Mark were set aside from the budget reserve, amounting to about 20 Mark per secular funeral: BLHA Potsdam, Rep. 601, No. 34044: *Beschluß des RdK Freienwalde*, 2–3.

26. EZA Berlin, Rep. 101, No. 2565, *Vergleich von Einzelleistungen beim KFA Leipzig 1977*.

27. StA Dresden, Rep. 9.1.14, No. 136: *Aktueller Stand von Rekonstruktionen und Neubau von Feier- und Leichenhallen in den Kreisstädten*, 11 November 1987, 1–2.

28. BA Berlin, DO 4, No. 892: *Prognose für die Entwicklung des Friedhofs und Bestattungswesens*, 31 January 1969, 46.

29. Grufman and Ingemark, *Feuerbestattung und Friedhofswesen in der DDR*, 7.

30. Even with regard to an antiquated legislative framework East Germany did not stand alone; in Britain to this day most aspects of funerals are still governed by the 1857 Burial Act. Despite announcements in 1999 and again in 2000 the Home Office has yet to publish proposals to redraft legislation for burials. There is also little political debate about the reuse of burial plots despite a looming crisis of availability of cemetery space. As an introduction see: O. Brukeman, 'Sensitive Britons Try to Bury Cemetery Crisis', *The Guardian*, 2 September 2000, 7.

31. In 1925 the first modern anonymous communal urn burial site was opened in Copenhagen. However, the price, unlike in the GDR, was always kept at a similar level to conventional forms of burial. Grave digging and the lease of a burial plot costs were 4,537 DKK in 2004, while cremation, the interment of the urn and lease of urn plot cost about 3,795 DKK. See also: C. Fogmoes, 'Cremation Developments in Denmark', *Pharos International*, 67:1 (2001), 45–47.

32. The introduction of the lawn cemetery (fields of headstones with no other vegetation but turf) in Britain after 1950 is an interesting case in point, because similar principles of economy and ease of maintenance played an important role in that process. 'Similarly, the practice of cremation took the corpse from a traditional milieu (the cemetery), and introduced a highly technical intervention that again defined its practitioners as specialists. The lawn cemetery, admittedly on smaller scale, aimed to effect a similar transition, in looking to remove the corpse from a family-controlled environment into one in which scientific principles and regulations were dominant.' For a detailed discussion see: Rugg, 'Lawn Cemeteries', 213–33.

33. SAPMO-BA Berlin, DY 30, No. 26343: *Probleme der sozialistischen Lebensweise und Intensivierung, ZISW (Zentralinstitut für sozialistische Wirtschaftsführung beim ZK der SED)*, 1975.

34. H. Zwahr, 'Kontinuitätsbruch und mangelnde Lebensfähigkeit – Das Scheitern der DDR', in Kaelble et al. (eds), *Sozialgeschichte der DDR*, 557.

35. Complaints about the Crematorium: StA Dresden, Rep. 9.1.14, No. 289: *Eingabeanalyse 1985*. The quoted complaint was written in regard to the UGA on the Heidefriedhof in Dresden: StA Dresden, Rep. 9.1.14, No. 288; *Eingabeanalyse 1979*.

36. Bauman, *Mortality, Immortality and Other Life Strategies*, 2.

BIBLIOGRAPHY

Primary Sources

Archives

Archiv der Kirchenprovinz Sachsen, Magdeburg (AKS Magdeburg)
   No. 903 d

Bundesarchiv, Berlin (BA)
   DA 5 Staatsrat, No. 8822
   DO 1 MdI, No. 31200
   DO 1 MdI, 2.3, No. 51891
   DO 1 MdI, 34.0, No. 26207
   DO 1 MdI, 34.0, No. 48678
   DO 1 MdI, No. 7500
   DO 1 MdI, No. 7800
   DO 4 Kirchenfragen, No. 2162
   DO 4, No. 863
   DO 4, No. 891
   DO 4, No. 892
   DQ 1, No. 11613
   NY 4036, No 30
   NY 4090, No. 700

Brandenburgisches Landeshauptarchiv, Potsdam (BLHA Potsdam)
   Rep 202, No. 498a
   Rep 401 RdB Potsdam, No. 6300
   Rep 401 RdB Potsdam, No. 6309
   Rep. 211 MfG, No. 1126
   Rep. 401 RdB Potsdam, No. 21780
   Rep. 520, NL W. Wittig, No. 8464
   Rep. 531, KL Brandenburg, No. 1295
   Rep. 531, SED KL Zossen, No. 892
   Rep. 601, No. 34043
   Rep. 601, No. 34044
   Rep. 801, RdB Cottbus, No. 25874

Evangelisches Zentralarchiv, Berlin (EZA Berlin)
  4/563
  4/716
  Rep. 101, No. 2565
  Rep. 101, No. 2567
  ZA 5109/02, No. 101/3377
  ZA 5109/02, No. 101/5221
  ZA 5109/02, No. 104/1216

Kreisarchiv Weimarer Land, Apolda (KA Weimarer Land)
  RdK Apolda, No. 3476

Landesarchiv Berlin, Berlin (LA Berlin)
  C Rep. 104, No. 607
  C Rep. 109, No. 1070
  C Rep. 110, No. 1068
  C Rep. 115, No. 215
  C Rep. 115, No. 220

Landeshauptarchiv Sachsen-Anhalt, Magdeburg (LHSA Magdeburg)
  Rep. K2 Ministerpräsident, No. 3885
  Rep. K2 Ministerpräsident, No. 7696
  Rep. K2, Ministerpräsident, No. 695
  P 13, SED-Bezirksleitung Magdeburg, No. 22810

Landeskirchenarchiv, Dresden (LKA Dresden)
  Bestand 1, No. 803
  Bestand 1, No. 806
  Bestand 2, No. 356
  Bestand 2, No. 3404
  Bestand 2, No. 34100
  Bestand 2, No. 34232

Landesarchiv Sachsen-Anhalt, Merseburg (LSA Merseburg)
  RdB Halle, No. 3800
  RdB Halle, 3. Ablage, No. 18530

Mecklenburgisches Landeshauptarchiv, Schwerin (MLHA Schwerin)
  RdB Schwerin, Abt. ÖVW, No. 36354
  Rep. 6.11-11 MdI, No. 1791
  Rep. 6.11-11 MdI, No. 561
  Rep. 7.1-1, RdB Schwerin, 1. Überlieferungschicht, No. 3995 a
  Rep. 7.1-1, RdB Schwerin, 1. Überlieferungschicht, No. 3995 b
  Z 77/90, RdB Neubrandenburg, Abt. Inneres, No. 426
  Z 77/90, RdB Neubrandenburg, Abt. Inneres, No. 867
  Z 77/90, RdB Neubrandenburg, Abt. Inneres, No. 900

Nordrhein-Westfälisches Staatsarchiv, Detmold (NWSA Detmold)
  D 1, Dezernat 24, No. 225
  D 106 Detmold, No. 2128
  D 106 Detmold, No. 2152
  D 106 Detmold, No. 436
  D 106 Detmold, No. 2146
  L 80 IC (Medizinalwesen Minden), Fach L.5, No. 9

Stiftung Archiv der Parteien und Massenorganisationen der DDR im Bundesarchiv,
    Berlin (SAPMO-BA Berlin)
  DY 30/J IV 2/2 A, No. 789
  DY 30, No. 26343
  DY 30/IV B 2/14/46 - Arbeitsgruppe Kirchenfragen am ZK der SED

Sächsisches Hauptstaatsarchiv, Dresden (SHSA Dresden)
  BT/RdB Dresden, 7.1., No. 6159

Sächsisches Staatsarchiv, Leipzig (SSA Leipzig)
  Bezirksleitung Leipzig, IV E-2/10/589
  BT/RdB Leipzig, No. 10521
  BT/RdB Leipzig, No. 18554
  BT/RdB Leipzig, No. 20679
  BT/RdB Leipzig, No. 21195
  BT/RdB Leipzig, No. 21420

Sächsisches Staatsarchiv, Chemnitz (SSA Chemnitz)
  RdB Karl-Marx-Stadt, Abt. Inneres, Personalwesen, No. 47109
  BT and RdB, Abt. Örtliche Wirtschaft

Stadtarchiv Bielefeld (StA Bielefeld)
  Akte FW 152–54: *Krematorium Sennefriedhof Vol. I – III.*

Stadtarchiv Dresden (StA Dresden)
  RdS, I/18/70
  Rep. 9.1.13, No. 737
  Rep. 9.1.14, No. 102
  Rep. 9.1.14, No. 126
  Rep. 9.1.14, No. 13
  Rep. 9.1.14, No. 130
  Rep. 9.1.14, No. 131
  Rep. 9.1.14, No. 136
  Rep. 9.1.14, No. 137
  Rep. 9.1.14, No. 189
  Rep. 9.1.14, No. 204
  Rep. 9.1.14, No. 205
  Rep. 9.1.14, No. 230
  Rep. 9.1.14, No. 288

Rep. 9.1.14, No. 289
Rep. 9.1.14, No. 299
Rep. 9.1.14, No. 373
Rep. 9.1.14, No. 381
Rep. 9.1.14, No. 644
Rep. 9.1.14, No. 731
Rep. 9.1.14, No. 761
Rep. 9.1.14, No. 812
Rep. 9.1.14, No. 825
Rep. 9.1.14, No. 826
Rep. 9.1.14, No. 1828

Stadtarchiv Eisenhüttenstadt
Sig. S 55
Sig. S 77

Stadtarchiv Greifswald (StA Greifswald)
Rep. 7.4., No. 300
Rep. 7.9., No. 260
Rep. 7.9., No. 287
Rep. 7.9., No. 298
VA 1390

Stadtarchiv Magdeburg (StA Magdeburg)
Rep. 41, No. 37
Rep. 41, No. 1433
Rep. 41, No. 1562

Stadtarchiv Halle (StA Halle)
Gebäudeakte Stadtgottesacker

Archiv der Hansestadt Rostock (StA Rostock)
Rep. 2.2.8, No. 10
Rep. 2.2.8, No. 12
Rep. 2.11, No. 5787

Stadtarchiv Schwerin (StA Schwerin)
Abt. MF, No. 82

Thüringisches Hauptsstaatsarchiv, Weimar (THSA Weimar)
AR BL, No. 3347
BPA Erfurt, B II / 2 / 14-001
BPA Erfurt, IV/B/2/5 – 200
BT Erfurt, Abt. Parteiorgane, No. 3347
Thüringischen Ministeriums des Inneren, Akten E 1545
Thüringischen Ministeriums des Inneren, Akten E 1551

Thüringisches Staatsarchiv, Rudolstadt (TSA Rudolstadt)
  BPA SED Gera, IV-A-2/9.01, No. 575
  RdB Gera, Rep. 2.2.2/20, No. 353

Thüringisches Staatsarchiv, Meiningen (TSA Meiningen)
  SED BL Suhl, No. IV/A-2.14/694

Vorpommersches Landesarchiv, Greifswald (VLA Geifswald)
  BL SED, IV / 215, No. 668
  Rep. 200 2.1, No. 1
  Rep. 200 4.3.1, No. 1
  Rep. 200, 2.2.2.1, No. 97
  Rep. 200, 7.1, No. 189

Unpublished

Arbeitsgruppe für weltliche Bestattungen im Bezirk Schwerin, *Leitfaden für die Gestaltung weltlicher Bestattungsfeiern.*

Bräuer, H., 'Die Ersten Drei Jahrzehnte der Ev. Friedenskirchengemeinde Eisenhüttenstadt – Erinnerungen, Selbstverlag'.

Brunnemann, G., *Zur Betreuung Hinterbliebener – Trauer und Trauerstörungen unter besonderer Berücksichtigung von Patienten- und Therapeutenverhalten*, PhD Thesis, Akademie zur Ärztlichen Fortbildung in der DDR, Berlin (circa 1985).

Frenz, P., *Die historische und gesellschaftliche Entwicklung des Bestattungswesen unter der Berücksichtigung der aktuellen Situation in der DDR*, PhD Thesis, Martin-Luther-Universität Halle-Wittenberg (1979).

IfK, *Analyse des Friedhofs- und Bestattungswesens mit Schlußfolgerungen und Vorschlägen zur Lösung der bestehenden Probleme* (Dresden: IfK,1976).

Provisorischer Arbeitskreis für Friedhofsgestaltung, *Der Friedhof – Gedanken für Alle* (1958).

Redlin, J., *Gegenwärtige großstädtische Bestattungsriten – eine empirische Untersuchung in der Hauptstadt der DDR*, Belegarbeit im Fach Ethnologie Humboldt Universität, Berlin (1985).

Published

Autorenkollektiv, *Der Friedhof: Gestaltung und Pflege* (Dresden: IfK, 1980).

Beneke, O., *Von unehrlichen Leuten: Kulturhistorische Studien und Geschichten aus vergangenen Tagen deutscher Gewerbe und Dienste*, Second Edition (Berlin: Hertz, 1889).

Bollenbach, G., 'Gemeinschaftsanlagen – aber wie?', *Informationen aus der Praxis für die Praxis*, No. 1/2 (1980).

Fischer, E. and Bärbig, K., *Die Sozialisierung des Bestattungswesens* – Veröffentlichung der sächsischen Landesstelle für Gemeinwirtschaft (Dresden: v. Zahn and Jaensch, 1921).

Freidank, G., *Alles hat am Ende sich gelohnt – Material für weltliche Trauerfeiern* (Leipzig: Zentralhaus für Kulturarbeit der DDR, 1975).

Grufman, N. and Ingemark, S., *Feuerbestattung und Friedhofswesen in der DDR – Schwedische Feuerbestatter berichten* (Berlin: Volks-Feuerbestattung e.V., 1972).

Hannig, G., 'Alte und Neue Friedhofskunst', *Der Friedhof,* 21:4 (1925), 46–48.

Hager, K., *Philosophie and Politik* (Berlin: Dietz, 1979).

———— *Zu Fragen der Kulturpolitik der SED – Referat auf der Sechsten Tagung des Zentralkomitees der SED* (Berlin: Dietz Verlag, 1972).

Hempelmann, J., *Die Praxis der Friedhofsgärtnerei, Anlage, Verwaltung und Instandhaltung von Friedhöfen und Gräbern* (Berlin: Parey, 1927).

IfK, *Dienstleistungen im Bestattungswesen* (Dresden: IfK, 1979).

———— *Gestaltung unserer Friedhöfe* (Berlin: Staatsverlag der DDR, 1963).

———— *Katalog der Bestattungsdienstleistungen* (Dresden: IfK, 1975).

———— *Rekonstruktion des Südfriedhofes Leipzig* (Dresden: IfK, 1978).

Kaiser, J.-C., *Arbeiterbewegung und Religionskritik – Proletarische Freidenkerverbände in Kaiserreich und Weimarer Republik* (Stuttgart: Klett-Cotta, 1981).

Kramer, M., (ed.), *Erarbeitungen von Vorschlägen und Normativen zur Erhöhung des Dienstleistungsniveaus im Bestattungswesens* (Dresden: IfK, 1974).

———— *Planung, Gestaltung und Pflege von Urnengemeinschaftsanlagen* (Dresden: IfK, 1985).

Kretzschmar, F., *Der Tag hat sich geneigt – Zur Gestaltung weltlicher Trauerfreiern* (Leipzig: Zentralhaus Publikation, 1982).

Müller, G., *Empfiehlt sich für kleine Stadtgemeinden die Errichtung von Krematorien?* Third Edition (Berlin: Volks-Feuerbestattungs-Verein, 1927).

Opitz, M., 'Können wir in der Bestattungswirtschaft mit der deutschen Sprachen auskommen oder müssen wir uns der Fremdwörter bedienen', in *Zeitschrift der Deutsche Bestattungswirtschaft,* 1933.

Schwarz, R., 'Aktive Einflußnahme in Leipzig – Wettbewerb zur Steigerung der Feuerbestattung', *Informationen aus der Praxis für die Praxis,* No. 3–4 (1970).

Statistisches Jahrbuch der Deutschen Demokratischen Republik [1955–1990] (Berlin-Ost: VEB Deutscher Zentralverlag, 1956–91, except 1960/61 published as one volume in 1962).

Statuen betreffend das Begräbniswesen der Stadt Jena (Jena: Universitäts-Buchdruckerei Neuenhahn, 1908).

'Zur Friedhofsanlage', *Blätter für lippische Heimatkunde* [published by *Lippischer Bund für Heimatschutz und Heimatpflege*], No. 2, April (1914).

Secondary Sources

Aaron, M., *Envisaging Death: Dying and Visual Culture* (Newcastle: Cambridge Scholars, 2013).

Ackermann, V., *Nationale Totenfeiern in Deutschland – Von Wilhelm I. bis Franz Josef Strauß – Eine Studie zur politischen Semiotik* (Stuttgart: Klett-Cotta, 1990).

AFD (ed.), *Grabkultur in Deutschland: Geschichte der Grabmäler* (Berlin: Reimer, 2009).

———— (ed.), Raum für Tote – *Die Geschichte der Friedhöfe von den Gräberstraßen der Römerzeit bis zur anonymen Bestattung* (Braunschweig: Thalacker, 2003).

Ahne, P., 'Rote Nelken für Lotte Ulbricht', *Berliner Zeitung,* 19 April 2002.

Ariès, P., *The Hour of Our Death* (Harmondsworth: Penguin, 1983).

———— *Western Attitudes to Death: From the Middle Ages to the Present* (London and New York: Marion Boyars, 1976).

Arnold, C., *Necropolis: London and its Dead* (London: Simon and Schuster, 2007).

Assheuer, T., 'Die neue Sichtbarkeit des Todes', *Die Zeit*, 19 November 2009.

Assmann, A., *Erinnerungsräume – Formen und Wandlungen des kulturellen Gedächtnisses* (Munich: C.H. Beck, 1999).

Baird, J., 'Goebbels, Horst Wessel and the Myth of Resurrection and Return', *Journal of Contemporary History*, 17:4 (1982), 633–50.

Barnett, M. and Rodriguez, S., 'Death Goes Global: An Examination of Foreign Direct Investment in the Death Care Industry' (Unpublished Position Paper, 2003).

Bauer, M. and Wickert, J., *Vorwärts immer, rückwärts nimmer – 4000 Tage BRD* (Berlin: Nicolai, 2004).

Bauman, Z., *Mortality, Immortality and Other Life Strategies* (Cambridge: Polity Press, 1992).

Becker, H., Einig, B. and Ulrich, P.-O. (eds), *Im Angesicht des Todes – Ein interdisziplinäres Kompendium I, Pietas Liturgica 3* (St. Ottilien: EOS Verlag, 1987).

Becker, U., Feldmann, K. and Johannsen, F. (eds), *Sterben und Tod in Europa* (Neukirchen-Vluyn: Neukirchener, 1998).

Behrens, C., 'Kremation im internationalen Kontext und am Beispiel Frankreichs', *Ohlsdorf – Zeitschrift für Trauerkultur*, 83:4 (2003).

Bendann, E., *Death Customs – An Analytical Study of Burial Rites* (London: Dawsons, 1969).

Berdahl, D., '"(N)Ostalgie" for the present: Memory, Longing and East German Things', *Ethnos*, 64:2 (1999), 192–211.

Bergmann, K., Baier, W., Casper R. and Wiesner G. (eds), *Entwicklung der Mortalität in Deutschland von 1955–1989* (Munich: MMV Medizin Verlag, 1993).

Besier, G., 'The German Democratic Republic and the State Churches, 1958–1989', *Journal of Ecclesiastical History*, 50:3 (1999), 523–47.

———— *Der SED-Staat und die Kirchen – Der Weg in die Anpassung* (Munich: C. Bertelsmann, 1993).

Bessel, R., *Germany 1945: From War to Peace* (London: Simon and Schuster, 2009).

———— *Nazism and War* (London: Weidenfeld and Nicolson, 2004).

Bessel, R. and Jessen, M. (eds), *Die Grenzen der Diktatur – Staat und Gesellschaft in der DDR* (Göttingen: Vandenhoeck, 1996).

Bessel, R. and Schumann, D. (eds), *Life after Death – Approaches to a Cultural and Social History of Europe During the 1940s and 1950s* (Cambridge: Cambridge University Press, 2003).

Binns, C.A.P., 'The Changing Face of Power: Revolution and Accommodation in the Development of the Soviet Ceremonial System, Part I', *Man: Journal of the Royal Anthropological Institute*, 14:4 (1979), 585–606.

———— 'The Changing Face of Power: Revolution and Accommodation in the Development of the Soviet Ceremonial System, Part II', *Man: Journal of the Royal Anthropological Institute*, 15:1 (1980), 170–87.

Black, M., *Death in Berlin: From Weimar to Divided Germany* (Cambridge: Cambridge University Press, 2010).

Blackbourn, D. and Eley G. (eds), *The Peculiarities of German History* (Oxford: Oxford University Press, 1984).

Blumenthal-Barby, K., *Betreuung Sterbender: Tendenzen, Fakten, Probleme* (Berlin: VEB Volk und Gesundheit, 1982).

Boehlke H. (ed.), *Wie die Alten den Tod gebildet – Wandlungen der Sepulkralkultur 1750–1850, Kasseler Studien zur Sepulkralkultur Vol. 1* (Mainz: Böhlau, 1979).

Bollwahn de Paez Casanova, B., 'Kampfgruß an Queen Mum der DDR', *taz*, No. 6729, 19 April 2002.

Borchert, W., *Draußen vor der Tür und andere ausgewählte Erzählungen* (Frankfurt: Suhrkamp, 1982).

Bottomore, T. (ed.), *A Dictionary of Marxist Thought*, Second Edition (Oxford: Blackwell, 1991).

———— (ed.), *Karl Marx – Early Writings* (London and New York: McGraw-Hill, 1963).

Bourgeois, R., 'De croque-mort à entrepreneur des pomper funèbres: La Martinme Funeral Directors' Association et la montée du professionalisme au début du 20ᵉ siècle', *Acadiensis (Fredericton)*, 31 (2002), 97–128.

Bowker, J., *The Meaning of Death* (Cambridge: Canto, 1993).

Boys, R., Forster D. and Józan, P., 'Mortality from Causes Amenable and Non-amenable to Medical Care: The Experience of Eastern Europe', *British Medical Journal*, 303 (1991).

Braune, G. and Fauser, P., *Lebensende – Kulturgeschichtlich-volkskundliche Aspekte von Sterben, Tod, Trauer, Bestattung* (Erfurt: Thüringer Hefte für Volkskunde, Band 8/9, 2003).

Brecht B., *Der Gute Mensch von Sezuan* (Frankfurt: Suhrkamp, 1982).

Brown, C., *Death of Christian Britain* (London: Routledge, 2000).

Brukeman, O., 'Sensitive Britons Try to Bury Cemetery Crisis', *The Guardian*, 2 September 2000.

Bundesminister für Gesundheit (ed.), *Indikatoren zum Gesundheitszustand der Bevölkerung in der ehemaligen DDR* (Baden-Baden: Nomos-Verlagsgesellschaft, 1993).

Camus, A., *The Collected Fiction of Albert Camus* (London: Hamish Hamilton, 1960).

Charmaz, K., Howarth G. and Kellehear, A., *The Unknown Country: Death in Australia, Britain and the USA* (Houndsmill: Macmillan, 1997).

Choron, J., *Death and Western Thought* (New York and London: Collier, 1963).

Clark, D. (ed.), *Sociology of Death: Theory, Culture, Practise* (Oxford: Blackwell, 1995).

Confino, A., Betts, P. and Schumann, D. (eds), *Between Mass Death and Individual Loss: The Place of the Dead in Twentieth-Century Germany* (New York: Berghahn, 2008).

Corner, P. (ed.), *Popular Opinion in Totalitarian Regimes. Fascism, Nazism, Communism* (Oxford: Oxford University Press, 2009).

Creuzberger, S., *Die sowjetische Besatzungsmacht und das politische System der SBZ* (Weimar: Böhlau, 1996).

Curl, J., *The Victorian Celebration of Death* (Stroud: Sutton Publishing, 2000).

Davies, D., *A Brief History of Death* (Oxford: Blackwell, 2004).

———— *Death, Ritual and Belief – The Rhetoric of Funerary Rites* (London and Washington: Cassell, 1997).

Davies, D. and Mates, L. (eds), *Encyclopaedia of Cremation* (Aldershot: Ashgate, 2005).

Deja-Lölhöffel, B., *Unbekannter Nachtbar DDR* (Arau and Stuttgart: AT Verlag, 1987).

Dethlefs, S., *Zur Geschichte der Friedhöfe und des Bestattungswesens in Münster* (Münster: Regensberg, 1991).

'Die Hadesmaschine', *Die Tageszeitung*, 21 May 2001.

Diederich, G., Schäfer B. and Ohlemacher, J., *Jugendweihe in der DDR – Geschichte und politische Bedeutung aus christlicher Sicht* (Schwerin: Landeszentrale für politische Bildung Mecklenburg-Vorpommern, 1998).

Eichhorn, W., *Von der Entwicklung des sozialistischen Menschen* (Berlin: Dietz, 1964).

Eliade, M., *The Sacred and the Profane – The Nature of Religion* (New York: Harper and Row, 1961).

Elias, N., *The Civilizing Process Vol. 2* (Oxford: Oxford University Press, 1982).

——— *The Loneliness of the Dying* (Oxford: Blackwell, 1985).

Eppelmann, R. et al. (eds), *Lexikon des DDR-Sozialismus* (Paderborn: Schöningh, 1996).

Eschebach, I. (ed.), *Die Sprache des Gedenkens: Zur Geschichte der Gedenkstätte Ravensbrück 1945–1995* (Berlin: Hentrich, 1999).

Feldmann, K., *Sterben und Tod – Sozialwissenschaftliche Theorien und Forschungsergebnisse* (Opladen: Leske + Budrich, 1997).

——— *Tod und Gesellschaft: Sozialwissenschaftliche Thanatologie im Überblick* (Wiesbaden: Verlag für Sozialwissenschaften, 2004).

Felicori M. and Zanotti, A., *Cemeteries of Europe – A Historical Heritage to Appreciate and Restore* (Bologna: Commune di Bologna, 2004).

Fetscher, M., *Die Reorganisation von Eigentumsrechten mittelständischer Unternehmen in Ostdeutschland*, PhD thesis, Universität Konstanz (2000).

Fischer, J. (ed.), *The Metaphysics of Death* (Stanford: Stanford University Press, 1993).

Fischer, N., *Geschichte des Todes in der Neuzeit* (Erfurt: Sutton, 2002).

——— 'Leitlinien einer neuen Kultur im Umgang mit Tod und Trauer', *Friedhof und Denkmal*, 44 (1999), 3–9.

——— *Vom Gottesacker zum Krematorium – Eine Sozialgeschichte der Friedhöfe in Deutschland* (Cologne: Böhlau, 1996).

——— *Wie wir unter die Erde kommen – Sterben und Tod zwischen Trauer und Tod* (Frankfurt: Fischer, 1997).

Fogmoes, C., 'Cremation Developments in Denmark', *Pharos International*, 67:1 (2001), 45–47.

Forman, W., et al. (eds), *Hospice and Palliative Care: Concepts and Practice* (Sudbury, MA: Jones and Bartlett, 2003).

Foucault, M., 'Des Espace Autres', *Architecture/Mouvement/Continuité*, October (1984).

Francois E. and Schulze H. (eds), *Deutsche Erinnerungsorte Vol. 1–3* (Munich: C.H. Beck, 2003).

Franz, A., '"Alles hat am Ende sich gelohnt"? – Christliche Begräbnisliturgie zwischen kirchlicher Tradition und säkularen Riten', *Liturgisches Jahrbuch*, 51:4 (2001), 190–211.

'Frauenpower: Ist "sie" der bessere Bestatter?', *Bestattung – Fachzeitschrift des VdZB*, 24 June 2010.

'Friedhöfe-Krematorien', *AW – Architektur und Wettbewerbe*, No. 192, December (2002).

Friedländer, S., *Kitsch und Tod – Der Widerschein des Nazismus* (Frankfurt: Fischer, 1999).

Friedrich, J., *Der Brand – Deutschland im Bombenkrieg 1940–1945* (Berlin: Propyläen, 2002)

Fulbrook, M., 'Fact, Fantasy and German History', *Bulletin of the German Historical Institute – Washington D.C.*, 26 (2000), 3–34.

———— 'New Historikerstreit, Missed Opportunity or new Beginning?', *German History*, 12:2 (1994), 203–7.

———— (ed.), *Power and Society in the GDR, 1961–1979 – The 'Normalisation of Rule'* (New York: Berghahn, 2009).

Gaedke, J., 'Friedhofs- und Bestattungsrecht in der DDR', *Deutsche Friedhofskultur – Zeitschrift für das gesamte Friedhofswesen*, 71 (1981).

Gebhard, U., 'Todesverdrängung und Umweltzerstörung', in U. Becker, K. Feldmann and F. Johannsen (eds), *Sterben und Tod in Europa* (Neukirchen-Vluyn: Neukirchener, 1998), 145–58.

Geißler, C., 'Unter der Erde der DDR', in K. Michel, *Todesbilder – Kursbuch 114* (Berlin: Rowohlt, 1993), 79–90.

Geyer, M. and Jarausch, K. (eds), *A Shattered Past: (Re-) Constructing German Histories* (Princeton: Princeton University Press, 2003).

Gorer, G., *Death, Grief and Mourning in Contemporary Britain* (London: Cresset, 1965).

Grainger, R., *The Social Symbolism of Grief and Mourning* (London and Philadelphia: Jessica Kingsley Publishers, 1998).

Grashoff, U., *"In einem Anfall von Depression": Selbsttötungen in der DDR* (Berlin: Ch. Links, 2006).

Gregor, N., '"Is He Still Alive, or Long Since Dead?" Loss, Absence and Remembrance in Nuremberg, 1945–1956', *German History*, 21:2 (2003), 183–203.

Groschopp, O., 'Weltliche Trauerkultur in der DDR – Toten- und Bestattungsrituale in der politischen Symbolik des DDR-Systems', *Sozialwissenschaftliche Informationen (SOWI)*, 29:2 (2000), 109–10.

Grossmann, G., 'Im Osten: Klassenkampf und Vergangenheitsbewältigung', *Deutsche Friedhofskultur (DFK)*, 8 (1995), 273–76.

Grundmann, S., *Bevölkerungsentwicklung in Ostdeutschland – Demographische Strukturen und räumliche Wandlungsprozesse auf dem Gebiet der neuen Bundesländer* (Opladen: Leske+Budrich, 1998).

Gumbert, H., Conference Report: 'Writing East German History: What Difference Does the Cultural Turn Make?', *Bulletin of the German Historical Institute – Washington DC*, 44 (2009), 137–41.

Habenstein, R. and Lamers, W., *Funeral Customs the World Over* (Milwaukee: Bulfin, 1974).

Haeckel, E., *Gibt es ein Weiterleben nach dem Tode? – Aus "Die Welträtsel"* (Berlin: Dietz, 1958).

Hallberg, B., *Die Jugendweihe – Zur Deutschen Jugendweihetradition* (Göttingen: Vandenhoeck and Ruprecht, 1979).

Hanke, S., *Tod – Was ist dein Sinn* (Stuttgart: Neske, 1990).

Happe, B., 'Anonyme Bestattung in Deutschland – Veränderungen in der zeitgenössischen Bestattungs- und Erinnerungskultur', *Friedhof und Denkmal*, 41:2 (1996), 40–52.

———— 'Die Nachkriegsentwicklung der Friedhofe in beiden deutschen Staaten', in AFD (ed.), *Raum für Tote – Die Geschichte der Friedhöfe von den Gräberstraßen der Römerzeit bis zur anonymen Bestattung* (Braunschweig: Thalacker, 2003), 195–224.

———— 'Die sozialistische Reform der Friedhofs- und Bestattungskultur in der DDR – Urnengemeinschaftsanlagen', in R. Sörries (ed.), *Vom Reichsausschuß zur Arbeitsgemeinschaft Friedhof und Denkmal* (Kassel: AFD, 2002), 185–213.

———— 'Grabmalgestaltung in der DDR – Der erzwungene Abschied vom persönlichen Grabmal', in AFD (ed.), *Grabkultur in Deutschland: Geschichte der Grabmäler* (Berlin: Reimer, 2009), 189–214.

———— 'Urnengemeinschaftsanlagen: Zur Friedhofs- und Bestattungskultur in der DDR', *Deutschlandarchiv*, 3 (2001), 436–46.

———— 'Veränderungen in der sepulkralen Kultur am Ende des 20. Jahrhunderts', *Friedhof und Denkmal*, 45:2 (2000), 9–20.

———— 'Zur Lage der anonymen Bestattung in Deutschland – eine Umfrage bei kommunalen und kirchlichen Friedhofsverwaltern', *Friedhof und Denkmal*, 43:2 (1998), 39–54.

Harsch, D., *Revenge of the Domestic: Women, the Family and Communism in the German Democratic Republic* (Princeton: Princeton University Press, 2007).

Heisenberg, W., *Quantentheorie und Philosophie* (Stuttgart: Reclam, 1959).

Herf, J., *Divided Memory – The Nazi Past in the Two Germanys* (Cambridge, MA: Harvard University Press, 1997).

Hermelink, J., 'Die weltliche Bestattung und ihre kirchliche Konkurrenz – Überlegung zur Kasualpraxis in Ostdeutschland', *Jahrbuch für Liturgik und Hymnologie*, 39 (2000).

Herzog, M. (ed.), *Totengedenken und Trauerkultur – Geschichte und Zukunft des Umgangs mit Verstorbenen* (Stuttgart: Kohlhammer, 2001).

Hoffjan, G., 'Existierte eine spezifische realsozialistische Friedhofgestaltung in der DDR und was waren ihre Charakteristika', in R. Sörries (ed.), *Vom Reichsausschuß zur AFD* (Kassel: AFD, 2002), 171–84.

Höge, H., 'Ehrengräber für die Elite', *taz*, No. 7257, 14 January 2004.

Howarth, G., *Last Rites – The Work of the Modern Funeral Direction* (Amityville, NY: Baywood Pub., 1996).

Howarth, G. and Leaman, O. (eds), *Encyclopaedia of Death and Dying* (London: Routledge, 2001).

Humm, A., *Auf dem Weg zum Sozialistischen Dorf? – Zum Wandel der dörflichen Lebenswelt in der DDR und der Bundesrepublik Deutschland 1952–1969* (Göttingen: Vandenhoeck and Ruprecht, 1999).

Imhof, A., *Leben wir zu lange?* (Cologne: Böhlau, 1992).

Jahresgesundheitsbericht 1989 für das Gebiet der ehemaligen DDR (Berlin, 1990).

Janetzky, B., 'Stille Beisetzungen trösten nicht – Die Notwendigkeit nichtkirchlicher Trauerfeiern', *Bibel und Liturgie*, 74 (2001).

Jeggle, U., 'In stolzer Trauer – Umgangsformen mit dem Kriegstod während des 2. Weltkriegs', *Tübinger Beiträge zur Volkskultur Volume 69* (Tübingen: Tübinger Vereinigung für Volkskunde, 1986).

Judt, M., *DDR Geschichte in Dokumenten – Beschlüsse, Berichte, interne Materialien und Alltagszeugnisse* (Berlin: Ch. Links, 1997).

Jupp, P. and Howarth, G. (eds), *The Changing Face of Death – Historical Accounts of Death and Disposal* (Houndsmill: Macmillan, 1997).

Kaelble, H., Kocka, J. and Zwahr, H., *Sozialgeschichte der DDR* (Stuttgart: Klett-Cotta, 1994).

Kamerman, J., *Death in Midst of Life – Social and Cultural Influences on Death, Grief and Mourning* (London: Prentice-Hall, 1988).

Kegan, R., *In Over Our Heads: The Mental Demands of Modern Life* (Cambridge, MA: Havard University Press, 1994).

Khalatbari, P. et. al. (eds, for Akademie der Wissenschaften der DDR), *Handbuch der Demographie in der DDR* (Oberlungwitz: VEB Kongreß- und Werbedruck, 1989).

Koch, S., 'Geschichte und Bedeutung des Friedhofes im Abendland', *Zeitschrift für Semiotik*, 11:2–3 (1989), 125–33.

Kortüm, A., 'Ordnung oder Uniformität', *Mitteldeutsche Neuste Nachrichten*, No. 274, 27 November 1958.

Koselleck, R. and Jeismann, M. (eds), *Der Politische Totenkult – Kriegerdenkmäler in der Moderne* (Munich: W. Fink, 1994).

Krause, T., *Der Umgang mit ethischen Problemen des Lebensende in der DDR und die Entstellungen Medizinischen Personals zu Sterbenden und zum eigenen Tod*, MD Dissertation, Faculty of Medicine, University of Leipzig (1995).

Krenzke, H.-J., *Magdeburger Friedhöfe und Begräbnisstätten* (Stadtplanungsamt: Magdeburg, 1998).

Krieg, N., *„Schon Ordnung ist Schönheit": Hans Grässels Münchner Friedhofsarchitektur (1894–1929), ein deutsches Modell?* (Munich: Herbert Utz, 1990).

Kübler-Ross, E., *On Death and Dying* (London: Tavistock, 1970).

Kuhn, T., *The Structure of Scientific Revolutions* (Chicago and London: University of Chicago, 1970).

Lacina, K., *Tod* (Vienna: Facultas WUV, 2009).

Laderman, G., *The Sacred Remains: American Attitudes towards Death, 1789–1883* (New Haven: Yale University Press, 1996).

Lange, I., 'Von der Wiege bis zur Bahre: Zur Geschichte Sozialistischer Feiern zu Geburt, Ehe und Tod in der DDR', *Kulturnation: Online Journal für Kultur, Wissenschaft und Politik*, 27:1 (2004).

Langer, I., *Das Ringen um die Einführung der fakultativen Feuerbestattung im Wiener Gemeinderat*, Diplomarbeit, Universität Wien (2008).

Lehmann, A., *Von Menschen und Bäumen: die Deutschen und ihr Wald* (Hamburg: Rowohlt, 1999).

Lichfield, J., 'Holocaust of the Elderly: Death Toll in French Heat Wave Rises to 10,000', *The Independent*, 22 August 2003.

Lichtensteiger, S. (ed.), *Last Minute – Ein Buch zu Sterben und Tod* (Baden: hier+jetzt, 1999).

Lindenberger, T., 'Alltagsgeschichte und ihr möglicher Beitrag zu einer Gesellschaftsgeschichte', in R. Bessel and M. Jessen (eds), *Die Grenzen der Diktatur – Staat und Gesellschaft in der DDR* (Göttingen: Vandenhoeck, 1996), 312–21.

——— (ed.), *Herrschaft und Eigen-Sinn in der Diktatur: Studien zur Gesellschaftsgeschichte der DDR* (Cologne: Böhlau, 1999).

Lisowski, F., 'The Practice of Cremation in China', *Eastern Horizon*, 19:6 (1980), 21–24.

Lüdtke, A. (ed.), *Herrschaft als soziale Praxis : Historische und sozial-anthropologische Studien* (Göttingen: Vandenhoeck and Ruprecht, 1991).

———'Blumen und Grabsteine – für alle Kriegstoten? Gedenken, Erinnern und Beschweigen in der DDR. Beispiele aus dem Berliner Umland', in I. Eschebach (ed.), *Die Sprache des Gedenkens: Zur Geschichte der Gedenkstätte Ravensbrück 1945–1995* (Berlin: Hentrich, 1999), 163–83.

Macho, T. and Marek, K. (eds), *Die neue Sichtbarkeit des Todes* (Paderborn: Wilhelm Fink, 2007).

Magistrat der Landeshauptstadt Magdeburg, *100 Jahre Westfriedhof Magdeburg* (Magdeburg, 1998).

Mählert, U., *Kleine Geschichte der DDR* (Munich: C.H. Beck, 1999).

Major, P., *Behind the Berlin Wall: East Germany and the Frontiers of Power* (Oxford: Oxford University Press, 2010).

Mann, B., 'Modernism and the Zionist Uncanny: Reading the Old Cemetery in Tel Aviv', *Representation* – Special Issue: Grounds for Remembering, 69 (2000), 63–95.

McLellan, D., *Marx* (London: Fontana, 1986).

——— *The Young Hegelians and Karl Marx* (London: Macmillan, 1969).

Merridale, C., *Night of Stone – Death and Memory in Russia* (London: Granta, 2000).

Michalka, W. (ed.), *Der Zweite Weltkrieg: Analysen, Grundzüge, Forschungsbilanz* (Munich: Piper, 1989).

Michel, M. and Spengler, T. (eds), *Todesbilder*, Kursbuch 114 (Berlin: Rowohlt, 1993).

Minois, G., *Geschichte des Atheismus von den Anfängen bis zur Gegenwart* (Weimar: Böhlaus Nachfolger, 2000).

Mitford, J., *The American Way of Death – Revisited* (London: Virago, 1998).

Moeller, R., *War Stories: The Search for a Usable Past in the Federal Republic of Germany* (Berkeley: University of California Press, 2001).

Moranda, S., 'Towards a More Holistic History? Historians and East German Everyday Life', *Social History*, 35:3 (2010), 330–38.

Mosler, H., *Verfassung des Deutschen Reichs vom 11. August 1919* (Stuttgart: Reclam, 1972).

Murray, H., *This Garden of Death – The History of York Cemetery* (York: Friends of York Cemetery, 1991).

Nawrodsi, J., 'Der Not gehorchend… – Handwerk in der DDR', *Die Zeit*, 20 August 1976.

Nipperdey, T., *Deutsche Geschichte 1866–1918, Vol. 1 – Arbeiterwelt und Bürgergeist* (Munich: C.H. Beck, 1994).

Niven, B. (ed.), *Germans as Victims. Remembering the Past in Contemporary Germany* (London: Palgrave, 2006).

Nolte, E., Scholz, R., Shkolnikov, V. and McKee, M., 'The Contribution of Medical Care to Changing Life Expectancy in Germany and Poland', *Social Science and Medicine*, 55:11 (2002), 1905–21.

Oberkrome, W., *Deutsche Heimat: nationale Konzeption und regionale Praxis von Naturschutz, Landschaftsgestaltung und Kulturpolitik in Westfalen-Lippe und Thüringen, 1900-1960* (Paderborn: Schöningh, 2004).

Overmans, V., *Deutsche militärische Verluste im Zweiten Weltkrieg* (Munich: R. Oldenbourg, 2004).

Pence, K., '"You as a Woman Will Understand": Consumption, Gender and the Relationship between State and Citizen in the GDR's Crisis of 17 June 1953', *German History*, 19:2 (2001), 218–52.

Peukert, D., *Inside Nazi Germany – Conformity, Opposition and Racism in Everyday Life* (New Haven: Yale University Press, 1987).

Podewin, N., 'Extrem Tüchtig', *Junge Welt*, 19 April 2003.

Pollack, D., *Kirche in der Organisationsgesellschaft* (Stuttgart: W. Kohlhammer, 1994).

Pommerin, R. (ed.), *Culture in the Federal Republic of Germany, 1945–1995* (Oxford and Washington: Berg, 1996).

Port, A., *Conflict and Stability in the German Democratic Republic* (New York: Cambridge University Press, 2007).

Praschek, H., 'Besonderheiten der amtlichen Statistik in der ehemaligen DDR', *Wirtschaft und Statistik*, 1 (2000).

Pritchard, G., *The Making of the GDR 1945–1952* (Manchester: Manchester University Press, 2000).

Prosenjak, F., 'Die Bewältigung der Totesproblematik im sozialistischen Begräbnis in Jugoslawien', *Liturgisches Jahrbuch*, 29:3 (1979), 143–56.

Prothero, S., *Purified by Fire – A History of Cremation in America* (Berkeley: University of California Press, 2001).

Pursell, T., 'The Burial of the Future': Modernist Architecture and the Cremationist Movement in Wilhelmine Germany', *Mortality*, 8:3 (2003), 233–50.

Radder S., '8. Mai 1945 – 60 Jahre Kriegsende – Bevölkerungszahlen aus den Jahren 1945 bis 1947', *Statistische Monatschrift – Berliner Statistik*, 5 (2005).

Rädlinger, C., *Der verwaltete Tod – Eine Entwicklungsgeschichte des Münchner Bestattungswesen* (Munich: Buchendorfer, 1996).

Ratschow, C., 'Erwarten wir noch etwas jenseits des Todes?', *Neue Zeitschrift für systematische Theologie und Religionsphilosophie*, 14:1 (1972), 112–29.

Redlin, J., *Säkulare Totenrituale: Totenehrung, Staatsbegräbnis und private Bestattung in der DDR* (Munich: Waxmann, 2009).

Richter, K., 'Der Umgang mit Tod und Trauer in den Bestattungsriten der Deutschen Demokratischen Republik', in H. Becker, B. Einig and P.-O. Ulrich, *Im Angesicht des Todes – Ein interdisziplinäres Kompendium I, Pietas Liturgica 3* (St. Ottilien: EOS Verlag, 1987), 229–58.

Rodden, J., *Repainting the Little Red Schoolhouse: A History of Eastern German Education, 1945-1995* (New York: Oxford University Press, 2002).

Rohkrämer, T., *Eine andere Moderne – Zivilisationskritik, Natur und Technik in Deutschland 1880–1933* (Paderborn: Schönigh, 1999).

Ross, C., *The East German Dictatorship: Problems and Perspectives in the Interpretation of the GDR* (London: Arnold, 2002).

Rugg, J., 'Defining the Place of Burial: What Makes a Cemetery a Cemetery', *Mortality*, 5:3 (2000), 259–75.

——— 'Lawn Cemeteries: The Emergence of a New Landscape of Death', *Urban History*, 33:2 (2006), 213–33.

Sachmerda-Schulz, N., 'Die *grüne Wiese* als Gottesacker? Eine religionssoziologische Studie zum Wandel der Bestattungsnormen und zur Normalisierung der

Anonymbestattung', *Arbeitstitel – Forum für Leipziger Promovierende*, 3:1 (2011), 65–66.

Schelenz, R. and Meinel, S., '"Sozialistische" Friedhofskultur in der DDR?', *Friedhof und Denkmal*, 41:1 (1996), 12–15.

Schiller, G., *Der organisierte Tod – Beobachtungen zum modernen Bestattungswesen* (Düsseldorf: Fachverlag des deutschen Bestattungsgewerbes, 1991).

Schmitz, H. (ed.), *A Nation of Victims? Representations of German Wartime Suffering from 1945 to the Present* (Amsterdam and New York: Rodopi, 2007).

Schoenfeld, H., *Der Friedhof Ohlsdorf: Gräber – Geschichte – Gedenkstätten* (Hamburg: Christians, 2000).

Schroeder, K., *Der SED-Staat: Partei, Staat, und Gesellschaft 1949–1990* (Munich: C. Hanser, 1998).

Schumann, D. et al., 'Death in Germany', *Bulletin of the German Historical Institute – Washington D.C.*, 34 (2004).

Schwartz, B., 'The Social Context of Commemoration – A Study in Collective Memory', *Social Forces*, 61:2 (1982), 374–402.

Scott, J., *Seeing Like a State – How Certain Schemes to Improve the Human Condition Have Failed* (New Haven and London: Yale University Press, 1998).

'Sensitive Britons Try to Bury Cemetery Crisis', *The Guardian*, 2 September 2000.

Skilling, H., 'Interest Groups and Communist Politics', *World Politics*, 18:3 (1966), 435–51.

Skilling, H. and Griffiths, F. (eds), *Interest Groups in Soviet Policy* (Princeton: Princeton University Press, 1971).

Sloane, D., *The Last Great Necessity – Cemeteries in American History* (Baltimore: John Hopkins University Press, 1991).

Smoltczyk, A., 'Ortstermin: Begräbnis der Witwe des ehemaligen Staatschef Walter Ulbricht in Berlin', *Der Spiegel*, No. 17, 22 April 2002.

Sørensen, T., 'The Presence of the Dead: Cemeteries, Cremation and the Staging of Non-place', *Journal of Social Archaeology*, 9:1 (2009), 110–35.

Sörries, R., 'Kontroverse um Sozialistische Friedhofskultur', *Friedhof und Denkmal*, 41:1 (1996).

———— 'Studienfahrt durch die Oberlausitz', *Friedhof und Denkmal*, 41:1 (1996).

———— *Ruhe sanft: Kulturgeschichte des Friedhofs* (Kevelaer: Butzon and Bercker, 2009).

———— (ed.), *Großes Lexikon der Bestattungs- und Friedhofskultur – Wörterbuch zur Sepulkralkultur, Vol.1* (Braunschweig: Thalacker, 2002).

———— *Vom Reichsausschuß zur Arbeitsgemeinschaft Friedhof und Denkmal* (Kassel: AFD, 2002).

Speitkamp W. (ed.), *Denkmalsturz: Zur Konfliktgeschichte politischer Symbolik* (Göttingen: Vandenhoeck and Ruprecht, 1997).

Statistisches Bundesamt, *Gesundheitswesen: Todesursachen in Deutschland – Fachserie 12, Reihe 4* (Wiesbaden: Statistisches Bundesamt, 2005).

———— (ed.), *Die deutschen Vertreibungsverluste – Bevölkerungsbilanzen für die deutschen Vertreibungsgebiete 1939/50* (Wiesbaden: Statistisches Bundesamt, 1958).

———— (ed.), *Statistik der natürlichen Bevölkerungsbewegung* (Wiesbaden: Statistische Bundesamt, 2005).

Statistisches Landesamt Mecklenburg-Vorpommern (ed.), *Statistisches Jahrbuch 2005* (Schwerin, 2005).

Stearns, P., *Childhood in World History*, Second Edition (London: Routledge, 2010).

Steininger, R., *Deutsche Geschichte seit 1945 – Darstellung und Dokumente, Vol. 1, 1945–1947* (Frankfurt: Fischer, 1996).

Stuut-Rothkegel, G., 'Friedhofskultur in den Niederlanden', *Friedhofskultur*, 91 (2001).

Tacke, C., *Denkmal im Sozialen Raum* (Göttingen: Vandenhoeck and Ruprecht, 1995).

Thalmann, R., *Urne oder Sarg? – Auseinandersetzung um die Einführung der Feuerbestattung im 19. Jhrt.* (Bern and Frankfurt: Lange, 1979).

'The Business of Bereavement: An Expensive Way to Go', *The Economist*, 4 January 1997.

Tillmann, M., "*Grundsätze und Erfahrungen bei der Gestaltung sozialistischer Feierlichkeiten um Geburt, Eheschließung und Tod in Stalinstadt" – Ein Beitrag zur Aufarbeitung von DDR-Geschichte*, Belegarbeit, Universität Potsdam (1993).

'Trends in der Feuerbestattung', *Das Bestattungsgewerbe*, No. 9, 1986.

Tumarkin, N., *Lenin Lives – The Lenin Cult in Soviet Russia* (Cambridge, MA: Harvard University Press, 1983).

Unfried, B. and Schindler, C. (eds), *Riten, Mythen und Symbole – Die Arbeiterbewegung zwischen "Zivilreligion" und Volkskultur* (Leipzig: AVA, 1999).

Venne, M., 'Anonym Bestatten – Digital Gedenken', *Friedhof und Denkmal*, 44:1 (1999), 17–34.

Vinen, R., *A History in Fragments – Europe in the Twentieth Century* (London: Little, Brown and Co, 2000).

Vollnhals, C. (ed.), *Sachsen in der NS-Zeit* (Leipzig: G. Kiepenheuer, 2002).

Walter, T., 'Death: Taboo or Not Taboo', *Sociology*, 25:2 (1991), 293–310.

————— 'La Visibilité des Morts dans la Société Moderne', *Proceedings of the Dying and Death in 18th–21st Century Europe International Conference* (Cluj-Napoca: Accent, 2009), 11–18.

————— *The Revival of Death* (London and New York: Routledge, 1994).

Werkentin, F., *Politische Strafjustiz in der Ära Ulbricht – Vom bekennenden Terror zur verdeckten Repression* (Berlin: C.H. Links, 1997).

Whaley, J. (ed.), *Mirrors of Mortality* (London: Europa, 1981).

Wheen, F., *Karl Marx* (London: Fourth Estate, 2000).

WHO, *World Health Statistics Annuals* (Geneva: World Health Organization, 1985).

Wilhelm-Schaffer, I., *Gottes Beamter und Spielmann des Teufels – Der Tod im Spätmittelalter und früher Neuzeit* (Cologne: Böhlau, 1999).

Winkler, E., *Tore zum Leben: Taufe, Konfirmation, Trauung, Bestattung* (Neukirchen-Vluyn: Neukirchener, 1995).

Winter, H., *Die Architektur der Krematorien im Deutschen Reich 1878–1918* (Dettelbach: Röll, 2001).

Wolle, S., *Die heile Welt der Diktatur – Alltag und Herrschaft in der DDR, 1971–1989* (Berlin: Ch. Links, 1998).

Wrede, B., 'Das Familiengrab ist voll', *Süddeutsche Zeitung*, 20/21 November 2004.

Zink, B., *Anyone, Anything, Anytime – A History of Emergency Medicine* (Philadelphia: Mosby, 2005).

Monographs in German History